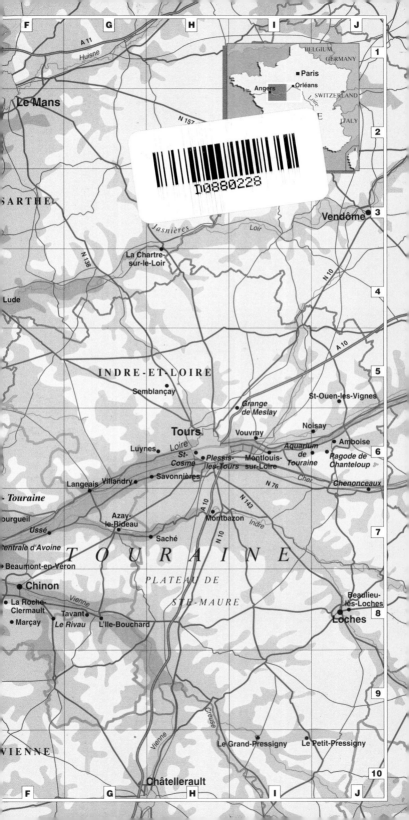

At the beginning of the century sand from the Loire was still hauled by hand before being transported to the port, where it was unloaded by barrow. A sifter then sieved it, using a large wire-mesh sieve.

"Happy, handsome and brave Touraine,
whose seven valleys flow in water and wine."
Honoré de Balzac (1799–1850)

The winter of 1879–80 was particularly harsh. The Loire was
completely iced over. As damage to bridges was feared, the
army dynamited the ice flow. Ten years later another bitterly
cold spell swept across Touraine, and the Loire remained
frozen for twenty-five days. The last memorable winter was that
of 1962–3, when the number of days of frost reached a record:
the Loire was entirely covered with ice for four weeks.

At the end of the 19th century a large part of the population of the Loire Valley was working in the vineyards or in associated industries. The methods and practices used by the cooper have barely altered over the centuries. He shapes the *douelles* (wooden staves), then assembles them on a "ring". The bending of the *douelles*, a delicate operation that determines the quality and longevity of the barrel, generally takes place over a wood fire.

THIS IS A BORZOI BOOK
PUBLISHED BY ALFRED A. KNOPF, INC.

Copyright © 1996 Alfred A. Knopf, Inc., New York

All rights reserved under International and Pan-American Copyright Conventions.
Published in the United States by Alfred A. Knopf, Inc., New York, and simultaneously in
Canada by Random House of Canada Limited, Toronto.
Distributed by Random House, Inc., New York.

Originally published in France by Nouveaux-Loisirs, a subsidiary of
Gallimard, Paris, 1996. Copyright © 1993 by Editions Nouveaux-Loisirs

THE LOIRE VALLEY – ISBN 0-679-76449-6
LC-96–77567

First published 1996

NUMEROUS SPECIALISTS AND ACADEMICS HAVE
CONTRIBUTED TO THIS GUIDE.

THE LOIRE VALLEY:
EDITOR: Anne-Josyane Magniant
assisted by Serge Gras, Cécile Gall, Philippe
Voyenne (history), Veronika Vollmer
(coordination practical information), Sylvie
Blanchard and Philippe Yvan (wines of the
Loire Valley)
LAYOUT: Olivier Brunot, François Chentrier,
Gérard Dumas, Carole Gaborit, Philippe
Marchand
PICTURE RESEARCH: Anaïck Bourhis
GRAPHICS: Élisabeth Cohat
THE LOIRE VALLEY (PAGES 12–13): René Maurice
NATURE: Philippe J. Dubois, Frédéric Bony *with*
René Chaboud, Alain Perthuis, Gérard Tardivo
HISTORY: Jeanine Labussière
ARTS AND TRADITIONS: François Icher, Denis Le
Vraud, Maurice Pommier, Cécile Vuatrin Duflot
ARCHITECTURE: Bruno Lenormand
with Anne Bourgne
THE LOIRE VALLEY AS SEEN BY PAINTERS:
Sylvain Bellanger, Marie-Christine Forest,
Yves Mauffrat, Véronique Moreau
THE LOIRE VALLEY AS SEEN BY WRITERS:
Lucinda Gane

ITINERARIES:
AMBOISE: Stéphane Gendron, Annie Gros
ANGERS: René Maurice
AZAY-LE-RIDEAU: Marie Latour, Anne-Josyane
Magniant
BLOIS: Bruno Guignard, Elisabeth Latrémolière,
Florent Texnier, Aude de Tocqueville
CHAMBORD: Jean Martin-Démézil, Françoise de
Person, Aude de Tocqueville
CHENONCEAUX: Stéphane Gendron
CHINON: Marie Latour
LOCHES: Paul-Jacques Lévêque-Mingam
ORLÉANS: René Maurice
SACHÉ: Bernard Briais
SAUMUR: René Maurice
TOURS: Christian Daumas, Stéphane Gendron,
Annie Gros, Jeanine Labussière, Marie Latour,
Elizabeth Latrémolière, René Maurice, Andrée
Moreau, Danièle Moreau, Véronique Moreau

PRACTICAL INFORMATION:
Alain Bradfer, Christian Daumas,
Veronika Vollmer

USEFUL ADDRESSES:
Jean-Claude Ribaut

ILLUSTRATIONS:
NATURE: Anne Bodin, Claire Felloni, Jean
Chevallier, Jean Philippe Chabot, Gismonde
Curiace, Bernard Duheme, François Desbordes,
Gilbert Houbre, Jean-Michel Kacedan,
Catherine Lachaud, Jean-Marc Pau, Sylvaine
Pérols, Pascal Robin, Frédérique Schwebel
ARCHITECTURE: Philippe Candé, Nicolette Castle,
Hugh Dixon, Bill Donohoe, Mick Gillot, Jean-
Marie Guillou, Trevor Hill, Roger Hutchins, Tuth
Lindsey, Ian Moores, Claude Quiec, Michael
Shoebridge, Ed Stuart, Tony Townsend
ITINERARIES: Grégory Baird, Philippe Biard,
Jean-Marc Lanusse, Bruno Lenormand, Philippe
Lhez, Dominique Mansion, Fabrice Moireau,
Jean-Claude Sénée
PRACTICAL INFORMATION: Maurice Pommier
MAPS: Vincent Brunot *with* Atelier de Bayonne,
Francine Callède, Dominique Duplantier ;
Éric Gillion
COMPUTER GENERATED MAPS: Patrick Alexandre,
Édigraphie, Sophie Compagne, Philippe
Doussinet, Cyrille Mallié, Patrick Merienne

PHOTOGRAPHY:
Éric Guillemot, Patrick Léger *with* Pierre
Aucante, Alain Beignet, Serge Chirol, Alain
Doron, Jean-Pierre Gislard, François Joly,
Patrick Lavaud, Michel Magat, Jean-Pierre
Moreau, Jean-Luc Pechinot, Jean-Philippe
Perraguin, Pierre Pitrou, Jean-Noël Thibault

WE WOULD LIKE TO THANK: Jacques Gérard,
Jacques Hesse, Pierre Huteau, Nicole Lagravère,
Paul-Jacques Lévêque-Mingam, Solange
Matheron, Mme de La Morandière, Marc
Philippe, Jean-Yves Pinon, Mr de Sainte-Marie,
Archives départementales, Galerie La Cymaise
(Paris), Bibliothèque départementale (Tours),
Bibliothèque Municipale (Tours), Château de
Blois, Musée de la Sologne (Romorantin-
Lanthenay), Musée des Beaux-Arts (Tours),
L'École Nationale d'Équitation, Saumur

TRANSLATED BY GILLES DESMONS AND SUSAN MACKERVOY.
EDITED AND TYPESET BY BOOK CREATION SERVICES, LONDON.
PRINTED IN ITALY BY EDITORIALE LIBRARIA.

THE LOIRE VALLEY

KNOPF GUIDES

CONTENTS

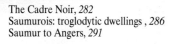

▲ THE LOIRE VALLEY

0   10   20 miles

░░ Forest

── Regional park

Loir

Segréen

Mayenne   *Sarthe*

Baugeois

Angers

A n j o u

Loire

Aubance

Regional park

Régional de

S a u m u r o i s

Saumur

Loire - Anjou - Touraine

Coteaux du Layon   *Layon*

Mauges

Thouet

Chinon

Vienne

T o u r a i n e

Tours   Ambo*

Indre

Loc*

The Loire Valley is
regarded as starting at Gien –
where the Loire begins its slow
meander westward – and
finishing at Angers, a border
town between the Paris Basin
and the Armorican Massif.
The historic provinces of the
Loire Valley – Orléanais,
Blésois, Touraine, Anjou – are
now divided administratively
into four départements (Loiret,
Loir-et-Cher, Indre-et-Loire
and Maine-et-Loire) and
two regions (Centre and Pays
de Loire). Nevertheless, the
old provinces have retained
their geographic characteristics,
and the only link between
them is provided by the river:
by river transport in the past,
and by tourism today.

ANJOU ● *37*, ▲ *277*
More of a historical
entity than a
geographical one,
Anjou is made up of
several regions. To
the west, bordering
the Armorican
Massif, the Segré and
Mauges regions are
known as Anjou Noir,
due to their schist and
sandstone terrain. To
the east the Beaugé
plateau and the plain
of Saumur make
up Anjou Blanc, with
its tufa, vines and
forests, while around
Angers the slopes
of the alluvial valley
are covered with
meadows, vineyards,
flower nurseries and
market gardens ■ *26*.

TOURAINE ● *77*,
▲ *193*
Nowadays Touraine
corresponds to the
Département of
Indre-et-Loire,
which has the well-
known university
town of Tours as its
capital. Spread
around the valleys
of the Loire and its
tributaries, this
gentle and luminous
region is home to
high-quality vineyards
■ *30*, which are one
of the chief sources
of its wealth. As in
Anjou troglodyte
dwellings ● *76*, ▲ *286*
are to be found here,
dug out in the white
tufa.

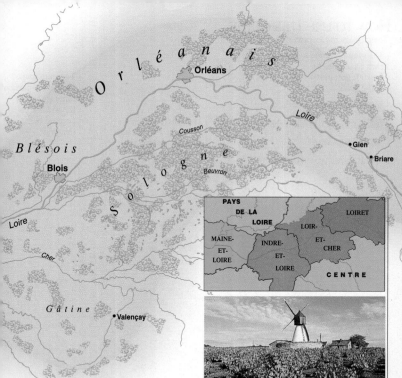

Orléanais
Orléans
Loire
Couisson
Blésois
Blois
Gien
Briare
Sologne
Beuvron
Loire
Cher
Gâtine
Valençay

PAYS DE LA LOIRE
LOIRET
LOIR-ET-CHER
MAINE-ET-LOIRE
INDRE-ET-LOIRE
CENTRE

AGRICULTURAL RESOURCES
Wine occupies
first place, closely
followed by the
cultivation of fruit,
vegetables and
flowers. Market
gardening ■ *26* has
become an important
addition to the vast
cereal farms of the
northern parts of
Blésois and
Orléanais.

THE WINES OF THE LOIRE ■ *30*
The vineyards of the
Loire valley have
been developed along
the river over the
centuries. Touraine
and Anjou (around
Saumur) are the two
most important wine
areas, producing a
variety of well-known
wines that admirably
complement the
varied range of
regional gastronomic
specialities.

*Above: windmill ● 79
at Thouard (Maine-et-
Loire). Center: views
of the towns of Gien
and Blois. Below: the
nuclear power station
at St-Laurent-des-
Eaux ▲ 139.*

ORLÉANAIS ▲ *111*
This region stretches
along the curve of the
Loire that reaches its
northernmost point at
Orléans, the capital
of Loiret. Here, more
than anywhere else,
the river unifies the
towns and the land
in a veritable mosaic:
the chalky Beauce
plain in the north is
succeeded to the
south by the sandy
Sologne, and to the
east by the splendid
Forest of Orléans
(c. 90,000 acres), the
clay soils of Gâtinais
and finally the valley
itself. There the river
enters on a sublime
display of landscapes
and châteaux.

BLÉSOIS ● *77*, ▲ *141*
Blois (above) is the
seat of the prefecture
of Loir-et-Cher. The
poor soils of Sologne
▲ *174*, the fertile
plains of Beauce, the
bocage of Perche and
the river valley, with
its great châteaux
such as Chambord
and Cheverny, afford
a remarkable diversity
of landscape.

INDUSTRY
The Loire Valley's
three nuclear power
stations – Avoine-
Chinon (1963),
Saint-Laurent-des-
Eaux (1969) and
Dampierre-en-Burly
(1980) – play a
central role in the
region's economy.

HOW TO USE THIS GUIDE
(Sample page shown from the guide to Venice)

The symbols at the top of each page refer to the different parts of the guide.

■ NATURAL ENVIRONMENT

● KEYS TO UNDERSTANDING

▲ ITINERARIES

◆ PRACTICAL INFORMATION

The itinerary map shows the main points of interest along the way and is intended to help you find your bearings.

The mini-map locates the particu[lar] itinerary within the wider area covered by the guide.

★ The star symbol signifies that a particular site has been singled out by the publishers for its special beauty, atmosphere or cultural interest.

At the beginning of each itinerary, the suggested means of transport to be used and the time it will take to cover the area are indicated:

🚤 By boat
🚶 On foot
🚲 By bicycle
🚗 By car
🕓 Duration

● ▲ ■ ◆
The symbols alongside a title or within the text itself provide cross-references to a theme or place dealt with elsewhere in the guide.

THE GATEWAY TO VENICE ★

PONTE DELLA LIBERTA. Built by the Austrians 50 years after the Treaty of Campo Formio in 1797 ● *34,* to link Venice with Milan. The bridge ended the thousand-year separation from the mainland and shook the city's economy to its roots as Venice, already in the throes of the industrial revolution, saw

🚶 Half a day

BRIDGES TO VENICE

NATURE

■ CLIMATE

The Loire in flood at
its junction with the Cher.

"Melancholic or radiant
according to the season, the skies are never obscured for long",
so said Joachim du Bellay (1522–60). The mild and temperate
Loire Valley spreads along either side of the river, the natural
border between the north and south of France. Near the river
the atmosphere seems continuously to hover between sun and
clouds; but the frequent morning mists rarely persist, the rain is
frequent but never abundant and there is plenty of sunshine,
especially on the hillsides overlooking the river. In the north of
Loir-et-Cher, toward the Perche hills, the climate becomes more
contrasted. In the southeast, the Sologne is characteristically
humid because of its numerous
forests and ponds.

Orléans
Blois
Angers Tours

Sea breezes

Galerne

Soulaire

The *galerne* is a westerly wind, whereas the
soulaire or *solaire* blows from the southwest
and brings maritime rains.

Heavy snowfalls and intense
droughts are unusual in the Loire Valley.
The temperate climate and the remarkable
light, hardly disturbed by the morning
mists, provide a perfect backdrop for
its Renaissance buildings.

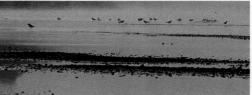

With its sandbanks and islets, the Loire provides an inviting habitat for migratory birds (ducks, gulls and waders . . .).

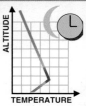

After nightfall the ground rapidly loses the heat accumulated during the day and cools down faster than the ambient air. During the night this cooling down process is transmitted progressively to the surrounding air, up to several hundred feet.

After a few hours of sunshine the ground warms up, and so does the surrounding air. The fog rises slowly . . . and clears away.

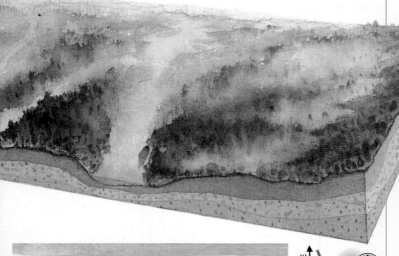

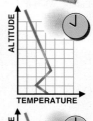

If the level of humidity in the air is great enough, the vapor condenses into minute drops. This is the phenomenon that creates fog, especially during clear and windless nights.

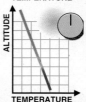

During the day the earth converts the sun's radiation into heat. The ground, being more conductive than the atmosphere, warms up more quickly. Some of this heat is then transmitted to the surrounding air by radiation from the earth.

THE LOIRE

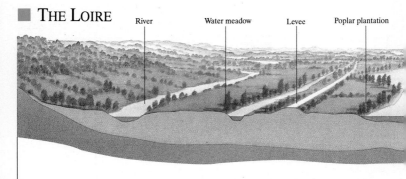

River   Water meadow   Levee   Poplar plantation

Set in a wide valley since the last glacial period, the majestic Loire, with its unpredictable floods, is partly constrained within embankments or levees built in the Middle Ages. These installations perceptibly altered the Loire landscape, with its soft hues and restful lines. With the passing of the seasons and variations of water level, the river is an extraordinary meeting place of water, sand and light. It provides an unusual variety of environments: islets, banks, dry meadows, water meadows and alluvial forests, which are home to remarkably diverse fauna and flora.

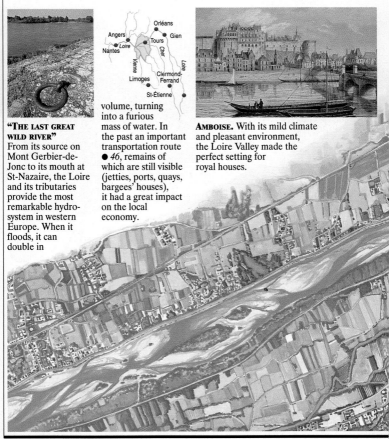

"THE LAST GREAT WILD RIVER"
From its source on Mont Gerbier-de-Jonc to its mouth at St-Nazaire, the Loire and its tributaries provide the most remarkable hydro-system in western Europe. When it floods, it can double in volume, turning into a furious mass of water. In the past an important transportation route ● *46*, remains of which are still visible (jetties, ports, quays, bargees' houses), it had a great impact on the local economy.

AMBOISE. With its mild climate and pleasant environment, the Loire Valley made the perfect setting for royal houses.

Secondary arm — Isle — Bank — Minor bed — Alluvial forest

Alluvial deposits (sandy clay)

Turonian limestone (Secondary Era)

There are several species of fauna and flora special to the
Loire: the hoplia, a blue metal scarab that was used as
a jewel in the past; the snowdrops that cover
forest floors with a white mantle late in
January; and the red osier, a pioneer
species, with golden stamens that
open on crimson catkins in the
first days of spring.

BLUE HOPLIA

SNOWDROP

RED OSIER

CORMORANT
This migratory
bird, originating
from the Low Countries and
Denmark, is seen from August to
April. It dives in the water to catch fish,
then dries its feathers and congregates
in the trees on the islets.

RIVER BANKS

WEASEL
This carnivore, partial to rodents, sometimes raids rabbit burrows and readily adds eggs and nestling birds to its diet.

As soon as spring comes, golden sandbanks appear in the shallow bed of the river. Their position varies according to the current, level and flow of the water. Small or large, they are sometimes isolated from the river banks by shallow channels. In spite of the surrounding water, these are arid areas which nevertheless shelter a pioneering life made up of fugacious plants, insects and arenicolous birds. They all contribute to the specific and rich ecosystems of the "last wild river" in France.

KINGFISHER
The only member of the kingfisher family found in Europe, this colorful bird nests in the river banks. Highly sensitive to pollution, it is a reliable indicator of water quality.

The golden banks of the Loire are made up of sand and gravel of varying sizes which originate mostly from erosion of the local rock (flint, chalk, burr) but also from the upstream geology (granite, basalt, gneiss, mica schist).

GRAY WILLOW
Its downy catkins are the first melliferous flowers of spring.

WOOD SANDPIPER, COMMON SANDPIPER, REDSHANK
These long-legged waders work different depths of water, depending on their size, and feed on animalcules found in the mud. The river banks provide these migratory birds with favorable conditions for their halts.

LITTLE RINGED PLOVER
This species nests on the sandy islets in large numbers, whenever the level of the river permits.

WILD RABBITS
The sand provides rabbits with an ideal place to dig their warrens.

SAND MARTIN
Steep, sandy river banks
and rockfaces in stone
quarries make ideal places
for these small sandy-brown
birds to excavate their
nest burrows.

LITTLE TERN
The Loire is an
important site for the
preservation of the population
of the smallest European tern, which
has become an emblem of
the river.

CHANGING BIOTOPES
The Loire's traditional
landscape has altered significantly. Trees and
bushes have been spreading fast, chiefly
because of the end of pastoralism and the
drop in the water level due to the dredging of
the river and eutrophication – excesses in
phosphates and nitrates
causing algae
to proliferate, thus
depleting the
supply of oxygen.

COMMON TERN
These long-distance
migratory birds arrive
from Africa late in March
to establish their breeding
colonies on the emerging
sandbanks.

PALUDINA
A viviparous water
snail that feeds on
algae and plankton.

CICINDELA OR TIGER BEETLE
A carnivorous insect
that likes to run across the
sand in the sun.

"GOMPHE SERPENTIN"
A central European
dragonfly. The Loire has
enabled its spread to the west.

F. Desbordes

Golden cyperus

Soapwort

Knot grass

Strapwort

Scirpus
michelianus

21

Like the perch,
the pike is a redoubtable
hunter: it eats three to
seven times its own weight
in fish per day.

So far as fishing is concerned, the Loire and its tributaries owe their reputation to migratory fish such as salmon, small and allis shad, river and sea lamprey, eels and mullet. In the past a greater number of professionals used to fish the river, but nowadays only a few license holders are authorized to install large nets across the Loire. A decline in the migratory fish population has been brought about by various causes, including the deteriorating quality of the water due to urban, industrial and agricultural pollution and the destruction of spawning grounds due to excessive extraction of sand and gravel.

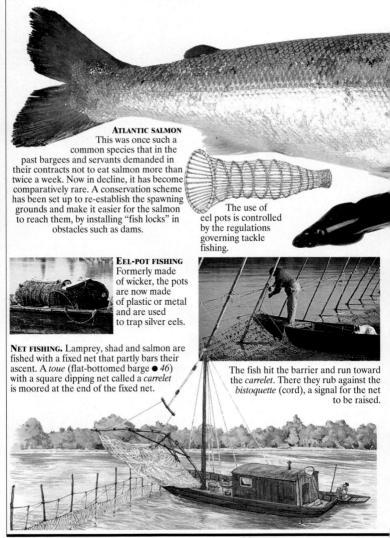

ATLANTIC SALMON
This was once such a common species that in the past bargees and servants demanded in their contracts not to eat salmon more than twice a week. Now in decline, it has become comparatively rare. A conservation scheme has been set up to re-establish the spawning grounds and make it easier for the salmon to reach them, by installing "fish locks" in obstacles such as dams.

The use of eel pots is controlled by the regulations governing tackle fishing.

EEL-POT FISHING
Formerly made of wicker, the pots are now made of plastic or metal and are used to trap silver eels.

NET FISHING. Lamprey, shad and salmon are fished with a fixed net that partly bars their ascent. A *toue* (flat-bottomed barge ● *46*) with a square dipping net called a *carrelet* is moored at the end of the fixed net.

The fish hit the barrier and run toward the *carrelet*. There they rub against the *bistoquette* (cord), a signal for the net to be raised.

PIKE
The pike population is diminishing because their preferred spawning grounds, the water meadows, are becoming rarer.

ALLIS SHAD. Related to sardines, these migratory fish leave the coastal waters in May and ascend the Loire to lay their eggs.

"TROUSSE-CULOTTE" FISHING
This involves tucking up trousers or skirts, standing thigh-deep in the water and stirring up the sand or gravel with one's feet. The resulting sand cloud attracts gudgeon, sparling and bleak.

BEAKED CARP. They come from eastern and central Europe and are very sensitive to pollution.

GUDGEON
Easily recognizable, this swift, gregarious fish is partial to invertebrates.

EEL. As soon as summer comes, eel go down the Loire for the long journey to the Sargasso Sea.

SPARLING
Small river fish that like sand and gravel.

CATFISH
Originating in North America, they are very small in Europe.

MULLET. These sea fish live in shoals and swim far up the Loire in search of food.

BREAM
They like calm, deep waters and enjoy foraging in muddy river beds to find their food.

RIVER LAMPREY
Primitive migratory fish, with a mouth shaped like a cupping glass. In common with their cousin the sea lamprey, they have now become extremely rare.

The Loire salmon has given rise to numerous local recipes, such as salmon in green sauce and salmon poached in stock with Vouvray wine.

WOODLAND AND FORESTS

SPOTTED SALAMANDER
You are most likely to encounter this amphibian on rainy nights.

The middle section of the Loire is surrounded by woods and forests, which are often very dense. Geological influences and human intervention have produced several kinds of landscape. Around Blois, for example, one can find magnificent plantations of sessile and pedunculate oaks; around Orléans Scots pines were introduced 200 years ago to create the largest national forest in France (almost 90,000 acres); and in the Sologne birches and chestnut trees complete the forest tapestry. Toward Anjou maritime pines reign supreme. Among the foliage, rich and diverse fauna and flora thrive in the woodland habitat.

Although perceived as natural landscapes, forests have to a large extent been shaped by human activity.

DEER
In early fall the forests resound with rutting calls. In the rutting season deer stop feeding for several weeks.

EUROPEAN WILD BOAR
The mature male (which has a dark, rough coat) leads a solitary life. Mature females lead groups consisting of several generations.

GOSHAWK
A clever forest hunter which keeps down pigeons, jays, rooks and squirrels.

HOLLY. It grows in the shady undergrowth.

MIDDLE-SPOTTED WOODPECKER
Declining in Europe, this typical inhabitant of the ancient oak woods is heard in the foliage, with its inimitable "twang".

JAY. Very fond of acorns, it is recognized as the premier European afforester.

F. Desbordes

AGRICULTURE AND HORTICULTURE

CUCUMBERS
Grown under glass, like tomatoes.

The quality of the soils in the Loire Valley (light, sandy and rich in silt), together with the mild regional climate, make it ideal for horticulture, market gardening and arboriculture. Large areas of the "Jardin de la France" are farmed (either in the open or under cover), flowers being the dominant crop. Market gardeners in the region specialize in a considerable variety of crops, including white and green asparagus, celery, lettuces, cauliflowers, gherkins and mushrooms. Other crops include soft fruit (strawberries, blackcurrants, raspberries . . .), grain, bulbs, pears and apples. In this way the Orléanais, Blésois, Touraine and Anjou regions contribute to the horticultural and agricultural reputation of the Loire Valley at the European level.

Mushroom caves dug in the chalk can be several hundred yards, or even more than a mile, deep. The mushrooms are grown on a bed of horse manure, straw and fertilizer. From sowing to harvesting takes three months.

CULTIVATED MUSHROOMS
Among the varieties developed from the meadow agaric are *albidus* (white), the most common, and *avelloneus* (blond).

BLACKCURRANTS
These are harvested with grape-picking machines and made into cassis syrup or liqueur.

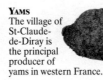

YAMS
The village of St-Claude-de-Diray is the principal producer of yams in western France.

ROSES
There has been a long tradition of rose-growing in the Loire Valley. Doué-la-Fontaine (Anjou) and Bellegarde (Orléanais) are the two main growers.

HEATHER
Heathers are cultivated on a large scale in Touraine (500,000 pots a year).

CHRYSANTHEMUMS
This flower is popular in France because it is in bloom for All Saints' Day. Anjou and Touraine are large-scale growers.

PELARGONIUMS
Zonal and ivy-leaved pelargoniums are well loved by gardeners. They are a specialty of the Orléans region.

THE "PLATISSOIRE"
A forgotten recipe has been revived in Rivarennes (Touraine) and Turquant (near Saumur): pears or apples are slowly dehydrated in the oven before being flattened and bottled in jars.

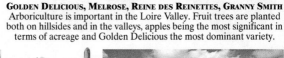

STRAWBERRIES
These are grown on mulched sandy soils, like asparagus and vines.

"ALBERGE DE TOURAINE" AND "PRÉCOCE DE SAUMUR"
Two varieties of apricot.

PASSE-CRASSANE, BEURRÉ-HARDY, CONFERENCE
Summer varieties, such as William, and winter varieties (Passe-Crassane) are losing ground to autumn pears such as Conference and Beurré-Hardy.

STE-CATHERINE PLUM
The flowering plum tree of Tours.

GOLDEN DELICIOUS, MELROSE, REINE DES REINETTES, GRANNY SMITH
Arboriculture is important in the Loire Valley. Fruit trees are planted both on hillsides and in the valleys, apples being the most significant in terms of acreage and Golden Delicious the most dominant variety.

Asparagus gouge

Cultivated in France since the 18th century, white asparagus has found ideal conditions in the sandy soils of the Loire Valley.

HARVESTING ASPARAGUS
Plastic mulching (above) has enabled early cropping. Asparagus is harvested from April to June. A special gouge (above, right) is used for cutting the spears.

CAULIFLOWERS
A traditional summer crop in Touraine. Varieties include "Frémont", "Linday" and "Nautilus".

LOLO ROSSA
A recent crop well liked by chefs.

LETTUCE
There can be three successive greenhouse crops.

GREEN ASPARAGUS
Traditionally a southern crop, green asparagus is now being grown in the Loire valley, especially in Loir-et-Cher.

ANIMAL FARMING AND BREEDING

Soil and know-how are the key to becoming a good goat's cheese maker.

Historically, the Loire Valley, from the area around Gien to Anjou, was a region dedicated to animal farming. Unfortunately with the progress of cereal-farming methods and a difficult economic situation, animal farming has been progressively abandoned in favor of corn crops, orchards, market gardening and poplar plantations. Cattle and horses are, however, still to be found in the more humid regions. Poultry, pigs and goats are raised intensively in accordance with the latest quality standards.

THE GÉLINE NOIRE OF TOURAINE
Originating from the French black chicken, its standard characteristics were defined in 1909.

BLACK TURKEY
This bird of American origin is now farmed in the Loire Valley – sometimes with the *label rouge* quality label, as in Touraine.

THE GÂTINAISE
The standard characteristics of this white chicken were defined in 1906. It is specific to the Loiret, and is bred for eating and eggs.

Now replaced by the tractor, the highly efficient draft horse was used for carting sand from the river, as well as for drawing barges along the Loire ● *46* and for ploughing the fields.

SOLOGNE SHEEP
Until the 19th century this extremely hardy and prolific breed, which is also an excellent walker, grazed in the water meadows beside the Loire and was the basis of a prosperous wool industry. The return of set-aside and rotation may revive it.

ALPINE GOAT
Most Loire herds consist of Saanen and Alpine goats. The small traditional herds are now giving way to the large herds of modern goat farming.

In the Loire Valley, as everywhere in France, the white Charolais has become the reference breed for meat.

WINE AND GOAT'S CHEESE

Goat's cheese can be eaten warm on a piece of toast or in puff pastry, or with a salad, or simply for the cheese course, accompanied by one of the Loire's excellent white wines, such as Cheverny, Saumur or Vouvray.

GOAT'S CHEESE

Much care is needed. Once the milk has been curdled with the addition of rennet, it is ladled into cheese strainers where it is left to drip and separate from the whey for twenty-four to forty-eight hours.

Although a few farms make cheese from yew's milk or cow's milk, most of the region's cheesemaking is based on goat's cheese. Well-known goat's cheeses include Selles-sur-Cher (Loir-et-Cher), the *bûche* from Ste-Maure (Indre-et-Loire) and the *pyramide* from Valençay. The first two are protected by an AOC.

THE MAINE-ANJOU

This cow is derived from the Mancelle breed, which was crossbred with the English Durham and the Shorthorn in the 19th century, resulting in the Durham-Mancelle in 1908. The standard characteristics of the Maine-Anjou were defined in 1925, and it became established on the borders of the Sarthe, Mayenne and Maine-et-Loire départements. Originally a mixed milk-meat breed, it is today raised almost exclusively for its fine marbled meat, which enjoys an excellent reputation. The herds are mostly in Anjou, though the largest ones (numbering some 85,000 head in 1996) are to be found in the United States and Canada.

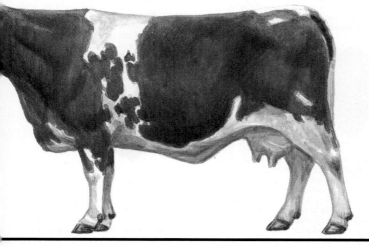

■ VINEYARDS

Grape picking – a source
of seasonal employment
and also an opportunity to
meet family and friends.

Present since Roman times, vineyards in the Loire Valley were given new life from the 9th to the 12th century thanks to the monasteries, in particular the famous abbeys of St-Benoît in the Orléans region, Marmoutier in Touraine, and Fontevraud in Anjou. The infatuation of the French kings with the Loire Valley contributed to this trend, and the river itself – where barges and lighters plied until the start of the 20th century – encouraged trading. Today the vineyards of the Loire Valley between Sancerre and Angers, covering 150,000 acres, constitute the fourth largest winegrowing area in France. The vines are spread, according to geological and climatic affinities, among some fifty *appellations d'origine contrôlée*, providing a wide choice of dry, sweet, sparkling and *pétillant* white wines, red wines for laying down or immediate drinking, and sweet or dry rosés.

MAIN APPELLATIONS

AOC (Appellation d'origine contrôlée): Anjou, Bonnezeaux, Bourgueil, Cheverny, Chinon, Coteaux-du-Layon, Coteaux-de-l'Aubance, Cour-Cheverny, Mennetou-Salon, Montlouis, Pouilly, Pouilly-Fumé, Quarts-de-Chaume, Quincy, Reuilly, St-Nicolas-de-Bourgueil, Sancerre, Saumur, Saumur-Champigny, Savennières, Touraine, Vouvray.

VDQS (Vin délimité de qualité supérieure): Cheverny, Côtes-de-Gien, Cour-Cheverny, Gris-Meunier de l'Orléanais, Valençay.

Angers

CÔT

This red-grape variety, known as Auxerrois in Cahors, was introduced in Anjou, Touraine and Blésois for making red and rosé Anjou and Touraine wines and also Valençay. It is used with Gamay, Cabernet and Groelleau to produce the finest Anjou rosés.

SAUVIGNON

This early grape variety forms the basis of some lively dry white wines that are spicy and highly aromatic. Its favorite terrain is Sancerrois, the home of Sancerre, Pouilly-Fumé and Mennetou-Salon. Grown in Anjou, Giennois, Blésois and Touraine, it combines well with Chenin Blanc and other grape varieties.

PINEAU-DE-LOIRE (CHENIN BLANC)

Already known in the time of Rabelais, this is the typical Loire-valley grape variety. Used alone, it gives such well-known white wines as Vouvray, Montlouis, Saumur, Savennières, Coteaux-du-Layon, Quarts-de-Chaume and Bonnezeaux. In association with Sauvignon, it contributes to Touraine and Cheverny wines and white Anjous.

GAMAY

Very much in fashion, this red-grape variety with white juice, from Beaujolais, has taken over numerous winegrowing areas, among them Anjou, Touraine and Blésois. It gives full, light, fruity wines and is perfectly adapted to the current vogue for young wines.

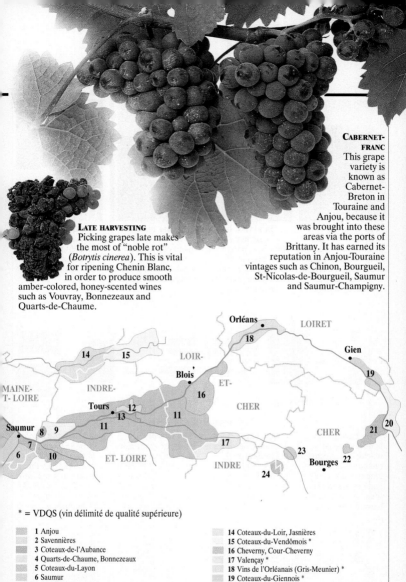

CABERNET-FRANC
This grape variety is known as Cabernet-Breton in Touraine and Anjou, because it was brought into these areas via the ports of Brittany. It has earned its reputation in Anjou-Touraine vintages such as Chinon, Bourgueil, St-Nicolas-de-Bourgueil, Saumur and Saumur-Champigny.

LATE HARVESTING
Picking grapes late makes the most of "noble rot" (*Botrytis cinerea*). This is vital for ripening Chenin Blanc, in order to produce smooth amber-colored, honey-scented wines such as Vouvray, Bonnezeaux and Quarts-de-Chaume.

Orléans
18
LOIRET
Gien
19
LOIR-
Blois
16
ET-
CHER
14   15
INDRE-
Tours
12
13
11
17
CHER
23   22
Bourges
21   20
MAINE-T-LOIRE
Saumur
8   9
7
6   10
ET-LOIRE
INDRE
24

* = VDQS (vin délimité de qualité supérieure)

1 Anjou
2 Savennières
3 Coteaux-de-l'Aubance
4 Quarts-de-Chaume, Bonnezeaux
5 Coteaux-du-Layon
6 Saumur
7 Saumur-Champigny
8 St-Nicolas-de-Bourgueil
9 Bourgueil
10 Chinon
11 Touraine (Azay-Le-Rideau, Amboise, Mesland)
12 Vouvray
13 Montlouis

14 Coteaux-du-Loir, Jasnières
15 Coteaux-du-Vendômois *
16 Cheverny, Cour-Cheverny
17 Valençay *
18 Vins de l'Orléanais (Gris-Meunier) *
19 Coteaux-du-Giennois *
20 Pouilly-Fumé, Pouilly-sur-Loire
21 Sancerre
22 Mennetou-Salon
23 Quincy
24 Reuilly

PINOT-NOIR
Famous in Alsace, Burgundy and Champagne, this grape variety plays a part in the production of the red wines of the Gien, Orléans and Sancerre areas.

ROCHE-AUX-MOINES AND COULÉE-DE-SERRANT (SAVENNIÈRES)
The Chenin Blanc cultivated on 70 acres of steep, picturesque shale slopes on the right bank of the Loire near Angers produces these two exceptionally fine vintages.

■ FROM VINE TO WINE

PRUNING THE VINE
Crucial for both quality and yield, the pruning is done in winter (see the legend of Saint Martin's donkey ● *104*).

BURSTING OF THE BUDS
The leaves burst from the buds in May. Grape picking takes place a hundred days after flowering.

GRAPE PICKING
Whether done by hand or by machine, this takes several weeks, starting in the middle of September.

BOTTLING
The wine undergoes a light filtration process before it is bottled.

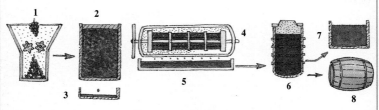

PRODUCTION OF RED WINES

After having been hand-picked or machine-harvested, the bunches of grapes are sorted and destalked (**1**), then left in a vat for between five and twenty days (**2**). The juice becomes colored through contact with the grape skins, and the sugars are fermented by the action of the yeasts. The fermented must, or grape juice, that collects at the bottom of the vat is drawn off; this is known as the *vin de goutte* (**3**). Next the *marc* is pressed (**4**), **and** then the *vin de presse* (**5**) **and** the *vin de goutte* (**3**) are mixed together (**6**) and poured into vats (**7**) or casks (**8**), where the wine is left to mature.

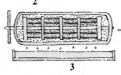

PRODUCTION OF WHITE AND ROSÉ WINES

The grapes, either white or black (for rosé), are destalked (**1**), then pressed (**2**) as quickly as possible in order to avoid any harmful oxidation. The juice or must (**3**) is put into a vat for carefully controlled fermentation (**4**). The settling process follows next, during which impurities are eliminated through filtration and racking (syphoning off). The must is then poured into vats (**5**) or casks (**6**) and the settling process continues, concluding with the final racking and clarification just before bottling (**7**). Clarification entails clearing the wine by adding a substance (generally either casein or egg white) that will precipitate any impurities still remaining in it.

SPARKLING AND PÉTILLANT WINES
The Loire's Chenin Blanc grapes are admirably suited to making sparkling and *pétillant* wines. The Crémant-de-Loire *appellation* extends from Angers (downstream) to Cheverny (upstream).

HISTORY

FROM CHARLES V TO LOUIS XVI
HISTORY, *36*

FROM CHARLES V
TO LOUIS XVI

1. The porcupine, Louis XII's emblem.
2. and **3.** The swan and the ermine, the emblems of Anne de Bretagne and her daughter Claude of France.

4. The salamander, emblem of Francis I.

*CHARLES V (1338–80) –

CHARLES VI – Isabel of Bavaria
(1368–1422)   (1371–1435)

CHARLES VII – Marie of Anjou
(1403–61)   (1404–63)

LOUIS XI – Charlotte of Savoy
(1423–83)   (1442–83)

Anne de Valois – Pierre de Beaujeu   **CHARLES VIII** – Anne de Bretagne   1. Jeanne de Valois –
(1461–1522)   (1438–1503)   (1470–98)   (1476–1514)   (1464–1505)
                                                                    2. Anne de Bretagne –
                                                                    (1476–1514)

FRANÇOIS II – Mary Stuart   **CHARLES IX** – Elisabeth of Austria   **HENRI III** – Louise of Lorraine
(1544–60)   (1542–87)   (1550–74)   (1554–92)   (1551–89)   (1553–1601)

ANNE DE BRETAGNE. Charles VIII had to stave off the intrigues of François II of Brittany, who wanted to marry his daughter and heiress, Anne, to Maximilian of Austria. Charles forced the young duchess to break off her engagement and dressed himself as a husband in Maximilian's place. Irrevocable commitments were made: if Anne had no male heir, she undertook to marry Charles' successor. And so she did: after Charles' death she married Louis XII, thus making Brittany part of France for ever ▲ *258*.

LOUIS XII. The son of Charles d'Orléans ▲ *114*, who was a refined man of letters, Louis XII was only three when his father died. Educated by his mother in history, literature and physical education, by the time he ascended the throne he had acquired a taste for socializing and a subtle knowledge of the human character.

4

1.

2.

3.

Jeanne de Bourbon (1338–77)

Louis, Duke of Orléans – Valentine Visconti
(1372–1407)   (1366–1408)

Charles, Duke of Orléans – Marie of Cleves   Jean d'Angoulême – Marguerite de Rohan
(1391–1465)   (1426–87)   (1404–67)   (?–1496)

Louis XII   Charles d'Angoulême – Louise of Savoy
(1462–1515)   (1459–96)   (1476–1531)

Claude of France – **François I**   Marguerite – Henri d'Albret, King of Navarre
(1499–1524)   (1494–1547)   (1493–1549)   (1503–55)

Henri II – Catherine de Médicis   Jeanne d'Albret – Antoine de Bourbon
(1519–59)   (1519–89)   (1528–72)   (1518–62)

1. Marguerite de Valois –
(1553–1615)
2. Marie de Médicis – **Henry IV**
(1573–1642)   (1553–1610)

Louis XIII – Anne of Austria
(1601–43)   (1601–66)

Louis XIV --Maria Theresa of Austria
(1638–1715)   (1638–83)

Louis, the Grand Dauphin – Marie Anne of Bavaria
(1661–1711)   (1660–90)

Louis, Duke of Burgundy – Marie Adelaide of Savoy
(1682–1712)   (1685–1712)

Louis XV – Marie Leszczynska
(1710–74)   (1703–68)

Louis of France – Marie Josephe of Saxony
(1729–65)   (1731–67)

Louis XVI – Marie Antoinette of Austria
(1754–93)   (1755–93)

*A family tree of reigning kings of France
from Charles V to Louis XVI.*

2500 BC to 1500 BC	52 BC Gauls
Dolmens and menhirs	rise against
	the Romans

| 500,000 BC | 50,000 BC | 10,000 BC | 5000 BC | 0 | 400 |

500,000 BC	80,000 BC TO 35,000 BC	7000 BC Farming at Fossé	58 BC Start of	258 AD to 260 AD
First human	Neanderthal man;	(near Blois) using wheat	the conquest of	Penetration by Franks
beings in the	beginning of the last	and millet seeds from the	Gaul by Julius	and Saxons into the
Loire Valley	Ice Age	Middle East	Caesar	Loire region

PREHISTORIC AND PROTOHISTORIC

The first human beings in the Loire Valley appear in the Paleolithic era and live by hunting, fishing and gathering. Around 10,000 BC global warming affects their nomadic way of life, causing them to settle down, to start to rear animals and to farm. Between 6000 and 4000 BC, in the Neolithic era, they clear the forests and improve their tool making. Besides flint, they work with wood, horn and bone. From around 2500 BC the countryside is dotted with megaliths for worshipping the dead. Dolmens (collective burial places) are numerous: almost 140 of them have been found in the four départements of the Loire Valley, among them the remarkable Grand Dolmen de Bagneux ▲ 290. The menhirs (monolithic stone blocks) are still shrouded in mystery; although many of them have been destroyed, there are still about 130 of them left. Cremation was practiced too, as evidenced by the field full of earthenware funeral urns discovered near Jargeau ▲ 126. Artefacts from the Bronze Age (around 1500 to 750 BC) are distinguished by their comparative luxury (sword handles and jewelry). From the Iron Age (750 to 50 BC), weapons and jewelry have survived.

THE GAULS

THE GAULS

Around 450 BC Celtic tribes from the east settle in the Loire Valley: the Andecavi ▲ 296 in what is now Anjou; the Turones ▲ 196 in Touraine; and the Carnutes ▲ 112 in the Orléans region. They build camps and fortified villages, such as the Châtelliers *oppidum* at Amboise ▲ 182.

THE ARRIVAL OF CHRISTIANITY
It would seem that Christianity developed in the Loire Valley in the 3rd century AD. By the 4th century Angers, Orléans and Tours have their own bishops. Saint Lidoire, first Bishop of Tours (337–70), is succeeded by Saint Martin ▲ 206. Combining his episcopal duties (371–91) with a life of meditation, he establishes a community at Marmoutier, near Tours. This becomes the cradle of the monasticism that would soon spread throughout Europe.

THE CONQUEST OF GAUL

In 58 BC Julius Caesar embarks on the conquest of Gaul. In the Loire Valley his soldiers meet with fierce resistance from the Andecavi and the Carnutes, allies of Vercingetorix. In retaliation, in 52 BC Caesar burns down Cenabum (present-day Orléans), capital of the Carnutes, then the center of Gaul. In the same year the taking of the city of Alesia and surrender of Vercingetorix marks the end of the Gallic Wars.

ROMANIZATION

Rome imprints its administrative and socio-cultural model on Gaul. Cities similar to Roman cities arise from Angers to Orléans. Caesarodunum (Tours) is founded in the year 20 AD. Large farms (*villae*) are set up. Today the imposing aqueduct of a private landowner is still visible in the middle of a field at Luynes ▲ 262. The Romans set up an intricate network of paved roads, sixteen of which radiate from Cenabum.

END OF THE "PAX ROMANA"

In the middle of the 3rd century AD the barbarians, hitherto restrained, cross the frontiers of the Empire. From 258 AD to 260 AD, the Franks and the Saxons ravage the Loire region, which in 274 AD suffers another Frankish invasion. Fortified walls are built to protect towns such as Orléans (in the 3rd century) and Tours (in the 4th century), where splendid ramparts still flank the Quai d'Orléans ▲ 196.

AD End of the Western ...man Empire. The barbarians ...e Rome – and Tours

751 AD Start of the Carolingian dynasty: Pepin the Short elected King of the Franks

Late 8th century to early 9th century The Carolingian renaissance

c. 972–1040 Foulques Nerra, Count of Anjou

486 Clovis, King of the Franks

507 Victory by Clovis over the Visigoths at Vouillé

732 Charles Martel, mayor of palace, defeats the Spanish Moors at Poitiers

800 Charlemagne becomes Emperor

987 Start of the Capetian dynasty; Hugues Capet, Count of Orléans and Étampes, elected King of France

THE EARLY MIDDLE AGES

THE BARBARIAN INVASIONS

In the 5th century Germans, Franks, Burgundians and Visigoths overrun Gaul. The population seeks refuge in fortified sites such as Orléans and Tours. In 451 the Huns unsuccessfully lay siege to Orléans; the Saxons are at Angers; and the Visigoths covet Tours. The barbarians carve out kingdoms throughout Roman Gaul.

THE FRANKISH KINGDOM

Franks and Visigoths fight for Touraine. Clovis, by his victory at Vouillé (507) over Alaric II ▲ *190*, King of the Visigoths, takes Tours and Aquitaine. On his death his sons indulge in fratricidal fighting, as related in *History of the Frankish Peoples* by Gregory of Tours ▲ *196*.

CROSS OF ANJOU
Created for Louis I of Anjou around 1377–9, it serves as the emblem of the Order of the Cross before becoming the Cross of Anjou ▲ *312*. In 1431 it takes the name "Cross of Lorraine" when René I inherits the duchy of Lorraine.

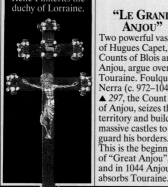

CAROLINGIAN RENAISSANCE

The Merovingian kings are gradually pushed out by the mayors of the palace, who exercise the real power. One of them, Pepin the Short (son of Charles Martel), is elected king of the Franks in 751. His son, Charlemagne (747–814), extends the frontiers of Christianity during his forty-six-year reign. His empire, with Aix-la-Chapelle as its capital, extends for nearly 400,000 square miles. At his bidding, the Basilica of St-Martin in Tours ▲ *204* becomes a royal abbey headed by the erudite Alcuin, who turns Tours into a major religious and intellectual center ▲ *205*. Charlemagne entrusts Alcuin and Theodulf ▲ *129*, Abbot of St-Benoît-sur-Loire, with the task of reviving the episcopal schools and of creating in each a *scriptorium* (scribe's workshop). St-Martin, in Tours, produces remarkable manuscripts during the 9th century.

NEW INVASIONS

The empire, divided and weakened, is threatened by new invaders: the Vikings. On six occasions between 853 and 903 they sail up the Loire from Angers to Orléans, plundering

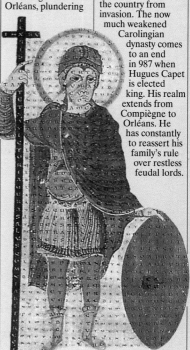

towns, churches and monasteries. The raids only cease when Charles the Simple gives Normandy to the Viking leader Rollo (911), in exchange for his promise to protect the country from invasion. The now much weakened Carolingian dynasty comes to an end in 987 when Hugues Capet is elected king. His realm extends from Compiègne to Orléans. He has constantly to reassert his family's rule over restless feudal lords.

THE ANGEVIN EMPIRE AND THE PLANTAGENÊTS

(1044–1259)

"LE GRAND ANJOU"

Two powerful vassals of Hugues Capet, the Counts of Blois and Anjou, argue over Touraine. Foulques Nerra (c. 972–1040) ▲ *297*, the Count of Anjou, seizes the territory and builds massive castles to guard its borders. This is the beginning of "Great Anjou", and in 1044 Anjou absorbs Touraine.

WISE WEDDINGS

The marriage, in 1110, arranged by Foulques V, Count of Anjou (1095–1143), between his son Geoffrey (1113–51) and Matilda, the daughter of King Henry I of England, brings the Angevins the county of Maine. After the marriage has been concluded, in 1129 Foulques V leaves for the Holy Land. Geoffrey, the first member of the Angevins to use the surname Plantagenet, initially a nickname, from the sprig of broom (*genêt*) with which he customarily decorates his cap, takes charge of the county of Anjou. In 1144 Geoffrey conquers the Duchy of Normandy, which he entrusts to his son Henry Plantagenet as early as 1150.

PLANTAGENETS V. CAPETIANS

On March 21, 1152 the marriage between the King of France, Louis VII (1120–80), and Eleanor of Aquitaine (1122–1204) is dissolved on grounds of "consanguinity". Two months later Eleanor marries the young Henry Plantagenet (1133–89), who in 1154 succeeds to the throne of England as Henry II. The couple are now at the head of a vast state rivaling that of the King of France, extending from the Scottish border to the Pyrenees, with Anjou at its heart. But in 1189 Henry II is obliged to accept a humiliating defeat near Azay-le-Rideau at the hands of his rebel son Richard the Lionheart (right), in alliance with Philippe-Auguste. He surrenders the crown of England to the former, and backs the territorial conquests of the latter. He dies at Chinon in the same year. Successive kings of France fight unceasingly to keep the domain of the Plantagenets under French tenure. With the Treaty of Paris (1259) Louis IX puts an end to what has been called the "First Hundred Years' War". He recovers Touraine, Anjou and Maine, and exacts homage from the King of England for Guyenne.

THE PLANTAGENETS' ACHIEVEMENTS

The Plantagenets left a lasting mark on the Loire Valley. They founded several abbeys, among them Fontevraud ▲ *227*, which houses their necropolis. The Hôpital St-Jean ▲ *308* in Angers, along with the Chartreuse at Liget ▲ *230*, were built by Henry II (below) in atonement for the murder of Thomas Becket. We owe to the Plantagenets the creation of law schools and the origins of the future University of Angers. Angevin vaulting ● *60* – also called Plantagenet vaulting – came into being during their reign, and embankments were raised to protect the Loire Valley from flooding.

THE HUNDRED YEARS' WAR (1337–1453)

THE ACCESSION OF THE VALOIS DYNASTY

In 1328 Philippe de Valois (1293–1350) ▲ *112*, nephew of Philip the Fair, succeeds his cousin Charles IV (the last direct Capetian descendant) under the name of Philippe VI. In 1337 Edward III, King of England, who is the vassal of the King of France for Guyenne, refuses to pay homage to Philippe VI; in return Philippe seizes the domain. In 1340 Edward, who is the grandson of Philip the Fair, claims the French throne. The Anglo-French conflict starts again: it will last 116 years, interrupted by numerous truces.

ARMAGNACS AND BOURGUIGNONS

The conflict starts again in 1337 in the name of the new King of England, Richard II (1367–1400), who is only ten years old. In France Charles VI (1368–1422), also a minor, reigns under the tutelage of his paternal uncles, the Duke of Anjou, the Duke of Berry, the Duke of Burgundy (Philip the Bold) and his maternal uncle, the Duke of Bourbon.

FROM CRÉCY TO THE 1375 TRUCE

In 1346 the English land in large numbers at Calais. Philippe VI and the cream of the French cavalry are decimated on August 26 at Crécy. Ten years later the King of France, Jean the Good (1319–64), son of Philippe VI, is taken prisoner at Maupertuis, near to Poitiers, by the Prince of Wales (the Black Prince) and is held captive in London for eight years. The Dauphin Charles, the future Charles V (1338–80), rules France during the internment of his father. The Treaty of Brétigny (1360) allows Jean to be set free in return for payment of a ransom. Furthermore, under the same treaty the English king agrees to abandon his claims to Anjou, Aquitaine, Normandy and the throne of France. Nevertheless, the war between England and France is resumed in 1369 when Charles V once again seizes Guyenne. Thanks to Du Guesclin (c. 1320–80), who is appointed High Constable in 1370, the French reconquer almost all their lost territories. The truce of 1375, imposed by the Pope, allows both parties to rebuild their armed strength.

1409 Birth of René I in Angers	**1415** French defeated at Agincourt	**1429** Joan of Arc breaks the siege of Orléans	**1431** Joan of Arc burned at the stake	**1440** Start of a royal presence in the Loire Valley
1400	**1410**	**1420**	**1430**	**1440**	**1450**
1407 Assassination of Louis d'Orléans by Jean the Fearless, Duke of Burgundy	**1418** Occupation of Paris by the Burgundians	**1420** Treaty of Troyes	**1429** French victory at Patay		**1453** End of the Hundred Years' War

In 1388, increasingly under the influence of his brother Louis d'Orléans (son-in-law of the Count of Armagnac), Charles VI replaces his uncles with his father's old counselors. In 1392 the king suffers an attack of madness, and his uncles take advantage of his fragile health to regain power. In 1407 the assassination of Louis d'Orléans by the new Duke of Burgundy, Jean the Fearless, stirs up the fight between the Burgundians and the Armagnacs. In 1414 Jean the Fearless forms an alliance with the English against the Armagnacs and the King of France. The English invasion starts in August 1415. After the defeat of the French troops at Agincourt (above) on October 25, 1415, the northern half of the kingdom is occupied by the English and the Burgundians. In May 1418 the Duke of Burgundy takes Paris and captures the king. The Dauphin Charles makes his escape, falling back first to Bourges, then to Chinon. By the Treaty of Troyes (May 25, 1420) Charles VI gives his daughter in marriage to King Henry V of England, whom he acknowledges as his heir, thus barring the "so-called Dauphin" – who stands accused by his mother, Isabel of Bavaria, of being an adulterer – from succeeding to the French crown. On December 1, 1420 the English enter Paris.

THE 1348 PLAGUE
In 1347 a scourge unknown in Europe since the 7th century arrives in Marseilles, brought by boat from the Crimea. The Black Death (bubonic plague) spreads over France during the following year. The Europe of 1349 to 1350 is in mourning. It is estimated that one out of three people in the kingdom has fallen victim.

THE RECONQUEST
In 1422 Charles VII proclaims himself King of France, but remains uncrowned. On October 12, 1428 the English lay siege to Orléans ▲ *116*. Then the unexpected happens – when Joan of Arc (below) leaves Domrémy, is given an audience by her king, on March 6, 1429 at Chinon ▲ *243*, and obtains his agreement to take up arms and go to Orléans. Eight days after her arrival the siege is lifted. After an even more decisive victory at Patay (May 8, 1429), Charles is crowned on July 17 in Reims. On September 21, 1435 he signs the Arras peace accord with the Burgundians, which at last confirms his legitimacy. His reign continues with twenty years of gradual reconquest, beginning in Paris in 1436 and culminating with the taking of Bordeaux in 1453. Thus the Hundred Years' War finally comes to an end, without any peace treaty having been signed.

1460	1470	1480	1500	1550	1600

1498 Louis, Duke of Orléans, King of France

1519 Death of Leonardo da Vinci at Clos-Lucé

1560 Conspiracy of Amboise

1598 Proclamation of the Edict of Nantes

1470 Foundation of silk industry in Tours

1491 Marriage of Charles VIII to Anne de Bretagne at Langeais

1523 Calvin at Orléans University

1588 Assassination of the Duke of Guise at Blois

THE GOLDEN AGE: THE 15TH AND 16TH CENTURIES

THE LOIRE, ROYAL RIVER

Starting with Charles VII (1403–61), who is disillusioned with the fickleness of Paris during the Hundred Years' War, the kings of France forsake the capital in favor of the Loire Valley, the itinerant court going from one château to another.

Charles VII sets up successively at Chinon ▲ 244, Loches ▲ 224 and Amboise ▲ 180, before settling near Tours ▲ 196. For eighty years the city becomes the political and religious capital of the kingdom. Louis XI (1423–83) makes Plessis-lès-Tours ▲ 259 (above) his "most visited" residence. Charles VIII (1470–98), husband of Anne de Bretagne ● 34, divides his time between Langeais ● 66, ▲ 268 and

Amboise, where he dies after an accident. Louis XII (1462–1515), who succeeds him, marries his widow and moves the court to Blois ● 67, ▲ 144. François I ● 35 (below) adds a wing to the castle ● 68 and persuades Leonardo da Vinci (opposite, bottom) to come to Amboise. The great man stays at Clos-Lucé ▲ 185 and advises on the design of Chambord ▲ 162. François' son, Henri II (1519–59), finishes the building. He gives Chenonceau ▲ 218 to his mistress, Diane de Poitiers, as a token of his love.

THE RELIGIOUS WARS

Early in the 16th century Luther and then Calvin denounce the privileges of the clergy and demand a reform of the Church. Books, now becoming more widely available thanks to the spread

of printing, and the spoken word help spread the thoughts of Calvin, who has frequently visited the University of Orléans ▲ 121. The Loire Valley is, after Paris, the fulcrum of the Reformation in France. From Gien to Angers, the Huguenots build Protestant churches. The conversion of famous families such as the Bourbons, the Condés and the La Rochefoucaults lends impetus to the formation of a Protestant "party", opposed to the increasingly frequent persecutions. The religious problem soon becomes a political one. Henry II's accidental death during a tournament in 1559 marks the start of a troubled period. His widow, Catherine de Médicis, is prepared to be tolerant, while the powerful Guise family fight for control of the Catholic "party".

In 1560 the Protestant princes attempt to kidnap the young Dauphin François II (1544–60), aged sixteen, to free him from the Guise influence. This is the savagely repressed Amboise conspiracy ▲ 183. The rupture between the Catholics and the Huguenots is now complete. Saint Bartholomew's Day (August 24) in 1572 is followed by the brutal massacre of Protestants in Angers. Then in 1588 Henry III (1551–89) has the Duke of Guise assassinated at Blois (below) in an effort to become the sole ruler of the Catholics. To escape the anger of the Catholic nobles, Henry III takes refuge at Tours, where he gathers his government. His assassination by the monk Jacques Clément in 1589 makes the Protestant Henry de Navarre (1553–1610) his legitimate successor. But the kingdom does not want a Protestant prince; he therefore agrees to convert to Catholicism and is crowned at Chartres, under the name of Henry IV. In 1598, by the Edict of Nantes, the new king ends forty years of civil war. His accession also marks the end of the royal presence in the Loire Valley.

1598 End of the royal presence in the Loire Valley	1648–53 Fronde	1685 Repeal of the Edict of Nantes	1709 Hunger riots in France	1745 Growing influence of Mme de Pompadour on Louis XV	1774 Louis XVI's reign
1610	**1650**	**1700**	**1725**	**1750**	**1775**
1610 Assassination of Henry IV by Ravaillac	1642 The Loire is linked to the Seine	17th and 18th centuries The Loire is a main commercial axis	1715 Death of Louis XIV		1774 Looting of boats transporting cereals

PROVINCIAL STAGNATION:
THE 17TH AND 18TH CENTURIES

ARTISTS AND WRITERS
The infatuation of the nobles and the prosperous trading and banking families with the new architecture leads to the building of numerous châteaux and *hôtels particuliers* ● *74* in the Loire Valley. Many of these are decorated by Touraine artists, such as Jean Fouquet ● *88* (above, *The Virgin of the Milk*), Jean Bourdichon ▲ *227* and François Clouet ▲ *220* (1505/10–72). There is also a lively interest in literature. Rabelais mentions his birthplace in *Gargantua* ▲ *250*. Ronsard ▲ *258*, the poet of love, dedicates poems to Cassandra ▲ *140* and Marie, and retires to St-Cosme ▲ *258*. Du Bellay is enthusiastic about the new school of poetry known as the Pléiade.

In spite of some disturbances during the early years of Louis XIII's reign (1601–43) and during the Fronde (1648–53), the Loire Valley stays outside the kingdom's political and religious troubles.

Shortly before the Revolution there is, as a general rule, a marked decline in the population of the towns. In a single century Blois has lost some 7,000 to 8,000 inhabitants; and Tours has lost as many as 13,000, as has Angers. Only Orléans has seen some measure of stability.

THE COUNTER-REFORMATION
The Protestants continue to cause unrest. In Saumur, a safe haven for the reformers, colleges and academies are training Protestant clerics. However, the Catholic Church is determined to reduce the influence of the Reformation. From 1614 the Oratorians turn Notre-Dame des Ardilliers ● *63*, ▲ *285*, in Saumur, into an important pilgrimage center; and in 1691 an episcopal seat is created at Blois. But while convents and colleges are being founded, Reformed churches are being closed. As a result, Protestants begin to emigrate ▲ *278*; the repeal of the Edict of Nantes in 1685 by Louis XIV (above) ● *35* accelerates the surge of emigration.

PROSPERITY AND DECLINE
Orléans has to rely on inland waterways for its trade with the Levant, the Antilles and England, and like Angers is seeking new openings; in the middle of the 17th century the city is linked to the Seine by a new waterway. In the period preceding the Revolution there are some thirty-two distilleries and two hundred vinegar factories ▲ *123* in Orléans, and also manufacturers of painted canvas. Blois has weathered the departure of the royal court (at the end of the 16th century) quite well, thanks to its trade in wine and spirits. However, the "decapitalized" city of Tours vegetates, its silk factories ▲ *260* rivaled by those of Lyon. Convents find the number of vocations is falling.

THE WORK OF THE "INTENDANTS"
The centralization started by the monarchy under Louis XIII relies on administrators (*intendants*) with wide-ranging powers. They leave their own mark on the Loire Valley. Du Cluzel, one of the *intendants* in the 18th century, is eager to give Tours the "most beautiful entry in the kingdom", with a stone bridge leading directly to the Rue Nationale. In Orléans another *intendant*, Perrin de Cypierre, opens up the Rue Royale with his famous arcades ▲ *121* that lead to a fine stone bridge. Blois is given a hump-back bridge ▲ *145* around which the life of the town seems to revolve in the 19th century.

41

1810 Talleyrand buys Valençay

1846 Hunger riots in Tours

1790   1800   1820   1830   1840   1850

1789 Start of the French Revolution

1793 Angers is taken by the Vendéens

1815 End of the First Empire

1829 Steamboats ply between Orléans and Blois

1849 The railway arrives at Orléans, Blois, Tours and Angers

FROM THE REVOLUTION TO THE THIRD REPUBLIC

REVOLUTION AND EMPIRE (1789–1815)

When Louis XVI (1754–93) convenes the États Généraux (States General) on May 5, 1789, the representative body loses no time in transforming itself into a revolutionary assembly to contest the supremacy of the monarchy. If the inhabitants of towns in the Loire Valley are won over by the arguments being put forward in favor of political and administrative reform (with a legislative assembly and four départements run by elected citizens), the peasant masses feel more and more let down. Religious reforms upset parish life, and the new fiscal regime in no way improves the lot of the peasantry. Discontent continues to grow with the sale of Church property and the requirement that the clergy must swear allegiance to the Constitution.

Finally September 21, 1792 witnesses the proclamation of the Republic, and Louis XVI is beheaded on January 21, 1793. Two months later, in March 1793, the Republic, now at war with the rest of Europe, decrees a mass conscription of the male population. This measure is

deemed provocative by the inhabitants of the Vendée and Anjou who, Royalist at heart, resort to arms. The "Whites" (the monarchists) and the "Blues" (the republicans) clash. Saumur falls, and then Angers. The terrible repression that follows leaves an indelible mark on the collective memory of western France. Napoleon Bonaparte (1769–1821), as First Consul, reacts to the political climate and manages to establish a religious peace, which is extended by the Concordat of 1801. After assuming the title of Emperor in 1804, he attempts to win the support of the monarchist département of Maine-et-Loire, but the renewed threat of conscription alienates the people of Anjou.

UNSTABLE REGIME

The Restoration (1815–30) and Louis-Philippe's "Monarchy of July" (1830–48) are unable to totally erase the advances made by the Revolution and the Empire. In the end Louis-Philippe is definitively ousted by the Revolution of 1848, which sees the birth of the Second Republic (1848–51). In December 1848 Louis-Napoleon Bonaparte, nephew of Napoleon I, is elected President of the Republic by universal franchise. On December 2, 1851 a coup d'état ushers in the Second Empire and he is crowned Napoleon III (left). Half-hearted efforts to liberalize his regime come too late to secure the future of the Empire.

| 1870 Tours serves as temporary seat of French government | 1875 Foundation of the Catholic University in Angers | 1876–83 Destruction of vineyards by phylloxera |

| 1860 | 1870 | 1880 | 1890 | 1900 | 1910 |

| 1870-1 Franco-Prussian war: operations by the Loire army | 1883 Foundation of the Franciade, France's first agricultural union, in Blois | 1902 The end of commercial traffic on the Loire between Orléans and Nantes |

THE THIRD REPUBLIC AND WORLD WAR TWO

A RESTRAINED APPROVAL

The Fench defeat at Sedan (September 1, 1870), at the hands of the Prussians, brings about the collapse of the Second Empire. The Third Republic is proclaimed on September 4 and is quickly adopted by the inhabitants of Indre-et-Loire, while those of Loir-et-Cher and Loiret tend to be more restrained. The situation is different in Maine-et-Loire; here the conservatism of the western regions derived from their historical monarchism and clericalism is still very much alive in the rural areas. With the introduction of laws on the secularization of schools and the separation of Church and State (1905), the syndrome of the "Whites" and the "Blues" is given a new lease of life.

The Prussians in Tours

THE DEFENSE OF THE LOIRE

In 1870 Gambetta escapes by balloon from Paris – which is under siege – to join the Government delegation in Tours, the temporary capital of France. Fighting takes place on the Loire at Orléans and Beaugency ▲ *139*. The inhabitants have to contend with requisitions, the cold and epidemics, most notably smallpox.

THE TOWNS OF THE LOIRE VALLEY IN THE 19TH CENTURY

Angers retains the image of an affluent town, proud of its school of engineering and its numerous private colleges. Its history has been marked by religious and aristocratic influence; this is less true of Tours, where there are numerous civil servants and railway employees. Blois struggles to make its mark, and Orléans experiences only average growth. Manpower from the countryside contributes to the growth of the towns.

INDUSTRIALIZATION AND THE RURAL ECONOMY

Rural depopulation worsens when the phylloxera infestation destroys the region's vineyards between 1876 and 1883. A third of them are not restored, being used for market gardening and as horticultural nurseries instead. The towns increase their activities. In Angers, Tours and Blois companies are founded that acquire a national or even worldwide reputation. Angers is the home of the Bessonneau textile empire and of Cointreau liqueurs ● *56*. Tours and Orléans both have pharmaceutical industries, while Blois is renowned for Poulain chocolate ● *56*. Loiret welcomes some remarkable foreign companies. The earthenware factory ▲ *134* started in Gien by Thomas Hall in 1821 enjoys its golden age in the second half of the 19th century. An American named Hutchinson brings the rubber industry to Montargis in 1853.

WORLD WAR TWO (1939–45)

In June 1940 history repeats itself. When the Germans occupy Paris, Tours becomes the capital for three days before the government withdraws to Bordeaux. During the Battle of the Loire, from Gien to Gennes, the cadets of Saumur ▲ *279*, ▲ *293* make a heroic stand against enemy forces. Towns with bridges over the Loire are bombarded and suffer considerable damage (more than 40 acres at Orléans). After the Armistice on June 22, 1940, the greater part of the four départements of the Loire Valley is under German occupation, which is completed by 1942. From 1943, and particularly during the spring of 1944, Allied bombs hit airfields and railway junctions, and the towns are hit again. Liberation takes place between August 10 and September 1, thanks to General Patton's 3rd Army, backed up by the French Resistance.

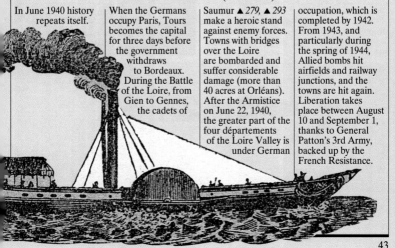

1940-4 Bombing of towns in the Loire Valley

1950-70 Postwar reconstruction and emergence of new towns

1986 The Halle aux Grains (grain market) in Blôis becomes a conference and cultural center

1920 ··· 1950 1960 ··· 1970 ··· 1980 ··· 1990

1920 Tours Congress: The French Socialist Party splits, birth of the PCF (French Communist Party)

1940 Tours is the capital of France for three days

1964 Avoine-Chinon nuclear power station starts operations

1972 Creation of the Centre and Pays de la Loire regions

1990 Start of TGV service between Paris and Tours

THE 4TH AND 5TH REPUBLICS: TOWARD THE THIRD MILLENIUM

The era of postwar reconstruction brings urban and industrial renewal accompanied by accelerated rural depopulation. To deal with the influx of people into the cities, new residential and industrial zones are created near the main towns (for example, Orléans purchases the 1,300-acre estate of La Source ▲ 124). There is considerable urban expansion: "Greater Angers" has 215,000 inhabitants; Tours, 282,000; Blois, 65,000; and Orléans, 244,000. Many of the region's older industries disappear, and are replaced by multinationals such as Thomson, Bull, Scania, SKF, Michelin and Matra. One of the most successful enterprises has been the Servier Pharmaceutical Products Laboratory: founded thirty years ago at Gigy with a total staff of nine,

it now employs some four hundred people, with factories in New York and Tokyo and a presence in 130 countries. The power stations beside the Loire ● 13 produce 25 percent of French nuclear electricity. The construction of new highways has made the region more dynamic. Thanks to the high-speed train (*TGV Atlantique*, below), in service since 1990, Tours is now less than an hour from Paris; TAT, the region's first private airline, has its offices in Tours. Universities, long lacking in the four départements, exist today: Orléans, seat of the Orléans-Tours Academy, has had a university since 1966; both Angers and Tours have possessed universities since 1971; and there has been a branch of Tours University in Blois since 1993. The organization of the country into new regions offered an opportunity to create a single entity from the four départements. However, the new administrative division has bought a resurgence of the old antagonisms. Maine-et-Loire has become

part of Pays de la Loire, while the three other départements have been assigned to

the Centre region, with a préfecture and regional council in Orléans ● 12.

REBIRTH THROUGH TOURISM

Tourism is benefiting from the new means of communication. There are now about a hundred châteaux in the Loire Valley open to the public. After Versailles, Chambord is the most visited historic site in France. The Briare canal bridge ▲ 137 celebrated its centenary in 1996, and the seven Rogny locks (which have survived from the

17th-century canal system) make an impressive staircase of water. Travel on the Loire itself has undergone a revival. The tributaries of the Maine (the Sarthe, Mayenne and Loir) are navigable for part of their length, and Angers makes a good base for cruises on these rivers. The Loiret ▲ 125 offers pleasant walks along its 8 miles.

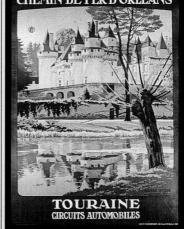

CHEMIN DE FER D'ORLEANS

TOURAINE
CIRCUITS AUTOMOBILES

ARTS AND TRADITIONS

● BOATS ON THE LOIRE

STEAMBOATS
A large number of steamboats were built from 1822 onward. Competition was tough between the different companies, such as Riverains Paquebots de la Loire and the famous Inexplosibles.

The quays and ports of the Loire are reminders of the importance of river transport, which reached its peak around 1860. At a time when the waterways were the principal means of communication, barges or lighters (*chalands*) were used to supply the towns with commodities such as wine, apples, salt, wheat, slates and tufa, and colonial products unloaded in Nantes. Sail navigation, which had adapted to the capricious river over the centuries, finally disappeared around 1900 when the railways arrived in the valley.

THE MERCHANTS' GUILD
From the 16th century onward bargees in the area banded together to fight against the excessive tolls imposed by local landlords and to press for necessary maintenance work on the Loire and its tributaries. Delegates from the riverside towns met every four years in Orléans. When the merchants' guild died out in 1772, responsibility for buoying, lights and maintenance was taken over by the highways department.

TRAVELING ON THE LOIRE
A river journey could take any length of time as the weather was so unreliable, and delays could be caused by floods, drought, ice or unfavorable winds. The Briare to Nantes journey, for instance, took around ten days downstream but more than three weeks upstream. On average, the river was navigable for 250 days a year.

THE "TOUE"
Some 50 feet long, this flat-bottomed boat was used as a short-distance carrier. Sand dredgers could load it with nearly 10 tons of sand. With a cabin and *carrelet* (square dipping net) it metamorphosed into the ideal craft for professional salmon or shad fishermen; floating tanks called *bascules* kept the fish alive until selling time.

THE "SAPINE"
Some 100 feet long, with a very shallow draught, the *sapine* was both carrier and cargo. Built upstream, without mast or sail, it made the journey downriver only once; on arrival it was dismantled, the wood being sold at the same time as its 40-ton cargo goods such as coal and china.

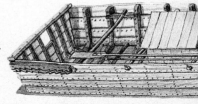

THE "FÛTREAU"
This small 30-foot craft could be rigged or not, depending on its use. It became a *bachot* for the bargee and ferryman,

and a *galiote* for the fisherman (it was then fitted with a fish tank). *Galiotes* were mostly used for catching perch.

GOING ABOUT
It was not uncommon for the large barges to dismast or haul down the rigging when approaching a bridge. For that purpose a powerful windlass, called a *guindas*, was used. The maneuver was not without danger: eight men were needed either to push (in which case they had to take care in order to avoid breaking the arms of the windlass) or to hang on (at the risk of losing hold).

"Let's sing to the Loire and its fleet, There's nothing like it on earth. On the way, when the sun rises Let's sing to the Loire and its fleet."

47

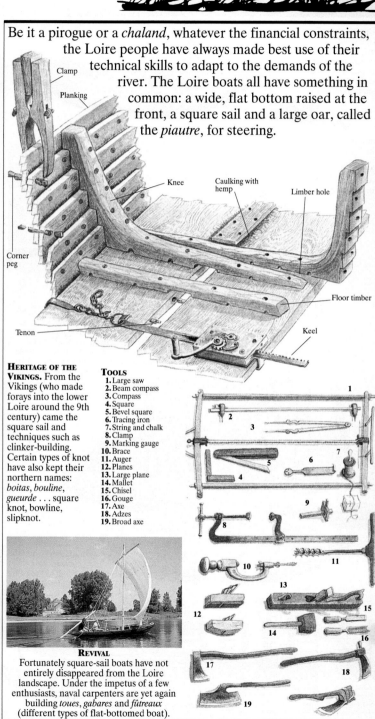

FROM PIROGUES TO LIGHTERS

Be it a pirogue or a *chaland*, whatever the financial constraints, the Loire people have always made best use of their technical skills to adapt to the demands of the river. The Loire boats all have something in common: a wide, flat bottom raised at the front, a square sail and a large oar, called the *piautre*, for steering.

Clamp

Planking

Knee

Caulking with hemp

Limber hole

Corner peg

Tenon

Floor timber

Keel

HERITAGE OF THE VIKINGS. From the Vikings (who made forays into the lower Loire around the 9th century) came the square sail and techniques such as clinker-building. Certain types of knot have also kept their northern names: *boitas*, *bouline*, *gueurde* . . . square knot, bowline, slipknot.

TOOLS
1. Large saw
2. Beam compass
3. Compass
4. Square
5. Bevel square
6. Tracing iron
7. String and chalk
8. Clamp
9. Marking gauge
10. Brace
11. Auger
12. Planes
13. Large plane
14. Mallet
15. Chisel
16. Gouge
17. Axe
18. Adzes
19. Broad axe

REVIVAL
Fortunately square-sail boats have not entirely disappeared from the Loire landscape. Under the impetus of a few enthusiasts, naval carpenters are yet again building *toues*, *gabares* and *fûtreaux* (different types of flat-bottomed boat).

EVOLUTION OF THE LOIRE BOATS

SINGLE-TRUNK PIROGUE

The trunk was dug out with a tool (axe or adze) or using fire. Ribs were left to provide rigidity.

THE ANCENIS PIROGUE

The single-trunk pirogue was split either deliberately or accidentally. The boat was widened with planks, and it was therefore necessary to peg several crosspieces together.

THE LIMOGES BOAT

This was constructed entirely of planks by a carpenter. The use of crosspieces, knees and ribs made it rigid.

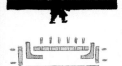

VIKING TECHNIQUES AND TOOLS

The Vikings brought clinker-building techniques to France (the planks overlapping one another like slates) and a tool, the *canap* (a large deep-bite clamp), to hold the planks together for pegging.

THE CLASSIC "CHALAND"

Its dimensions were restricted by the length of the tree trunk and the shallowness of the water.

49

The Loire bargees led a strange life, forever at the mercy of the capricious river, but they maneuvered skillfully. Those of the "lower country", leading a train of barges upstream, had to wait for a propitious sea wind, find a channel and dismast at bridges; those of the "upper country" had to wait for a rise in the water level in order to rush downstream on a coal-loaded *sapine* ● 46.

"They also wore gold or gold-plated earrings which were shaped like one-franc coins adorned with an anchor in the middle.**"**
Pierre Mondanel

Tie pin.

FEAST CLOTHES
The bargees' everyday clothes consisted of a blue smock, corduroy trousers, a scarlet-flannel belt and a wide-brim felt hat; on feast days they wore a white shirt which set off the brooches bearing the distinctive signs of their profession. As for the cashmere scarf, it came from India, via Nantes.

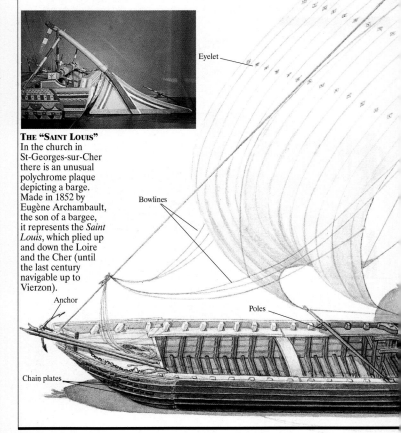

Eyelet

THE "SAINT LOUIS"
In the church in St-Georges-sur-Cher there is an unusual polychrome plaque depicting a barge. Made in 1852 by Eugène Archambault, the son of a bargee, it represents the *Saint Louis*, which plied up and down the Loire and the Cher (until the last century navigable up to Vierzon).

Bowlines

Anchor

Poles

Chain plates

"TREMPÉE AU VIN" (DUNKED IN WINE)
Put some stale breadcrumbs in a bowl. Moisten and sweeten as required. Just before serving, add a large quantity of cool red wine. Stir and eat with a spoon.

Jug for walnut oil.

Salt herrings.

A drop of cheap liquor.

WATER NOMADS
Lively and independent, barge people were always on the go. Their entire fortune was kept in a chest which they decorated themselves. Jovial drinkers and often bawdy, they would invoke their patron saints (Saint Clement, Saint Nicholas etc.) when carrying out a dangerous maneuver or during a sudden storm.

A bargee's casket.

A two-ring stove in front of which the *cuit-pomme* (apple tart) was placed.

THE "GUIROUÉ"
Normally an ordinary flag was enough to tell the direction of the wind, but each boat had its own weather vane for special occasions. The *guiroué* was carved during the long winter evenings and was the pride of the crew.

Leach

COOKING ON BOARD
Barge crews liked to eat well: cured meat, meat balls, soup, fish, *matelote* (fish stew), stuffed carp . . . the whole lot washed down with some fine wine "borrowed" from the cargo.

Food safe.

Mast stay

Lashing block

Strap

Windlass

THE "PIAUTRE"
The large steering oar, or tiller, is one of the most original components of the Loire *chaland*. It stands on the stern and is held firmly by an array of ropes. It can be adjusted according to the displacement and depth of the water, and can be taken out when the barge is in a "train".

Tiller

Hunting, or venery, is the art of pursuing game with hounds. It has been practiced in France since the 12th century on a regular basis, and in the Loire Valley was the favorite sport of the French kings in the 15th century. Today several thousand lovers of the chase perpetuate a tradition that has become codified by centuries of custom.

HUNTING TERMS
According to the situation, one talks of the *bien-aller* ("tally-ho") – when the *veneur* (Master of the Hounds) sounds the *bien-aller* the hounds are directed either with the voice or the horn – of "starting" the quarry, losing the scent, tracing the drag, changing forests, breaking away, sounding the *mort* (the kill) among others.

"ACCESSOIRES"
In this picture by Henry Koehler (1991) one can see a horn, a whip, a knife, a hat and a belt, all essential items of equipment for the huntsman.

THE "DÉFAUT"
by Karl Reille (1960). A *défaut* means the hounds have lost the scent (*voie*) of the quarry.

BUTTONS AND "BUTTONS"

Each hunt is distinguished from the others by the buttons on the waistcoat (*gilet*) and tunic (the hunter's uniform) – hence the name *boutons* (buttons) sometimes given to the members of the hunt.
Right: the button of the Cheverny Hunt ▲ *172*.

THE PATRON SAINT OF HUNTING

In the 8th century Saint Hubert had a vision of a deer carrying a cross between its antlers.
His saint's day is celebrated on November 3.

"MORT"

by René Princeteau (19th century).
This hunting cry means the animal is at bay.

SMALL OR LARGE GAME

Small-game hunting is for foxes, hares or rabbits.
Large-game hunting is for red deer, roe deer or wild boar.

"HONORS"

It is customary after a kill for one of the followers of the hunt to be "honored" (presented) with a foot or sometimes the antlers.

THE HUNT AND THE HOUNDS

The Master of the Hounds leads the hunt and is helped by the *boutons* (the members of the hunt). The *piqueux* (whippers-in) are responsible for the hounds during the hunt and in the kennels. The pack is made up of about sixty hounds for large-game hunts, and about twenty for small-game hunts. The most sought-after breeds are Anglo-French or English (beagles and harriers). The "followers" (guests) follow the hunt either on horseback or by car.

FOOD:
FISH TERRINE

"In a language difficult to constrain, a style of cooking that is clear, simple and logical, inspired by Rabelais' spirit and Descartes' genius, in a land of gourmets" – that is how the great gastronome Curnonsky described Touraine cuisine. Renowned for its charcuterie, its goat's cheeses, its confectionery and its wines, Touraine is also a land of rivers, so is well endowed with mouthwatering recipes for preparing and cooking fish.

2. Let the stock simmer for 15 minutes, reduce by half and strain.

3. Poach each fish separately in the stock for 8 minutes. Transfer the fish into a large tureen, pour the stock over it and leave to cool.

6. Place the perch fillets in a terracotta dish, then add the chopped egg whites.

8. Add the eel fillets, then cover with the chopped yolks and diced lemon.

9. Leave in a refrigerator overnight and serve with mayonnaise to which some tomato sauce has been added.

INGREDIENTS:

3–4 lb perch	1 or 2 eggs
2–3 lb salmon	1 lemon
3–4 lb eel	Tarragon

STOCK:

Fish bones	
and heads	1 bouquet garni
5 shallots	2 large onions
2 leeks	1 large mushroom
3 carrots	Half a glass of dry
2 oz butter	white wine
	Salt and pepper

1. To prepare the stock: chop all the ingredients, put them in a pan, add the wine and cover with water.

4. Fillet each fish.

5. Hard-boil the eggs, then chop the whites and yolks separately. Peel the lemon and cut it into small cubes.

7. Add the salmon fillets and the tarragon.

● SPECIALTIES

TRADITIONAL VINEGARS FROM ORLÉANS

They say in Orléans that it takes a great wine to make a great vinegar – so it is wine from the greatest vineyards, such as Chinon, and Bourgueil, that fills the 220-litre casks used for the three-week transformation period. The vinegar is then aged for six months in oak tuns.

COTIGNAC D'ORLÉANS

A specialty of St-Ay enjoyed since the 15th century, this quince jelly comes in a box, traditionally made of spruce, with the effigy of the "Maid of Orléans" on it. Benoît Gouchault is the last maker of this sweet amber-colored delicacy.

REGIONAL PRESS

La Nouvelle République du Centre-Ouest covers the news for all the départements of the Loire Valley, while the *Magazine de la Touraine* deals with the history of the area.

RILLONS AND RILLETTES

Four centuries old, these specialties are made from diced rib and loin pork, simmered over a wood fire. The largest pieces are taken out to make *rillons*; the smaller ones are mashed with a fork to make *rillettes*.

LIQUEURS OF ANGERS

In 1849 the Cointreau brothers, who were confectioners, founded a company to make their celebrated Guignolet using fruits from Anjou. In 1875 Louis, a worthy descendant, created the famous Cointreau liqueur from orange peel.

POULAIN CHOCOLATE

The famous brand, much appreciated by chocolate lovers, is still made in Blois ● *47* and ▲ *145*.

"CHAMPIGNONS DE PARIS"

These have been grown in the Loire Valley since 1895, mainly in the limestone caves around Saumur ▲ *292*.

VALLEY OF VINEYARDS

The region's vineyards ◆ *322* encompass some sixty appellations and about 200,000 acres of vines ■ *30*. You can find very drinkable table wines here as well as noble vintages; consistent, generous, fresh white wines, with a flinty taste and a flowery bouquet; and full-bodied, ruby-colored reds that have a hint of iris, violets or honey.

56

ARCHITECTURE

RELIGIOUS ARCHITECTURE
THE ROMANESQUE PERIOD

In the Romanesque period the Loire Valley, particularly Touraine, enjoyed a period of building activity during which a large number of religious edifices were erected. Ecclesiastical architecture was influenced by building methods from Poitou, Aquitaine, Burgundy and Berry: pier-buttressed apses, domes over the transept, doors lacking a tympanum, carvings, etc. The bell towers, however, are original to the region – topped by a spire flanked by pinnacles at the base. Carvings are almost exclusively reserved for capitals, cornice modillions and door arches; murals are relatively common, especially in the crypts.

DOORWAYS
(Church of Chênehutte-les-Tuffaux ▲ 292, 12th century)
The decoration of the main portal was often the most ornate part of the church. The arches are made of a series of voussoirs carved with foliage or geometric motifs. The absence of a tympanum is typical of the Loire Valley.

FRESCOS
(Below: Church of Tavant, ▲ 251, second quarter of the 12th century)
The Christ in Majesty enthroned in a mandorla (above), which can be seen in the apse of the choir at Tavant, belongs to the so-called *fonds clairs* school (characterized by the use of a light background with a strong vigorous line).

CRYPTS
(Church of Tavant ▲ 251, late 11th century)
Many of the churches of this period have richly decorated crypts. The reason for this was probably the worship of saints and their relics, which the crypt housed or should have housed. The crypts often had an entrance and an exit in order to regulate the flow of pilgrims.

CHEVETS
(Abbey of St-Benoît-sur-Loire ▲ 129, 1067–80)
A ground plan featuring an ambulatory and radiating chapels is characteristic of churches designed to receive large processions. Most Benedictine churches were built to this design. The plan of St-Benoît-sur-Loire (right) is particularly ambitious, with two of the chapels making a kind of small second transept. The structure of the chevet (apse and ambulatory) is similar to that of St-Étienne-de-Nevers in Burgundy. The chancel was originally flanked by twin bell towers.

ROMANESQUE ELEVATION

(Collegiate Church of St-Aignan ▲ 217, late 11th century)
The porch opens onto a nave of four bays with aisles. The transept is surmounted by a dome and a bell tower. The ambulatory opens onto three apsidioles.

THE SCHOOL OF AQUITAINE

(Fontevraud Abbey ▲ 227, 12th century)
With its single nave topped by a series of domes on pendentives, the church at Fontevrault reveals the links between Aquitaine and Anjou in Plantagenet times ● 38. The transept and chancel precede the nave – on the Benedictine model, with ambulatory and radiating chapels.

THE BELL TOWER

(Notre-Dame de Cunault ▲ 292, late 11th century)
This is the prototype of Romanesque bell towers in the Loire Valley. The first of the three tiers of windows is blind, while the alternating pilasters and columns of the top one provide diversity. The squat polygonal spire is stabilized by the surrounding turrets.

Gothic architecture, introduced in France in the 12th century,
was characterized by a new treatment of mass and space;
stained-glass windows provided a new interplay of light, and
décor became less representational. Anjou devised its own style
of vaulting, with extra ribs between the main cross ribs and the
diagonals. Soaring pillars and high ribbed vaults, from the north
(Chartres), stayed in vogue from the 13th to the 15th century.
Until the 14th century Gothic architecture was relatively sedate;
but the 15th century saw the advent of the Flamboyant style,
facilitated by using soft stone, such as tufa.

IN SEARCH OF VERTICALITY
(Chapel of St-Hubert
▲ *184*, Amboise,
1491–6) The chapel's
chevet is emphasized
by an *avant-corps*
(forebuilding) on top
of the castle wall.
The ornamentation
is reminiscent of
a Flemish reredos;
the Flamboyant
style of the north is
also manifest in
the fine tracery of
the windows.

1. Diagonal rib, or ogive
2. Wall rib, or formeret
3. Transverse arch
4. Cell, or web
5. Lierne
6. Keystone
7. Capital

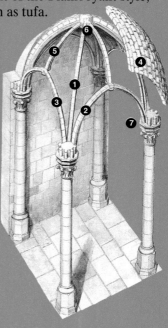

THE ANGEVIN OR PLANTAGENET VAULT
(Church of St-Serge ▲ *307*, Angers) This
abbey church is characterized by high convex
vaults supported by diagonal ribs (**1**), wall ribs
(**2**) and transverse arches (**3**), to which extra
ribs, the liernes (**5**), were added to strengthen
the cell (**4**). The large number of ribs gave rise
to the vogue for bosses at the intersections.

FRESCOS
(Chapel of the
Château de Pimpéan
▲ *293*, 15th century)
The frescos are
concentrated around
the ribs. The eight
sections bounded by
the ribs and liernes
of the vault illustrate
various episodes from
the life of Christ.

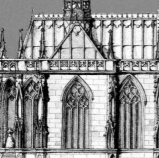

FLYING BUTTRESSES
(Ste-Croix Cathedral ▲ *114*, Orléans)
During the Gothic period the powerful pier
buttress gave way to the flying buttress,
an arch or half arch that transferred the thrust
of the vault to an outer support or pier.
Pinnacles were placed on top of the slender
buttresses to give them added weight,
which helped to stabilize the structure by
means of the vertical load.

FLAMBOYANT GOTHIC
(St-Gatien Cathedral
▲ *196*, Tours)
The façade was simply
superimposed on the
frame of the old one.
This is a good
illustration of the
Flamboyant style:
the cathedral's three
tall splayed doors,
with their intricate
ornamentation, have
a kind of "miniature
architecture" of
their own.

THE SPIRE
(Ste-Croix Cathedral
▲ *114*, Orléans)
The spire, in the
shape of a slender
pyramid, is the
culminating point of
the bell tower.
This spire, rebuilt in
1858, is a copy of
the one at Amiens
Cathedral.

RELIGIOUS ARCHITECTURE
FROM THE RENAISSANCE TO CLASSICISM

A MIXTURE OF STYLES (capital from the chapel at Ussé ▲ *270*)
The inspiration of this Renaissance capital is classical (Doric),
but the imaginative treatment is clearly medieval.

The chief creations of the Renaissance and of the classical period were often nothing but an update of earlier buildings. The churches of the 16th century were decorated in the Italian style, with basket-handle or semicircular arches and numerous niches containing statues. In the 17th century religious architecture became more majestic, with superimposed classical Greek orders, doors surmounted by pediments, stately domes and grandiose arched doorways and window frames.

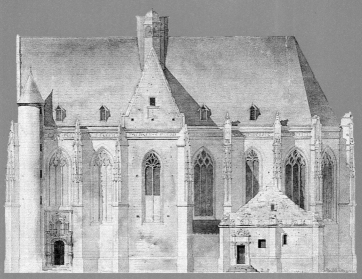

A NEW DECORATIVE ORDER
(Collegiate Church of St-Jean-Baptiste ▲ *231*, Montrésor, 1522–41)
To the Gothic ground plan and elevation were added a new decorative order, visible around the doors, the tracery of the windows, the cornices and the moldings. The ornamentation was inspired by Antiquity: fluted pilasters and ornate Corinthian capitals. The façade is similar to that of the chapel of the Château d'Ussé ▲ *270*.

FRAMES
(side door of the Collegiate Church of St-Jean-Baptiste ▲ *231*) Door and window frames were the chosen place for ornamentation.

TRIUMPHAL COMPOSITION

(Convent Church of the Minimes, 3, rue de la Préfecture, Tours, 1627–35) This doorway, built like a Roman triumphal arch, heralded the end of the large Gothic towers that previously framed church doors. This style marks the transition between façades that merely have decorative portals and fully integrated classical façades such as that of St-Vincent at Blois (below).

CLASSICISM

(Church of Notre-Dame des-Ardillers ▲ 285, Saumur, 17th century) The classical ground plan imitated the centered plan with a dome that was a characteristic of the Italian Renaissance. Associated with it is the strict use of the classical orders. Each of the three façades of this church has a Doric portico with four columns, surmounted by a triangular pediment. Crowning the edifice is a dome, roofed with slates, surmounted by an elegant lantern.

Ground plan of the Church of St-Vincent at Blois.

THE COUNTER-REFORMATION

(façade of the Church of St-Vincent, Blois, 1625–78) Reacting against the Protestant reformation and its emphasis on austerity, the architects of the Counter-Reformation cultivated a grandeur and flamboyance that led to the Baroque. The majesty of the orders and the basilica plan were borrowed from Antiquity. Here the three main orders (Doric, Ionic and Corinthian) are visible, superimposed one above the other. The single nave flanked by four small chapels is crowned by a cupola.

63

CASTLES AND KEEPS
11TH TO 14TH CENTURY

MACHICOLATIONS
(below, detail of the Porte des Cordeliers
at Loches ▲ 229, 15th century)
Machicolations replaced wooden
palisades at the level of the wall walk,
which were used until the 14th century
for bombarding attackers below.

In Romanesque times the rectangular or square keep, no doubt based on the wooden structures of the past, was the principal element of the medieval castle. During the Gothic period the keep lost some of its importance, and from the 13th century castles were sometimes built without a keep. After the Crusades progress in offensive techniques meant that defense systems had to be reviewed. Important innovations were introduced; tall stone walls were erected, protected by bastions, watchtowers, wall walks, battlements, machicolations and moats.

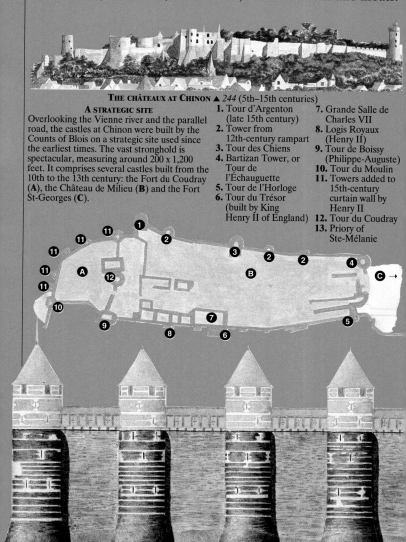

THE CHÂTEAUX AT CHINON ▲ *244* (5th–15th centuries)

A STRATEGIC SITE

Overlooking the Vienne river and the parallel road, the castles at Chinon were built by the Counts of Blois on a strategic site used since the earliest times. The vast stronghold is spectacular, measuring around 200 x 1,200 feet. It comprises several castles built from the 10th to the 13th century: the Fort du Coudray (**A**), the Château de Milieu (**B**) and the Fort St-Georges (**C**).

1. Tour d'Argenton (late 15th century)
2. Tower from 12th-century rampart
3. Tour des Chiens
4. Bartizan Tower, or Tour de l'Échauguette
5. Tour de l'Horloge
6. Tour du Trésor (built by King Henry II of England)
7. Grande Salle de Charles VII
8. Logis Royaux (Henry II)
9. Tour de Boissy (Philippe-Auguste)
10. Tour du Moulin
11. Towers added to 15th-century curtain wall by Henry II
12. Tour du Coudray
13. Priory of Ste-Mélanie

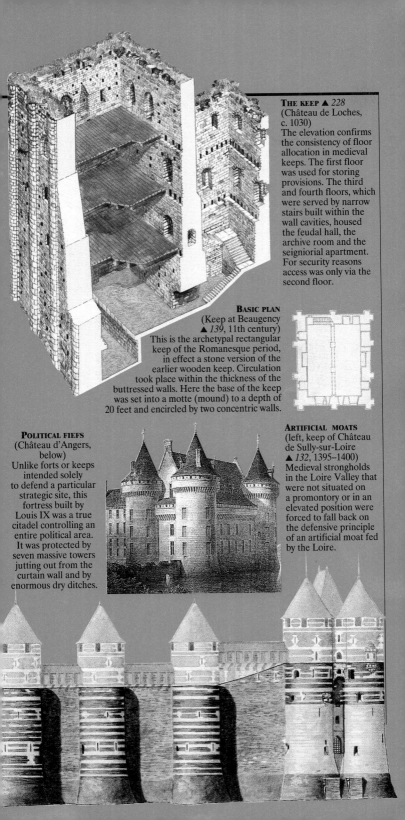

THE KEEP ▲ *228*
(Château de Loches,
c. 1030)
The elevation confirms
the consistency of floor
allocation in medieval
keeps. The first floor
was used for storing
provisions. The third
and fourth floors, which
were served by narrow
stairs built within the
wall cavities, housed
the feudal hall, the
archive room and the
seigniorial apartment.
For security reasons
access was only via the
second floor.

BASIC PLAN
(Keep at Beaugency
▲ *139*, 11th century)
This is the archetypal rectangular
keep of the Romanesque period, in
effect a stone version of the
earlier wooden keep. Circulation
took place within the thickness of the
buttressed walls. Here the base of the keep
was set into a motte (mound) to a depth of
20 feet and encircled by two concentric walls.

POLITICAL FIEFS
(Château d'Angers,
below)
Unlike forts or keeps
intended solely
to defend a particular
strategic site, this
fortress built by
Louis IX was a true
citadel controlling an
entire political area.
It was protected by
seven massive towers
jutting out from the
curtain wall and by
enormous dry ditches.

ARTIFICIAL MOATS
(left, keep of Château
de Sully-sur-Loire
▲ *132*, 1395–1400)
Medieval strongholds
in the Loire Valley that
were not situated on
a promontory or in an
elevated position were
forced to fall back on
the defensive principle
of an artificial moat fed
by the Loire.

**GROUND PLAN OF THE
CHÂTEAU DE CHAUMONT**
The red line corresponds to
the north wing demolished in
the 18th century to give
the building an unimpeded
view of the Loire.

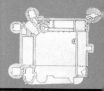

The end of the Hundred Years' War (1453) and the popularity of the Loire Valley with the kings of France resulted in a new kind of château design. Although castles built in the second half of the 15th century often still had battlements and the look of medieval fortresses, this arose not so much from a need to exhibit power and strength as from a desire for decoration. Interiors were adapted to a new lifestyle centered on comfort: the residential block became more spacious, the windows were enlarged and reinforced with mullions, and the number of rooms increased. The château had evolved from feudal stronghold to luxury residence.

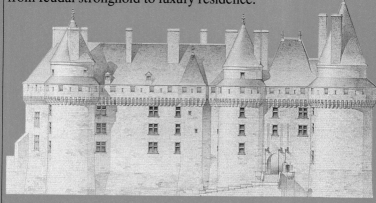

THE LAST GREAT FORTRESSES
(above, Château de Langeais, ▲ 268, c. 1465)
A continuous *chemin de ronde* (wall walk) and massive walls are evidence of the military aspect of the Château de Langeais. However, the mullioned windows, installed almost immediately after the completion of the building, show that the château had already lost some of its defensive function. The two *corps de logis* (residential blocks) with high-ceilinged bedrooms overlooking the wall walk are significant of the new emphasis on residential comfort.

THE PREMISE OF A FRENCH RENAISSANCE
(below, Château d'Amboise ▲ 184, c. 1491)
Charles VIII had new buildings looking out over the Loire erected on the site of the ancient fortress, and commissioned the laying out of new gardens. This was in answer to the changing requirements of residential life. Nevertheless, the ground plan and elevation remain rooted in the Flamboyant style, as is witnessed by the tall dormer windows and the ornamental elements.

POLYCHROME BRICKWORK
(above, Château de Gien ▲ *133*, 1494–1500)
The decorative principle is not based on sculpture, as in Italy, but on the diamond-pattern diapering of the polychrome brickwork. A number of Gothic elements have been retained, notably the L-shaped ground plan and the elevation.

PROGRESSIVE REFURBISHMENT
(below, Château de Chaumont ▲ *177*, 1465–1510)
This château was built in two phases: the west wing in 1465–75, and the east and south wings in 1498–1510.
The original medieval plan was of a square flanked by towers and gatehouse. Of the later modifications, only the grand staircase reflected the burgeoning influence of the Italian Renaissance. Opening the château onto the Loire was an 18th-century idea, in order to offer a view of the landscape, as at Valençay ▲ *232*.

BETWEEN GOTHIC AND RENAISSANCE
(Louis XII Wing at the Château de Blois ▲ *149*, 1498–1515)
Still submitting to the Gothic rationale, the architect has shifted the door of the spiral staircase to the side. The Renaissance influence is clearly visible in the vertical alignment of the centered windows, an impression reinforced by the dormer with gable and pinnacles. The only obviously Italianesque feature is the gallery.

● THE RENAISSANCE CHÂTEAU

During the 16th century the military aspect
disappeared and was replaced by a preoccupation
with comfort. The château, at once in harmony with and open
to nature, left the hills and nestled in the valley. Water
was now an essential part of the design. Steeply pitched
roofs covered spacious attics lit by large dormers. A
grand staircase in the center of the façade, with
straight banisters and a coffered ceiling above
it, replaced the corner turret. An elegant Italian-
style gallery opened onto the main courtyard.

THE STAIRCASE
(Château de Blois ▲ *150*)
Although staircases with
straight banisters in the
Italian style were beginning
to make their appearance
(as at Azay-le-Rideau), the
spiral staircase set back
from the main edifice was a
French tradition. But the
architects' great innovation
was to multiply its turns and
remove the walls between
the corner posts, so that a
playful aspect was grafted
onto its functional role.
At Blois three stories of
balconies overlook the
courtyard, a design that
reached its apogee at
Chambord ▲ *160*.

DORMER WINDOWS
(Château de Chambord ▲ *158*, after 1519)
France was still enamored of big roofs.
This handsome dormer has retained its
Gothic structure but has been enriched with
a Renaissance ornamental vocabulary. It is
embellished with geometric motifs in slate,
instead of the Tuscan marble used in Italy.

IN SEARCH OF SYMMETRY (Château de Villesavin ▲ *166*, 1537)
The carefully balanced design echoes the Italian villa and anticipates the so-called classical château. The buildings between the courtyard and the gardens are one story high. Square pavilions have replaced the towers of the past, emphasizing the nobility of the building without compromising its horizontality. The tall dormer windows follow the Loire Valley tradition.

AN ORDERED COMPOSITION (plan for the Château de Chenonceau ▲ *218*, 1556)
The gallery-bridge acts as an axis of symmetry, reinforcing the perspective. Its original purpose was to provide access to a group of pavilions and gardens on the other side of the Loire.

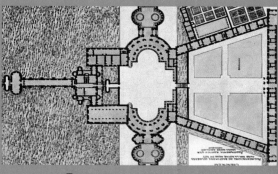

THE GALLERY
(The Façade des Loges, Château de Blois ▲ *150*, 1515–19)

The Italian influence is clearly evident in this part of the François I Wing. The two tiers of loggias with basket-handle arches could have been inspired by Bramante's Vatican loggias (16th century). Above them is a scalloped cornice; and above that a *promenoir*, or long covered balcony. The decorative motifs were drawn from the classical Italian repertory.

ŒIL-DE-BŒUF (detail from the façade of Cheverny ▲ *170*)
The ornamental possibilities of the dormer were enriched
by the introduction of œil-de-bœuf windows.

Abandoned by the court, in the 17th century the
Loire Valley ceased to be France's architectural
playground. Nevertheless, the aristocracy still
enjoyed staying there and built fine châteaux characterized by a
rigorously balanced treatment of space. The prevailing classical
fashion implied the use of pediments, domes and Greek orders.
Châteaux continued to be country houses looking out onto a
courtyard and a classic French garden, but in the 18th century
parks and secondary buildings, such as orangeries, follies, and
other curiosities, were often added, reflecting the naturalist
mood of the century of Enlightenment.

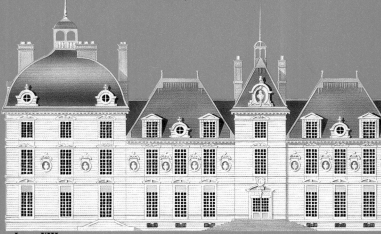

LOUIS XIII STYLE
(Château de Cheverny
▲ *170*, c. 1625–9)
The Louis XII style is
characterized by a
compact plan with
juxtaposed pavilions.
The Château de
Cheverny (above) is
one of the finest
examples of that style.
The main façade is
composed of five
pavilions, arranged
symmetrically around
a central pavilion
which houses the
monumental staircase.
Each of the pavilions
is roofed individually,
a system that gives the
building a verticality
which is very French.
The somewhat severe
effect is relieved by
the bossed horizontal
facing punctuated
by niches.

LOUIS XIV STYLE: THE VERSAILLES MODEL
(Château de Valençay ▲ *232*, 1770)
The west wing (below), on the park side, was modified and enlarged in
the 17th century; on the courtyard side it was faced in the classical
style with ionic pilasters in the 18th century. The entrance was
embellished with twin pilasters supporting a tympanum with Rocaille
ornamentation. The Mansard roof, a newly adopted design
(with two distinct slopes, the lower steeper than the upper one),
has segmental arches and pediments over the dormer windows, which
alternate with œil-de-bœuf windows and urns topped by flames.

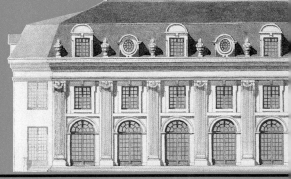

THE FRENCH TRADITION
(Château de Blois ▲ *150*, 1635 onward)
Closing the courtyard, the Gaston d'Orléans Wing was
built according to Mansart's plans. It was one of
the first examples of classical architectural principles
applied to a French château. In order to show
off better the central bay and the main entrance, the
avant-corps was raised slightly in relation to the
façades, and curved porticos were installed to lessen
the severity of the outline. Segmental and triangular
pediments punctuate the entablature.

THE VOGUE FOR FOLLIES
During the century of Enlightenment follies
became the fashion. These small allegorical
buildings peppered parks and gardens in a
Rousseau-like vision of an ideal natural
world. At the Château de Menars ▲ *140*
the "Rotunda of Abundance" (above)
was built in 1764 by Jacques Germain
Soufflot (1713–80) to link the château
with the Orangery. The elegant pagoda
at the Château de Chanteloup ▲ *191*,
built from 1773 to 1778, reflects the
infatuation of the time with the exotic,
like its celebrated counterpart in
Kew Gardens, London.

URBAN ARCHITECTURE
TIMBER-FRAMED HOUSES

GOTHIC STYLE
(Maison d'Adam ▲ 303, Angers, c. 1500) Wood is an ideal medium for decorative carvings, be they religious or secular. This couple, still medieval in inspiration, evoke courtly love.

At the end of the Middle Ages the Loire Valley experienced a population explosion resulting mainly from the end of the Hundred Years' War (1453) and the presence of the king and his court. In towns building plots were becoming smaller, and corbeled timber-frame houses were built out of necessity. The overhang increased usable space, sheltered the lower part of the house from rain, and had certain structural advantages. Merchants' premises or craftsmen's workshops often occupied the first floor, while the upper floor served as living space.

DECORATIVE PURSUIT
(Maison Rouge ▲ 246, Chinon, 15th century) The timbering, arranged in a grid or X-pattern, exemplifies the contemporary search for new decorative elements, though the overhanging truss is as much a part of the construction technique as it is part of a concern with esthetics. The arch-braced roof has no ridge.

(below, house at 15, rue St-Laud, Angers ▲ *306*) No more corbels, instead carved motifs: foliage and pilasters ornament the façades. However, little change is discernible in terms of building technique.

THE HOUSE OF A WEALTHY BOURGEOIS
(Maison d'Adam ▲ *303*, Angers, c. 1500) This large, handsome corner house witnesses the comfortable lifestyle of its owner. It also shows how versatile timber-frame houses could be: it has three gables on the street side, a double façade, six corbeled tiers, a remarkable corner bartizan and an abundance of richly carved decoration.

THE END OF THE TIMBER-FRAME HOUSE
At the end of the Hundred Years' War vast deforestation took place to convert land to farming, so there was an ample supply of wood. But in the 17th century, to reduce fire risks, laws were passed banning timber-frame houses.

THE NOGGINGS
Depending on what natural resources were available and the wealth of the owners, the noggings could be made of wattle and daub, lath and plaster, pisé (rammed earth), tufa, ashlar or bricks, and they were sometimes rendered. The bricks could be laid in a pattern (horizontally, vertically, or in a herringbone design) and were often used for a colorful effect. Their essential function, however, was to reinforce the timber structure.

CREATING DECORATIVE EFFECTS
In the half-timbered houses built during the 15th and 16th centuries the story-high posts sometimes rested on a stone plinth (**16**), and they could be corbeled (**12**). The façades were made to look extremely diverse by using various kinds of noggings, studs (**8**) and braces (**9**): the timbers themselves were arranged in grids, Saint Andrew's crosses or lozenge patterns, and the brick noggings were often used to create decorative patterns.

THE MAISON ROUGE
▲ *246* (Chinon, 15th century)
1. Crown post
2. Collar beam
3. Arched brace
4. Principal rafter
5. Hammerbeam
6. Wall plate
7. Angle brace
8. Studs
9. St Andrew's cross
10. Lower purlin
11. Cross brace
12. Lintel
13. Post
14. Fanlight
15. Cross beam
16. Bay window
17. Running support
16. Wall plinth

CLADDING
(house at 26, rue de la Monaie, Tours, above and right) The noggings of the weather-beaten east and west façades of timber-frame houses were sometimes either rendered or clad with slates to provide protection against bad weather.

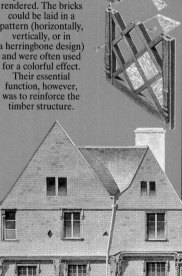

● TOWN HOUSES

HÔTEL PIERRE DU PUY, TOURS ▲ *209*
With its gabled front facing the street and its central
courtyard, this has the appearance of an ordinary house,
but the fact that it has two separate wings built around a
central staircase and gallery makes it an *hôtel particulier*.

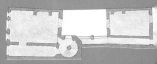

Inspired by the royal residences, from the 15th century onward
the aristocracy and the wealthy bourgeoisie built themselves
magnificent stone mansions known as *hôtel particuliers*. The
design, based on the characteristic layout of the château, set
between front courtyard and gardens, had to be adapted to
the restricted space available in towns. The 17th and 18th
centuries saw the development of town-planning schemes.
Although the austere style known as the "architecture of
the engineers" characterized the first half of the 18th
century, a return to ornamentation marked
the end of the century.

FLEMISH GOTHIC
(Hôtel Pierre du Puy ▲ *209*, Tours, c. 1460–70)
The bricks, the crow-stepped gable and the magnificent spiral
staircase known as the "Vis de St-Gilles" were inspired
by Flemish building styles and are evidence of the commercial
links between the Loire Valley and Flanders. The portico
with rib vaulting and pendant keystones, the corbels of the
dripstones of the windows and the moldings of the ogee arch
over the door are all part of the Flamboyant Gothic style.

THE L-PLAN
(Hôtel Pincé ▲ *306*,
Angers, 1530–8)
This grand L-shaped
mansion is composed
of two wings linked
by a tower where,
following medieval
tradition, the stairs
were housed.

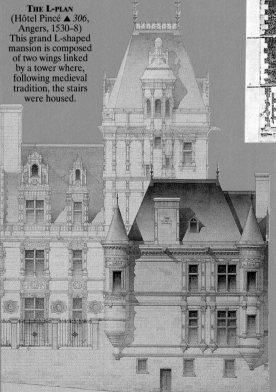

EARLY RENAISSANCE
(Hôtel Pincé ▲ *306*,
Angers, 1530–8)
The façade (left) is
a brilliant showpiece,
exploiting the vast
decorative repertory
of the times. The
concept of profusion,
which was seen as a
virtue, was dear to the
Italian Renaissance.
Human and animal
figures, arabesques,
foliage, shells, friezes
and pilasters enliven
the building's walls.
The overhanging
turrets, supported by
squinches, highlight
the boldness of
the architect,
Jean de L'Espine.

LATE RENAISSANCE
(Hôtel Cabu ▲ *119*,
Orléans,
mid 16th century)
The courtyard façade,
which is attributed
to Jacques Androuet
Du Cerceau (1520 to
c. 1585), presents two
lateral avant-corps
with superimposed
orders. This is one of
the earliest examples
of a Henri II style
building in Orléans.

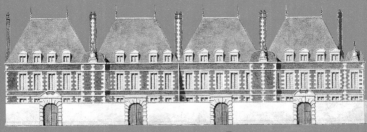

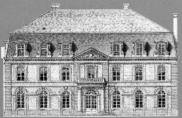

TOWN PLANNING SCHEMES
(Pavillons d'Escures ▲ *120*, Orléans,
before 1614)
This fine ensemble of four identical houses is
characteristic of the town-planning schemes
of the times. The houses are linked by stone
piers and are not dissimilar to the houses of
the Place des Vosges in Paris. Each has a
courtyard with a gateway to the main street,
and another courtyard with outbuildings and
a porte-cochère at the rear. They are
reminiscent of Du Cerceau's work ▲ *118*.

**THE "ARCHITECTURE
OF THE ENGINEERS"**
(Ancien Évêché
at Blois ▲ *154*,
early 18th century)
On the courtyard side
this rather austere
edifice comprises two
elegant stories.
A large pediment
tops the avant-corps.

MANNERISM
(Hôtel Lefebvre
de Montifray
▲ *214*, c. 1772)
In the center of the
façade two twin
pilasters crowned with
a pediment jut out, in
effect constituting a
false avant-corps. The
windows are profusely
adorned with Rocaille
cartouches and
mascarons – evidence
that ornamentation
was back in vogue.

The variety of farm buildings in the Loire Valley reflects micro-regional differences as well as the wide range of geological resources and building materials. Although tufa, in its various forms, remains the common element, brick and slate (from Blois to Gien) and schists (around Angers) add a cheerful dash of color to farm houses and other agricultural buildings.

THE GATEWAY
In the 16th and 17th centuries the richer farmers generally built walls around their property. An arched gateway gave a farm the look of an estate. This trait was sometimes reinforced (as above) by the addition of a timber-framed pigeon loft with stone noggings.

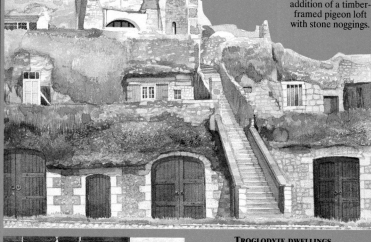

TROGLODYTE DWELLINGS
Whether on a hillside ▲ 286 or in the plain ▲ 287, troglodyte dwellings were a by-product of quarrying tufa and falun, and provided cheap accommodation.

MATERIALS
Tufa and falun ▲ 286 are the principal building materials in the Loire Valley, but schist (in the area around Angers) and brick (in Orléanais and the Sologne) also contribute to the appearance of the buildings. The Loire and its tributaries helped to spread these materials and give free rein to the interplay of colors.

BLÉSOIS (the region around Blois)
As in other parts of the Loire Valley, this winegrower's house has a single elongated story. The various windows and doors give an idea of the rooms' uses. The walls of limestone-rubble masonry were usually rendered.

THE SOLOGNE ▲ *174*
Builders made good use of the variety of tone and pattern offered by brick. There is an almost infinite range of colors, resulting from the type of earth used in making the bricks and their position in the oven. Bricks were laid in many different ways, the most common design being the Flemish bond (with alternating headers and stretchers).

CHINONNAIS
(the Chinon region) In the 19th century a new prosperity, resulting from agriculture, gave rise to more sophisticated buildings like the one below. The walls were thinner and built of white stone blocks. String courses, moldings and pilasters adorned the façades. The attic roof was covered with slates brought by rail from Anjou.

TOURAINE
Simple buildings like the one shown above are purely functional. The window with the shutter, the door on the left, with the flat stone lintel, and the chimney stack indicate the living quarters. The central door is the entrance to the barn, while the door on the right opens into the cowshed.

The first water mills were established at a very early date. In the 15th century windmills appeared in waterless areas or were added to the existing installations; there are several kinds in the Loire Valley, including one type specific to the area, the cave windmill. To the east of Blois there are numerous remains of brickyards and tileries, attesting that these industries were in existence as early as the 12th century and were widespread from the 15th century onward.

WATER MILLS WITH A VERTICAL WHEEL
The mill is said to have either a *roue de dessus* or a *roue de dessous*, depending on the height at which the water flows into the wheel. The side mill wheel (above), with the water level just below the wheel axle, enabled the use of small heads of water.

PIVOT WINDMILL
This type of windmill has a wooden "cage", or cabin, that pivots on a wooden or stone base. Inside the cabin can be found the windshaft and the millstones, in the upper part, and the bolter in the lower part. The millstones have their own axle.

TOWER WINDMILL
The main body of the mill is built in tufa masonry. All the machinery is located under the roof, at the top of the tower. The axis of rotation, which is identical to that of the millstones, enables the miller to set the sails into the wind, thanks to an outside shaft descending from the top of the mill to the ground.

The sails (**1**) drive the windshaft (**2**), on which is mounted the sheave (**3**); this transmits the movement vertically to the millstones (**4**). The whole grain contained in the hopper (**5**) is poured mechanically and ground between the fixed and running millstones. The ground grain is then poured into the bolter (**6**), a large muslin sac where the flour is graded as pure or coarse flour and bran.

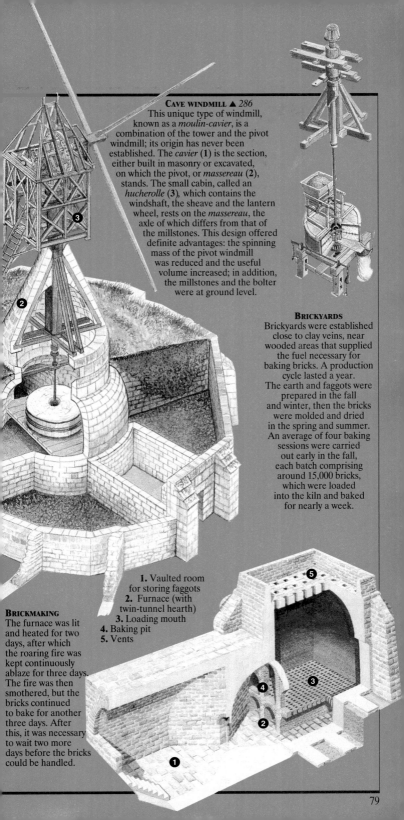

CAVE WINDMILL ▲ 286

This unique type of windmill, known as a *moulin-cavier*, is a combination of the tower and the pivot windmill; its origin has never been established. The *cavier* (1) is the section, either built in masonry or excavated, on which the pivot, or *massereau* (2), stands. The small cabin, called an *hucherolle* (3), which contains the windshaft, the sheave and the lantern wheel, rests on the *massereau*, the axle of which differs from that of the millstones. This design offered definite advantages: the spinning mass of the pivot windmill was reduced and the useful volume increased; in addition, the millstones and the bolter were at ground level.

BRICKYARDS

Brickyards were established close to clay veins, near wooded areas that supplied the fuel necessary for baking bricks. A production cycle lasted a year. The earth and faggots were prepared in the fall and winter, then the bricks were molded and dried in the spring and summer. An average of four baking sessions were carried out early in the fall, each batch comprising around 15,000 bricks, which were loaded into the kiln and baked for nearly a week.

1. Vaulted room for storing faggots
2. Furnace (with twin-tunnel hearth)
3. Loading mouth
4. Baking pit
5. Vents

BRICKMAKING

The furnace was lit and heated for two days, after which the roaring fire was kept continuously ablaze for three days. The fire was then smothered, but the bricks continued to bake for another three days. After this, it was necessary to wait two more days before the bricks could be handled.

● SMALL FARM BUILDINGS

WELLS
The form may vary, but wells are common on the limestone plateaus, where farmers have to dig deep to find water. This well backs onto a troglodytic dwelling cut into a hillside.

Near farms and in the midst of cultivated land one often finds rudimentary buildings either designed to house agricultural equipment or with a utilitarian function, such as wells. The variety of building materials used corresponds to the local resources and sometimes produces remarkable results – such as the large *loges*, or vegetable sheds, found near farm buildings. Dovecotes and winegrowers' cottages are more traditional.

DOVECOTES
▲ *140, 166*
Dovecotes, called *fuyes*, are generally either round or polygonal. Pigeon breeding was a seigniorial right. Pigeons were raised both for food and for their *colombine* (droppings). Within the masonry there are nesting holes, the *boulins*, where the pigeons roost. A ladder, attached by crosspieces to a pivoting central pole, provides access to the nesting holes.

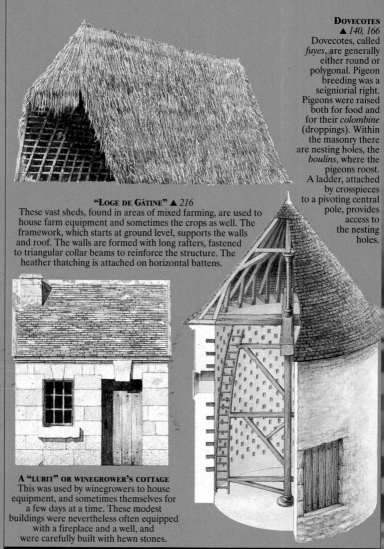

"LOGE DE GÂTINE" ▲ *216*
These vast sheds, found in areas of mixed farming, are used to house farm equipment and sometimes the crops as well. The framework, which starts at ground level, supports the walls and roof. The walls are formed with long rafters, fastened to triangular collar beams to reinforce the structure. The heather thatching is attached on horizontal battens.

A "LUBIT" OR WINEGROWER'S COTTAGE
This was used by winegrowers to house equipment, and sometimes themselves for a few days at a time. These modest buildings were nevertheless often equipped with a fireplace and a well, and were carefully built with hewn stones.

THE LOIRE VALLEY
AS SEEN BY PAINTERS

Many artists have been inspired by the Loire, with its soft changing light and huge meadows rolling down to the edge of the river. Edouard Debat-Ponsan (1847–1913) was inspired by the pale sandbanks (1). At the end of the 19th century the silhouette of the poplars painted by Bobeau (2) evoked the serenity of Loire landscapes, while Paul Fachet (b. 1885) filled vast skies with post-impressionist clouds (3) and, around 1895, Gabriel Firmin-Rogier painted fishermen at work (4).

E. DEBAT-PONSAN

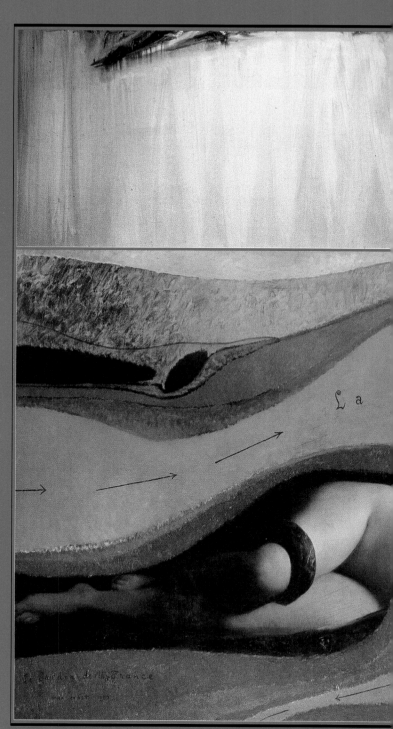

"THE LOIRE IS A WOMAN IN LOVE AND IN RAPTURES
BUT SWIFT TO FLEE IN WILD CAPRICES,
HER PERFIDIOUS LANGUOR ASLEEP ON THE RUSSET SANDS,
KISSES THE CURVES OF ITS CHARMED BANKS."

JULES LEMAITRE

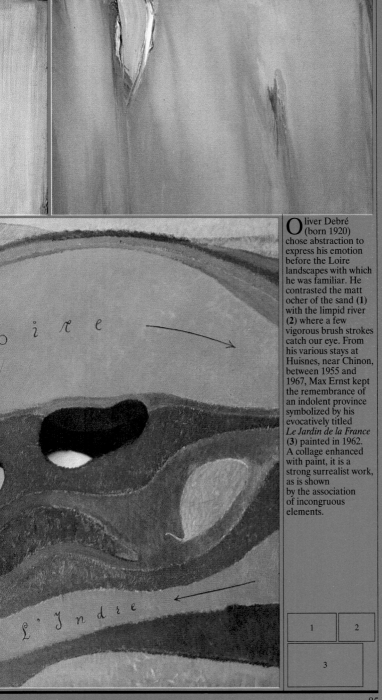

O liver Debré (born 1920) chose abstraction to express his emotion before the Loire landscapes with which he was familiar. He contrasted the matt ocher of the sand (1) with the limpid river (2) where a few vigorous brush strokes catch our eye. From his various stays at Huisnes, near Chinon, between 1955 and 1967, Max Ernst kept the remembrance of an indolent province symbolized by his evocatively titled *Le Jardin de la France* (3) painted in 1962. A collage enhanced with paint, it is a strong surrealist work, as is shown by the association of incongruous elements.

1	2
3	

Dupuis 1853.

"ALONG THE ROUNDED HILLS AND THE NOBLE VALES
THE CHÂTEAUX ARE STREWN LIKE PROCESSIONAL ALTARS . . ."

CHARLES PÉGUY

Monuments are all-important in the works of artists who came to the Loire Valley, including celebrated landscape painters such as Turner (1775–1851) and Théodore Rousseau (1812–67). Étienne Dupuy (1805–60) moved to Blois around 1849 where he became an art teacher and, in his own words, "a miniature painter". His *Château de Chambord* (1) is part of a series of five pictures painted in 1853, depicting Chambord, Blois, Amboise and Chenonceau. One of the great châteaux of the département, partly built during the reign of François I, the Château de Blois enjoyed a tremendous resurrection thanks to the restoration work of Félix Duban between (1797–1870). Several European architects were fascinated by the site, including the architect John Gregory Grace (1809–89) who was responsible for the British rediscovery of the Renaissance. His representation of Blois (2, 3, 4) in 1600 was inspired more by the famous engraved drawings of Jacques Androuet du Cerceau (c. 1510–c. 1585) kept in London than by the château as it was when he discovered it in 1847. In contrast his compatriot William Burges (1827–81), a disciple and friend of Viollet-le-Duc (1814–79), concentrated on château interiors (5).

"THE FALL OF JERICHO"
This miniature by Jean Fouquet (c. 1415 to c. 1480), from a fine edition of Josephus' *Jewish Antiquities* (c. 1475), is an illustration of the storming of Jericho by the Israelites, from the fourth chapter of Joshua. Seven priests, blowing seven ram's horns, precede the Ark of the Covenant. The blowing of the trumpets causes the immediate collapse of the high walls, thus giving the city over to the Israelites.

Jean Fouquet ▲ *231*, a native of Tours, transposes the famous biblical scene from the Jordan Valley to the Loire Valley, easily recognizable by the slate and tile roofs of the Renaissance houses and by the gentle light of the hilly landscape. In the foreground, thanks to the vivid colors and an extremely precise line (used, for example, for the ornaments on the Ark), the seven protagonists stand out against a landscape rendered infinite by soft tones and an

ashen atmosphere. Little is known of the artist's life or training. During his lifetime he was greatly honored (he was the official painter to the courts of Charles VII and Louis XI). Fouquet was then completely forgotten until he was rediscovered in the 19th century and recognized as the greatest French artist of the 15th century. His renewed fame was due to the discovery by Georges Brentano, at the beginning of the 19th century, of forty miniatures from

the *Heures d'Étienne Chevalier*, which led to major scholarly studies of Fouquet's work. The artist was probably influenced by Flemish art, and certainly by Italian art: we know, for instance, of his stay in Rome from 1444 onward, where he painted a portrait of Pope Eugenius IV. Among his most famous works are his portrait of Charles VII and the *Virgin of the Milk* (the model for the Madonna being Charles VII's celebrated mistress, Agnès Sorel ▲ *227*).

THE LOIRE VALLEY
AS SEEN BY WRITERS

THE GARDEN OF FRANCE

A WELL-TENDED GARDEN

Hippolyte Taine (1828–93), philosopher, historian and literary critic, is perhaps best known for his influential theories on human thought and development, but his travel writings both in France and abroad, imbued with his characteristic lucidity, provide the reader with fascinating, and often charming, insights into the places and people he encountered. He visited Touraine in 1863 during a spell as an admissions examiner for the Military School at Saint-Cyr, and was clearly seduced by the landscapes of the Loire.

❝The country is transformed; the wild and succulent verdure ceases. There are no more oaks; the moisture grows less abundant. We pass the Loir, and presently come in sight of the Loire.

There is a wide plain, a stream with no defined course, which is often in flood and often runs partly dry, amidst eyots of shingle and long banks of sand. The sandbanks have a certain vegetation, and there are broad lands covered with stunted pines.

But, especially after passing Tours, nothing could be more cheerful, or give better indication of comfort and prosperity. There are beautiful meadows, abundant crops, fruit trees, and rows of poplars, with every now and then a peaceful farm. Hemp, corn, various kinds of fruit, are plentiful; there is no more buckwheat, as in Brittany. The sky adds to the pleasantness and cheerfulness of the country. The velvet southern sky begins at this point, a radiant blue infused with light, like the clearest crystal. This lovely colour, sparkling and tender, sheds a glow of happiness over the trees, over the long stretch of fertile fields; the whole landscape resembles a garden, not the formal, plotted, economised garden of England, but somewhat casually tended, with a suggestion of neglect, though man's light-hearted negligence robs him of no whit of earth's prodigality. A few white castles, with picturesque turrets, perched like pigeons amongst the foliage, raise their blue pointed roofs and survey the plain from their vantage-ground. They bring to mind the happy life of the Valois, Diana of Poitier and Francis I. and Rabelais, the careless, gallant ways of life, the hunting, the boating-parties on those bright and wayward streams.❞

HIPPOLYTE TAINE, *JOURNEYS THROUGH FRANCE – BEING IMPRESSIONS OF THE PROVINCES*
PUB. T. FISHER, UNWIN, LONDON, 1897

A METAPHOR FOR LOVE

Honoré de Balzac (1799–1859) was born in Tours. Set mostly in the valley of the Indre, his novel "The Lily of the Valley" details the intense but unrequited love of a young man for a chatelaine – a love expressed through the beauty of nature.

❝Nature has certain effects of boundless meaning, rising to the level of the greatest intellectual ideas. Thus, a blossoming heath covered with diamonds of dew that hang on every leaf sparkling in the sun, a thing of infinite beauty for one single eye that may happen to see it. Or a forest nook, shut in by tumbled boulders, broken by willows, carpeted with moss, dotted with juniper shrubs – it scares you by its wild, hurtled, fearful aspect, and the cry of the hawk comes up to you. Or a scorching sandy common with no vegetation; a stony, precipitous plateau, the horizon reminding you of the desert – but there I found an exquisite and lonely flower, a pulsatilla waving its violet silk pennon in honour of its golden stamens; a pathetic image of my fair idol, alone in her valley! Or again, broad pools over which nature flings patches of greenery, a sort of transition between animal and vegetable being, and in a few days life is there – floating plants and insects, like a world in the upper air. Or again, a cottage with its cabbage garden, its vineyard, its fences overhanging a bog, and surrounded by a few meagre fields of rye – emblematic of many a humble life. Or a long forest avenue, like the nave of a cathedral where the pillars are trees, their branches meeting like the groins of a vault, and at the end a distant glade seen through the foliage, dappled with light and shade, or glowing in the ruddy beams of sunset like the painted glass window of a choir, filled with birds for choristers. Then, as you come out of the grove, a chalky fallow where full-fed snakes wriggle over the hot, crackling moss, and vanish into their holes after raising their graceful, proud heads. And over these pictures cast floods of sunshine, rippling like a nourishing tide, or piles of grey cloud in bars like the furrows on an old man's brow, or the cool tones of a faintly yellow sky banded with pale light – and listen! You will hear vague harmonies in the depth of bewildering silence.**"**

HONORÉ DE BALZAC, *THE LILY OF THE VALLEY*,
TRANS. JAMES WARING, PUB. J.M. DENT & CO., LONDON/NEW YORK, 1897

OLD ROOFS

Less impressed with the local countryside, Edith Wharton (1862–1937) conjures up, in her travel writings, the sublime views to be enjoyed from the lofty vantage points of Blois.

"A short afternoon's run carried us through dullish country from Chartres to Blois, which we reached at the fortunate hour when sunset burnishes the great curves of the Loire and lays a plum-coloured bloom on the slate roofs overlapping, scale-like, the slope below the castle. There are few finer roof-views than this from the wall at Blois: the blue sweep of gables and ridge-lines billowing up here and there into a church tower . . . or breaking to let through the glimpse of a carved façade, or the blossoming depths of a hanging garden; but perhaps only the eye subdued to tin housetops and iron chimney-pots can feel the full poetry of old roofs.**"**

EDITH WHARTON, *ABROAD – SELECTED TRAVEL WRITINGS, 1888–1920*
PUB. ROBERT HALE, LONDON, 1995

NOSTALGIA

Maurice Genevoix (1890–1980) was an Orléanais but made frequent visits to friends near Brinon-sur-Sauldre in the Sologne region, where he got to know some of the local poachers. His experiences lent an air of authority to his novel "Raboliot", the story of a peasant who has an ambivalent relationship with the animals he kills.

"Memories came flooding to him in great waves: all the smells of the woodlands, the acrid scent of the damp earth covered by fermenting leaves, the light exhalation of resin, the floury aroma of a mushroom crushed in passing; all the murmuring, rustling and sudden flight in the branches, the noise of birds winging across the groves or soaring low over the furrows; and the cries of twilight, the grating screech of the cock-pheasants, the partridges calling to each other, the short chirps of the nightjars, and at nightfall a grinding sound passing close to one's head as the first sparrow-owl flies out hunting . . .

The lagoon of Chanteloup threw up a great limpid reflection. The surrounding reeds, and a few still leafless hedgerows, cast their warm tints of ochre, red and burning russet, against the solid blue of a pine-grove that closed the horizon. The sky touched the tops of the pines, it seemed, to be poised upon them, leaning there

indefinitely like a globe of green crystal . . . Raboliot breathed slowly, his flesh penetrated by a vegetable well-being, so absolute that he no longer felt his body. He lived only through a few sporadic thoughts, images scattered on the surfaces of dreams like islets on a lake. It was the fifth evening that he had returned thus to the edge of the great plain. And as on the other evenings, in front of this familiar space, memories passed through him, visions of the recent past today all gentle, that he saw slipping onto the shores of his being, soft and slow, barely melancholy . . .

With the month of March, the terrible cold returned from the north, the harsh sleet and the frost nights when the great trees cracked and crackled from top to toe, in the limpid blue air beneath the greenish fires of the stars. During those nights he went walking, across leagues of countryside. And thus roaming, always towards the north, he came to the edge of a flat and fertile valley, where the roofs of the houses and the clusters of acacias and poplars were no more than purple and reddish shapes, blurred behind a veil of fine mist bathed in a gentle light . . . And from then on, an insidious nostalgia slipped into all his being, slowly penetrating it. He turned back towards the south, towards the pinewoods and the fields of broom, the copses of birch and oak where the abundant game was there to nourish anyone who could catch it, and where – so long as it had not rained too much – the ditches under the brushwood offered a warm and dark sanctuary to the fugitive.**99**

MAURICE GENEVOIX, *RABOLIOT*, ÉDITIONS DU SEUIL, PARIS 1980

TWO TURNINGS

"Le Grand Meaulnes", by Alain-Fournier (1886–1914), is a classic French "coming-of-age" novel with chilling descriptions of landscape and character.

66When he had traversed the village, leaving the school-house behind, he had a choice of two turnings. He hesitated. He knew vaguely that to get to Vierzon one must bear to the left – but there was no one to ask. So he pushed on at a steady gait down a road which turned out to be narrow and badly surfaced. For a while he skirted a wood of firs and at length met a carter to whom he shouted out an inquiry. But the mare was pulling hard and kept trotting. The carter may not have understood the question. At any rate he made a vague reply with a gesture no less vague, and Meaulnes decided to take a chance on the road he was on.

Then once more he was surrounded by a vast frozen plain devoid of landmarks: no living thing in sight but now and then a magpie which rose in alarm and flapped away to perch on the stump of an elm. Wrapping the heavy blanket around him like

a cape, the traveller now stretched out his legs and, leaning against the side of the carriole, fell into a sleep that must have lasted for some time . . .

. . . When at length, chilled through in spite of the blanket, he came to his senses, the scene was transformed. It was no longer a landscape of distant horizons merging into a boundless white sky, but a patchwork of fields, still green, behind high enclosures. On either side were ditches in which water was flowing beneath the ice. Everything pointed to the proximity of a river. And between the hedgerows the road was now merely a rough narrow lane.

The mare had left off her jog-trot some distance back. Meaulnes used his whip, but nothing would induce her to move faster than a slow walk. Then, leaning forward, his hands on the dashboard, he bent down and discovered that she was limping – something was wrong with one of her hind legs. He drew up and got down in some alarm, muttering to himself:

'We'll never get to Vierzon in time for that train.'

He hardly dared knowledge the most alarming thought of all: that he might have lost his way, that the road he was on might not be the road leading to his destination.**

ALAIN-FOURNIER, *THE LOST DOMAIN (LE GRAND MEAULNES)*,
TRANS. FRANK DAVISON, PUB. OXFORD UNIVERSITY PRESS, OXFORD/NEW YORK, 1986

THE LOIRE

A BENEFICENT STREAM

The American-born novelist Henry James (1843–1916) settled in England in 1877 and embraced European culture, in both his life and literary works. He visited France in 1882, and relates his experiences in a charming volume entitled "A little tour in France", of which ten chapters are given to his time spent in Touraine. His account of the Loire Valley and surrounding countryside is scrupulous in contemporary detail, and timeless in its sense of place.

**[Touraine] is, moreover, the heart of the old French monarchy; and as that monarchy was splendid and picturesque, a reflection of the splendour still glitters in the current of the Loire. Some of the most striking events of French history have occurred on the banks of that river, and the soil it waters bloomed for a while with the flowering of the Renaissance. The Loire gives a great 'style' to a landscape of which the features are not, as the phrase is, prominent, and carries the eye to distances even more poetic than the green horizons of Touraine. It is a very fitful stream, and is sometimes observed to run thin and expose all the crudities of its channel – a great defect certainly in a river which is so much depended upon to give an air to the places it waters.

But I speak of it as I saw it last; full, tranquil, powerful, bending in large slow curves and sending back half the light of the sky. Nothing can be finer than the view of its course which you get from the battlements and terraces of Amboise. As I looked down on it from that elevation one lovely Sunday morning, through a mild glitter of autumn sunshine, it seemed the very model of a generous, beneficent stream. The most charming part of Tours is naturally the shaded quay that overlooks it, and looks across too at the friendly faubourg of Saint Symphorien and at the terraced heights which rise above this. Indeed, throughout Touraine it is half the charm of the Loire that you can travel beside it. The great dyke which protects it, or protects the country from it, from Blois to Angers, is an admirable road; and on the other side as well the highway constantly keeps it company. A wide river, as you follow a wide road, is excellent company; it brightens and shortens the way. **99**

HENRY JAMES, *COLLECTED TRAVEL WRITINGS: THE CONTINENT*,
PUB. THE LIBRARIES OF AMERICA, NEW YORK, 1993

AN ENCHANTING SIGHT

In an account of her trip to La Charité, Matilda Betham-Edwards (1836–1919) gives this description of the magnificent landscape of the Loire.

66Hardly had we reached our rooms in the more than old-fashioned Hôtel du Grand Monarque, than from a side window, we caught sight of the Loire; so near, indeed, lay the bright, blue river, that we could almost have thrown pebbles into its clear depths; quitting the hotel, half a dozen steps, no more were needed, an enchanting scene burst upon view.

Most beautiful is the site of La Charité, built terrace-wise, not on the skirts but on the very hem of the Loire, here no revolutionary torrent, sweeping away whole villages, leaving only church steeples visible above the engulfing waters, as I had once seen it at Nantes, but a broad, smooth, crystal expanse of sky-blue. Over against the handsome stone bridge to-day having its double in the limpid water, we see a little islanded hamlet crowned with picturesque church tower; and, placing ourselves midway betwen the town and its suburban twin, obtain vast and lovely perspectives. Westward, gradually purpling as evening wears on, rises the magnificent height of Sancerre, below, amid low banks bordered with poplar, flowing the Loire. Eastward, looking towards Nevers, our eyes rest on the same broad sheet of blue; before us, straight as an arrow, stretches the French road of a pattern we know so well, an apparently interminable avenue of plane or poplar trees. The river is low at this season, and the velvety brown sands recall the sea-shore when the tide is out. Exquisite, at such an hour, are the reflections, every object having its mirrored self in the transparent waves, the lights and shadows of twilight making lovely effects. **99**

MISS BETHAM-EDWARDS, *EAST OF PARIS*,
PUB. HURST AND BLACKETT, LTD, LONDON, 1902

A MAGNIFICENT PAST

ROMANCE OF A BYGONE ERA

In his verse autobiography "The Prelude – or growth of a poet's mind", William Wordsworth (1770–1850) reflects both upon the present and upon a glorious past steeped in rich history and legend.

> **66**Along that very Loire, with Festivals
> Resounding at all hours, and innocent yet
> Of civil slaughter was our frequent walk
> Or in wide Forests of the neighbourhood,
> High woods and over-arch'd with open space
> On every side, and footing many a mile,
> In woven roots and moss smooth as the sea,
> A solemn region. Often in such place
> From earnest dialogues I slipp'd in thought
> And let remembrance steal to other times
> When Hermits from their sheds and caves forth stray'd
> Walk'd by themselves, so met in shades like these . . .
>   And when my Friend
> Pointed upon occasion to the Site

Of Romorentin, home of ancient Kings,
To the imperial Edifice of Blois
Or to that rural Castle, name now slipp'd
From my remembrance, where a Lady lodg'd
By the first Francis wooed, and bound to him
In chains of mutual passion; from the Tower,
As a tradition of the Country tells,

Practis'd to commune with her Royal Knight
By cressets and love-beacons, intercourse
'Twixt her high-seated Residence and his
Far off at Chambord on the Plain beneath:
Even here, though less than with the peaceful House
Religious, 'mid these frequent monuments
Of Kings, their vices and their better deeds,
Imagination, potent to enflame
At times with virtuous wrath and noble scorn,
Did also often mitigate the force
Of civic prejudice, the bigotry,
So call it, of a youthful Patriot's mind,
And on these spots with many gleams I look'd
Of chivalrous delight. "

WILLIAM WORDSWORTH, *THE PRELUDE, BOOK 9: RESIDENCE IN FRANCE*
PUB. OXFORD UNIVERSITY PRESS, LONDON/NEW YORK, 1970

A MAID IN ARMOR
In this passage from Maurice David-Darnac's history of the life of Joan of Arc, Joan receives the gift of a suit of armor and retrieves a holy sword.

❝In Tours Joan was being equipped for battle. The king had a suit of armour made for her. This must have given her much pleasure, as fine arms delighted her throughout her career. In any case the present was a sign of her new status and of the confidence which was now placed in her, as well as marking a definitive separation from the peasant girl she had once been. A full suit of armour, not only because of its connotations, but because it was so expensive, was the thing which most conspicuously set the knight apart from the rest of those who surrounded him. Joan was also offered a sword, but for this she insisted on sending back to Sainte-Cathérine-de-Fierbois. She asked for a weapon which she knew to be concealed at a particular spot within the church:

How did you know this sword was there?
I knew it was there from my voices. I had never seen the man who went to look for it. I wrote to the churchmen of the place to ask for the sword, and they sent it to me. It was not deep in the earth. It was, as I think, behind the altar; but I am not certain whether it was in front of the altar or behind it.

Joan added that, when the sword was found, it was rusty, but 'the clergy rubbed it, and the rust readily fell off'. She also said that she had a great liking for this weapon 'because it had been found in the church of St Catherine, whom she loved well'.❞

MAURICE DAVID-DARNAC, *THE TRUE STORY OF THE MAID OF ORLEANS*,
TRANS. PETER DE POLNAY, PUB. W.H. ALLEN, LONDON, 1969

A MEETING WITH THE DAUPHIN
During her travels Virginia Woolf visited the castle at Chinon, where Joan of Arc first met the Dauphin, later to become King Charles VII of France.

❝Explored castle alone . . . Saw the high unroofed room in wh. Jeanne stood before the King. The very chimney piece perhaps. Walls cut through by thin windows. Suddenly one looks down, down on the roofs. How did the middle ages get through the evenings? A stone crypt in wh. J. lived: people carve their names everywhere. River silken serpentine beneath. Liked the stone roofless rooms; & the angular cut windows. Sat on the steps to hear 2 struck by the clock wh. has rung since the 13th Century: wh. J. heard. Rusty tone. What did she think? Was she mad? a visionary coinciding with the right moment.❞

TRAVELS WITH VIRGINIA WOOLF, ED. JAN MORRIS,
PUB. THE HOGARTH PRESS, LONDON, 1993

GLORIOUS FOOD

RECOLLECTION OF PLEASURES PAST
Vernon Lee was the pseudonym of Violet Paget (1856–1935), the English essayist and novelist who spent most of her life in Italy

❝It is impossible to speak adequately of Touraine, to recall its charm at all adequately (indeed, it was a true instinct which caused me to describe that charm by the word 'flavour') without mentioning things to eat and drink. I confess to not thinking much about my dinner in other countries, save as one of the inevitable bothers of life; but I think about it a great deal, and as a permeating essence of life, in Touraine. It has a right to permeate, because, as I have said, this land has turned it into a poetry. The *déjeuner à la fourchette* at the inn of Saumur was as essential a part of that old town's charm as the discreet Balzac *portes-cochères*, overhung by creepers, and the lovely turreted house built by King René for his daughter. I remember, and shall remember, the beautiful long loaves of bread, like blond cactuses, off which one cut colossal hunks, as well as anything else, at Langeais. And as to the Château de St Avry, it sums up all the special poetic prose of the Loire-side in a draught – a draught out of a silver wine-taster's mug – of ten-year-old Vin de Chinon. "

VERNON LEE, *GENIUS LOCI – NOTES ON PLACES*,
PUB. JOHN LANE, THE BODLEY HEAD/JOHN LANE COMPANY, NEW YORK, 1908

A BITTER AND VIOLENT CONFLICT OVER PANCAKES ("FOUACES")

One of Touraine's greatest writers, François Rabelais (c. 1494–1553) gives this satirical, yet affectionate portrayal of ordinary folk at their most vulgar and ridiculous

"At that time, which was the season of Vintage, in the beginning of Harvest, when the countrey shepherds were set to keep the Vines, and hinder the Starlings from eating up the grapes; as some cake-bakers of *Lerne* happened to passe along in the broad high way, driving unto the City ten or twelve horses loaded with cakes, the said shepherds courteously intreated them to give them some for their money, as the price then ruled in the market; for here it is to be remarked, that it is a celestial food to eat for breakfast hot fresh cakes with grapes, especially the frail clusters, the great red grapes, the muscadine, the verjuice grape and the luskard, for those that are costive in their belly; because it will make them gush out, and squirt the length of a Hunters staffe, like the very tap of a barrel; and often-times thinking to let a squib, they did all-to-besquatter and conskite themselves, whereupon they are commonly called the Vintage-thinkers. The Bunsellers or Cake-makers were in nothing inclinable to their request; but (which was worse) did injure them most outragiously, calling them pratling gablers, lickorous gluttons, freckled bittors, mangie rascals, shiteabed scoundrels, drunken roysters, slie knaves, drowsie loiterers, slapsauce fellows, slabberdegullion druggels, lubbardly lowts, cosening foxes, ruffian rogues, paultrie customers, sycophant-varlets, drawlatch hoydons, flouting milksops, jeering companions, staring clowns, forlorn snakes, ninnie lobcocks, scurvie sneaksbies, fondling fops, base lowns, sawcie coxcombs, idle lusks, *scoffing Braggards, noddie meacocks, blockish grutnols, doddi-pol-jolt-heads, jobernol goosecaps, foolish loggerheads, slutch calf-lollies, grouthead gnat-snappers, lob-dotterels, gaping changelings, codshead loobies, woodcock slangams, ninnie-hammer flycatchers, noddiepeak simpletons;* Turdie gut, shitten shepherds, and other such like defamatory epithetes, saying further, that it was not for them to eate of these dainty cakes, but might very well content themselves with the course unraunged bread, or to eat of the great brown houshold loaf. To which provoking words, one amongst them, called *Forgier*, (an honest fellow of his person, and a notable springal,) made answer very calmly thus: How long is it since you have got homes, that you are become so proud? indeed formerly you were wont to give us some freely, and will you not now let us have any for our money? This is not the part of good neighbours, neither do we serve you thus when you come hither to buy our good corn, whereof you

make your cakes and buns: besides that, we would have given you to the bargain some of our grapes, but *by his zounds*, you may chance to repent it, and possibly have the need of us at another time, when we shall use you after the like manner and therefore remember it. Then *Marquet*, a prime man in the confraternity of the cake-bakers, said unto him, Yea Sir, thou are pretty well crest-risen this morning, thou didst eat yesternight too much millet and bolymong, come hither *Sirrah*, come hither, I will give thee some cakes: whereupon *Forgier* dreading no harm, in all simplicity went towards him, and drew a sixpence out of his leather sachel, thinking that *Marquet* would have sold him some of his cakes; but in stead of cakes, he gave him with his whip such a rude lash overthwart the legs, that the marks of the whipcord knots were apparent in them; then would have fled away, but *Forgier* cried out as loud as he could, O murther, murther, help, help, help, and in the mean time threw a great cudgel after him, which he carried under his arme, wherewith he hit him in the *coronal* joynt of his head, upon the *crotaphick* arterie of the right side thereof, so forcibly, that *Marquet* fell down from his mare, more like a dead then living man. Mean-while the farmers and countrey-swaines, that were watching their walnuts near to that place, came running with their great poles and long staves, and laid such load on these cake-bakers, as if they had been to thresh upon green rie. The other shepherds and shepherdesses hearing the lamentable shout of *Forgier*, came with their slings and slackies following them, and throwing great stones at them, as thick as if it had been haile. At last they overtook them, and took from them about foure or five dosen of their cakes; nevertheless they payed for them the ordinary price, and gave them over and above one hundred egges, and three baskets of mulberries. Then did the cake-bakers help to get up to his mare *Marquet*, who was most shrewdly wounded, and forthwith returned to *Lerne* changing the resolution they had to go to *Pareille*, threatning very sharp and boistrously the cowherds, shepherds, and farmers of *Sevile* and *Sinays*. This done, the shepherds and shepherdesses made merry with these cakes and fine grapes, and sported themselves together at the sound of the pretty small pipe, scoffing and laughing at those vain-glorious cake-bakers, who had that day met with a mischief for the want of crossing themselves with a good hand in the morning. Nor did they forget to apply to *Forgiers* leg some faire great red medicinal grapes, and so handsomly drest it and bound it up, that he was quickly cured. **99**

FRANÇOIS RABELAIS, *GARGANTUA AND PANTAGRUEL*,
TRANS. SIR THOMAS URQUHART AND PIERRE LE MOTTEUX,
PUB. EVERYMAN'S LIBRARY, LONDON, ALFRED A. KNOPF, NEW YORK, 1994

POUILLY-FUMÉ
In his book "Bouquet de France" Samuel Chamberlain describes the many culinary delights that France has to offer. Here he praises the Pouilly nectar.

66Vineyards begin to ribbon the riverbanks near the town of Cosne and become thicker as one approaches Pouilly. The carefully tended vines are blue-green with spray. They were growing grapes on these same chalky slopes a millennium ago, for the archives have records of a large vineyard which thrived near Pouilly in the year 859. It takes time to develop a wine as

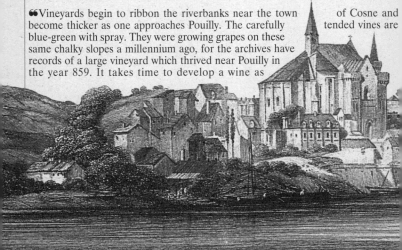

seductive as Pouilly-Fumé! The town itself is an unpretentious place along the river, with no particular charm. Every street, every dead-end alley seems to be devoted to wine. Confusion is bound to result from the fact that another fine white wine, this one from the Beaujolais country, carries the name of Pouilly-Fuissé. Nobody seems to have invented a formula to remember which is which. But you'll never forget Pouilly-Fumé if you taste it cool from a cellar in Pouilly-sur-Loire! This clean, immensely palatable wine has a rich, fruity bouquet underlying its dryness. As a result, it makes a perfectly splendid *apéritif*. It would be unthinkable in the Pouilly region to drink anything but white wine of a café terrace. Parisian motorists jam on their brakes and follow a sudden inspiration to enjoy a cool bottle of Pouilly-Fumé before proceeding on their journey. No other wine in France possesses quite the mysterious perfume which a subtle combination of sun and rocky soil produces here. The nostril detects the same flinty aroma common to other Loire wines, but there is an added touch of softness, which caresses the throat and rejoices the spirit. The wine of Pouilly *"chaugge le bonhomme,"* as the natives say – fills him with sunshine and then departs, diuretic and beneficial. Why have a *carete des vins*, they ask, when a single wine suffices for everything? Before, during, and after your meal – a glistening goblet of Pouilly's lemon-gold glory!

Just to get the record straight, there are two distinct wines from this region. The great one is Pouilly-Fumé, so-called because of the smoky-blue color of its Sauvignon grape, or Blanc-Fumé. The mysterious chemistry of the vine produces the rich, golden, liquorous Château d'Yquem from the same plant. How different is pale Pouilly-Fumé, the result of the Sauvignon when it grows on a bank of Kimmeridgian chalky clay! The wine called Pouilly Blanc comes from another grape, the Chasselas, and is more closely akin to Muscadet, the dry wine which flourishes near the mouth of the Loire. It has much the same fresh, faintly flinty bouquet and almost as much finesse as the Fumé. Either is an enchantment on a warm summer's day. **"**

SAMUEL CHAMBERLÀIN, *BOUQUET DE FRANCE: AN EPICUREAN TOUR OF THE FRENCH PROVINCES*, PUB. HAMISH HAMILTON, LONDON

CHÂTEAUX OF THE LOIRE

TALCY

The châteaux of the Loire are famed for their elegance and beauty. The delightful château at Talcy appears to be one that has been undeservedly overlooked.

"Talcy is another of the greatly underestimated châteaux, yet it is certainly fit to take place in the second rank of them, if not in the first. It was built, about 1520, by a Florentine, Bernard Salviati, cousin of Catherine de Médicis, at the time when François I was busy with the Italianate wing of the château of Blois, when everything Italian was the very height of fashion, and the transalpine architects had not yet assimilated the gentle light and delicate colourings of the Loire valley. Yet, and in this it is almost unique, it is built away from the river in the most unpromising position of La Beauce, scorning all the natural advantages of the magnificent river setting to be found so few miles away. Built for an Italian, it is as remote from Italy as it is from Persia or Cathay. It is, almost alone of its date, uncompromisingly French. It occupies the site of a small fortress of the twelfth century, from which it inherited a certain strength; not enough to make it a fort, yet sufficient to make it a manor house easily defended. There is a strong, square tower, surmounted by a corbelled sentry-walk and carrying three turrets with the rather self conscious air of a serious somebody-in-the-city wearing a comic hat to please the children.

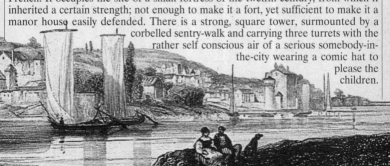

Simple, rectangular, unornamented almost, it stands amongst the other châteaux (if the metaphor may be allowed to change sex) like the county lady who, having found a style to suit her, refuses thereafter to pander to the fashion of the day. If the outside is uncompromising, the inner courtyard is soft and feminine to the point of prettiness. In the middle of it is a dome-covered well; the corner of the too-massive keep is rendered surprisingly effeminate by a turret staircase, looking the more delicate for the direct comparison with its heavy neighbour; the main building is lightened by a four-arcaded gallery, severe enough for a monastery, were it not lightened by two fanciful gables. To what extent Bernard Salviati was ruled by his wife, history does not tell, but the evidence of Talcy is that he arranged the exterior to his liking, but his wife asserted her ideas when it came to the courtyards. The second courtyard is difficult to see, so much is it dominated by an immense dovecote, apparently contemporary with the main building, yet still in splendid condition. It has some 1,500 pigeon-holes, if that is the right word in a dovecote; the French *alvéoles* is distinctly more poetic. We know that they were early risers in those days, and well must they have needed to be at Talcy, for the awakening of a thousand doves must have driven all but the dead from their sleep.**

VIVIAN ROWE, *CHATEAUX OF THE LOIRE*, PUB. PUTNAM, LONDON, 1958

A RELUCTANT SIGHTSEER

In these diary entries the novelist Evelyn Waugh (1903–66) makes it perfectly clear that viewing castles is not his favorite pastime.

It continues to be hot, but not intolerable. We are leading a lazy and agreeable life; getting up late, lunching heavily, perhaps going to visit a château, perhaps doing some shopping in Tours and having tea at Massie and going to the cinema at the Café de Commerce, dining heavily and then sleeping heavily. I am reading Richard's *Principles of Literary Criticism* again. My French is making no progress. On Saturday we went to Chenonceaux for luncheon where the *pâté de maison* was excellent. I do not much like seeing over châteaux. We then went to Chaumont and arrived at Amboise just too late to go over the château. Instead we drank some wine at a restaurant to which an importunate little boy directed us. There is little temptation to dine out as the cooking here is so excellent . . . It has rained a good deal in the last few days, bringing all manner of rank smells out of the country. On Monday we did a big round of châteaux, Azay-le-Rideau, Langres, Chinon, Langeais, Ussé. They were less crowded than on Saturday. The chapel at Ussé is very fine. I do not much like seeing châteaux. . . . On Saturday we set out for Blois in the two motor cars, but the Frazer Nash broke its springs. We arranged to spend the night at Bois at an hotel called Angleterre. We saw the château and rested and ate a dreadful dinner and then Julia and I went off in search of a music hall and we found a fair all along the Loire where we were photographed. We also saw a patriotic drama and Julia fell in love with a redheaded American girl chewing nuts. When we got back to the hotel we were told that Richard and Elizabeth had gone back to Tours. I may be old-fashioned, but it seemed to me an improper proceeding, particularly as the manageress could only very hardly [?] be persuaded that Julia and I did not want to sleep together. I went for a walk round the town. Next day I went to see a very beautiful church called, as far as I could make out, St Nichole and St Laurent. We lunched at the Angleterre, paid an immense bill, and drove to Chambord – a monstrous building with what the book on Touraine calls 'a dream city' on its roof. Yesterday we pottered about Tours drinking tasteless French beer.

EVELYN WAUGH, *THE DIARIES OF EVELYN WAUGH*, ED. MICHAEL DAVIE, PUB. BOOK CLUB ASSOCIATES, LONDON, 1976

PEOPLE AND PLACES

AMBOISE

The English philosopher John Locke (1632–1704) spent some years traveling through France. His assertion that Amboise was built by Dogabert is thought to be pure legend; as for his warning about the price of good wine . . . it's best to find out for yourself.

Thurs. May 27. From Tours to Amboise 6 leagues through a sandy valley by the side of the Loire, full of rie and poplar trees: are not 12 ordinary English miles. Amboise is a litle, stragleing towne. There is a manifacture of woolen stuffs, an old Chasteau, built by Dogabert, which stands high over the towne, wherein is a chappell where are hung up the mighty pair of Stag's hornes, 15 foot high & 7½ broad, the stag, they say, kild in the Forest of Arden in Francis the Ist time, & a round tower where, in a spirall ascent a coach may drive up to the top. In the midle or nave of this winding ascent is a well, & a cart might goe down the same way to fetch up water. The ascent not very steep, nor the tour very large. A la Corne excellent coole wine, but make your bargain before hand or expect an extraordinary reconing.**

John Locke, *Locke's Travels in France, 1675–1679*,
Cambridge University Press, Cambridge, 1953

Watching the weather in Saumur
Honoré de Balzac exercises his aptitude for detailed characterization on the burghers of Saumur, in his novel "Eugénie Grandet" (1833). He exposes their mundane hopes and fears – and, with some irony, their propensity for downright nosiness – with an unflinching scrutiny alleviated only a little by a dark vein of humor.

**Here, as in Touraine, the whole trade of the district depends upon an atmospherical depression. Landowners, vinegrowers, timber merchants, coopers, innkeepers, and lightermen, one and all are on the watch for a ray of sunlight. Not a man of them but goes to bed in fear and trembling lest he should hear in the morning that there has been a frost in the night. If it is not rain that they dread it is wind or drought; they must have cloudy weather or heat, and the rainfall and the weather generally all arranged to suit their peculiar notions.

Between the clerk of the weather and the vine-growing interest there is a duel which never ceases. Faces visibly lengthen or shorten, grow bright or gloomy, with the ups and downs of the barometer. Sometimes you hear from one end to the other of the old High Street of Saumur the words, 'This is golden weather!' or again, in language which likewise is no mere figure of speech, 'It is raining gold louis!' and they all know the exact value of sun or rain at the right moment.

After twelve o'clock or so on a Saturday in the summer time, you will not do a pennyworth of business among the worthy townsmen of Saumur. Each has his little farm and his bit of vineyard, and goes to spend the 'week end' in the country. As everybody knows this beforehand, just as everybody knows everybody else's business, his goings and comings, his buyings and sellings, and profits to boot, the good folk are free to spend ten hours out of the twelve in making up pleasant little parties, in taking notes and making comments, and keeping a sharp look-out on their neighbours' affairs. The mistress of a house cannot buy a partridge but the neighbours will inquire of her husband whether the bird was done to a turn; no damsel can put her head out of the window without being observed by every group of unoccupied observers.

Impenetrable, dark, and silent as the houses may seem, they contain no mysteries hidden from public scrutiny, and in the same way everyone knows what is passing in every one else's mind. To begin with, the good folk spend most of their lives out of doors, they sit on the steps of their houses, breafast there and dine there, and adjust any little family differences in the doorway. Every passer-by is scanned with the most minute and diligent attention; hence, any stranger who may happen to arrive in such a country town has, in a manner, to run the gauntlet, and is severely quizzed from every doorstep. By dint of perseverance in the methods thus indicated a quantity of droll stories may be collected; and, indeed, the people of Angers, who are of an ingenious turn, and quick at repartee, have been nick-named 'the tattlers' on these very grounds. 99

HONORÉ DE BALZAC,
EUGÉNIE GRANDET,
TRANS. ELLEN MARRIAGE,
PUB. EVERYMAN'S LIBRARY,
LONDON, ALFRED A. KNOPF,
NEW YORK, 1992

RECOLLECTIONS OF CHILDHOOD

Sidonie-Gabrielle Colette (1873–1954) was an exotic character who spent her early life as a music-hall actress. Her bisexuality and risqué dancing won her few friends among the staid bourgeoisie, but she became a respected writer in later years. She was admired for her sensuous prose, and her rich appreciation of mankind and Nature.

66 August, in my northern country, was a month for long patience. Like me deprived of school, the children found the days long. They crowded together during their interminable leisure in the shade at the foot of the houses, for they were tired of the shorn stubble and the silent woods. As the sun rotated they folded up their dusty legs to shield them from it. They played, we played, at spinning the knife, three pebbles, knuckle-bones. They bit into the first half-green peaches – I don't write 'we bit' because, as always, I was an expert on the taste of ripe juicy fruit. We watched the upward growth on the waste land of those thistles, fit for carding, whose flower, armed overall, takes fire with a violet flame just before the expiration of summer. Mulleins also climbed there, all covered – hairy leaves, buff-coloured flower – with the dustiness of those sultry days. Sated with idleness, listless from missing school and from concealing it, we counted the days and lied: 'My word, doesn't it go quickly!'. . .

Down there the pale, blackhaired women grape-harvesters put on large hats, turn down their sleeves to the wrists, and affect fearfulness: 'Oh, there's a spider! Holy Mother, a snake!' With equal affectation the men shed their coats and throw off their shirts. While the men go handsomely half-naked, the women laugh freely and sing on the paths. Fine, high voices, which the west wind carries from one bay to the next . . . The wasps, drunk and defenceless, adhere to the sticky tubs; the September sun is as good as August's . . . 99

COLETTE, *LOOKING BACKWARDS*, TRANS. DAVID LEVAY, PUB. PETER OWEN, LONDON, 1975

ANOTHER LITERARY FIGURE

The eccentric and perhaps immoral behavior of another French novelist, George Sand (Amandine-Aurore Lucille Dupin, 1804–76), scandalized bourgeois society and won her the distrust and disapproval of her country neighbors.

❝La Châtre also has a Famous Literary Figure. George Sand (1804–76) did not live in the town itself but in the pretty, turreted manor house known grandly as her 'château' two or three miles up the road, at Nohant. It is La Châtre that figures, street for street, in several of her novels, and the surrounding countryside was the inspiration of much of her writing.

In her lifetime many of her country neighbours were wary of her, regarding her as an eccentric woman with an immoral personal life and given to dangerous idealistic enthusiasms – an upper-class type that was by then well established. Her father was an office in Napoleon's Grand Army, her mother had been a camp-follower and was the child of a man who sold birds on the streets of Paris. Her paternal grandmother, who largely brought her up, was herself the child of an illegitimate son of the King of Poland. Present-day Anglo-Saxon attempts to set George Sand up as as feminist icon, an original rebel against the 'bourgeois morality', are misconceived. But it must be said that the twentieth-century French tendency to canonize her not only as a Great Writer but as *la Bonne Dame de Nohant*, as if she had been some kind of country saint ministering to the poor and beloved by all, is equally wide of the mark. In life George Sand had local enemies as well as admirers; her numerous novels are variable in quality and hardly qualify as 'great'. What matters most about her today is that she was the first person in France to write about the rural and artisan classes with personal knowledge and sympathy. Unlike her contemporary Balzac, who made his own contribution to the enduring French urban idea of the brutal peasantry, and Zola, who added it later in the century from a position of metropolitan ignorance, George Sand regarded the country people as individuals like herself. Her stories such as *La Mare au Diable*, *François le Champi* and *Le Meunier d'Angibault*, are a fountain of incidental local information concerning the world we have lost – and which was being lost even as she was depicting it.**❞**

GILLIAN TINDALL, *CÉLESTINE,*
VOICES FROM A FRENCH VILLAGE,
PUB. SINCLAIR-STEVENSON, LONDON, 1995

AT THE MERCY OF THE PEASANTS OF BERRY
This passage from George Sand's "Le Meunier d'Angibault" shows the difficulty of negotiating the Loire terrain, even for the local people .

❝When the sun had set, the darkness came on rapidly in these hollow ways, and the last peasant whom they addressed answered carelessly:

'Go on! go on! you have only a short league more, and the road is all good.'

Now this was the sixth peasant who, within about two hours, had stated that there was only a short league more, and this good road was such that the horse was exhausted, and the travellers at the end of their patience. Marcelle herself began to fear an overturn; for if the patachon and his nag needed all their skill to choose their passage in broad day, it was impossible that in dark night they should avoid the false openings which the unequal nature of the ground renders as dangerous as picturesque, and which are liable to sudden terminations, exposing you to a fall of ten or twelve perpendicular feet. The lad had never penetrated so far into the Black Valley; he lost patience, and swore furiously every time that he was forced to retrace his steps to recover the way; he complained of thirst, of hunger, groaned over the fatigue of his horse, beating him unmercifully meanwhile, and cursed the savage country and its stupid inhabitants, with all the airs of a little cockney.

More than once, seeing the road steep, but dry, Marcelle and her servants alighted; but they could not walk five minutes without coming to a hollow where the road narrowed, and was entirely occupied by stagnant springs on the level of the ground, forming a liquid mud impossible for a delicate woman to pass on foot. The Parisian Suzette had rather be overturned, she said, than leave her shoes in these sloughs; and Lapierre, who had passed his life in pumps upon polished floors, was so awkward and confused, that Mmm. de Blanchemont dared not let him carry her son.

The usual answer of the peasant, when asked the way, is, 'Go straight on, always straight on.' This is simply a joke – a sort of pun – which means that you are to walk straight on your legs; for there is not a straight road in the Black Valley. The numerous ravines made by the Indre, the Vauvre, the Couarde, the Gourdon, and a hundred lesser streams which take different names in their course, and have never borne the yoke of any bridge or dike, force you to a thousand turns to find fordable places, so that you are often obliged to turn you back upon the spot you wished to reach.

When they came to an angle of the road surmounted by a cross – a sinister locality always peopled by the peasant imagination with demons, sorcerers, and fantastic animals – our embarrassed travellers addressed themselves to a beggar, who, seated upon the death-stone, cried to them in a monotonous voice, 'Charitable souls, have pity on a miserable creature!'**

GEORGE SAND, *THE MILLER OF ANGIBAULT*,
PUB. WELDON & CO., LONDON, 1848

A CALL OF NATURE AND A VISIT TO MOULINS

The Swedish chemist John Jakob Berzelius (1779–1848) gives his particular impression of the highs and lows of his trip through France.

**I slept quite well all night long, not waking until we arrived at Nevers, at 8 in the morning. At this point the filthiness of France began to grow indescribable, and it continued in this way southwards. This applies particularly to the inconvenience of the kind of convenience known in France as *commodit*. Either it is lacking altogether and you are referred to the dunghill, or else it is so decorated that your cleanest and most convenient recourse is to use the floor beside it. 'La méthode est drôle', said one of my fellow passengers, together with whom I had the honour of repaying our debt to nature; but slithering backwards the same instant, he added: 'et mauvaise'. I crave my friends' forgiveness for mentioning these things, but it is impossible to divert attention altogether from subjects which, in every street and courtyard, present themselves in heaps to both eye and foot.

The coach pulled out of Nevers. The country grew increasingly beautiful and fertile. For several miles, ever since the previous day, we had been following the River Loire, which we crossed at Nevers. The road soon brought us to the River Ailler, which debouches into the Loire. We arrived at Moulins, on the shore of the Aillier, at 3 of the afternoon. After taking a dinner which, though mean, was served in three courses, my fellow-passengers went to rest but I, having slept well in the coach, took a guide and went to see the monuments of the town. It is quite a beautiful, well-built town. The most remarkable thing I saw was a tomb of the Duke DE MONTMORENCY in the chapel belonging to le Collège Royal. In accordance with the stage coach timetable, we stayed on until 12 at night, so that after completing my walk I had plenty of time for rest, until we were told that the coach was harnessed.**

CARL GUSTAF BERNHARD, *THROUGH FRANCE WITH BERZELIUS: LIVE SCHOLARS AND DEAD VOLCANOES*, PUB. PERGAMON PRESS, OXFORD, 1989

ITINERARIES
IN THE LOIRE VALLEY

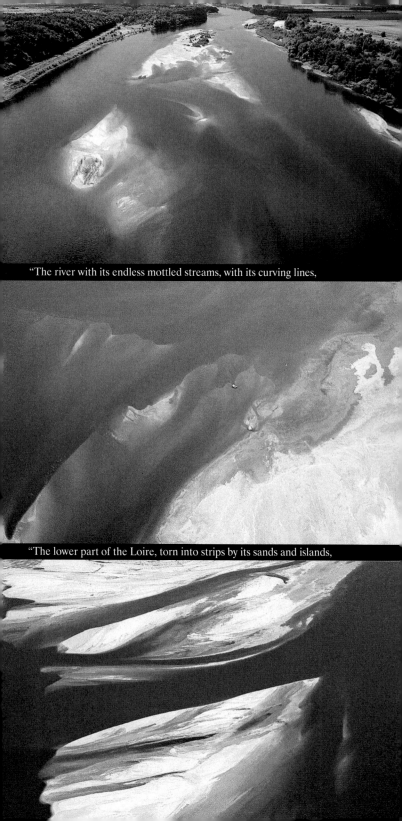

"The river with its endless mottled streams, with its curving lines,

"The lower part of the Loire, torn into strips by its sands and islands,

sometimes dramatic . . . sometimes indolent in appearance" *Charles Péguy*

looked from afar like those silver trails which snails leave across gardens" *René Boylesve*

▲ Château de Chaumont.

▲ The Pagoda at Chanteloup.   Château d'Azay-le-Rideau. ▼

▲ Château de Fougères-sur-Bièvre.

▲ Château de Cheverny.   Château de Beauregard. ▼

▲ Sandbank on the Loire.

▲ The Loire near the Château de Menars.　　　　The Loire in winter. ▼

In and around Orléans

BOULEVARD
ALEXANDRE-MARTIN
BOULEVARD ROUGET-DE-LISLE
PLACE DU MARTROI
17
6
PLACE DU Gᵃˡ-DE-GAULLE
16
15
QUAI CYPIERRE
RUE ROYALE

ORLÉANAIS
From north to south, the loosely defined region of Orléanais stretches from Beauce to the Sologne and (further to the east) from Gâtinais to Gien. It has a very rich historical heritage. In the 10th century the county of Orléans was annexed to the French kingdom by the first Capetians. Their successor, Philippe VI de Valois (above), made the province into a duchy in 1344: the title was traditionally given to the second son of the King of France. This flat region, divided by the Loire and situated between the Forest of Orléans (almost 90,000 acres) ■ 24 and the Sologne ▲ 174, covers almost exactly the same area as today's département of Loiret ● 12.

RÉPUBLIQUE FRANÇAISE
LA POSTE 1995
2,80
ORLÉANS
68ᵉ Congrès · Fédération Française des Associations Philatéliques

HISTORY OF THE TOWN

One of the principal towns of the Loire valley, Orléans is located at the apex of the river's bend, at the confluence of two small tributaries (one of them the Loiret). From an early stage the town had a vital strategic function, mainly because it stands at a major crossroads and also possesses a large river port.

CLASSICAL TIMES AND THE MIDDLE AGES. In the 1st century BC Orléans (then named Cenabum) was one of the main strongholds of the Carnutes, a powerful Gallic tribe. Under Roman rule it was renamed Aurelianum. Clovis captured the town in 498 and held the first Council of France here in 511. The coronations of Charles the Bold and Robert the Pious (son of Hugues Capet) took place here in 848 and 987 respectively, reflecting the town's growing political and religious stature. Orléans became an important bishopric and also a renowned intellectual center, with a university that continued the Carolingian academic tradition established by Theodulf ● 129. The region's growth was underpinned by its rich natural resources: wheat from Beauce, sheep from the Sologne, wood from the Forest of Orléans. Joan of Arc's famous victory of May 8, 1429, when she liberated the town from the English, became an enduring symbol of French resistance to invaders ● 116.

FROM PROSPERITY TO DECLINE. During the Renaissance phases of growth and construction ▲ *74* alternated with extended periods of turbulence due to the Wars of Religion. In the 17th and 18th centuries Orléans was a flourishing provincial capital and one of the six richest towns in France ▲ *116*. However, the revolutionary era and Napoleonist centralism dealt severe blows to this prosperity. The town's fortunes did not revive until the 3rd Republic, when major urban-development projects were undertaken. In June 1940 the center of the old town (around 42 acres) was destroyed by German bombing.

A MODERN CITY. Between 1950 and 1970 Orléans was gradually rebuilt; and in 1959 a new town, Orléans-la-Source, was developed on the south bank of the Loire. Today the city has a population of around 250,000. It has a strong horticultural sector and a lively university, and is active in engineering, electronics and pharmaceuticals.

HIDDEN TREASURES
Here more than elsewhere in the Loire Valley, visitors must be prepared to delve below the surface. Although the charm of Orléans is apparent at first sight, those willing to explore can discover the many historic and artistic treasures hidden away in this old royal city.

FAMOUS BISHOPS
The town's first
heroic bishop was
Anianus, later
Saint Aignan. Along
with Saint Euverte,
he played an
instrumental role in
repelling Attila's
Huns in 451.
Later bishops who

contributed to the
region's intellectual
and religious
development included
Theodulf ▲ *128* from
738 to 818, Jonas
from 818 to 843, and
Agius from 843 to
868.

POET PRINCE
Charles d'Orléans
(1394–1465) inherited
the duchy from his
father, Louis
d'Orléans, and
distinguished himself
at the Battle of
Agincourt in 1415.
He was captured by
the English and
imprisoned in
London from 1415 to
1441. To pass the time
he devoted himself to
writing poetry. He left
around one hundred
ballads and laments,
which fell into
oblivion for two
centuries before
being brought to light
by the Abbé Salier in
1734.

THE CATHEDRAL

Construction of Orléans' Cathédrale Ste-Croix took nearly
550 years to complete – from 1287 to 1829 – and yet the result
lacks neither grandeur nor elegance. The cathedral's unusual
towers are decorated with intricate stonework; its huge
Gothic nave rests on simple, elegant pillars.

DISASTERS. Over the centuries the cathedral suffered a series
of disasters. The first cathedral (4th–5th century) was

destroyed by fire in 989. The second
building, in the Romanesque style
(11th–12th century), partly collapsed in
1278. The Gothic cathedral (late 13th
century, early 16th century) was
destroyed by the Huguenots in 1568. It
was rebuilt under Henri IV from 1599
onward, but the spire of the transept was
demolished in 1691 when it looked likely
to collapse. The cathedral was finally
inaugurated on May 8, 1829.
Unfortunately the vault of the shrine collapsed in 1904,
crushing the altar under tons of masonry.

TOUR OF THE CATHEDRAL. The towers, in the neo-Gothic style,
were rebuilt between 1708 and 1829. The present-day central
spire is also neo-Gothic, dating from 1858. Two 16th-century
bays (the third and fourth) survive in the upper nave
(1601–1829), presenting an unusual mixture of Gothic and
classical styles. Stained-glass windows in the right side aisle
(1893–6) depict five episodes from the life of Joan of Arc.
The choir (1605–23) is decorated with splendid 18th-century
wood carvings and carved stalls. The great vault of the apse
was modeled on that of Notre-Dame-de-Cléry ▲ *138*.
Excavations undertaken in
1890 uncovered the pillars
of the Romanesque
building, which can be
seen in the crypt today.
The Tour Ste-Croix
(to the
left of
the

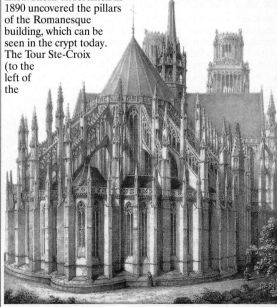

cathedral entrance) is a fragment of the 4th-century Gallo-Roman wall. Partially demolished and then buried, it was rediscovered in 1980.

AROUND THE CATHEDRAL

PLACE STE-CROIX. This square first came into being when the Rue Jeanne d'Arc was built in 1840; it was completed in 1976. The cathedral is framed by the Musée des Beaux-Arts and the town hall on one side, and by the regional authority for the central Loire valley on the other. The buildings opposite have neoclassical façades.

MUSÉE DES BEAUX-ARTS. The museum was founded in 1823 and initially housed in the Hôtel des Créneaux. It moved into this contemporary building in 1984. It has an exceptionally rich collection, and the displays of paintings, drawings, prints,

sculptures and objets d'art are changed regularly, presenting a fairly comprehensive overview of European art from the 16th to the 20th century. Look out for the Cabinet des Pastels (pastels room), the displays of French painting from the 17th and 18th centuries (Le Nain, Philippe de Champaigne, La Tour, Watteau, Boucher) and the impressive international collections (Correggio, the Carracci, Ruysdael, and Velásquez's famous *Saint Thomas the Apostle*). The museum is also the proud owner of Gauguin's *Fête Gloanec* (above). One room is dedicated to the poet Max Jacob ▲ *131*.

ANCIEN ÉVÊCHÉ. This private residence (no. 1, rue Dupanloup) was built for Alphonse Elbène, Bishop of Orléans from 1646 to 1655. In the 19th century a leading representative of the liberal wing of the Church, Bishop Félix Dupanloup (1802–78), lived here.

RUE DU BOURDON-BLANC. The Collège Jeanne d'Arc (at no. 2) occupies the buildings of the former Grand Séminaire (1705–20), which was built over the Collegiate Church of St-Avit. Only the 11th-century CRYPT of the church survives.

CAMPO-SANTO. Until 1786 this site (in Rue Fernand-Rabier) was the main cemetery of Orléans. A corn market was built here in 1824. Today the building with its lovely arcaded galleries (15th century) is used for a wide range of events, including Orléans' extremely popular jazz festival.

THE "BASTARD OF ORLÉANS"
Jean, Comte de Longueville et de Dunois (1403–68) was the natural son of Louis d'Orléans ● *39*, hence his nickname. A valiant warrior, he defeated the English at Montargis in 1427, and led the defense of Orléans both before Joan of Arc's arrival and subsequently by her side ▲ *116*. He made a vital contribution to France's liberation by taking a number of towns (Chartres in 1432, Paris in 1436, Dieppe in 1443) and through his campaigns in Normandy and Guyenne (1448–53).

THE HISTORICAL MUSEUM ▲ *119*
Popular prints made in Orléans showed a highly original

response to the Revolution. Above: Liberty, a print dedicated to "the sans-culottes of Orléans".

▲ JOAN OF ARC "THE MAID OF ORLÉANS"

The name of Joan of Arc (1412–31) has been linked with Orléans since May 8, 1429, when she rode victorious into the town, which had been besieged by the English since October 12, 1428. A humble peasant girl from the Lorraine, only seventeen years old and very religious, she claimed she was guided by the "voices" of Saint Michael, Saint Catherine and Saint Margaret. Orléans has fêted its heroine every year since May 8, 1430. After her martyrdom at Rouen two years later, she became a figurehead for the whole of the nation. The semi-legendary story of how the "Maid of Orléans" miraculously saved the French kingdom is imprinted in the minds of all French people, of whatever political or religious inclination.

THE SIEGE OF ORLÉANS

Ten thousand English soldiers, under the Earl of Salisbury, Lord Talbot, the Earl of Suffolk and William of Glasdale, laid siege to Orléans in October 1428, with the aim of gaining control of the town's river crossing. They erected a number of bastions, cutting the town off from the southern bank of the Loire. The Comte de Dunois (the "Bastard of Orléans" ▲ 139), La Hire, Xaintrailles, the Comte de Clermont and Admiral Louis de Culant led the town's defense.

FROM CHINON TO ORLÉANS ▲ 243, 244, 245

The day after the "Battle of the Herrings", Joan left Vaucouleurs to meet the Dauphin at Chinon ▲ 244. After being interrogated for three weeks she finally left for Tours, where her armor ▲ 199 and standard were made. She then took up position at the head of the army defending Orléans.

"BATTLE OF THE HERRINGS"

On February 12, 1429 an attempt to intercept a convoy of enemy supplies turned to disaster for the inhabitants of Orléans. The fatal "Day of the Herrings" seemed to mark the end of any hope that the Dauphin's armies might save the town ● 39, ▲ 245.

THE LIBERATION OF ORLÉANS

The town was about to succumb to famine when Joan appeared at the head of the royal reinforcements. At nightfall on April 29, 1429 she entered Orléans without meeting any opposition from the English. She stayed in the house of Jacques Boucher ▲ *139*. On April 30 Joan sent a challenge to the English, who replied with insults. On May 4 the French conquered the bastion of St-Loup; and on May 6 the English lost another of their fortifications, at St-Jean-le-Blanc. Close on the heels of this victory, Joan and La Hire recaptured the Augustinian convent; and on May 7, despite having been hit by an arrow, Joan led her companions in an attack on the bastion of Les Tourelles which blocked the bridge to the town. Talbot ordered the English to retreat and Orléans was saved.

AFTER ORLÉANS, THE LOIRE CAMPAIGN

Joan rested for a few days and then, together with the Duc d'Alençon, set off in pursuit of the defeated English armies. During their Loire campaign they captured Jargeau, Meung and Beaucency. On June 18, 1429 the English troops were routed at Patay, thus avenging Agincourt ● *39*.

"THE MAID OF ORLÉANS"
(Battle of Patay)
Frank Craig, 1907.

HÔTEL GROSLOT. Since 1790 the town hall has
been housed in this huge red-brick Renaissance
mansion (above), with diamond-pattern diapering and
ornamental window gables, which was restored and
redecorated around 1850. Attributed to Jacques Androuet
Du Cerceau (see left), it was built between 1549 and 1555 for
Jacques Groslot, bailiff of Orléans. The porch of the Chapel
of St-Jacques (late 15th/early 16th century), which once stood
in the Place du Châtelet, now
stands in the small garden; it was
moved here, after being rescued
from demolition, in 1883.

RUE JEANNE-D'ARC. Although this
street was first planned in 1767 by
Monseigneur de Jarente, Bishop of
Orléans, it was not built until 1840, following
plans by François Pagot. The Centre Jeanne
d'Arc is at no. 24, in the former Collège Royal
(1847); its monumental façade does not detract from the
restrained, regular appearance of the
street as a whole. This stylistic austerity
makes an extremely effective backdrop
for the intricate architecture of the
cathedral.

PLACE DU GÉNÉRAL DE GAULLE. The
square has several houses with 16th-
century façades that were either
reconstructed or transferred here after
the bombardments of World War Two.
The façades of nos. 3 and 5 (1539–45)
were moved here from the neighboring
Rue Tabour in 1945. At no. 7 is the
Maison de Jeanne d'Arc, dating from
1425, which was the residence of Jacques
Boucher, treasurer to the Duke of
Orléans; Joan of Arc is said to have
stayed here from April 29 to May 9, 1429.
The house's half-timbered façade ● 72
was meticulously reconstructed in 1965.

HÔTEL GROSLOT
In the main courtyard
is a statue of Joan
of Arc by Marie
d'Orléans, daughter
of Louis-Philippe
(1773–1850).

THE OLD TOWN

The area between the cathedral and the Loire is the oldest
quarter of the town, with medieval houses and Renaissance
residences.

PLACE ABBÉ-DESNOYERS. The square has noteworthy
houses on two sides, and Rue Ste-Catherine makes up the

third side. Maison de la Pomme (late 16th century) presents a lovely façade of brick and stone; this house, which once stood at no. 43 Rue Ste-Catherine, was moved when the street was widened in 1931 and rebuilt on the square. Maison du Sancier (1540–94), which consists of a single room built over a passageway, was moved here from Rue du Poirier, also in 1931.

HÔTEL CABU AND MUSÉE ARCHÉOLOGIQUE ET HISTORIQUE DE L'ORLÉANAIS ● 75. The Hôtel Cabu (right), also known as the Maison de Diane de Poitiers, dates from 1548. It was built by Jacques Androuet Du Cerceau for Philippe Cabu, a lawyer of the town. Legend has it that Diane de Poitiers, mistress of Henri II, stayed here in 1549. The court façade has two lateral forebuildings; the one on the left houses a spiral staircase. The archeological museum was established here in 1862. Its prize exhibit is the treasure discovered at Neuvy-en-Sullias (between Jargeau and Sully-sur-Loire) in 1861, consisting of a collection of Gallo-Roman bronzes (left, *The Dancer*). Also on show are sculptures, enamels, ivories and tapestries from the Middle Ages; and there is a section devoted to historical displays of local ceramics, earthenware, porcelain and glass. Do not miss the gallery showing popular prints of the 18th and 19th centuries: this genre developed in a markedly original way in Orléans, especially in its response to revolutionary events ▲ *115*.

RUE STE-CATHERINE. There is a lovely half-timbered house at no. 14. However, it is the HÔTEL DES CRÉNEAUX (1503–13) which catches the eye, built in a mixture of Renaissance and Flamboyant styles. The main wing overlooks Rue Ste-Catherine, while the rear of the building opens onto Place de la République. The 17th-century Passage du Saloir leads from the square to the street, passing underneath the building. The Hôtel des Créneaux was Orléans' town hall until 1790; today it is an annexe of the Conservatoire de Musique. Its belfry tower is older: it was built between 1445 and 1448, over the remains of the Gallo-Roman wall.

MAISON "DU CERCEAU". One of the loveliest houses of the old town, no. 6, rue Du-Cerceau ▲ *120* dates from the second half of the 16th century. The three upper stories of this Renaissance

HÔTEL CABU
Section of the façade overlooking Rue Charles Sanglier; and detail of the courtyard façade.

RÉPUBLIQUE FRANÇAISE
LA POSTE 1996
6,70
TRÉSOR DE NEUVY-EN-SULLIAS
LOIRET · BRONZE GALLO-ROMAIN

TREASURE OF NEUVY-EN-SULLIAS
A quarry worker discovered the Neuvy hoard, which was buried deep in the ground. This rare collection of Gallo-Roman art includes some surprisingly stylized figures of animals and people – for example, *The Dancer* (left). The impressive statue of the horse-god Rudiobus (above) has a dedication to the god on the base.

119

ÉTIENNE DOLET
Born in Orléans on
August 3, 1509, the
French humanist
(right) studied first in
Paris then in Padua
and Venice. Highly
quarrelsome, even
with his friends, he
was condemned to
death for his heretical
ideas.

**MAISON
"DU CERCEAU"**
Like Maison Sancier
▲ *119*, this house has
a Latin inscription
over the door: *Pax
huic domui* (Peace
to this house).

mansion have elegant
windows framed by pilasters
surmounted with cartouches.

RUE ÉTIENNE-DOLET. The street is named after Étienne Dolet
(right), the local printer and freethinker of the Renaissance
(1509–46) who was burned for heresy in Paris. At
no. 11 is the Maison des Chevaliers du Guet,
built in 1547 for the widow Marie Brochet;
its decorative brickwork with black
glazed diapering is a relatively late
example of its type ● *67*.

RUE DE BOURGOGNE. This street, with
its half-timbered houses (nos. 264, 266,
268 and 270), is one of the oldest in
Orléans. It once ended at the Porte de
Bourgogne, the eastern entry to the
town's fortifications (near the intersections
with Rue du Bourdon-Blanc and Rue de la
Tour-Neuve), where Joan of Arc entered Orléans on April 29,
1429.

HÔTEL HECTOR-DE-SAUXERRE. This house, on the corner of
Rue de la Poterne, was built between 1543 and 1545. It has an
unusual corbeled room on the second story: this was the
library of Hector de Sauxerre, an educated resident of the
town who lived during the reign of François I.

HÔTEL DE LA PRÉFECTURE. The Préfecture of Loiret moved
into a former Benedictine abbey (below) in 1800. The abbey,
Notre-Dame-de-Bonne-Nouvelle, was built in 1653 and
abandoned after the Revolution.

SALLE DES THÈSES. This old library, in Rue Pothier, was built
in the Gothic style between 1411 and 1417; it is all that

survives of the medieval university, dissolved in 1793. The university's students included Rabelais, Calvin and Charles Perrault.

COLLEGIATE CHURCH OF ST-AIGNAN. The crypt, in Rue Neuve St-Aignan, is all that remains of the 11th-century building. Several kings of France, from Charles VII to Louis XII, contributed to the magnificent collegiate church, which was destroyed by Protestants in 1567. Only the transept, the choir and five chapels survived the Revolution.

TOUR BLANCHE. This tower, in Rue Tour-Neuve, was part of the fortifications of the Gallo-Roman town.

COLLEGIATE CHURCH OF ST-PIERRE-LE-PUELLIER. This collegiate church (Rue de l'Université/Rue St-Gilles) was built, from the 12th to the 16th century, near a convent – to which its name, derived from *puella* (the Latin for "girl"), refers. It became national property under the Revolution. Disused since 1958, it has since been restored.

PONT GEORGE-V. Today's bridge, leading from the Quai du Châtelet, was built between 1751 and 1760. It replaced the medieval bridge which played a famous part in the town's liberation in 1429.

RUE ROYALE. This street was built between 1754 and 1760, leading up to Place du Martroi. The Chancellerie was all that survived of the lovely 18th-century arcaded buildings after the bombings of 1940. The façades and arcades (above) have been restored with considerable care.

PLACE DU CHÂTELET. In medieval times a fortress stood here, overlooking a large marketplace.

MAISON "DE LA COQUILLE". The shell (right) on the façade of the 16th-century house at no. 7, rue de la Pierre-Percée is derived from the sign on an earlier house built in 1511.

CHAPELLE NOTRE-DAME-DES-MIRACLES. This chapel, in Rue Saint-Paul, was built in 1629 and restored in 1915. Along with the bell tower (1620–7), it is all that remains of the Church of St-Paul destroyed in June 1940.

MAISON "DE LA COQUILLE" (left, and detail above). The external design of this house is similar to that of the house at no. 6, place du Châtelet known as the Maison de Jean Dallibert.

121

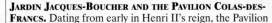

HÔTEL TOUTIN
(1536–40), courtyard.

JARDIN JACQUES-BOUCHER AND THE PAVILION COLAS-DES-FRANCS. Dating from early in Henri II's reign, the Pavilion Colas-des-Francs was used for storing silverware, money and archives; its ornate interiors have survived.

CHURCH OF NOTRE-DAME-DE-RECOUVRANCE. This church, in Rue Notre-Dame-de-Recouvrance, was built between 1513 and 1519 and badly damaged during the Wars of Religion. Its vaulting was restored in the 17th century, and the choir rebuilt in the troubadour style in the 19th century.

HÔTEL TOUTIN. The house at no. 26, rue Notre-Dame-de-Recouvrance was built between 1536 and 1540 by Guillaume Toutin, who was valet de chambre to Dauphin Henri, son of François I. The building has two wings – one facing the street, the other facing the courtyard (above) – connected by a gallery supported by columns with capitals.

HÔTEL EUVERTE-HATTE, CENTRE CHARLES-PÉGUY. This house, in Rue du Tabour, is one of the city's jewels of François I architecture. It was built between 1524 and 1529 for Orléans merchant Euverte Hatte. From the internal courtyard visitors can admire a magnificent two-story covered gallery. Today the building houses the Centre Charles Péguy, which includes a library and documents relating to the writer's life and works.

THE "VILLE OPULENTE"

In this district 17th-century buildings stand side by side with more recent constructions, reflecting the commercial expansion and prosperity of the town during the 18th century and the first half of the 19th century.

PLACE DU MARTROI. Buildings from several architectural periods, from the 18th century to the modern day, border this square at the heart of the town. With its cafés and brasseries with pavement terraces, the Place du Martroi (above) is a favorite meeting place.

PORTE BANNIER. Remains of the medieval town walls (14th–15th century) were unearthed when a car park was being built beneath Place du Martroi in 1986.

STATUE OF JOAN OF ARC. The bronze equestrian statue at the center of the square was made by sculptor Denis Foyatier in 1855. The bas-reliefs (also 1885) by Vital-Gabriel Dubray around the base recount the life of the heroine of Orléans.

CHARLES PÉGUY ● 99
Born in Orléans on January 7, 1873, Charles Péguy enrolled as a student at the École Normale Supérieure in Paris in 1894. A socialist and ardent defender of Dreyfus, he founded and published a fortnightly journal, the *Cahiers de la Quinzaine*, despite financial difficulties. He turned to Christianity in 1908 and wrote some important poetic and mystical texts, including the *Mystère de la charité de Jeanne d'Arc* (1910).

THE CHANCELLERIE AND CHAMBRE DE COMMERCE. The façade of the Chancellerie, dating from 1754, was the only part of the original building to survive the destruction of June 1940. The building was formerly used to house the archives of the Duke of Orléans. The Chamber of Commerce was built in the neoclassical style as a counterpart to the Chancellerie, in 1863.

ANCIEN COUVENT DES MINIMES. The church and cloisters of the former Monastery of the Minims were completed in 1621. The last monks were forced to leave the monastery under the Revolution. Since 1913 the building has housed the Departmental Archives.

PAVILLONS D'ESCURES ● 75. Rue d'Escures is bordered by private houses dating from the Renaissance and the early 17th century. Next to the Caisse d'Épargne building (in Third Empire style) is a small 16th-century house formerly owned by the Chevaliers de St-Lazare. At nos. 2, 4 and 6 are the Pavillons d'Escures, a group of four private houses built in the 17th century for an eminent local figure, Pierre Fougeu d'Escures (1554–1621), who was mayor of Orléans and a friend of Henri IV. The brick-and-stone buildings, separated by domed pavilions in the Imperial style, are reminiscent of the buildings on Place des Vosges in Paris. They are a rare example of 17thcentury town planning.

CHURCH OF ST-PIERRE-DU-MARTROI. This church was built in the 16th century during the reign of François I; it is the only religious building in Orléans made of bricks. Rebuilt after the Wars of Religion, it contains a number of old paintings, including those attributed to Jean Restout (1692–1768) on the altarpiece of the high altar (1738).

DISTINGUISHED VISITORS
There have been many distinguished visitors to the city. Emperor Charles V came to Orléans on December 20, 1539, accompanied by the French king François I: he inspected 4,000 troops on Place du Martroi before proceeding to Place de l'Étape. Prince Louis-Lucien Bonaparte visited the town in 1804; the Russian and Austrian emperors came here in 1815, and King Ludwig II of Bavaria in 1870.

PLACE DU MARTROI

ORLÉANS VINEGAR ● 56
Casks of wine commonly turned sour during shipment on the Loire, so the citizens of Orléans decided to turn this to their advantage. High-quality vinegar was manufactured here from 1394 onward, and in the reign of Louis XVI the town had two hundred master "vinaigriers". Maison Desseaux became the leading local vinegar manufacturer in 1826. The famous scientist Louis Pasteur (1822–95), son-in-law of a family of printers in Orléans, often came to the town to study acetic fermentation. Today Orléans still produces half the vinegar consumed in France.

A JEANNE D'ARC
LA VILLE D'ORLÉANS
AVEC LE CONCOURS
DE LA FRANCE ENTIÈRE

JEAN ZAY (1904–44)
Born in Orléans, Jean Zay was a brilliant lawyer who served as a radical-socialist deputy for Loiret from 1932 to 1940

and contributed to the victory of the Popular Front in 1936. As a young minister for education and culture (up to September 1939), he took steps toward making the arts and teaching profession more democratic. When Pétain sued for peace Zay boarded *Le Massilia*, in order to continue the war, but was arrested in Morocco by the Vichy government. Condemned to deportation in 1940 following a sham trial, he was interned at Riom and handed over to the militia, who assassinated him at Cusset on June 20, 1944.

HORTICULTURE ■ 26
The horticultural industry of Orléanais ▲ 13 goes back to the 15th century. By 1750 more than 30,000 fruit trees were being grown in the region's nurseries, and exports flourished with the commercial expansion of the 19th century. Today the region accounts for two-thirds of the horticultural trade in the Loire valley, and each year local growers sell some five to six million rose bushes.

HÔTEL POMMERET. This sober, harmonious 17th-century residence was owned by the Pommeret family from 1789 to 1978; it was modified under Louis XV and again under the Restoration.

RUE DE LA RÉPUBLIQUE. This semi-pedestrianized street which connects Place du Martroi with Place Albert Ier was built in 1895, to develop the area around the station (built in 1843). The blocks which line the street were erected between 1897 and 1904. The Hôtel Moderne at no. 37 was built for Émile Dindault in 1902, designed by Louis Duthoit in the Art Nouveau style: it is reminiscent of the famous Lavirotte building on Avenue Rapp in Paris.

RUE ALSACE-LORRAINE. The 19th- and early-20th-century buildings create a strikingly unified, harmonious effect.

PLACE ALBERT-Ier. A new shopping center (reached by a flight of steps) has replaced the town's old railway station, which was the terminus of the Paris-Orléans line. To conclude your tour of the city, take a stroll on the tree-lined Boulevard Alexandre-Martin (named after a former mayor).

ORLÉANS-LA-SOURCE

Orléans-la-Source, an extension of Orléans to the south of the Loire, was built in 1959 on a 1700-acre site reclaimed from the Sologne. Features of this "garden suburb" include a remarkable flower park and the new university campus. The latter, opened in 1963 to cater for 10,000 students, covers an area of some 450 acres.

THE PARC FLORAL. During the Orléans flower festival in 1967 nearly 2,300,000 visitors discovered the delights of this floral park, created from 86 acres of woodland in 1963. Today visitors can admire some 150,000 rose trees, begonias, dahlias, rhododendrons and other plants. Since 1995 new floral and woodland areas have been created within the park, including the Jardin de la Source, the Gloriette aux Papillons (butterfly garden) and an iris garden.

THE SOURCES OF THE LOIRET. This tributary of the Loire has given its name to the whole département, although it is only 8 miles long. It has its source in two springs at the heart of the Parc Floral: the Bouillon (the main spring) and the Grande Source or Abîme.

CHÂTEAU DE LA SOURCE. This building, which now stands in the Parc Floral, was rebuilt in 1622. In 1962 it became the first wing of the new university.

OLIVET   (O2)

Olivet was once a village of fruit-tree nurseries and market gardens. Although

> **"NO DAZZLING ATTRACTIONS, NO OSTENTATIOUS GRANDEUR. IT IS NO MORE THAN A VALLEY ... WITH THE LOIRE WINDING THROUGH IT UNDER THE SKY. BUT WHAT GENTLE LIGHT, AND WHAT PURITY IN THE LONG TRANQUIL CONTOURS OF THE LANDSCAPE."**
>
> MAURICE GENEVOIX

THE ACADÉMIE DE LA SOURCE
Henry St John, Viscount Bolingbroke (1678–1751), a friend of Swift and Voltaire, became the new tenant of the château in the 18th century. He made it into a very lively literary center, which his friends dubbed the "Académie de la Source". Voltaire read a few verses of his *Henriade* here in 1722.

it is now a residential suburb of Orléans, it has retained something of its horticultural character. The Sentier des Prés and then the Chemin des Moulins (which connects the old mills of St-Julien, St-Samson, Les Béchets, La Mothe and Le Bac) offer a charming countryside walk along the Loiret.

LA FERTÉ-ST-AUBIN (P4)

Although this town is on the edge of the Sologne, it has been influenced economically and culturally by the nearby city of Orléans.

THE CHÂTEAU. The first fortress which guarded the crossing of the Cosson was destroyed in 1562 and replaced by a second château, built for François de St-Nectaire between 1590 and 1620: this is the "petit château" which survives in the left-hand section of the present-day building. St-Nectaire's son Henri, Maréchal de France, instructed Théodore Lefèvre, architect to the Duke of Orléans, to reorganize and extend the château in 1630. The "grand logis" (main building), the second level of the terrace and the two pavilions flanking the entrance, which have Imperial-style roofs, are attributed to Lefèvre. The outbuildings of the château appear to date from this period, although those on the right are more recent in style and were probably built from 1746 onward for the Comte de Loewendal (1700–55), Maréchal de France.

A PERFECT MOVIE SET
The Château de La Ferté-St-Aubin was used as a movie set for Jean Renoir's *La Règle du jeu*, made in 1939; a scene from the movie is shown

below. The leading actors were Marcel Dalio, Julien Carette, Jean Renoir and Paulette Dubost.

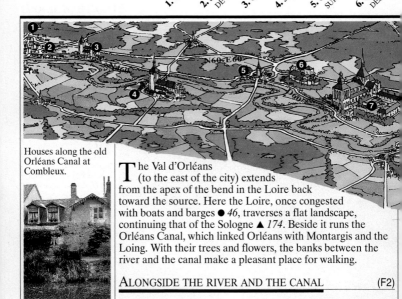

Houses along the old Orléans Canal at Combleux.

The Val d'Orléans (to the east of the city) extends from the apex of the bend in the Loire back toward the source. Here the Loire, once congested with boats and barges ● *46*, traverses a flat landscape, continuing that of the Sologne ▲ *174*. Beside it runs the Orléans Canal, which linked Orléans with Montargis and the Loing. With their trees and flowers, the banks between the river and the canal make a pleasant place for walking.

ALONGSIDE THE RIVER AND THE CANAL   (F2)

ST-JEAN-DE-BRAYE. This little town perched on the hillside overlooking the Loire is an important historical site. The place known as the Pointe St-Loup was Attila's encampment in 451; it was also the site of an English bastion during the siege of Orléans in 1429 ▲ *116*. The Abbey of St-Loup (14th century) was destroyed by the French army to prevent the English from taking refuge there: only the chapel and a few buildings are still standing.

LOCAL WRITER
The writer Maurice Genevoix (1890–1980) lived in Châteauneuf-sur-Loireat at no. 2b, rue St-Nicholas (named after the patron saint of sailors). He was a member of the Académie Française from 1946 and wrote a number of books inspired by the Sologne and the Loire, notably *Raboliot* (winner of the Prix Goncourt, 1925), *La Loire* and *Le Bestiaire enchanté* (1970).

THE FONDERIE BOLLÉE ★. This is one of the last three bell foundries in France (right). Its museum of campanology is one of the few museums tracing the history of bell founding.

COMBLEUX. Its flowers and its situation beside the Orléans Canal make Combleux a charming town. The towpath from St-Jean-de-Braye to the lock at Combleux offers wide views over the open landscape (above).

ST-DENIS-DE-L'HÔTEL AND JARGEAU   (G2)

These sister-towns stand on either side of the river: their churches have identical square bell towers. At St-Denis-de-l'Hôtel is the MAISON MAURICE GENEVOIX, opened in 1984 and devoted to the author of "romans de la nature" (see left). Jargeau, on the left bank of the river, is famous for its andouilles (sausages). Its collegiate church, St-Vrain (11th–14th century), has a rare wrought-iron pulpit from 1755.

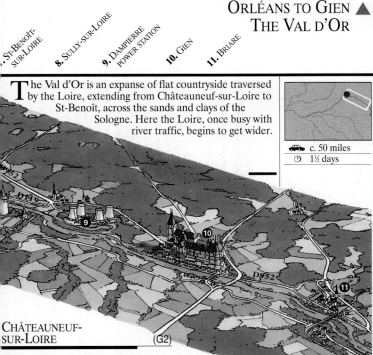

7. ST-BENOÎT-SUR-LOIRE **8.** SULLY-SUR-LOIRE **9.** DAMPIERRE POWER STATION **10.** GIEN **11.** BRIARE

The Val d'Or is an expanse of flat countryside traversed by the Loire, extending from Châteauneuf-sur-Loire to St-Benoît, across the sands and clays of the Sologne. Here the Loire, once busy with river traffic, begins to get wider.

🚗 c. 50 miles
🕐 1½ days

CHÂTEAUNEUF-SUR-LOIRE (G2)

Famous for its rhododendrons, Châteauneuf-sur-Loire was a busy river port until the advent of the railway brought about its decline.

THE CHÂTEAU. Although the château originated in the 11th century, it was rebuilt in the 17th century for the Marquis Louis Phélipeaux de la Vrillière, who was Secretary of State under Louis XIV. All that remains today is a group of outbuildings – an attractive architectural ensemble consisting of a Mansart-style stable block (17th century), an orangery (18th century) and a domed octagonal rotunda which now houses Châteauneuf's town hall. The arboretum in the park contributes to the town's horticultural reputation.

MUSÉE DE LA MARINE DE LA LOIRE. This unique museum, in the former guardroom, was opened to the public in 1962; it tells the story of navigation on the Loire ● *46.*

BALADE DES MARINIERS ★. This historical trail starts from the museum and leads through the old town, showing visitors buildings and landmarks which illustrate the life of bargemen on the Loire. The quaysides of the Rampe du Haut-du-Quai give an impression of how this lively port must have looked in the past. The Colonne des Mariniers on the Place du Port was erected in 1847 to commemorate the bravery of the bargemen during the devastating floods of October 1846.

CHURCH OF ST-MARTIAL. This was once the church of the hamlet of La Ronce (12th century); it was rebuilt several times and restored in the 1940's. It houses the tomb of Louis Phélipeaux de la Vrillière, which is attributed to Dominico Guidi (1628–1701), a follower of Bernini.

HALLE ST-PIERRE. This building (behind the church) was originally a boat house: erected in 1854, it was subsequently converted into a corn exchange.

LADY OF THE STAMP The Musée de la Fondation Oscar Roty (1846–1911), in Jargeau, is named after the engraver of La Semeuse (The Seed-sower), a famous image used on French coins and stamps in the earlier part of the 20th century.

THE ARMENIAN INFLUENCE
The churches which most closely resemble the oratory at Germigny in terms of architectural style are those of Armenia – such as the Church of Bagaran and the Cathedral of Edjmiatsin, although both of these have a circular ground plan. Armenian architects like Odo, who built the oratory, were regarded as the best in the world at this time.

VISIGOTHIC ARCHES
The arches at Germigny are of a special type. They are not Romanesque (semicircular), or Arabian (slightly narrower): they are the horseshoe-shaped arches of the Spanish Visigothic style.

ALABASTER FILTERS
The muted light created by the translucent alabaster in the narrow windows of the lantern tower provides the perfect setting for the Carolingian mosaic, which was probably created by a Byzantine artist.

GERMIGNY-DES-PRÉS ★ (G3)

This Carolingian oratory, set in a tiny village on the right bank of the Loire, is visited by more than 100,000 tourists every year. The Romanesque tiled roof and the cypress trees around the building give it an Italian air.

HISTORY OF THE ORATORY. It was built in 806 for Theodulf, Abbot of Fleury (the original name of the nearby Abbey of St-Benoît-sur-Loire), Bishop of Orléans and one of the *missi dominici* of the Emperor Charlemagne. Originally this private oratory was part of Theodulf's opulent villa, which was destroyed by the Normans; like the oratory of Charlemagne's palace at Aix-la-Chapelle, it was built by Armenian architect Odo (see left). In 1868 the oratory at Germigny was restored by Juste Lisch, who made major alterations to both the surface and the structure of the building. The two apsidioles of the eastern apse were removed, the western apse was replaced by a long nave, and the lantern tower (belfry) was shortened by 10 feet.

EXTERIOR. The top section of a 16th-century lantern and a 17th-century wrought-iron cock can be seen in the grounds of the oratory. In the presbytery is a small 12th-century enameled shrine, which was made in the workshops of Limoges.

ARCHITECTURE OF THE ORATORY. The original church, in the shape of a Greek cross, was built on a square ground plan with three naves and three bays; the addition of apses in the middle of each side created a quatrefoil design. The contour of the demolished western apse is indicated by large floor slabs. The original entrance was to the right of the northern apse. The pillar piscina with a cable molding dates back to the Carolingian church.

THE MOSAIC. The 19th-century alterations were designed to highlight the superb mosaic in the rounded vault of the eastern apse. The apse was originally framed by two niches: one for the preparation of bread and wine, the other for sacred vessels and liturgical vestments. It now functions almost like a choir, drawing visitors toward the brightness of the mosaic, whose glass cubes are the only area of color in the monochrome church. The 9th-century mosaic is extremely beautiful, and is unique of its kind in France. It is made of 130,000 small squares of glass (blue, purple, white, green, black and gold) and depicts the Ark of the Covenant: two large angels swoop graciously, set against a gilded blue background showing the hand of God. A 16th-century wooden Pietà has been placed below the mosaic: it was carved by a sculptor from the Burgundian school.

ST-BENOÎT-SUR-LOIRE ● 58 (H3)

The town of St-Benoît-sur-Loire was once a port of call for bargemen on the Loire, and old fishermen's houses still line the riverside. However, St-Benoît is chiefly famous for its Benedictine abbey; the town, originally called Fleury, was renamed after the abbey in the 11th century. In the words of the writer Max Jacob (▲ 131), St-Benoît is "a plain leading off into the distance, broken by houses and clumps of trees, a plain for harvest and vegetables. This beautiful landscape is made of more than just contour and color: it is infused with the spirit which reigns over all of St-Benoît, and the source of this spirit is the basilica. . . ."

THEODULF ● 37, 112
Theodulf was born around 760, into a great Spanish Visigothic family. He studied in Aquitaine and stayed at the Abbey of St-Benoît-d'Aniane, not far from St-Guilhem-le-Désert (in the Hérault region). He was appointed Bishop of Orléans in 798 and became abbot of several abbeys, including St-Benoît at Fleury. He was the most important of Charlemagne's *missi dominici* (provincial inspectors) and one of the emperor's advisers. Theodulf was an educated, civilized man, an educational reformer and one of the outstanding figures of the Carolingian Renaissance. In 814, on the death of Charlemagne, he served as a counselor to Charlemagne's successor, Louis the Pious. Falsely accused of conspiracy, he was imprisoned in a monastery in Angers in 818, where he remained until his death in 821.

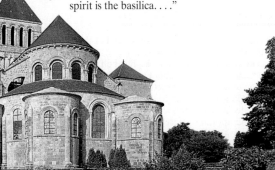

ABBEY OF ST-BENOÎT-SUR-LOIRE
View of the chevet ● 58.

SUDDEN DEATH
In the 9th century the abbey was sacked by the Viking Rynaldus. The patron saint of the abbey punished him with immediate death. To commemorate this event, his snarling face is carved as a decorative mask on the west wall of the transept.

Belfry porch of the Abbey of St-Benoît details of the columns and carvings.

THE LIFE OF SAINT BENEDICT
The saint was born around 480 and died in 543 or 547 at Monte Cassino in Italy. In 578 the monastery there was destroyed by the Lombards, and his tomb buried under the ruins. His life as a hermit in Subiaco and on Monte Cassino is recounted in the second book of *Dialogues* by Pope Gregory the Great. The relics of Saint Benedict were brought back from Italy by the monks of Fleury around 670–2.

HISTORY OF THE ABBEY OF FLEURY. The abbey was founded in 651 by Leodebold, Abbot of St-Aignan-d'Orléans, and placed under the patronage of Saint Benedict; at this stage it was called the Abbey of Saint-Benoît-de-Fleury. At the end of the 7th century, after the monk Aigulf was sent from Fleury to Italy to bring back the relics of Saint Benedict, the abbey took the name of St-Benoît-sur-Loire.

GOLDEN AGE. The abbey flourished under the rule of Theodulf ▲ *129*, the builder of Germigny. From the 10th to the 12th century – under Odon, Abbot of Cluny, Abbon (a monk from Reims) and Gauzlin (later Archbishop of Bourges) – St-Benoît's reputation continued to grow, attracting pilgrims and students to the town. Philippe I, King of France, was buried here in 1108.

DECLINE. The abbey's decline began in the 13th century, not long after the basilica was completed (it was dedicated on October 26, 1218). From 1486 onward the tradition of commendatory appointments, whereby the abbey's benefices were granted to a layperson chosen by the king, produced a series of conflicts. During the course of one of these, in 1527, François I had the Tour Gauzlin knocked down by his troops. The abbey was sacked by Protestants during the Wars of Religion. Later St-Benoît saw a revival in its fortunes when it was given in commendam to Richelieu. When religious orders were suppressed in 1790, the monks dispersed. Two years later the monastery was partially destroyed.

RESTORATION AND REVIVAL. In 1865 four monks from the Monastery of Pierre-qui-Vire in Burgundy moved into the parish, cleared the crypt, restored the paving of the church and reconsecrated it. It was not until October 11, 1944, however, that a monastic community was re-established at St-Benoît. The monks undertook an extensive programme of restoration, as a result of which the monastery regained its former status as an abbey in 1959. Today the Abbey of Fleury has thirty-five monks, as well as some visiting brothers, notably from Africa. The monks have a Benedictine library and meet in the church for services, where Gregorian chants are sung.

ARCHITECTURE OF ST-BENOÎT

The abbey church stands at the far end of the village square, on the site of two earlier churches.

BELFRY PORCH (details left) ★. The belfry porch is called the Tour Gauzlin, after the abbot who built it in the 11th century. It is the oldest surviving section of the abbey, and serves as a forebuilding to the church. Its sixteen pillars are decorated with historiated capitals, carved in a striking, expressive style which incorporates references to Carolingian and classical art and also to the decorative repertoire of illuminated manuscripts.

> **"ST-BENOÎT OF THE OLD VINE,
> YOUR PEACEFUL PLAIN AND THE BENIGN LOIRE
> WILL MAKE ME FORGET
> THE ATTRACTIONS OF PARIS."**
>
> MAX JACOB

CHOIR AND TRANSEPT. These were built between 1067 and 1107. The tall, deep choir is a beautiful example of Romanesque architecture. It is the main shrine of the abbey, with its altar dedicated to the Virgin Mary. The columns stand on a platform surmounted by a blind arcature and clerestory windows; a semicircular vault covers the whole ensemble. The high, rounded apse over the crypt has four small chapels (two radiating and two aligned, the latter crowned by a minuscule Romanesque bell tower). The high altar is surrounded by decorative paving (below), created under Abbot Gauzlin early in the 11th century, which was

MAX JACOB AT ST-BENOÎT
Max Jacob (1876–1944), a writer and converted Jew, spent the last twenty years of his life at St-Benoît, seeking to escape the Montmartre of his Bohemian youth. He was arrested by the Gestapo in 1944 and taken to the prison camp at Drancy, where he died a few months later. His works include *Saint Benoît et l'abbaye de Fleury* (1938). The house where the writer lived is now the local tourist office; on the second story there is a permanent exhibition devoted to him.

uncovered during excavations. This is a work of opus sectile – mosaic made of relatively large pieces of multicolored marble laid out in geometric patterns, with larger discs of different sizes to vary the effect.

NAVE. The vast nave was the last section of the church to be built, probably from 1144 to 1218. It is built in the transitional Romanesque style, although it looks Gothic at first sight. It has seven two-story bays and two side aisles with rib vaulting. The carved portal (especially the lintel) in the left side aisle is one of the masterpieces of the period. At the crossing of the nave and the transept is a magnificent group of 15th-century stalls, including a splendid panel depicting the Annunciation.

CRYPT. The 11th-century crypt is reached by means of a staircase situated to the east of the side aisles of the choir. Excavated in 1958–9, it extends across the area covered by the small transept and the apse and ambulatory. Its structure converges on the central pillar, which is hollow and contains the relics of Saint Benedict. The relics are kept in a contemporary shrine designed by D. de Laborde, a monk from the Abbey of Solesmes. Around it are fifteen lamps, symbolizing the congregations of the Benedictine Order.

CHAPEL OF ST-MOMMOLE. The southern end of the crypt leads to this 10th-century chapel; situated under the sacristy, it predates the rest of the church.

> " In the ever quiet shades
> Of Sully, this peaceful place,
> I am a thousand times happier
> Than the great prince who has exiled me."
>
> Voltaire

SULLY-SUR-LOIRE (R3)

The château of Sully-sur-Loire, a plain-fortress on the left bank of the river, retains something of its medieval air. It is surrounded by a moat, which is fed by the small river Sange and separated from the Loire by a bank of earth and sand.

HISTORY OF THE TOWN. The town flourished from the 10th century onward as its position allowed it to control both the river traffic and the road between the royal territories and the Massif Central. Sully-sur-Loire suffered considerable damage in the Wars of Religion, then again during the siege of 1563 and the Protestant uprising of 1621. Nearly three-quarters of the town was destroyed during battles for control of the bridge in June 1940 and by bombardments in 1944. Apart from the château and the religious buildings, the only surviving remnant of the old town is the 16th-century house at no. 8, rue du Grand-Sully.

THE CHÂTEAU. All that survives of the original château, dating from 1102, is the layout of the rooms. From 1395 onward a new château was built at the request of the Trémoille family by Raymond du Temple, architect of the Château de Vincennes. Further alterations were made, from 1602 onward, by the new owner, Maximilien de Béthune, a minister of Henri IV better known as the Duc de Sully, or simply as Sully. In 1611, a year after the king's assassination, Sully retired to his estate. Voltaire stayed here in 1716 and in 1719, when exiled from Paris by the regent Philippe d'Orléans (1674–1723).

THE ARCHITECT OF VINCENNES
Raymond du Temple, the military architect who transformed the royal château at Vincennes for Charles V, displayed his innovative and progressive talents at Sully in 1395.

Whereas Vincennes had square corner towers, which were rather old-fashioned, Du Temple decided on round towers for Sully, relying on his master mason, Colin des Chapelles, to execute the design.

THE BRIDGE OF SULLY-SUR-LOIRE
The bridge (right) built in 1836 was carried away by the terrible floods of 1856. It was made vulnerable by the access ramps leading to the suspended roadway: unfortunately they blocked part of the river bed, which was very narrow at this point.

ARCHITECTURE OF THE CHÂTEAU. The castle consists of two buildings, surrounded by the moat: one from the 14th century, built by Guy VI de la Trémoille, and the other from the 16th century, built by Sully.

THE OLD CHÂTEAU OR KEEP (1395–1400). This impressive rectangular building flanked by four circular towers stands facing the Loire, with Sully's additions between it and the river. The Salle des Gardes, on the ground floor, has enormous stone fireplaces. The annual music festival of Sully-sur-Loire is held here.

THE "PETIT-CHÂTEAU". This comprises the *corps de logis* or residential wing (to the east of the château) added by Sully in the 16th century and fortifications that include the Tour de Rosny and the large Tour de Béthune. The latter, built by Sully in 1606, looks toward the town, which he regarded as a potential source of trouble.

THE DUC DE SULLY
Maximilien de Béthune, Baron of Rosny (1559–1641), was a Protestant whose fortunes were linked with Henri de Navarre's. Serving him in a military capacity, he became his Superintendent of Finances in 1598 and was made Duc de Sully in 1606.

COLLEGIATE CHURCH OF ST-YTHIER. Despite the damage suffered during World War Two, the church still has important architectural features and furnishings dating from the 16th and 17th centuries, including painted wooden statues and stained-glass windows.

T he Val du Giennois traditionally marks the start of the Loire valley for those following the course of the river from its source. In the Middle Ages the first bridge and the first château on this royal route were at Gien. The Val is a border region, set between the Pays Fort and the Sologne on the left bank, and between the Forest of Orléans and Puisaye on the right.

GIEN (S4)

The town (right), which became known for its earthenware ▲ *134* thanks to an Englishman, is best viewed from the left bank of the Loire.

HISTORY OF THE TOWN. Gien stands beside the river, rising in tiers to the château and the Church of Ste-Jeanne-d'Arc. As the ancient Celtic town of Diomagus, it served as a trading place for the Gallic tribes of the Carnutes and the Eduens. In medieval times Gien became the capital of a county annexed to the French kingdom by Philippe-Auguste in 1199.

WORLD WAR TWO
In June 1940 the French armies retreated to the Loire, pursued by German forces. Both soldiers and civilians took refuge in Gien, and from 15 to 17 June enemy aircraft bombarded the town. The old quarters below the château were hit and the center of the town soon became an inferno. The bridge over the Loire was blown up, and the church destroyed. Only a storm saved the château, after its roofs caught fire.

▲ GIEN EARTHENWARE

Below: archery trophy (11) with hand-painted decoration, dated 1869.

The Gien factory was founded by the Englishman Thomas Hulm, known as Thomas Hall, in 1821. From 1834 onward it produced "opaque china" (fine earthenware or *faïence*) similar to Staffordshire pottery, popular in France in the 18th century. Initially the factory concentrated on making everyday crockery, but after 1855 it turned toward the production of decorative pieces. Later it was hugely successful at the Universal Exhibitions of the late 19th century, with numerous artists contributing to its output. The largest earthenware factory in France, it is still innovative today. Since 1970 the best examples of Gien earthenware have been exhibited in the factory's museum.

THE CRAFT ...

The earthenware pieces are made of terracotta (composed of clay, kaolin and quartz), coated and decorated with enamels based on lead and pewter.

... AND ITS HISTORY

This craft first appeared in the Near East in classical times, and later became established in Spain. By the late Middle Ages, Malaga and Valencia were exporting their pottery on Majorcan ships to Italy, where it was called "majolica". The French word for fine glazed earthenware, "faïence", comes from Faenza, the main Italian center of production, along with Florence, during the Renaissance.

The first French factories were founded by Italian potters in the 16th century, in Lyon and Nevers, during the reign of François I. In the 17th century the main centers of production were Rouen, Strasbourg, Marseille and Moustiers in France; Delft in the Netherlands; Hamburg and Hanau in Germany; and Bristol and Liverpool in England.

ALLIANCE OF ART AND TECHNIQUE

Gien's success was based on the use of modern mechanical processes and on the talent and number of its artists (some 200 of the 1,000 workers in 1878). This ensured both mass production and high-quality design.

11

1

2

3

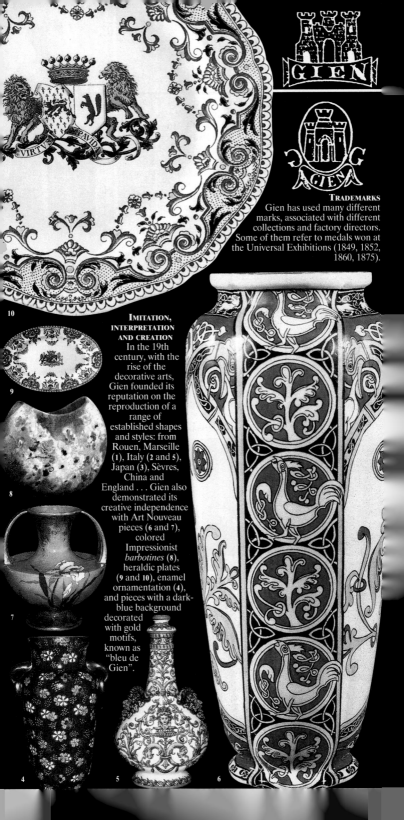

TRADEMARKS
Gien has used many different marks, associated with different collections and factory directors. Some of them refer to medals won at the Universal Exhibitions (1849, 1852, 1860, 1875).

IMITATION, INTERPRETATION AND CREATION
In the 19th century, with the rise of the decorative arts, Gien founded its reputation on the reproduction of a range of established shapes and styles: from Rouen, Marseille (**1**), Italy (**2** and **5**), Japan (**3**), Sèvres, China and England . . . Gien also demonstrated its creative independence with Art Nouveau pieces (**6** and **7**), colored Impressionist *barbotines* (**8**), heraldic plates (**9** and **10**), enamel ornamentation (**4**), and pieces with a dark-blue background decorated with gold motifs, known as "bleu de Gien".

9

8

7

4

5

6

ANNE DE BEAUJEU
Anne de France (1461–1522), the daughter of Louis XI and Charlotte de Savoie, was married at the age of twelve to Pierre II de Beaujeu, Duc de Bourbon, who gave her the county of Gien. Her father appointed her as regent during the minority of her brother Charles VIII: she ruled with a firm hand and succeeded in overcoming a feudal revolt led by the Duc d'Orléans, later Louis XII ● 34. Anne de Beaujeu undertook various projects in Gien from 1481 to 1522: she raised the town wall, restored the bridge, rebuilt the collegiate church, and made attractive modifications to the château.

Joan of Arc passed through Gien nine times in 1429, during her expedition to liberate Orléans ● 116. However, the town's golden age was the era of Anne de Beaujeu, daughter of Louis XI, regent of France and Countess of Gien (right). She altered and enlarged the château; and restored the old stone bridge across the Loire, with its thirteen arches. The young Louis XIV took refuge in Gien for a few days during the Fronde. In the 18th century the town's fortunes revived, boosted by the earthenware industry with which its name is still associated. The bombardments of June 1940 and July 1944 inflicted catastrophic damage on the town; it was rebuilt very tastefully after the war, prompting the writer Jules Romain to call it the "jewel of French reconstruction".

THE CHÂTEAU. The château dominates the town. Its distinctive black-and-red color scheme ● 67 is created by the glazed bricks used to form diamond, checkerboard and herringbone patterns on its walls; light stone frames around the doors and windows accentuate the effect. The only remnant of the feudal fortress is the façade overlooking the river, with its square tower (12th–13th century). The other buildings, set at right angles, were added by Anne de Beaujeu between 1484 and 1500.

MUSÉE DE LA CHASSE. The château was converted into an international museum of hunting in 1952. The rooms display hundreds of trophies, weapons, paintings and tapestries, all of them relating to hunting.

CHURCH OF STE-JEANNE-D'ARC. The present-day church on Place du Château replaced the 15th-century Collegiate Church of St-Étienne, which was rebuilt by Anne de Beaujeu. The original building was almost completely destroyed in 1940: all that remains is the large square bell tower, around which the new brick-built church was constructed.

THE BRIDGE. This lovely bridge was built in 1734 to replace the 13th-century bridge, which had suffered severe damage during the floods of May 28, 1733. The present-day bridge has only twelve arches; its predecessor had thirteen.

MUSÉE DE LA FAÏENCERIE. The museum on Place de la Victoire was created to mark the factory's 150th anniversary in 1970. It is housed in one of the factory buildings and displays a magnificent collection of fine earthenware from the early 19th century, as well as large display pieces produced for the Universal Exhibition held in Paris in 1900.

The main hall of the Musée de la Chasse has superb exposed beams; it is dedicated to the animal painters François Desportes (1661–1743) and Jean-Baptiste Oudry (1686–1755).

EXCURSION TO BRIARE ★ (T4)

Briare's exceptional location, at the meeting point of the Loire and several canals, makes it a town dominated by water – with no less than two ports, fourteen bridges and seven locks.

THE CANAL-BRIDGE. This bridge over the Loire carries a canal, not a road. It was built to link the Canal Henri IV (or Canal de Briare) with the canal running alongside the Loire. This masterpiece of engineering, which connects the Seine and Saône basins, is an impressive structure of iron and stone: some 725 yards long, including 660 yards spanning the Loire, it is the longest metal canal bridge in the world. Built between 1890 and 1894 by the Daydé et Pillé company, it was opened in 1896; Gustave Eiffel's company assisted with the foundations. In many ways the bridge's decoration (right) is reminiscent of the Pont Alexandre III in Paris.

CHURCH OF ST-ÉTIENNE. The church dates from 1895. The Briare enamels on the façade and the interior were intended to demonstrate the skills of the town's craftsmen.

HÔTEL DE VILLE. The town hall is housed in the 17th-century château of the "Seigneurs du Canal" (see right), in a lovely setting surrounded by water. Opposite the town hall is the Musée de la Mosaïque et des Émaux (Museum of Mosaic and Enamels), which traces 150 years of local industrial history.

THE "SEIGNEURS DU CANAL"
This was a group of seventeen (later thirty-three) citizens of Briare who in 1638 decided to complete the Canal de Briare, construction work having come to a halt after the assassination of Henri IV in 1610. The canal was opened in 1642, and was such a success that the untitled members of the group were given noble status. Each of the "Lords of the Canal" was granted use of the château (now the town hall) for a year.

"MODERN LIGHTING"
From the beginning the canal bridge was lit by electricity, using two turbines driven by the water falling into the canal beside the Loire, 26 feet below. The pilasters bear the coats of arms of the towns served by the canal.

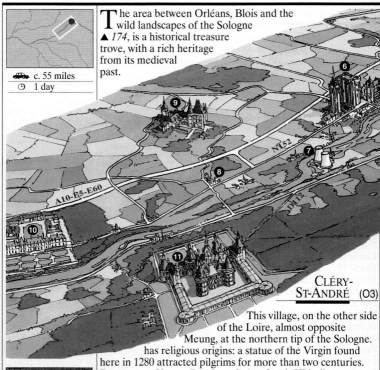

c. 55 miles
1 day

The area between Orléans, Blois and the wild landscapes of the Sologne ▲ *174*, is a historical treasure trove, with a rich heritage from its medieval past.

CLÉRY-ST-ANDRÉ (O3)

This village, on the other side of the Loire, almost opposite Meung, at the northern tip of the Sologne, has religious origins: a statue of the Virgin found here in 1280 attracted pilgrims for more than two centuries.

BASILICA OF NOTRE-DAME DE CLÉRY. Louis XI built a new church here where another one had been destroyed during the Hundred Years' War, after having dedicated himself to the Virgin of Cléry during the Battle of Dieppe against the English, on August 15, 1443. He made it a royal chapel, so that he could be buried here; destroyed by Protestants, his tomb was rebuilt on the order of Louis XIII. The great square tower to the north is all that remains of the 14th-century building.

JEAN DE MEUNG
Jean Chopinel, known as Jean de Meung (c. 1240–1305), from the Gâtinais region, wrote a sequel to the *Roman de la rose*, the courtly poem composed by another writer from the Loiret, Guillaume de Lorris (c. 1200–10 to c. 1240). The poem was a great success with the aristocracy throughout the Middle Ages. Jean de Meung wrote a second part of some 18,000 lines between 1275 and 1280, adding to the 4,000 lines of the original poem.

MEUNG-SUR-LOIRE (N3)

This little town dominated by its château has served a variety of purposes – it was a residence for the bishops of Orléans, the headquarters of the English army before they were expelled by Joan of Arc ▲ *116*, one of the places in which the poet François Villon (c. 1431–63) was imprisoned, and the holiday retreat of the famous Inspector Maigret, created by the Belgian writer Georges Simenon.

THE CHÂTEAU. The building has a medieval façade (built in the 12th century by Manassès de Garlande, Bishop of Orléans) and a residential wing dating from the 16th and 17th centuries.
CHURCH OF ST-LYPHARD. The ground plan of this 13th-century church takes the form of a trefoil design, unique in the region. Some Romanesque elements ● *58* survive, along with an 11th-century belfry.
THE TOWN. The Porte d'Amont, a fortified gateway that was altered in the 17th century, opens onto streets lined with stone and half-timbered houses ● *72* and old mills ● *78*.

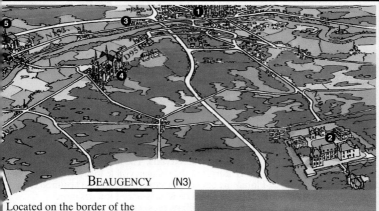

BEAUGENCY   (N3)

Located on the border of the
départements of Loir-et-Cher and Loiret,
Beaugency (right) is a typical Loire town.
The quayside lined with plane trees, the
old tile and slate roofs, its tall bell towers
and the massive keep combine to make a
very attractive picture, best viewed from
the left bank of the Loire.

THE BRIDGE. With its irregular arches, this
is the only medieval bridge that has
survived in the middle section of the Loire. Although modified
over the centuries, it still has several of its Gothic arches and a
large archway for boats to pass through. The Tour du Diable
on the quayside, downstream from the bridge, was once part of
the fortifications of the Abbey of Notre-Dame.

CHURCH OF NOTRE-DAME. Dating from the late 11th century,
this was once the church of an Augustinian abbey that attracted
pilgrims throughout the Middle Ages. The nave and choir
form a majestic example of Romanesque architecture ● 58.
Badly damaged by the Huguenots in 1567, the church was
reroofed in 1665 using wooden vaulting that slightly distorts its
intended proportions. The abbey buildings, between the
church and the Loire, date from the 17th century.

CHÂTEAU DUNOIS. The château (right) was modernized by the
Bastard of Orléans ▲ 115 – Jean, Comte de Dunois,
companion in arms of Joan of Arc
▲ 116 – in the second half of the 15th
century, and then by his descendants
in the 16th century. Today it houses a
museum featuring the history,
everyday life and folk art of the
Orléanais region.

HÔTEL DE VILLE. This elegant
building (left) from 1526 is said
to be the work of master mason
Pierre Biart, who built the Hôtel
Hector de Sanxerre ▲ 120 in
Orléans, which would explain
similarities between them.
Displayed in the council chamber
are some splendid 17th-century
tapestries.

BEAUGENCY
The courtyard of the
Château Dunois.

**NUCLEAR POWER
STATION OF
ST-LAURENT-DES-
EAUX ● 12**
St-Laurent-des-Eaux
was the second
nuclear power station
built by Électricité de
France, following the
one at Chinon (Indre-
et-Loire). It began
operations in 1969.
The site was chosen
for its proximity to
the Loire, since an
abundant supply of
water is needed for
electricity production.

139

▲ ORLÉANS TO BLOIS

LOVE AND POETRY AT TALCY
In the 16th century Cassandra, the

daughter of Bernardo Salviati and Françoise Doulcet, was the first love of the poet Pierre de Ronsard ▲ *258*, immortalized in his sonnets *Les Amours de Cassandre*. Later the château witnessed the long and unrequited love of the Huguenot poet Agrippa d'Aubigné ▲ *183* for Cassandra's Catholic niece Diana.

TALCY (M3)

This charming village halfway between Beaugency and Blois is principally known for its château, which stands between the Loire and the Loir, set slightly off the beaten track in the "petite Beauce".

THE CHÂTEAU OF THE SALVIATI. The lords of Talcy go back to the 13th century, but the château visible today was created by the Florentine banker Bernardo Salviati, who acquired it on November 8, 1517. The Renaissance façade is more ornamental than military, presenting a large square tower above an entrance porch, two hexagonal turrets crowned with machicolations, and a covered wall walk. The two wings of the building are set at right angles, overlooking a charming courtyard with a well that adds to the tranquil atmosphere of the place. The château has one of the most remarkable dovecotes ● *80* in the region, with 1,500 nesting holes.

THE CHÂTEAU DE MENARS (M4)

HISTORY OF THE BUILDING. The original château was built around 1646 by Guillaume Charron, a finance minister under Louis XIII; the main building and two pavilions survive today. From 1760 onward the château was altered and enlarged by the Marquise de Pompadour (below), mistress of Louis XV. She added two wings and the buildings around the main courtyard, designed by Ange-Jacques Gabriel (1698–1782), as well as redesigning the gardens and creating sumptuous interiors. Her brother, the Marquis de Marigny, director of the king's buildings, inherited the château in 1764 and appointed Germain Soufflot, the architect of the Panthéon, to add a low forebuilding in front of the central façade. The terraced gardens overlooking the Loire are graced with statues and elegant follies, such as the "Rotunda of Abundance" ● *71* and the Orangery.

❝Whatever the weather, from the windows of the château you can let your eyes and mind wander over the water and the great expanse of countryside, where there is always some kind of diversion.❞
André Félibien

Mme de Pompadour (right) acquired Menars in 1760, but was not to enjoy the château for long, as she died in 1764.

BLOIS

Blois

RUE GALLOIS

RUE DU

⑤

EAN·LAIGRET

③

④

⑤

①

⑧

QUAI DE L'ABBÉ DE LA S

1. Château
2. Church of St-Nicolas
3. Anne de Bretagne Pavilion
4. Church of St-Vincent
5. Hôtel d'Alluye
6. Cathedral of St-Louis
7. Garden of the Ancien Évêché
8. Place Louis XII
9. Vienne

②

Hôtel d'Alluye ▼

RUE PORTE CHARTRAINE

⑤

PAPIN

PONT JACQUES-GABRIEL

CHURCH OF ST-NICOLAS ▼

RUE DES MARCHANDS

Bust dating from the 1st century, found at Blois during excavations.

Figures from an anonymous 16th-century painting (right).

Gaston d'Orléans.

Louis XII's signature.

HISTORY OF THE TOWN (M4, 5)

ORIGINS. The site where Blois now stands was inhabited from the Protohistoric era onward. Archeologists have established that a town was founded between the Loire and the hillside in the 1st century AD. By the early 3rd century the town was well developed, with baths, sewers and a port. It was the capital of a Merovingian *pagus* (district), first mentioned in 584. However, it did not expand significantly until it became the seat of the Counts of Blois-Champagne around 950. From the 10th to the 13th century the town increased in size, as the counts became more powerful and early villages that had grown up around churches were joined together within a single city wall. The first bridge over the Loire was built at the end of the 11th century; and the castle was extended and embellished, symbolizing the town's prosperity and its political and economic status.

CAPITAL OF THE FRENCH KINGDOM. The town was sold to Louis d'Orléans in 1391. The accession of Charles d'Orléans in 1440 marked the start of a new phase of expansion and prosperity through the 15th century. This rise accelerated dramatically when Louis II d'Orléans became king of France, reigning as Louis XII. For a century Blois was a royal residence, which brought many of the king's officers and servants to the region. The town was scarred by the Wars of Religion and was sacked by Huguenots in 1568, leading to the exile of part of the Protestant population. The town retained its allegiance to the kings of France, who stayed here frequently up to the end of the century.

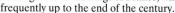

PROVINCIAL EXILE. Gaston d'Orléans, brother of Louis XIII, was exiled to Blois and kept a court in the town; though certainly more modest than the king's, this was large enough to maintain the illusion that Blois was a capital city. During this time a number of convents were founded outside the city walls, a Jesuit college was built, old abbeys were restored and a hospital founded – all reflecting both the prince's generosity and the strength of the Catholic Counter-Reformation. After the prince's death in 1660, Blois lost its dynamism: neither the creation of a bishopric (1698) nor the reconstruction of the bridge (1724) roused the town from its slumbers.

MODERN TIMES. Although the town's architectural heritage suffered considerable damage during the Revolution, at that time Blois became the seat of the préfecture of Loir-et-Cher. Most of the administrative buildings connected with its new civic function were built during the first half of the 19th century, even though this was a time of economic depression. The Préfecture, Palais de Justice, Halle aux Grains, Séminaire and Asile Départemental were all built between 1826 and 1850. The advent of the railway in 1846 brought further changes, and the town's fortunes began to improve significantly under the Second Empire. Mayor Eugène Riffault had roads built to connect the upper and lower town, and Blois' economy benefited greatly from the enterprise of two local industrialists: Auguste Poulain (1825–1918), who founded a chocolate factory, and Louis-Edme Rousset, who mechanized the production of shoes.

BLOIS TODAY. Badly damaged by bombing in June 1940, the center was rebuilt after the war and a new town grew up on the plateau. Today Blois is a medium-sized town, with a rich architectural heritage that has been fully restored. The river flowing through it weaves Blois into the surrounding landscape, making it one of the most attractive towns in the region.

THE BRIDGE ▲ *155*
The earlier bridge was washed away in February 1716, when the Loire thawed after a frost. Philippe d'Orléans commissioned the design for a new bridge from the famous architect Jacques Gabriel, the first Royal Engineer of Bridges and Roads.

WATCHMAKING AT BLOIS
Luxury industries like watchmaking grew up here in the 16th and 17th centuries, benefiting from the largesse of royal patrons. In 1640 Blois had forty-six watchmakers, who were renowned throughout Europe for the quality of their work.

The first Poulain chocolate factory ● *57*, between the station and the château, opened in 1864.

145

BY GOD HE'S SO TALL! SO TALL!
HE SEEMS EVEN LARGER DEAD THAN ALIVE.

HENRI III

(BEFORE THE CORPSE OF THE DUC DE GUISE)

Henri III, son of Henri II and Catherine de Médicis, ruled over a France which from 1574 onward was divided by the Wars of Religion. This troubled period was also marked by the slaughter of Protestants in the horrific St Bartholomew's Day massacre. It revealed the power of a man who would do anything to reassert the supremacy of Catholicism in France: the Duc de Guise, commander of the Holy League created in 1576 to oppose the king's concessions toward the Huguenots. The death of the king's brother, the Duc d'Alençon, on June 10, 1584, made Henri de Navarre the heir to the throne. Whereupon a new conflict broke out. The Duc de Guise refused to countenance the possibility of a non-Catholic king, and in the face of an increasingly impotent monarchy he swiftly took control of Paris and prepared to deal his final blow.

THE SECOND ÉTATS GÉNÉRAUX, OCTOBER 1588
Seeking to restore his authority, Henri III convened the second États Généraux (parliament) at Blois. Knowing the Duc de Guise was supported by many of the deputies, the king decided to have him killed, along with his brother the Cardinal de Lorraine.

ASSASSINATION OF THE DUC DE GUISE
Before the murder Henri III declared: "When passion is wounded, finally it turns to fury. Let them not put me to it." The commander of the League did not heed this ominous warning. On the morning of December 23, 1588 the Duc de Guise was summoned by the king and while crossing the royal chamber fell under the blows of Henri's notorious assassins, the "Quarante-Cinq". The king, who had been hiding behind a curtain, emerged to witness his rival's death.

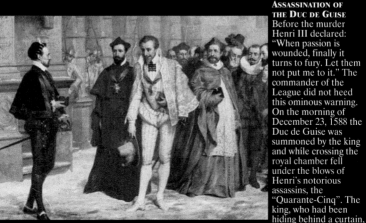

CONFRONTATION. The two men met at the Château de Blois a few days before these dramatic events, in a highly charged atmosphere.

HENRI III
The political situation became untenable for the king (on the left). He was driven from Paris by the League in May 1588 and took refuge at Blois.

THE DUC DE GUISE
Lieutenant General of the French kingdom and commander of the Holy League, the duke coveted the French throne and plotted against the king.

THE INSIGNIA OF POWER
Henri III's aim was to reassert the authority of the monarchy in France, where the Catholic League had seized the initiative (with the support of Spain). He joined forces with his cousin Henri de Navarre to lay siege to Paris (July 1589). On August 1, 1589 he was stabbed by the monk Jacques Clément, a member of the League. The following day, as he lay mortally wounded, the French king – who was the last of the Valois line – appointed as his successor Henri de Navarre, head of the House of Bourbon and a direct descendant of Saint Louis. A 16th/17th-century tapestry (left) commemorates the event: the dying king hands over the royal insignia to his successor, who kneels by the bedside. Henri de Navarre became Henri IV of France.

François I staircase.

AUDACIOUS ESCAPE
Marie de Médicis, who had been exiled to Blois, escaped from the castle by sliding down a rope during the night of February 21–2, 1619. Rubens re-created the episode in a painting (right).

Seal of Louis II.

Chapel of St-Calais, in the château.

HISTORY OF THE CHÂTEAU ● 68, 75, 86

Few buildings enjoy such a rich historical and architectural heritage as the Château de Blois. The first reference to a *castrum* (fort) on this site dates from the 6th century.

THE CASTLE OF THE COUNTS OF BLOIS. In the 9th century the Counts of Blois built a fortress here, which was constantly modified over the course of subsequent centuries. Today the oldest surviving sections of the château date from the early 13th century. The Salle des États, the Tour du Foix and several sections of ramparts give some idea of the scale of this early building.

ROYAL RESIDENTS. When Louis II d'Orléans became king of France in 1498, ruling as Louis XII, he established the political capital of the kingdom at Blois, the town where he was born. Taking up residence here, he embarked on a complete reconstruction of the castle, as well as creating magnificent gardens to the northeast. Work was completed with the consecration of the chapel in 1508 ● *60*.

François I, who succeeded Louis II, began to rebuild the north wing in 1515. Four phases of building work followed, but construction came to a halt with the death of Claude de France in 1524. After that date François I spent little time at Blois. Henri III convened the États Généraux here in 1576 and 1588. It was during the second session that he had the Duc de Guise assassinated ▲ *146*. After the royal court departed, at the end of the 16th century, the château served as a place of exile for Marie de Médicis and then for Gaston d'Orléans. In 1635 the latter embarked on a reconstruction scheme devised by the famous

architect François Mansart, but this was abandoned three years later. After the death of Gaston d'Orléans (1660) the château fell into oblivion.

CHANGING FORTUNES. The château was scheduled for demolition in 1788; but was saved only by being assigned for military use. Regiments of cavalry and engineers occupied the château for eighty years, causing substantial damage to the buildings. In 1842, as a result

> "SPARE THE CHÂTEAU,
> THOUGH DARK AND FEARSOME,
> THOUGH IT IS STAINED WITH BLOOD"
>
> VICTOR HUGO

of the efforts of the Romantic writers, the château was classified as a historical monument. As with many French monuments, Félix Duban was entrusted with its restoration; he aimed to re-create the way it looked at the end of the 15th century. Today the château houses a number of museums.

Cul-de-lampe on the façade of the Louis XII wing.

LOUIS XII WING ● 67

FROM THE PLACE DU CHÂTEAU. The large gable on the right is that of the Salle des États: it was rebuilt in 1860, following the demolition of the old roof of the château, which provided access to the entrance courtyard. The main portal is surmounted by an equestrian statue of Louis XII made by Seurre in 1858, based on an earlier one destroyed in 1792. The Gothic decoration of the niche contrasts with the setting of the porcupine, the king's emblem, which bears the mark of Renaissance influence. To the left of the portal, two culs-de-lampe framing the first window on the ground floor depict a courtly scene.

THE COURTYARD FAÇADE. On the courtyard side is a gallery supported by square pillars decorated with candelabras. This motif, of Northern Italian inspiration, is typical of the early Renaissance and is the earliest example of its kind in France. By contrast the ornamentation of the windows, and the combination of polychrome brick and stone, is typical of the 15th-century Franco-Flemish tradition.

CHAPEL OF ST-CALAIS. The chapel built by Louis XII has suffered considerable damage over the centuries. The nave was demolished in the days of Gaston d'Orléans. What remains of the choir was divided into three stories during the military occupation. The interior decoration, restored by Félix Duban in the 19th century, was ruined by bombing during World War Two. Today the chapel has a beautiful collection of stained-glass windows (right) created in the workshop of master glassmaker Max Ingrand and dedicated in 1957. The windows depict major events in the château's history, including Joan of Arc's visit in 1429.

TOUR DU FOIX. The tower's terrace offers a lovely view over the town, the Church of St-Nicholas and the Loire valley. The tower was originally part of the medieval fortress, Gaston d'Orléans had an astronomical observatory installed here. The fountain in the middle of the terrace has three marble panels and a marble basin that came from the old gardens of the château.

THE ORIGINAL EQUESTRIAN STATUE OF LOUIS XII
The original statue showed the king wearing a hat, instead of the crown he bears in the 19th-century replica. Below it was a Latin inscription by Faust Andrelini, which read: "Where Louis was born by the grace of the gods, he holds the royal scepter with a noble hand. Happy the day which shone announcing such a king! Gaul was not worthy of a higher prince."

▲ BLOIS
THE CHÂTEAU

BLOIS EARTHENWARE
Ulysse Besnard (1826–99) established the reputation of this typical Blois craft

when he founded the town's first earthenware factory in 1862. The tradition lasted until 1953, when the last factory was closed.

THE FAÇADE DES LOGES
"It has many small galleries, small windows, small balconies and small ornaments, combined without order or regularity: the whole effect is grand, and pleasing." This is how Jean de La Fontaine described the façade, which has been compared with those of Italian palaces.

FRANÇOIS I WING ● 68

This wing of the château was constructed scarcely fifteen years after the Louis XII Wing.

THE STAIRCASE. "The famous spiral staircase . . . is a kind of carved cylinder, with large openings which make it effectively an open-air staircase." This is how it was described by Henry James in the 19th century. In addition, it is worth mentioning the decorative detail, which includes buttresses adorned with fine carvings, with motifs such as classical profiles, trophies and candelabras.

THE APARTMENTS. The great staircase leads to the royal apartments on the second story. Their current appearance is the product of Félix Duban's restoration work. In his attempt to re-create the original setting, Duban drew on the few historical remains (pieces of door frames, fragments of painted decorations) and in particular on manuscript sources. The result is not so much an authentic reproduction of the 16th-century interior as a reflection of 19th-century preoccupations and the Romantic interest in the Renaissance. The most striking features are the painted decorations, probably inspired by late-15th-century manuscripts, and tiling reminiscent of Italian majolica. The carvings on the fireplaces and above doorways reveal an expert knowledge of Renaissance ornamentation. We do not know with certainty what each room was used for in the 16th century. We know only that the rooms overlooking the courtyard had a more public function than those opening onto the Façade des Loges, where the royal residents lived. In the late 16th century the second story was occupied by Catherine de Médicis, while Henri III lived on the third story. Each apartment included an antechamber, a wardrobe, a bedroom, an oratory and a *cabinet* (study). The *cabinet* was where the king or queen worked, but it was also used for exhibiting precious objects, jewelry, medals and exotic curiosities. The famous secret cupboards in Catherine de Médicis' study were in fact used for this purpose. It was many years later, in the 19th century, that Alexandre Dumas *père*, in his novel *La Reine Margot* (1845), depicted them as poison cupboards, giving rise to a remarkably persistent legend.

"BLOIS OFFERS A STRIKING
SYNTHESIS OF THREE PERIODS
OF FRENCH ARCHITECTURE."

HENRI GUERLIN

THE GASTON D'ORLÉANS WING ● 71

This part of the château, at the far end of the courtyard, was designed by Mansart. This makes it one of the earliest classical châteaux in France. Gustave Flaubert's verdict was hasty and unjust when he called it "a building of the most idiotic kind . . . [designed] in a detestable manner with its half-baked classicism . . . in execrable taste." In fact this is a beautifully proportioned and elegantly designed work of architecture. The architect employed a number of devices to accentuate the central bay and the main entrance of the château: the forebuilding is slightly higher than the façades, and curved colonnades draw the viewer's gaze to the center; triangular and rounded pediments are used to give emphasis to the portico. Inside, the staircase is in the Baroque style. The crowning dome is seen through a semi-cupola halfway up, which accentuates the perspective and increases the majestic effect of the whole. The skillful use of light, a wealth of decorative carvings by the best artists of the time (though these were not completed), and the high quality of the masonry make this one of the masterpieces of French Baroque art.

THE SALLE DES ÉTATS

The tour of the château concludes in a room that survives from the castle of the Counts of Blois. It was constructed at the same time as Chartres Cathedral. The room, one of the oldest feudal halls in France, is divided into two naves by a row of elegant columns.

"One of the fireplaces (in the François I Wing) has as its central motif two medallions containing a salamander and an ermine, each borne aloft by four cherubs. Between the medallions are beautifully crafted candelabras; above them is a frieze composed of scallops alternating with cherubs bearing garlands.**"**
Dr Frédéric Lesueur

HISTORICAL NAME
The Salle des États owes its name to the two sessions of the États Généraux ▲ *148* held here during the reign of Henri III.

The porcupine,
royal emblem
of Louis XII.

MUSÉE DES BEAUX-ARTS

Housed in the château from the outset, Blois' museum of fine arts has always been somewhat overshadowed by the celebrity of its setting. The restoration of the château in 1845 gave new impetus to the artistic life of the town, prompting the establishment and development of the museum.

MANY ACQUISITIONS. Like so many of the provincial museums that came into being in the mid 19th century, the museum was created by a combination of municipal efforts and donations from local citizens. The French state and the Louvre have also given pictures to the museum, among them *François I Armed by Bayard* (Louis Ducis, 1817) and *The Meeting of Henri III and the Duc de Guise* (Charles Comte, 1855). The museum reflects the importance in the town's history of the Valois family and the assassination of the Duc de Guise ▲ 146. Paintings on both these subjects have been collected here since the 19th century.

THE WORKS. The sculptors Daniel Dupuis, Alfred Jean-Baptiste Halou and Henri Varenne are well represented in the museum's collection of statues, part of which is on display. The museum also has some 16th-century Italian paintings, featuring works by the school of Leonardo including a polyptych by Marco d'Oggiono (detail below) and *Colombine*, attributed to Francesco Melzi. French painting of the 16th century is represented by artists such as Antoine Caron, Jean Cousin and Corneille de Lyon. Notable among the extensive 17th-century collections are *Eliazer and Rebecca* by Sébastien

MADELEINE OF SCOTLAND
This portrait of François I's daughter, painted by Corneille de Lyon, has a pale green background, typical of this Dutch artist.

Virgin and Child, detail from a polyptych by Marco d'Oggiono.

Bourdon, *The Visitation* by Michel Corneille and, from schools outside France, *The Death of Adonis* by Maarten De Vos, *Flemish Market* by Anton Polcke and *Hercules and Omphale*, attributed to Antonio Zanchi. From the 18th century there is an outstanding collection of medallions by the sculptor Nini ▲ 177 and *Psyche Receiving the Divine Honors* by François Boucher, along with splendid furniture from the Korewo collection. The 19th-century collections include paintings by Luminais, Bezard, Cormon, Ingres, Compte-Calix and Chassériau. In addition to watches and ceramics from Blois, the museum has large collections of tapestries and ironwork. The very modern arrangement of Louis XII's apartments can still be clearly appreciated by visitors; six rooms (restored by Duban) are served by one of the earliest galleries in France (pre-1501). The recently opened Lapidary Rooms display a splendid collection of sculptures from the 15th and 16th centuries that were removed from the château during the 19th century.

THE ANNE DE BRETAGNE PAVILION
This pavilion, built on a terrace of the gardens in the reign of Louis XII,
is one of the oldest garden buildings known in France. To its right is the
orangery, a reminder that citrus trees were introduced into the Loire
valley at the end of the 15th century, after the Italian campaigns.

AROUND THE CHÂTEAU

In medieval times the Place du Château was the farmyard of the fortress. Later it was bordered by the Collegiate Church of St-Sauveur, where Joan of Arc ▲ *116* had her standard blessed. Some private houses from the 16th century can still be seen. The large house at the eastern end of the square was built in the mid 19th century; from 1997 it will house the Maison de la Magie, featuring a theater for events and performances as well as an exhibition of objects from the collection that belonged to Blois magician Robert-Houdin (see right), including automata and other intriguing devices.

CHURCH OF ST-NICHOLAS ★. The church of the former Benedictine abbey, founded in 924, was built in two phases. The choir, the transept and the first bay of the nave were built in Early Gothic style between 1138 and 1186, whereas the nave and western façade date from the early 13th century and were modeled on Chartres Cathedral. Inside, visitors can trace the development of Gothic style from the chapels of the ambulatory (still clearly influenced by Romanesque) to the Chapelle de la Vierge (mid 14th century), built in the High Gothic style. The transept crossing is surmounted by a dome on pendentives, in a striking design. The abbey buildings nearest to the Loire are still standing; most of them date from the 17th or 18th century.

TOWARD THE GARDENS. From Rue des Fossés-du-Château there is a good view of the impressive external façade of the Gaston d'Orléans Wing. A path leads down the embankment of the château to the Jardin du Roi, from where you can admire the Façade des Loges ▲ *150*. In 1992 a space was cleared below the Jardin du Roi for a reconstruction of the gardens that Louis XII had laid out here in the early 16th century.

ROBERT-HOUDIN, MAGICIAN OF BLOIS (1805–71)
This suave illusionist was born Jean-Eugène Robert in Rue Porte-Chartraine, once a main street of the city. He was famous for his mechanical inventions and spectacular tricks using electricity. He performed before fashionable Parisian society, at the Théâtre du Palais-Royal, and toured throughout Europe. In 1849 he moved to St-Gervais, near Blois. Escapologist Harry Houdini adopted his name.

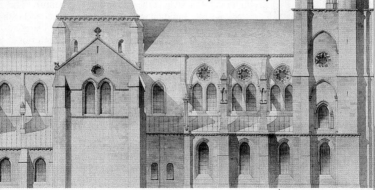

THE UPPER TOWN

This section of the town, set on the hillside, features many charming steep alleyways and streets with steps.

🔲 PETITS DEGRÉS DU CHÂTEAU

RUE ST-HONORÉ. The Hôtel d'Alluye ★ at no. 8 (at the top, on the left-hand side) was built for Florimond Robertet, Baron d'Alluye, a powerful man, open to new ideas, who served as treasurer, notary and secretary under three kings: Charles VIII, Louis XII and François I. He had the house built around 1505, and received a Florentine embassy here in 1508. The street façade, which was heavily restored at the end of the 19th century, is similar to the Louis XII façade of the château. The courtyard (which can be visited on weekdays) is better preserved and displays features that were completely new in France at the time: galleries built one above another, uncompromisingly Italianate décor, and terracotta medallions with classical profiles. At the top of the street the Escalier Denis Papin (above) commemorates the inventor of steam power, who was born at Blois in the 17th century. From here there is a wide view over the roofs of the lower town, the château and the ruins of the medieval castle. Rue du Palais, which has lovely 18th-century portals at nos. 3 and 5, leads to Place St-Louis. On this square (at no. 3) is the Maison des Acrobates (late 15th century), decorated with figures dressed in costume of Louis XI's era, whose liveliness and state of preservation is remarkable.

BLOIS "GLORIOUS IN FOUNTAINS AND RICH IN AQUEDUCTS"
Eight fountains supplied Blois with water from the 16th century onward. However, by the 18th century the town's needs had outstripped their capacity, and in 1749 a vast cistern, known as Le Gouffre ("the abyss"), was dug out under Place Louis XII to supply the lower town, including the Louis XII fountain (below). The first pumping of water from the Loire began in 1852.

CATHEDRAL OF ST-LOUIS. This complex building is a former collegiate church, founded in the 10th century under the name of St-Solenne. Construction of the façade and the two stories above the bell tower (the base dates from the 12th century) began in 1544: they represent one of the first attempts at classical religious architecture in France.

The nave was destroyed by a hurricane in 1678 and was rebuilt in Gothic style at the end of the 17th century. The building was completed around 1860 with the neo-Gothic Chapelle de la Vierge. The beautifully proportioned interior houses remains of the early 10th-century church, in the crypt under the choir. The organ case was donated by Louis XIV in 1704, the year in which the church became a cathedral.

THE ANCIEN ÉVÊCHÉ. The town hall of Blois was formerly the episcopal palace, built in 1700, following plans by Jacques Gabriel (the comptroller of the king's buildings at Chambord), for Mgr de Bertier, the first bishop of Blois.

The terraced gardens ★ (opposite, center) overlook the Loire valley and offer a lovely view of the town and the humpback bridge, which was also built by Gabriel.

The Pente du Côteau

Between the cathedral and the Loire is a picturesque quarter laid out in tiers over the hillside. In the 16th century the wealthy citizens and court dignitaries of Blois lived here; later it remained largely unaffected by changes to the town center. It was renovated between 1970 and 1980, and now gives a good idea of how the town looked in the 16th century.
Place Louis XII ★. On Saturday mornings a colorful market is held in this square, which is dominated by the château walls. Huge steps lead from the square to the Place du Château. The 15th-century Louis XII Fountain (opposite, bottom left), designed in the Flamboyant style, once stood against a wall. In 1451 Antoine Astesan described it as "a beautiful stone fountain with bright silvery water that supplies the whole town". Below this, near to the covered market, is the former Jacobite convent founded by Jean de Chatillon, Count of Blois, in the 13th century. It now houses the Musée d'Histoire Naturelle (containing local and exotic fauna) and the Musée Diocésain d'Art Religieux (religious objects, statues and liturgical ornaments).

Vienne

Vienne, on the left bank of the Loire, is a very old suburb, inhabited since the Roman era.
Church of St-Saturnin. An ancient pilgrimage in honor of Notre-Dame des Aydes, patron saint of Blois, ends at this church. Evidence of this can be seen in the large number of *ex votos* in the northern side aisle. The church was partially rebuilt in the 15th century thanks to Anne de Bretagne; however, the project was left incomplete when she died, in 1514. The church was burned down by Protestants in 1568 and restored in the 17th century; a section of the nave was rebuilt, and a roof added to the bell tower.
Cloisters of St-Saturnin ★. This is in fact a monumental cemetery, standing opposite the church. It was built in 1516 and is one of the few to survive in France; today it houses a Lapidary Museum.

PONT JACQUES-GABRIEL
Blois had a bridge as early as the 11th century. In 1508 Louis XII gave permission to build on the bridge "for the good, profit and use, decoration and ornamentation of our town and of the said bridge". The present bridge, designed by the architect Jacques Gabriel, was opened in 1724. The central arch is surmounted by a pyramid; the cartouche bearing the king's arms at the base was carved by Guillaume Coustou, who sculpted the famous Marly horses on Place de la Concorde in Paris. Damaged during the two world wars, the bridge has been faithfully restored.

CLOISTERS OF ST-SATURNIN
The stone pillars of the south gallery have capitals depicting funerary themes, such as skulls and bones.

🚗 c. 30 miles
⏱ 1½ days

BLACK WOODPECKER
This bird, the largest
member of the
woodpecker family,
has lived in the
forests around
Chambord and
throughout the
Sologne for the last
thirty years ▲ *174*.

THE CHAMBORD ESTATE

The Château de Chambord stands at the
heart of dense woodland and is perfectly
suited to its natural setting, the Forest
of Boulogne. Today the estate
(covering 13,500 acres) is the
largest enclosed forest park
in Europe; the wall that
surrounds it is some 20
miles long.

THE NATURE RESERVE.
The park has
been a national
nature reserve
since 1947. Only
part of the park
(around 1,700 acres)
is open to the public;
the rest is reserved for
the study of wildlife. Around
seven hundred red deer and a thousand
wild boar (the numbers fluctuate depending on
the season), roe deer, mouflon, foxes and other species
live here in complete freedom. The bird life is also
rich and varied, with one hundred nesting species
– including three species of eagle and six species
of woodpecker. The forest has been maintained
and developed (in 1820 it covered only half the
estate) with a view to protecting these animals.
Hunting ● *52* is forbidden, although sixteen
official hunts are held annually as a means of
population control; animals are also captured alive in
order to repopulate other territories.

PARC DE CHAMBORD

    PUBLIC ACCESS TO THE ESTATE. The estate has six
    entrance gates, each of which is guarded by a forester's
    cottage crowned by a stag's head (the symbol of
    Chambord). At each entrance a wide grille over a
    ditch across the road (similar to a cattle grid) deters
    the larger animals from leaving the reserve. Visitors
    can watch the wild animals from observatories in
    the area open to the public. The deers' rutting
    season, from mid September to mid October, is
    an especially interesting time. There are
    footpaths and bridleways through the estate;
    and the foresters organize guided tours with
    commentaries, ranging from a few hours to a
    whole day. Animal photographers can obtain
    permission for access to some of the restricted
areas between April 1 and July 31.

SAINT-DYÉ, PORT OF CHAMBORD   (D4)

    François I's decision to built a château at
    Chambord in the early 16th century had
    a dramatic effect on the fortunes of
    St-Dyé. The initial intention was to
    divert a branch of the Loire; however,
    this project was soon abandoned and

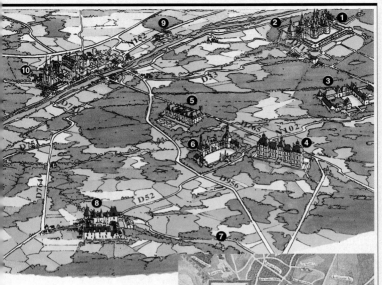

the architects chose the nearest point on the river for unloading supplies, which was the port of Dyé. Whole bargeloads of lead, Trélazé slate ▲ *312*, and stone from Apremont-sur-l'Allier or even from Bourré in the Cher valley (which had to come via Tours) were unloaded here. From this time St-Dyé's fortunes and activities were closely bound with those of the château. The town flourished as a result: new houses were built and the church was renovated. From the 17th century onward the wine business was another source of income: vineyards were set up around the village, and barrels of wine were sent along the river by the hundred to supply the cafés and restaurants of Paris. Wood was another important cargo. This was the heyday of river transport on the Loire ● *50*, and a new port was built to meet the demand. The present-day port dates from the second half of the 18th century, and the quayside was extended upriver in 1806. The whole area was extensively renovated in 1984, enhancing the effect of the spacious quaysides lined with plane trees, running alongside the river for half a mile. The town is a delightful place for a stroll: in its streets, which run down to the port or across the hillside, you will come upon old inns and Renaissance buildings such as La Salamandre, the Maison du Galet (the love nest of Maréchal de Saxe ▲ *165*) and the Maison de la Prée. Remains of the old ramparts can be seen at various points around the town.

ON THE RIVER BANKS
Local tradition has it that Joan of Arc stopped in the town on April 26, 1429, on her way to Orléans ● *116*. After passing along the right bank of the Loire, she went up to the church to pray at the altar of the Virgin, then continued on her journey, heading toward St-Laurent-des-Eaux.

157

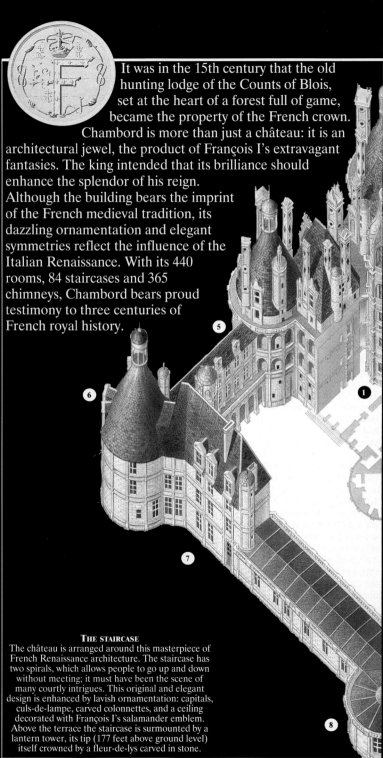

It was in the 15th century that the old
hunting lodge of the Counts of Blois,
set at the heart of a forest full of game,
became the property of the French crown.
Chambord is more than just a château: it is an
architectural jewel, the product of François I's extravagant
fantasies. The king intended that its brilliance should
enhance the splendor of his reign.
Although the building bears the imprint
of the French medieval tradition, its
dazzling ornamentation and elegant
symmetries reflect the influence of the
Italian Renaissance. With its 440
rooms, 84 staircases and 365
chimneys, Chambord bears proud
testimony to three centuries of
French royal history.

THE STAIRCASE
The château is arranged around this masterpiece of
French Renaissance architecture. The staircase has
two spirals, which allows people to go up and down
without meeting; it must have been the scene of
many courtly intrigues. This original and elegant
design is enhanced by lavish ornamentation: capitals,
culs-de-lampe, carved colonnettes, and a ceiling
decorated with François I's salamander emblem.
Above the terrace the staircase is surmounted by a
lantern tower, its tip (177 feet above ground level)
itself crowned by a fleur-de-lys carved in stone.

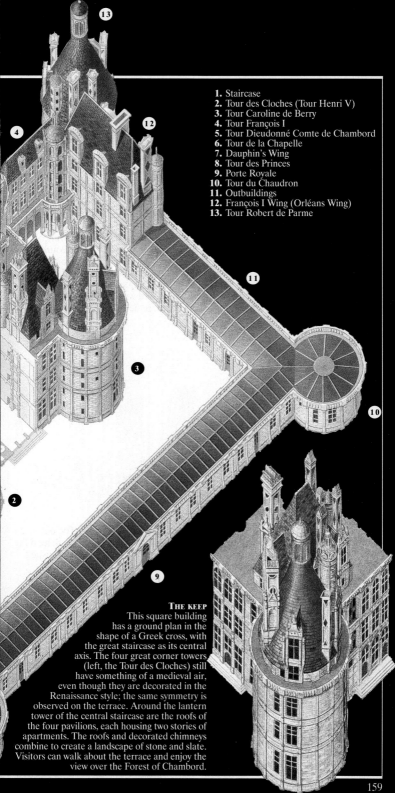

1. Staircase
2. Tour des Cloches (Tour Henri V)
3. Tour Caroline de Berry
4. Tour François I
5. Tour Dieudonné Comte de Chambord
6. Tour de la Chapelle
7. Dauphin's Wing
8. Tour des Princes
9. Porte Royale
10. Tour du Chaudron
11. Outbuildings
12. François I Wing (Orléans Wing)
13. Tour Robert de Parme

THE KEEP
This square building
has a ground plan in the
shape of a Greek cross, with
the great staircase as its central
axis. The four great corner towers
(left, the Tour des Cloches) still
have something of a medieval air,
even though they are decorated in the
Renaissance style; the same symmetry is
observed on the terrace. Around the lantern
tower of the central staircase are the roofs of
the four pavilions, each housing two stories of
apartments. The roofs and decorated chimneys
combine to create a landscape of stone and slate.
Visitors can walk about the terrace and enjoy the
view over the Forest of Chambord.

159

HISTORY OF THE CHÂTEAU ● *40, 68*, (P4)

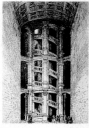

INTERPRETING THE TEXTS. When French historians began to study Chambord in the mid 19th century, they soon realized how much had been lost: only a small number of documents relating to the building of the château survived. They did establish, however, that François I's decision to build "a beautiful and sumptuous palace at Chambort [*sic*], according to edict and estimation" dated from September 6, 1519. They also discovered the names of some of the key figures: François de Pontbriant, superintendent of the works, Jacques Sourdeau, master mason, Clotet, the treasurer, all of them from the Loire Valley. Pontbriant was old and soon resigned his post; Sourdeau died in 1552. The war against Charles V was resumed, and work on Chambord was suspended from 1524 to 1526; in 1525 the French were defeated at the Battle of

Pavia, and the king was held captive in Madrid. The old 12th-century castle at Chambord had been built to defend the ford at the bend of the river, and this had to be demolished before work could begin. The 17th-century historians Jean Bernier and André Félibien des Avaux state construction of the château began in 1526, but it is probable that work on the building itself had scarcely begun at this

Elevation of the lantern tower of the great staircase.

"I know nothing comparable with this fantasy in stone . . . an incredible profusion of little domes, bell towers and chimneys of all shapes, some covered in mosaics of colored stone."

Prince
Pükler-Muskau,
Journal de Voyage

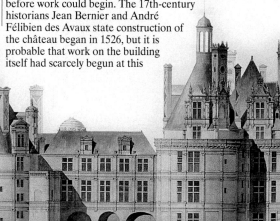

THE VOICE OF THE ROMANTICS
Chateaubriand paid homage to Chambord
as it stood empty and neglected. He saw
in it only "Clorinda resting on the
ruins" – the ruins of the monarchy.

time. The king had envisaged a site by the edge of the river,
which would be flooded when the water level was high.

FRANÇOIS I – ARCHITECT OF HIS OWN PALACE? In 1526, on his
return from captivity, François I stayed at Chambord. We
know that he was an impatient man: his workers found this to
their cost, except for Antoine de Troyes,
appointed comptroller after the death of
Jacques Sourdeau (Sourdeau himself was
succeeded as master mason by Pierre
Trinqueau, who held the post until his death in
1538). Charles de Chauvigny was appointed
superintendent by the king and held the post
until the 1540's. All the 19th-century
historians, including Viollet-le-Duc, viewed
Chambord as a thoroughly French work of
architecture: they saw it as the last of the great
plain-fortresses, a younger brother of
Vincennes built by the descendants of the
Loire Valley's great master masons, of whom
they were proud. François I had whiled away
the tedium of his long captivity in Madrid by
reading, and had been captivated by a Spanish
chivalric novel, *Amadis de Gaule* (a 14th-century
work adapted by Garcia Rodriguez de Montalvo).
When he returned to France, the king had the novel
translated. The hero of the epic lived in the
Château de l'Île Ferme, set in grounds
inhabited by a thousand strange creatures, with
a river winding its way through the greenery:
this must have seemed a fairy-tale version of
Chambord. The name of Chambord's
architect, the designer of this grand plan
combining French and Italian architectural
styles, is not mentioned in any of the
surviving documents. However, the
role of François I is alluded to repeatedly.
He decided to have a wall built around the château's grounds
and personally staked out its course during the winter of
1523–4; at that time the land on the right bank of the Cosson
had not yet been acquired. The site continued to expand: in
January 1530 he again took part in staking
it out, and then again, for the last time, in
December 1539. François also followed
up another project in person: after his
return from captivity he appointed
an engineer, Pietro Caccia, at
Chambord. In July 1529 he

FRANÇOIS I. The
king engraved on a
bedchamber window:
"Woman's often
fickle, man's a fool to
trust her."

The hundreds of
chimneys rising from
the summit of the
château are crowned
and decorated with
royal motifs,
surmounted by
statues and adorned
with slate
lozenges. Their
silhouettes
stand out
against the
backdrop of
roofs and
domes.

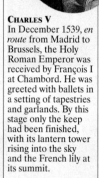

CHARLES V
In December 1539, *en route* from Madrid to Brussels, the Holy Roman Emperor was received by François I at Chambord. He was greeted with ballets in a setting of tapestries and garlands. By this stage only the keep had been finished, with its lantern tower rising into the sky and the French lily at its summit.

The Forest of Chambord was perfect for the traditional sport of kings: hunting.

summoned Caccia to question him regarding "the means necessary to divert part of the Loire river to pass through Chambord". However, the plans were altered repeatedly over the years: the château as it stands today bears the marks of these changes. The idea of diverting the course of the Loire was never carried out; attempts to alter the course of even the smaller Cosson river only succeeded in enlarging the marshes, a problem that was not resolved until the mid 18th century. Perhaps the real architect of Chambord was François himself.

SILENT GENIUS. Acceding to François I's insistent requests, the aging Leonardo da Vinci arrived at Amboise during the winter of 1516–17; the great painter, engineer and architect lived at Clos-Lucé (then called Cloux), which had been renovated for him by the king. François had at first thought of building a palace at Romorantin, where he spent his childhood; sketches for the project survive in Leonardo's notebooks. This idea was later abandoned in favor of the very different plan for Chambord: a hunting château on a centralized ground plan, consisting of four sections of apartments joined by the four corner towers, with intersecting rooms in the shape of a cross at the center of the building. The king had "several plans drawn up before undertaking anything". A wooden model of Chambord, already badly eroded, was discovered in the 17th century: this was a preliminary model of Leonardo's design,

apparently made by Dominico da Cortona. Cortona, who had come to Amboise with Charles VIII, produced a whole series of architectural models for François I at the beginning of his reign, including this one of Chambord. Leonardo's fragile state of health most probably did not allow him to visit the site; he died in May 1519, and it was not until September of the same year that the building supervisors were appointed.

The king made several visits to Amboise during this time – and may well have had meetings with Cortona and Melzi, Leonardo's companion, in an attempt to discover any further information that might have been left by Leonardo. However, that is purely conjecture.

GASTON D'ORLÉANS. The brother of Louis XIII was exiled to Blois (1634–44) and subsequently, from 1652 until his death in 1660, was wholly isolated from court affairs. He shared François I's passions for architecture and hunting ● 52, and was strongly drawn to Chambord. By this time the waters of the Cosson had created a marsh in front of the château, which required urgent attention: three flying buttresses on the lantern tower had collapsed, requiring immediate repair; the terraces of the keep were leaking; and the great casement windows lighting the cross-shaped rooms were falling into ruin, as were the arches under the terraces, and the roofs. These repairs were covered by an estimate of 1641–2; the architectural ornaments on the arches were also to be restored to their original state. However, the work came to a halt due to lack of funds; it was eventually completed by Louis XIV.

LOUIS XIV AT CHAMBORD. Louis XIV was also captivated by Chambord, visiting a number of times to enjoy the pleasures of hunting and court life in a rural setting. Molière and Lully presented two comédies-ballets here: *Monsieur de Pourceaugnac* (1669) and *Le Bourgeois gentilhomme* (1670). In 1668 Louis XIV decided the royal apartments of François I were not grand enough. In a scheme that made nonsense of

Sketch of the lantern tower (centre) by Leonardo da Vinci.

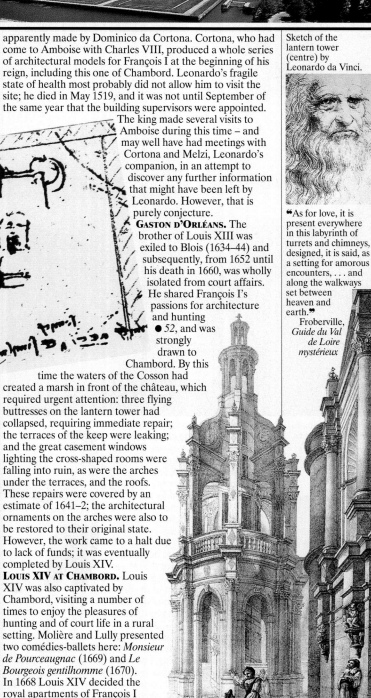

"As for love, it is present everywhere in this labyrinth of turrets and chimneys, designed, it is said, as a setting for amorous encounters, . . . and along the walkways set between heaven and earth."

Froberville,
Guide du Val de Loire mystérieux

Louis XIV organized huge hunting parties at Chambord ● 52.

"LE BOURGEOIS GENTILHOMME"
Molière staged the first performance at Chambord in 1670, in the presence of Louis XIV.

the original design, he turned the northern section of the cross-shaped room on the second story into a vestibule; the northeastern apartments were altered, and the tower room adjoining the king's room was reserved for the queen. These apartments were later restored by the architect Jules Hardouin-Mansart. Inelegant stable buildings were put up to the west of the château in 1681 (they were demolished in 1755), and more parts of the interior restored; later the Cosson was canalized. Major excavations in front of the northern façade created large gardens alongside the canalized river, which was diverted to supply moats at the foot of the castle's northern and eastern façades. A royal gateway (the Porte Royale) was built into the southern wing, opening onto a great esplanade flanked by huge outbuildings and stables. The building work finally ceased in 1685, and Louis did not return to Chambord. However, the château was saved from ruin thanks to Colbert's reorganization of the Service des Bâtiments du Roi, which was responsible for maintaining royal buildings.

MARÉCHAL DE SAXE (1696–1750)
Maurice de Saxe was appointed Maréchal de
France in 1744 and distinguished himself by
defeating the English in the Battle of
Fontenoy. Louis XV gave him Chambord as
a reward. He moved into the château in
1748, and died there two years later.

THE 18TH AND 19TH CENTURIES. Residents at Chambord
during the 18th century included Stanislas Leszcynski, the
deposed king of Poland and father-in-law of Louis XV, who
was not happy here, and then Maréchal Maurice de Saxe,
who from 1748 until his death in 1750 gave a good deal of
attention to managing the forests and carrying out drainage
works. The king sent large carved panels from Versailles to
Chambord for the former bedchamber of Louis XIV, now
occupied by the Maréchal. Enormous earthenware stoves
were also sent to heat the rooms of the central cross; one
of these survives today. During the
Revolution, when all symbols of royalty
were earmarked for destruction, this
"haunt of vultures" was nearly
demolished. The furniture was sold
off, and there was some pillaging of
paneling from the apartments and
lead from the roofs. Napoleon first
assigned Chambord to the 15th cohort
of the Légion d'Honneur, then in 1806
gave it to Maréchal Berthier (later
Prince de Wagram). In 1821, after
the death of Berthier, Chambord was
acquired by national subscription for
Henri de Bourbon, the son of the Duc
de Berry. His successors held Austrian
nationality; consequently the château
was sequestered during World War
One. The estate was eventually
purchased by the French state in 1930,
although the château and park had
been classified as a historical
monument since 1840.

**HENRI DE BOURBON
(1820–83).** The fifth
Henri de Bourbon
(below), Duke of
Bordeaux and Count
of Chambord, was the
last legitimate
claimant to the
throne of France.

CHAMBORD THROUGH THE CENTURIES. The château's design,
with its massive corner towers and spiral
staircases, was already outdated by the
conclusion of François I's reign, and
variations around the theme of the
central keep had done nothing to
remedy this. Nevertheless, as the
17th-century historiographer Félibien
des Avaux noted: "neither Gothic nor
modern", Chambord "can be regarded as
one of the most magnificent buildings
erected by the kings of France". This
remains true of the keep today, with the
spirals of its magnificent openwork
staircase, its soaring lantern tower, and
the matching stylistic features elaborated
on the four sections of terracing by Antoine
de Troyes. Chambord
represented a new
phase of architectural
development, in which the flamboyant
superstructures of the 14th-century
châteaux were reworked using the
picturesque stylistic language of the
early Renaissance.

"PEAU D'ÂNE"
Catherine Deneuve
played the heroine
in Jacques Demy's
film, made at
Chambord in 1969.

▲ CHÂTEAUX OF THE SOLOGNE WINE REGION

THE MEDALLIONS AT VILLESAVIN
On the wall of the main court are terracotta medallions from Bologna, depicting six Roman emperors.

CHATEAU DE VILLESAVIN
This horseshoe-shaped château consists of a single story, in the style of Italian villas, and is crowned by high slate roofs. Restoration work has progressed steadily. The moat was restored around ten years ago, and the bridge rebuilt using old stone; the original mullions of the windows have also gradually been restored.

BUST OF FRANÇOIS I
The wall that joins the left-hand pavilion of the Château de Villesavin to the main building, at the far end of the main court, has a gateway surmounted by a bust of François I dating from the late 18th or early 19th century.

CHÂTEAU DE VILLESAVIN ● *69* (P5)

CONVENIENT FOR WORKING AT CHAMBORD. In 1527 Jean Le Breton, one of the superintendents in charge of work on Chambord, decided to build himself a relatively modest residence near the site of the new palace. Le Breton decorated Villesavin in a simple style, but to the highest standards of workmanship, using the Florentine sculptors who were working on Chambord. The dormer windows are beautifully carved, some depicting humorous characters or the Muses (music, comedy, and so on). A tall white Carrara marble basin dating from the 16th century still stands in the main court. The chapel was decorated with frescos (1530), which were marked with a black band, as a sign of mourning, when Le Breton died. The interior is rustic in character, with some impressive fireplaces (including a kitchen fireplace with an enormous roasting jack). At either end of the château are two charming closed courtyards that emphasize its intimate atmosphere. In one of them, under the shade of an old lime tree, there is a collection of horse-drawn carriages, including some intriguing items, among them an 18th-century Central European carriage that was drawn by eight horses, a Second Empire *coupe de ville* magnificently lined with Russian leather, and children's donkey carts. With its sumptuously ornamented dormer windows, its Ionic pilasters and its carved medallions, the Château de Villesavin displays a clear kinship with Chambord ▲ *158*. However, this long, low, Italian-style country villa has its own special charm, which owes a good deal both to its early-Renaissance architecture and to its romantic and somewhat mysterious forest setting. Its distinctive, homely atmosphere sets it apart from the "chateau museums" to be seen elsewhere.

RICHES FROM PIGEON DROPPINGS. The château has a dovecote ● *80* with a revolving ladder (above), still in perfect condition. Pigeon droppings were a good source of income at a time when chemical fertilizers were not available. The dovecote is made of local stone and has 1,500 nesting holes. The number of nesting holes was an indicator of a landlord's wealth, each hole representing an *arpent* (about an acre). The landlord must therefore have owned some 1,500 acres here, as well as a further 1,000 acres represented by a second dovecote on a farm. On the garden side of the château a wide lawn runs down to the Beuvron river; in the nearby meadows you can see peaceful Poitou donkeys, an endangered species which the proprietor's son is keen to preserve. In the distance the Forest of Boulogne leads toward Chambord.

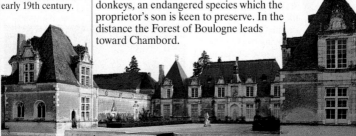

> **"THIS HOUSE HAS SOMETHING REMARKABLE AND DISTINCTIVE ABOUT IT THAT LED THE PEOPLE OF THE BLOIS REGION TO CALL IT BEAUREGARD-LE-ROYAL."**
>
> BERNIER

CHÂTEAU DE DE BEAUREGARD (M5)

The Château de Beauregard is set in the peaceful Beuvron valley, hidden way at the heart of the Forest of Russy, on the edge of the winegrowing area of the Sologne. Fields stretch out around it: an unusual sight in the highly populated region around Blois.

AN APPROPRIATE NAME. The château was built in the mid 16th century and extended in the 17th century; it was never intended as a ceremonial palace. It was built by Jean du Thier, Secretary of State to Henri II, who was not aiming to compete with his neighbors at Chaumont or Chambord. He was a man of taste, a friend of the poet Ronsard, and he made this an elegant residence, built in a simple style with refined ornamentation. We do not

The Cabinet des Grelots at Beauregard.

Aerial view of the Château de Beauregard.

know the name of the architect who designed the sober façades and the arcaded gallery of the main building. However, we do know that Niccolo dell'Abbate was responsible for the decorations in the chapel (sadly destroyed in the 19th century), and that the cabinetmaker Scibec de Carpi created the famous Cabinet des Grelots. This small paneled room is named after the *grelots* (bells) that appear as motifs on the coffered ceiling and in between the finely carved wall panels. Bells featured in Du Thier's coat of arms, which explains this unusual choice. Paintings illustrate the owner's various pursuits: music, silversmithing, sculpture and games. In the 17th century Beauregard was acquired by the Ardier family, another family of politicians. Paul Ardier retired to this peaceful retreat after serving three kings (Henri III, Henri IV and Louis XIII) and added what is still the showpiece of the château: the gallery of historical portraits ▲ *168*.

A DELIGHTFUL SETTING. The Château de Beauregard was built on a wooded hill beside the Beuvron, a slow-moving river popular with anglers; it stands in a large, well laid-out park. The current owners, who inhabit part of the building, have planted oaks and cedars. Irises, lupins, foxgloves and other flowering plants have been arranged in the old kitchen garden, delighting visitors with a riot of color. Each spring a plant fair is held in the grounds, which attracts both amateur and professional gardeners. In addition an annual Book Fair is held in the 17th-century outbuildings behind the château, drawing publishers and booksellers from the entire region.

Part of the numerous collections at Beauregard, this clock can be seen in one of the rooms on the ground floor.

167

The Galerie des Illustres is the showpiece of the Château de Beauregard, and a remarkable example of a genre that was very much in vogue in the 17th century: the gallery of historical portraits. It was devised by Paul Ardier, the state councillor who owned Beauregard at the time, and it contains no less than 327 portraits of people who played an important role in French court or political life over three centuries, from Philippe de Valois to Louis XIII. The three rows of pictures form a pageant of kings, ministers and courtesans, including foreigners who had an influence on the destiny of the French kingdom. There are some amusing surprises: for example, Catherine de Médicis is placed next to François II and Charles IX (she was regent during the latter's minority) and not with her husband Henri II, who is next to his mistress Diane de Poitiers.

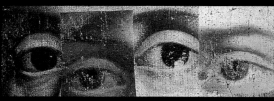

A MASTERPIECE REVEALED

It was discovered that the portrait of Paolo di Venetia has Henri de Navarre's eyes. The underlying portrait is to be restored.

RESTORATION OF THE PORTRAITS

Around one hundred portraits in the Galerie des Illustres have already been restored. This demanding, time-consuming project is due to be completed in the year 2000. The restorers' aim is to achieve both historical truth and visual quality. Underneath the portrait of the Count of Fuentes (a mediocre work dating from the 19th century), X-rays have revealed the face of a woman who may well be Catherine de Bourbon. Historians have yet to deliver their verdict; so for the time being she remains the "Unknown Lady of Beauregard".

SEBASTIEN · ROY · DE · PORTVGAL.

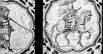

CHEVERNY ● *70* (M5)

Cheverny's pure Louis XIII architecture is in contrast to the many Renaissance châteaux of the Blois region. Completed in 1634, it was built on the site of a medieval castle at the edge of a somber forest; its dazzling white, symmetrical façade stands out boldly against the green carpet of the lawn.

AN UNFORTUNATE JOKE. It was the second wife of Henri Hurault who supervised the building of the château: its imposing white mass is relieved by ornamental niches, balustrades and statues, creating an impression of feminine elegance. The son of Count Philippe Hurault, he was the governor of Blois and a faithful servant of Henri IV. The château was built following a tragic episode, recorded by one of Cheverny's owners in the 18th century. A domineering character, Hurault had shut his young wife away in the old fortified castle at Cheverny. One day, as a joke for the amusement of his courtiers, Henri IV made the cuckold's sign behind Hurault's head. Hurault saw the gesture in a mirror. Furious, he leapt on his horse and galloped straight to Cheverny, where he discovered his wife in the arms of a page. He drew his dagger and killed her lover, then offered his unfaithful wife the choice of dying by poison or the sword. An hour later she was dead.

The intricate carvings on the main staircase (above) feature fruit and plant motifs.

Detail of the ceiling in the guardroom (below).

Henri IV was not at all pleased with this act of rough justice, and sentenced Hurault to "house arrest" on his estate.

A NEW CHÂTEAU. Hurault's second wife was a more docile and obedient woman. Doubtless wishing to eradicate the memory of the unhappy episode, Hurault demolished the old Cheverny and gave his second wife free rein to build a new residence in the modern style. The increasing power of the monarchy had made the old style of fortifications superfluous. Cheverny was beautifully decorated by the architect-sculptor Boyer and the famous Blois painter Jean Mosnier; most of the 17th-century decorations survive today. The Grande Mademoiselle (daughter of Gaston d'Orléans ▲ *145*), who was an honored guest here, wrote: "Nothing is more elegant, more comfortable and more splendid than the interior." The elegantly decorated main staircase with straight banisters is reminiscent of the examples at Chenonceaux ▲ *218* and Azay-le-Rideau ▲ *234*. Cheverny is exceptional in that the rooms display their

The imposing white façade of the Château de Cheverny, facing onto the main court.

original furniture: this is highly unusual among the châteaux of the Loire, which are mainly furnished with acquisitions from museums and later collections. To the right of the staircase is the dining hall, hung with Cordoba leather. This room was restored at the end of the 19th century but has retained most of its original decoration, partly produced by Mosnier, who was born in Blois in 1600. He produced fifteen of the thirty-four painted panels that decorate this room, illustrating fantastic episodes from *Don Quixote* (which Cervantes completed in 1615). The SALLE D'ARMES (guardroom) on the second story possesses a French-style ceiling made of wooden panels with colored paintings including a variety of motifs (cherubs, mythological and symbolic subjects). The Chambre du Roi (King's bedroom) is even more opulently decorated: the tapestries, designed by Simon Vouet, illustrate the adventures of Ulysses, as do the paintings on the coffered ceiling and the monumental fireplace; all these works date from the 17th century. Returning to the ground floor, we reach the GRAND SALON with its magnificent furniture and a portrait of the Countess of Cheverny by Nicolas Mignard (1606–68). The château is beautifully preserved, on both the interior and the exterior; for this we are largely indebted to the owner in the early part of this century, who opened the building to the public in 1922. This was a bold idea at the time and attracted much criticism, though in later years it was widely admired.

MODEL FOR MARLINSPIKE. Around forty years ago Hergé, the creator of Tintin, was on holiday in the region. One day he took the road from Contres to Cheverny, formerly the main approach road to the château, and came across the main building without seeing the two corner pavilions, which were concealed by trees. Hergé was captivated by Cheverny's classical style of architecture and asked permission from the owner to make this the model for Marlinspike, the famous castle of Captain Haddock. He also used Cheverny's great staircase, which the irascible but likeable captain tumbles down so frequently in *The Castafiore Emerald*; and the guardroom, which figures in *The Secret of The Unicorn* and *Red Rackham's Treasure*.

A GHASTLY SURPRISE . . .
Captain Haddock: "Thundering typhoons! Am I dreaming! It's Marlinspike Hall! . . . Marlinspike, my family estate! It's impossible! . . ."
Tintin: "Well, captain, it's quite simple: your family castle is for sale? . . . you must buy it back!"
Red Rackham's Treasure

▲ Châteaux of the Sologne wine region

This curious figure is one of many stone carvings to be seen at the Château de Troussay.

The décor of the Chambre du Roi (above); and the Cheverny Hunt.

❝I followed the invitation of a little caretaker, neat and proper, who sat with two children taking a breath of fresh air by the door of her cottage; she told me to continue a little further and then to turn to the right. I followed her instructions to the letter and as I turned I saw a house with the charm of an old fairy-tale manor.... A charming and elegant residence overlooked a green lawn, beds of flowers and groups of trees.❞

Henry James

A FAMILY BUSINESS. Cheverny is unusual among the châteaux of the Loire Valley in that it has belonged to the same family for five centuries. The descendants of the Hurault family, who still live in part of the château, are keenly aware of the importance of their historical heritage and are constantly developing new activities to make Cheverny better known. A highly sophisticated *son et lumière* performance is held at the château each summer, with six hundred actors and many special effects, splendidly re-creating the history of France as seen through the fortunes of the Hurault family.

A REPUTATION FOR HUNTING ● *52.* The famous pack of hounds (of the Anglo-Poitevins breed) is still kept in the kennels next to the Salle des Trophées, which holds some two thousand stag's antlers and hunting trophies belonging to the Cheverny Hunt. During the season, hunts are held in the neighboring forests. The Forest of Cheverny is an integral part of the estate and is managed with great professionalism. An 18-hole golf course, complete with copses and lakes, was recently built alongside the forest.

LOCAL WINES ■ *30.* The flat countryside of this part of the Sologne is scattered with vineyards, as well as forests. Winegrowers of the twenty-three parishes around Cheverny produce white and red wines that are classified as VDQS (Vins Délimités de Qualité Supérieure). The red wines are light, fruity and pleasant to drink. The whites are highly prized throughout the region; dry and fruity, they are made from Sauvignon, Chardonnay and Romorantin grapes (Romorantin being a local variety).

CHURCH OF ST-ÉTIENNE. This 12th-century church stands opposite the entrance to the château. It is notable for having retained its *caquetoir*, a lovely wooden porch where churchgoers could gather for a chat (*caqueter*) after mass, sheltered from the weather. The porch was also used as a meeting place (for collecting tithes, for auctions, and so on). It is arguably one of the most beautiful porches in France.

Château de Troussay   (M5)

The elegant Renaissance manor house of Troussay is tucked away among ancient trees, in the midst of vineyards and woodland, two miles from Cheverny. This small château with charming outbuildings gives a good idea of what the small estates of the Sologne must have looked like in the past.

> **"I HAD A RAPID AND PARTIAL GLIMPSE OF CHEVERNY, BUT IT WAS A FLEETING REVELATION OF PERFECTION"**
>
> HENRY JAMES

A DIMINUTIVE CHATEAU. Troussay has a tall main building, framed by towers with diamond-shaped bricks, and large outbuildings; the superlative quality of its decoration is comparable with the great châteaux of the Loire. Originally a modest 15th-century manor house, it was renovated for the first time in the 16th century. In the 19th century the historian Louis de La Saussaye inherited the house from his uncle Christophe de Réméon; he found it in a very dilapidated state, as it had stood unoccupied since the Revolution. He turned to his friend the architect Jules de La Morandière and then had the idea, not common at that time, of decorating the building (on both the exterior and the interior) with ornaments from historical buildings in the region that were falling into ruins. In this way he was

CHATEAU DE TROUSSAY
Louis de La Saussaye, rector of the Académie de Lyon, brought this old manor house back to life.

able to save them from destruction and relocate them in an appropriate context. Thus the capital to the left of the entrance is from the Château de Bury, and the porcupine on the northern façade from the former residence of Hurault de Cheverny at Blois. The collection of early-16th-

century stained-glass windows once adorned the Hôtel Sardini ▲ *141* and the Hôtel de Guise at Blois ▲ *138*. The carved wooden door of the Oratory from the same period, which is the pride of Troussay, came from the Château de Bury. This door was sent to Japan in 1972 for an exhibition on the Loire Valley. Original features of Troussay's decoration that have survived include Louis XII floor tiles on the ground floor

and splendid woodcarvings on the doors and windows. The period furniture (16th to 18th century) and old paneling give the château a homely atmosphere. Troussay also benefits from its delightful woodland setting. It is still inhabited, and has changed hands only twice since the 15th century.

DECORATIONS OF THE CHATEAU DE TROUSSAY
The entrance door of the house is framed by two capitals: the capital on the left comes from the former Château de Bury, as does the door of the Oratory.

RECONSTRUCTION OF TRADITIONAL SOLOGNE LIFE. A little museum of Sologne country life has been set up in the authentic setting of the old outbuildings that were at one time the hub of Troussay's economic activities. Old domestic and agricultural objects are exhibited in the beautiful beamed rooms, some of which are used today for exhibitions and receptions.

CHATEAU DE ROUJOUX. The "magic castle" of Roujoux, situated between Cheverny and Fougères, on the road to Contres, cannot rival its royal neighbors. However, this attractive Louis XIII style residence has been open to visitors since 1986, and makes a pleasant stop, with its park and water-filled moats. The owners have set up a series of historical displays in the rooms, which are almost empty of furniture. Set into the recesses of the library are twenty-seven puppet scenes recounting the history of Roujoux since the arrival of the Vikings.

▲ THE SOLOGNE

For a long time the Sologne region was viewed as a barren land of little commercial value: its acid soils, which were often waterlogged, were ill-suited for agriculture. In the 18th century sheep-rearing became a widespread practice, and the moors used for pasture were extended at the expense of woods and fields. Drainage of the ground was neglected creating unhealthy marshes. The region experienced a recovery under the Second Empire, when drainage, reforestation and the development of agriculture created the basis of its present-day appearance.

THE SOLOGNE AREA
This small region of the old kingdom of France is situated between three départements: Loir-et-Cher, Cher and Loiret. Each of the different areas within it has its own distinctive character: the winegrowing area to the west, lakes in the center, and the Berry district further to the east.

REDEVELOPMENT OF THE SOLOGNE
During the time of the Second Empire Napoleon III did a good deal to revitalize the Sologne. Trees were planted and experimental farms established as part of the rehabilitation program. The emperor's interest in the region attracted wealthy industrialists to come and live here.

THE FOREST ■ *24*
Half of the Sologne is
covered by forest,
which is still the
major feature of the
landscape. It consists
of oaks and birches,
as well as many
varieties of conifer
(including maritime
pines, Scots pine and
larch).

MOORLAND LAKES
These lakes were mostly
created at the instigation
of religious communities,
on marshes left by the
great land-clearing of the
Middle Ages. The
moorland here is
covered with a mixture
of gorse and broom.

SOLOGNE MUTTON ■ *28*
The meat of the region was
once highly prized by Parisian
butchers and was
distinguished by its
own appellation.
Today only a
handful of sheep
farmers
continue to
breed the
local stock.

Legend has it that a lord of Fougères once shut his wife up in one of the towers of the château, before killing her out of jealousy...

CHATEAU DE FOUGÈRES-SUR-BIEVRE. Its charm derives from the picturesque buildings around the main courtyard: towers and turrets, dwellings, the curtain wall, a pavilion and gallery, and a feudal chapel.

RENAISSANCE DECORATION OF FOUGÈRES. The carved decoration of the two Louis XI style accolade doors is of very high quality: on the lintel of the first, Saint Michael and three angels, carved in an elegant, slightly mannered style, guide the visitor through the room toward the chapel; the two warriors on the second represent the defense of the postern guarding the entrance to the staircase. This is the legacy of Pierre de Refuge at Fougères.

FOUGÈRES-SUR-BIÈVRE (LM6)

It is a surprise on arriving in this small village to discover a massive fortress in the medieval style that is generally overlooked in traditional tours of the châteaux of the Loire. The castle, an archetypal child's image of a fortress, is solidly planted in the middle of the village.

★ A FORTIFIED CASTLE BUILT IN THE RENAISSANCE ★. Contrary to all appearances, Fougères does not date from medieval times. It was erected on the site of a building destroyed earlier in the 15th century. Around 1475 Pierre de Refuge, treasurer of Louis XI and owner of the estate, obtained permission from the king "to rebuild the Château de Fougères as a fortress": As a result, it is the only Renaissance château of the Loire Valley to have a fortified keep complete with drawbridge, machicolations and loopholes – built some twenty years after the fortifications at the Château de Blois had been replaced with the more cheerful style of decoration suited to a place of residence. In the 16th century the arrow slits of this little fortress were replaced by windows with carved pediments and the moats were filled in, somewhat softening the austere appearance of the façades. The building was converted into a mill in the 19th century, a process which took years to complete, and the Bièvre was diverted to pass below the chapel. Later Fougères became a hostel for destitute families, before being acquired by the state in 1932.

A SHOWPIECE OF LOCAL BUILDING. Although from the outside the château retains its fortresslike appearance, the rounded lines of its interior court give it a distinct charm. A low gallery in the Flamboyant style is surmounted by windows with Italianate decoration, which may well have been copied from the Charles d'Orléans gallery at Blois. The tall slate roofs, the intimate scale of the courtyard and the simplicity of the décor combine to create a charming and authentic impression of rusticity. Local builders and craftsmen were employed for the structural work and the decoration, making Fougères a showpiece of their skills. The rooms are large, bare of furniture, with fine beams. The château fell into oblivion for many years; steps are now being taken to make it better known.

> **"Yes, this is an admirable sight, but how much I prefer my gutter in the Rue du Bac . . ."**
>
> Madame de Stael, who spent the summer of 1810
> at Chaumont, having been exiled from Paris by Napoléon

CHAUMONT-SUR-LOIRE ★ ● 67 (L5)

The Counts of Blois built a castle on their territory in the 10th century, to ward off invaders from Anjou. It stood on a steep hill with a striking view over the Loire.

THE CASTLE OF THE AMBOISE FAMILY. The Amboise family acquired the castle through marriage and kept it for five centuries, during which time it suffered many changes of fortune. In 1465 Louis XI had it razed to the ground, to punish its owners for having joined the league of discontented nobles led by Charles the Bold. Pierre and Charles I of Amboise soon returned to favor and began to rebuild their castle, but they only had time to re-erect the north and west wings. The west wing still stands today, with a corner tower which could serve as a defensive retreat. The north wing housed a great hall overlooking the river. In the late 15th century Charles II (son of Charles I) planned to complete the building. However, he was called to Italy by the high offices entrusted to him by Louis XII, and delegated supervision of the building work to his uncle, the patron and minister Georges I of Amboise. The south and east wings were built at this stage, but sadly they have been greatly altered since and robbed of their main attraction: the two great overhanging cornices that ran along the interior façade of the new building, displaying the full repertoire of Italian decorative motifs. The great cornice of the François I Wing at Blois was a pale reflection of these bold innovations.

THE PRICE OF REVENGE. In 1560 Catherine de Médicis forced Diane de Poitiers (formerly the mistress of her husband, Henri II, who had died a year before) to exchange Chenonceaux ▲ 218 for Chaumont, which she did not even legally own yet. And what a pity! The deaths of Georges d'Amboise and his nephew, in 1510 and 1511 respectively, had left the upper parts of the building unfinished; the task of restoration fell to Diane, who made a brave effort but died in 1566 before the work could be completed.

THE LE RAY ERA. After a variety of modifications, the château entered another decisive period when Jacques Donatien Le Ray acquired it in 1750: Le Ray was famous for trading with the New World and for his business deals with Benjamin Franklin. He had the north wing demolished, along with the beautiful cornices that joined onto it, in order to open up the view from the courtyard over the river valley. He also destroyed the great staircase, which was doubtless in poor condition, to suit the elevation of the south wing; he completed the latter by adding a portico and the upper story that had been missing since the 16th century. The ceiling of the chapel was also the work of this prudent businessman, who created a small factory for pottery and glass in the old outbuildings. He hired the services of the Italian artist Giambattista Nini (1717–86) to produce medallions here. The château fell under threat of demolition during the Revolution, and some of the coats of arms were mutilated. After this, peace returned.

DIANE DE POITIERS
Catherine de Médicis took her time to finalize the forced "exchange" of Chaumont for Chenonceaux and to pay the death duties due to the exchequer at Blois. As a result, Diane was not able to take possession of her new home until 1562.

NINI'S MEDALLIONS
Some of Nini's terracotta medallions depicting famous figures of the age can still be seen at the château.

An old well in the château courtyard.

The château is built on the highest hill of the river bank, surrounding the broad summit with its high walls and its enormous towers; tall slate bell towers rise above them, giving the building that religious air common to all our old châteaux . . .
Alfred de Vigny,
Cinq-Mars

Paul-Ernest Sanson, an architect popular with the aristocracy and the political and financial élite, was entrusted with the refurbishment of the château at the end of the 19th century: he installed modern conveniences and refurbished both the interior and the exterior, creating magnificent stables and redesigning the castle approaches.

THE 19TH CENTURY: RESTORATIONS AND GREAT FORTUNES.

Restoration work began in 1833, and took a new turn when Viscount Walsh enlisted the devoted collaboration of the architect La Morandière. The latter, in a first phase of restoration work completed in 1852, rebuilt the great staircase and modified the far end of the west wing in the "troubadour style", to the complete satisfaction of his client. However, the Commission for Historical Monuments was far less happy with his work and Prosper Mérimée, the commission's inspector, had to lay down strict guidelines for the restoration of the south wing. The south wing was altered again after 1875, the year in which the château was acquired by Marie-Charlotte Say, heiress of a huge sugar fortune and later the wife of Prince Amédée de Broglie. This couple entrusted the building to one of the most renowned architects of the era,

Paul-Ernest Sanson. Sanson rebuilt one of the two cornices of the east wing in an inspired neo-Renaissance style, as well as its covered walkway. The château became the setting for extravagant festivities and huge receptions to which the leading figures of the day were invited. There were some surprises: a maharaja, for example, brought an elephant as a gift, a charming if cumbersome creature answering to the name of Miss Peggy. The threat of financial ruin put an end to the festivities, but even cutbacks and economies were not enough to avert disaster.

LATEST DEVELOPMENTS. In 1938 the state bought the building (by which stage some of the furniture had been sold off), and maintenance work was restarted on a small scale. In 1947 to 1948 several rooms were subjected to "derestoration" work, which had been planned as early as 1943: all or some of the 19th-century decorations were removed in favor of a more austere effect. Sanson's modifications were accorded no better treatment than those of La Morandière: in 1991 his alterations to the ground floor of the east wing were eradicated. An interesting feature, unconnected with the château itself, is the splendid new garden opened in 1992, which is the setting for an international garden festival.

Amboise

▲ AMBOISE

1. CHÂTEAU
2. CLOS-LUCÉ
3. HÔTEL DE VILLE
4. GRENIERS DE CÉSAR
5. CHURCH OF ST-FLORENTIN
6. POSTAL MUSEUM
7. ABBEY CHURCH OF SAINT-DENIS
8. MAX-ERNST FOUNTAIN
9. ÎLE D'OR

QUAI GÉNÉRAL-DE-GAULLE

RUE JEAN-JACQUES-ROUSSEAU

RUE BRETONNEAU

HISTORY OF THE TOWN (K6)

EARLY SETTLEMENTS. Amboise was the site of several fortified settlements over the course of the centuries. For over five centuries the Turones (one of the peoples of Gaul) had their capital on the Éperon des Châtelliers, the spur of land on which the château stands today. Their *oppidum* (citadel) was followed by a Merovingian fort, which may have dated from the late Roman Empire (3rd and 4th centuries AD). The first reference to the citadel of Ambatiacum dates from the 6th century, in the writings of Gregory of Tours. This fortress appears to have been destroyed three times during Norman invasions of Touraine, and then rebuilt by Ingelger, Count of Anjou. It was one of the sites fought over by the armies of Blois and Anjou. Foulques Nerra built the Collegiate Church of St-Florentin (demolished in the 19th century) here around 1030.

ROYAL BUILDING PROJECTS. When the Hundred Years' War forced the French kings to leave the banks of the Seine for the Loire, the French court relocated to Amboise. Charles VII confiscated the fortress from Louis d'Amboise in 1434, extended it and added the St-Michel Chapel to the Church of St-Florentin in 1446. He gave the town special privileges and exemptions. Louis XI moved his family to Amboise and rebuilt the château, adding a new wing to the south. He was particularly fond of this place, of which he said: "The estate of Amboise is large and beautiful, in a beautiful and fertile region." Charles VIII, born at Amboise in 1470, built the château's two enormous feudal towers: the Tour des Minimes and the Tour Hurtault. He brought back a score of Humanists from his Italian campaigns, including artists and craftsmen such as Pacello di Mercogliano ▲ *188*, who designed terraced gardens for him between the palace and the dry moat.

THE SALAMANDER
This was the emblem of Charles VIII and of his cousin Charles d'Angoulême, who passed it on to his son, François I. Only their mottos, which generally accompanied the emblem, differed.

THE EARLY RENAISSANCE. When Charles VIII died, Louis XII moved his cousin Louise de Savoie to Amboise, along with her children: François d'Angoulême (later François I) and his sister (later Marguerite de Navarre), who was one of the most learned women of her time. Building work continued on the north wings and the Tour Hurtault, and the gardens were extended. François I was especially fond of this place, where he had grown up: "We lived and were raised for most of the time at Amboise, a place for which we have always had particular love and affection." After 1530, when his mother died, he gradually deserted Amboise in favor of Chambord and Fontainebleau.

> **"WE AND OUR PREDECESSORS HAVE HAD PLEASURE AND AMUSEMENT AT THE MAGNIFICENT CASTLE BUILT IN THIS TOWN."**
>
> FRANÇOIS I

THE AMBOISE CONSPIRACY. Henri II and Catherine de Médicis, who moved into the château in 1551, sought to restore the French court to its former splendor and make it a center for all the arts. In 1560, during the brief reign of their son, the young François II (below, as a child), Amboise was the setting for a tragic episode. A Protestant gentleman named La Renaudie in the pay of the Prince de Condé gathered together a group of Reformers. They planned to demand the freedom to practice their faith from the king (then staying at Blois) and probably also to neutralize the Duc de Guise, their most virulent adversary. The plot was betrayed; the king took refuge at Amboise (a castle that was easier to defend) and organized its repression. The conspirators were killed as they arrived – either decapitated, drowned, or hanged from the balcony of the château. These tragic events cast a shadow over Amboise's prestige.

DECLINE. Louis XIII converted the château into a royal prison after confiscating it from his brother, the unruly Gaston d'Orléans ▲ *145*. The financier Nicolas Fouquet and the libertine Duc de Lauzun were held prisoner here under Louis XIV. Later Napoleon gave the château to Senator Pierre-Roger Ducos, who had most of it demolished between 1806 and 1810 since no funds were provided for its maintenance. The future Louis-Philippe inherited Amboise in 1821, and made modifications to turn it into a summer residence. After the 1848 revolution the estate was confiscated again. The first serious restoration work (though carried out with some license) was started at the end of the 19th century by Victor and Gabriel Ruprich-Robert, the official architects responsible for historical monuments.

TODAY. Since 1974 the château has been managed by the Fondation St-Louis, whose president is the Comte de Paris; it is visited by many tourists. The town is pursuing a development strategy to make the most of its historical heritage and attract new businesses to the area.

TERRIBLE REPRESSION
The violence of the punishment exacted on the Amboise conspirators had a profound effect on contemporaries. Agrippa d'Aubigné (1552–1630) was scarred for life by the memory. He was traveling to Paris with his father, from his home of Saintonge, and arrived in Amboise the day after the tragedy. His horrified father made him swear to avenge the Huguenots who had been massacred.

ABD-EL-KADER (1808–83)
This Arab Emir led the resistance to France's invasion of Algeria between 1832 and 1847. After many defeats, he yielded in 1847. He and his followers were held at Amboise from 1848 to 1852, when Napoleon III released him (below).

THE CHÂTEAU

The best view of the château is from the Île d'Or ▲ *190*. The entrance is approached via a covered ramp to the southwest of the rampart.

TOUR DES MINIMES. This enormous circular tower to the north of the château was built at the end of the 15th century. It was named after the Minims' convent that stood between the tower and the Loire. The tower has a ramp for horses and carriages, which winds around its central core leading up to the terraces.

TOUR HURTAULT. This has survived intact, without restoration. It is surmounted by a walkway and a conical roof, and has an entrance ramp. The interior decorations are clearly Italianate.

CHARLES VIII WING. The façade of this wing facing the Loire has a great gallery with seven arcades, seven high windows and a roof with dormer windows, which have been restored. The building stands above a basement of defenses which were freely "improved" by 19th-century architects. The carvings in the Salle des États were completely revamped by the Ruprich-Roberts, in Gothic style with early-Renaissance features. It is in this room that judgment was passed on the Protestants who took part in the Amboise conspiracy.

LITTLE SURVIVES
The scale of the destruction can be seen by comparing the plan of the château of Amboise (right) depicted by Jean Androuet du Cerceau in *Les Plus Excellents Bastiments de France* (1576–9) with a modern photograph (above). The area covered by the château today is only one-fifth of what it was in the 16th century. Only the Charles VIII and François I wings, the Chapel of St-Hubert and part of the rampart survive.

LOUIS XII/FRANÇOIS I WING. This wing has four stories facing the courtyard and three facing the garden. Its elegant early-Renaissance décor is typical of the first part of François I's reign.

CHAPEL OF ST-HUBERT ● *60.* The chapel originally opened on to the galleries of a building that has now disappeared. Built between 1491 and 1496 (the date of Charles VIII's return from Italy), it stands on a forebuilding, which gives its chevet particular prominence, and has magnificent lacework stone ornamentation on two levels. The lintel is decorated with bas-reliefs depicting the legend of Saint Christopher

(patron saint of travelers) and Saint Hubert (patron saint of hunters). Leonardo da Vinci ▲ *162* is now buried here.

THE PORTE DES LIONS. This gate stands at the eastern end of the gardens; its name was taken from an earlier one surmounted by two statues of lions, probably alluding to the menagerie which Charles VIII kept in the dry moat.

CLOS-LUCÉ

This manor house was known as the Château de Cloux until the 17th century. Built of brick and stone, in 1477, it consists of two main buildings standing at right angles to each other on either side of an octagonal tower.

LEONARDO DA VINCI AT CLOS-LUCÉ. The Italian genius moved to the Château de Cloux in the spring of 1516, at the invitation of François I, and spent the last three years of his life here. The king made extensive funds available to him, "so that he can achieve all that his genius is capable of producing". Despite suffering from malaria, Leonardo continued to work hard, took part in organizing court festivities and devoted himself to projects relating to the region's hydrography (connecting the royal residences by water, diverting the course of the Loire and draining the marshes of the Sologne). He advised on a royal residence that was to be built at Romorantin, and the initial ideas for Chambord have been attributed to him. He died at Clos-Lucé on May 2, 1519 at the age of sixty-seven and was buried in the château's Collegiate Church of St-Florentin. After the Revolution the manor house became a carpet factory, and another wing was added. Today it houses a museum devoted to Leonardo.

CHÂTEAU-GAILLARD. This house, below Clos-Lucé, was built in the 15th century for Pacello di Mercogliano, who introduced Italian garden design to France. Charles VIII required flowers for his terraces and fruit for his table – and Mercogliano created a special garden and greenhouses for the purpose. The first orange trees in France are said to have been planted here.

View of the château from the west.

THE LEONARDO DA VINCI MUSEUM Clos-Lucé is now a museum displaying models of some forty machines ▲ *186* designed by Leonardo. There is a video presentation on his life and work; and his bedroom, with its lovely hooded fireplace, has been restored to its original state. The walls of the chapel, which was Anne de Bretagne's oratory, still have traces of frescos painted by Leonardo or one of his pupils.

REPUBLIQUE FRANÇAISE
1.00
POSTES 1973
LE CLOS-LUCÉ A AMBOISE

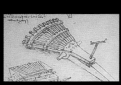

MILITARY GENIUS
Leonardo produced a series of sketches and studies of war machines – among them firearms with several barrels (left), projectiles, grapeshot missiles, huge crossbows, and canons with multiple openings – anticipating the designs and devices that make up the war arsenal of our own time.

"Leonardo was truly admirable and divine . . . Nature had favored him to such a degree that he achieved excellence in all the areas to which he directed his mind, his thought and his soul. To everything he did he gave a mark of sensitivity, brilliance, goodness, beauty and grace as has never been equalled."
Giorgio Vasari

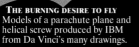

THE BURNING DESIRE TO FLY
Models of a parachute plane and helical screw produced by IBM from Da Vinci's many drawings.

THE LAST HOURS OF A GENIUS "MUCH PRAISED AND MUCH CRITICIZED"
Leonardo's amazing ideas, which had not found favor in Rome, fascinated François I and his court. "Vasari has him say, in that famous description of his glorious death tenderly watched over by the king (below), that it pains him to have 'offended God and men by not working in art as he should have done'. When you look for the artist you find a scientist, a 'thinker'; when you look for the painter you find an architect, a sculptor, an engineer; and when you finally do find the painter he is held back by the ideas and experiments of the theorist."
André Chastel

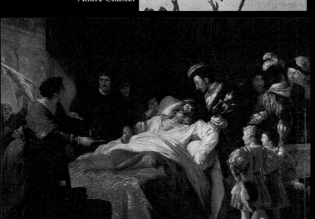

LEONARDO'S "SERENE AND SEVERE FEATURES"
This red pencil drawing, universally attributed to Leonardo, is most probably a self-portrait. Da Vinci was sixty years old at the time of the drawing, which dates from 1512.

PROJECT FOR AN "AERIAL SCREW", ANCESTOR OF THE HELICOPTER. "I thought that it was possible . . . to build a screw that would lift itself into the air as it turned . . . but how to keep this flying spinning top fixed to its support, and to the mechanism below?"
Ralph Steadman

Mary Magdalene, in the
Church of St-Denis.

**THE DROWNED
WOMAN OF THE
CHURCH OF ST-DENIS**
This recumbent
figure of a woman's
naked and decaying
corpse is strikingly
realistic: some say it
depicts Marie Babou,
the mistress of
François I who
drowned herself in
the Loire.

A 19th-century
lithograph of a view
from the main road
between Blois and
Tours.

TOWARD THE CHURCH OF ST-DENIS

TOUR DE L'HORLOGE. The narrow Rue Mably with its old
stone markers leads to the Tour de l'Horloge, formerly the
Porte de l'Amasse, one of six gateways in the medieval
rampart which protected the town. The early wooden portal
was demolished under Louis XI, then replaced in 1497 by the
present stone clock tower. It has two stories, with mullioned
windows on one side, and is crowned with a lantern. In a

niche under the porch
stood a 14th-century
Virgin and Child in
colored terracotta, now in
the Musée de l'Hôtel de
Ville (opposite, right).
MUSÉE DE LA POSTE. This
museum is housed in the
Hôtel Joyeuse, once the
home of the Italian artist
Fra Giovanni Giocondo,
who was brought to
Amboise by Charles VIII.
Both the house and the
street bear his name,
Giocondo being translated into French as "Joyeuse". The
house, which has two small Louis XIII pavilions, features a
beautiful carved cornice from the 15th century. The garden,
laid out on three terraces, was restored in 1900: it aims to
reproduce the garden designed for the house by Pacello di
Mercogliano ▲ *182*. At the center water pours into an
ornamental lake from an Italian-style basin. The museum
retraces the history of the postal service from its beginnings,
with models of inn signs, stagecoaches, old trunks, uniforms
and coachmen's gear.
MAISON ENCHANTÉE. Around two hundred animated figures
are used here to create some twenty tableaux, including
historical scenes, comic ones and fantasy.
ABBEY CHURCH OF ST-DENIS ★. This church was begun in
1107, apparently to replace one founded by Saint Martin ▲ *206*
on the site of a former pagan temple. The choir, which has a
polygonal chevet, and the transept both date from this time;
the nave and two side aisles were added thirty years later.
The two vaults between the bays of the nave are

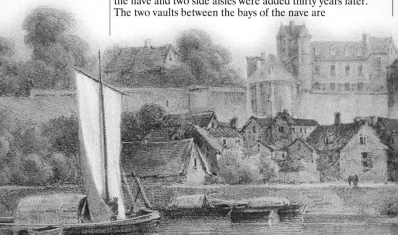

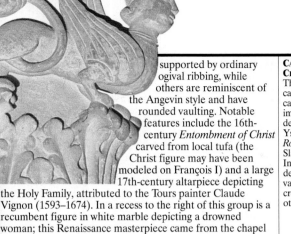

supported by ordinary ogival ribbing, while others are reminiscent of the Angevin style and have rounded vaulting. Notable features include the 16th-century *Entombment of Christ* carved from local tufa (the Christ figure may have been modeled on François I) and a large 17th-century altarpiece depicting the Holy Family, attributed to the Tours painter Claude Vignon (1593–1674). In a recess to the right of this group is a recumbent figure in white marble depicting a drowned woman; this Renaissance masterpiece came from the chapel of the Babou family near Montlouis-sur-Loire.

CAPITALS OF THE CHURCH OF ST-DENIS
The decorative carvings on the capitals are rich and impressive. They depict Saint Denis, Ysengrin from the *Roman de Renart*, the Slaughter of the Innocents, the deadly sins, and a variety of fantastic creatures (left) and other figures.

THE QUAYSIDE

Virgin and Child, displayed at the Hôtel de Ville.

HÔTEL DE VILLE. This Renaissance building at the southern end of the bridge was built in the late 15th century for Pierre Morin, treasurer of France and mayor of Tours. Subsequently the Duc de Choiseul ▲ *209*, who had been appointed governor of Touraine, installed the law courts here when he acquired the estate of Amboise. Around 1776 the building was partially reconstructed using old plans, as it was falling into ruin. Nevertheless, carvings from the early 16th century have survived; and the interior has partition walls of bare brickwork and a 16th-century fireplace. The MUSÉE DE L'HÔTEL DE VILLE features documents relating to the history of the town, furniture from Chanteloup and a collection of paintings, including one by Emmanuel Lansyer ▲ *229*. The Salles des Mariages, with its monumental fireplace, has a magnificent view over the Loire and the neighboring hills.

CHURCH OF ST-FLORENTIN. This church was built against the town rampart, close to the Hôtel de Ville, in 1484. It was called Notre-Dame-de-Grève until the château's Church of St-Florentin was destroyed; it then took over the name. It has two side entrances, to the north and south. The top of the bell tower and the Renaissance-style ornamentation were renovated in the 16th century. Inside is a striking 15th-century font decorated with thistles.

LEONARDO DA VINCI ON THE ÎLE D'OR
This bronze statue depicting Leonardo da Vinci was produced by an anonymous artist a short time before World War Two. In the 1970's the city of Paris donated it to Amboise, the great man's final home.

THE DUC DE CHOISEUL (1719–85)
A favorite of Louis XV, Choiseul became a minister thanks to the support of Madame de Pompadour. He directed France's foreign policy for twelve years (1758–70).

MAX ERNST FOUNTAIN ● *83.* (Quai du Général-de-Gaulle.) Michel Debré, mayor of Amboise, asked Max Ernst (1891–1976) to produce a fountain for the town in 1968. Painter, sculptor, etcher and writer, Ernst took up residence in Touraine, near Huismes, in 1955. A prominent member of the Surrealist movement in Paris from 1921 onward, he experimented with a variety of art forms and invented new techniques of painting involving collage, frottage and transfers.

GRENIERS DE CÉSAR ★. Behind the Hôtel Choiseul there is an unusual construction: a dozen or so caves cut into the tufa rockface. The first of these is now used for exhibitions. Beyond it are the huge and mysterious brick silos known as Caesar's Granaries. The silos do indeed recall methods of grain storage that were used in early antiquity: when a silo was filled with grain it produced carbon dioxide, which prevented fermentation and killed off pests. The sheer size of the complex suggested that only the Romans could have been capable of creating it. However, recent research has shown that the silos have nothing to do with Caesar: they probably date from the 16th century.

MAISON DES PAGES DE CHARLES VII. This half-timbered house below the castle is built of brick and stone; it has two stories and a staircase turret. Carvings can be seen on the façade.

ÎLE D'OR

The Île d'Or (also known as Île St-Jean) divides the Loire into two. It was here, around 504–5, that Clovis and Alaric II ● *37* met to define their territories. The view over the château and the town is magnificent. The island has various leisure facilities, including a picnic area.

CHAPEL OF ST-JEAN. This chapel was built in the 12th century, at which stage it belonged to the Order of Saint John of Jerusalem. From the outside you can see a Romanesque window and the chevet with three irregular openings. The keystones, in the Angevin style, are carved and painted. There was a second chapel on the island: the Chapel of St-Sauveur, which housed poor people suffering from contagious diseases. It was completely destroyed by flooding in the 18th century.

CHURCH OF NOTRE-DAME-DU-BOUT-DES-PONTS (right bank). This was built under François I to provide a parish church for the

THE MAX ERNST FOUNTAIN
The frog and the tortoise (the
heroes of La Fontaine's *Fables*)
are the dominant components of
the work, reflecting Max Ernst's
vision of childhood.

suburb, which was separated from the Church of St-Denis
by the Loire. The single nave has five bays with ogival
vaulting; to the south it is flanked by a square staircase
turret. The façades of the old houses around the church
retain their original carvings, including a 16th-century
bas-relief depicting a knight giving alms.

The Loire at the
Île d'Or.

THE CHANTELOUP PAGODA ★   ● *71* (K6)

In 1713 Jean d'Aubiny, Master of the Waters and Forests of
Amboise, had a château built at Chanteloup, an estate to the
south of the town. The architect was Robert de Cotte,
brother-in-law of Mansart. The Duc de Choiseul (opposite)
acquired Chanteloup in 1761 and added it to his estate at

Amboise. He extended the château and surrounded it with
formal gardens designed by Le Camus. In his 10,000 acres
of forest he created a network of intersecting avenues,
including seven broad avenues converging in front of the
château. A few years later the original gardens were
replaced by ones landscaped in the English style, with
winding paths, an artificial grotto, a river with waterfall,
exotic trees and orange trees. The famous pagoda in the
Anglo-Chinese style is Choiseul's crowning achievement;
it was "built by the Duke in commemoration of the persons
who visited him in his exile" (Arthur Young, *Travels in
France in 1787, 1788 and 1789*). Similar to the pagoda in
London's Kew Gardens, it was erected between 1773 and
1778, following plans drawn up by Le Camus. It was
reflected in a vast semicircular lake covering more than
18 acres, connected to the Étangs de Jumeaux by a canal
7 miles long. This is all that remains of the magnificent
estate, the setting for a brilliant court that attracted the
famous and fashionable from Paris, London, Vienna and

**❝The apartments
of the château are
arranged in a
comfortable and
splendid manner;
those on the
ground floor
have been so
well gilded that
they are brighter
than those created
in our own time.
The château is
decorated with
beautiful
colonnades on
either side.❞**
Élisabeth
Vigée-Lebrun,
Souvenirs

Right and below: details of the pagoda.

Berlin. The château itself was demolished between 1823 and 1825. The pagoda, which is 130 feet high and 50 feet wide, has seven stories; each is smaller than the one below and contains a domed octagonal room. Although exotic motifs can be seen on the balustrades and the geometric designs of some windows, the greater part of the ornamentation is in Louis XVI style.

THE PAGODA, A PROTEST AGAINST THE KING'S FICKLENESS
The exiled Duc de Choiseul was very popular, and the pagoda features testimonies to his friends. It has a dedication by the Abbé Barthélemy (1716–95), author of *Voyage du jeune Anacharsis en Grèce* (1788), and Chinese inscriptions meaning "gratitude" and friendship".

AROUND AMBOISE

CHARGÉ. The MUSÉE DE LA BATAILLE DE LOIRE ET DE LA RÉSISTANCE, opened in 1986, records the events of the Battle of Chargé (June 17–20, 1940).

POCÉ-SUR-CISSE. This town, arranged around the 16th-century Church of St-Adrien (below), has a number of châteaux and manor houses.

LIMERAY. The base of the square bell tower is the oldest section of the Church of St-Saturnin (11th century). Two styles can be seen side by side here: the rounded vaulting of the apse is Romanesque, whereas the vault of the choir is Plantaganet. A curious narthex was recently added to the 16th-century nave – consisting of six marble colonnettes from Amboise and a Romanesque capital from the Abbey of Moncé. A 19th-century abbot virtually turned the church into a museum, collecting fragments of columns, capitals and twenty or so statues from the 15th and 16th centuries. The town's bridge over the Cisse still has its ogival arches dating from the 14th century.

ÇANGEY. The simple gable and the nave of the CHURCH OF ST-MARTIN date from the 11th and 12th centuries. Inside there are historiated capitals, and stained-glass windows made around 1540.

TOURS

10. Basilica of St-Martin
11. Les Halles (market)
12. Chapel of St-Éloi
13. Hôtel de ville
14. Palais de justice
15. Railway station
16. Palais des Congrès
17. Jardin des
Prébendes d'Oé

The town's coat of arms.

HISTORY OF THE TOWN (H6)

GREGORY OF TOURS
Gregory was Bishop of Tours from 573 to 594. He produced his *History of the Frankish Peoples* and *Books of Miracles* with the aim of glorifying Saint Martin; without them two centuries of western history would be virtually unknown today.

TOMB OF THE CHILDREN OF ANNE DE BRETAGNE AND CHARLES VIII
Formerly located in the Collegiate Church of St-Martin, the tomb was transferred to the Cathedral of St-Gatien in 1810. The recumbent figures of the princes Charles and Charles-Orland were carved in the Gothic style in the early 16th century by Guillaume Regnault, a pupil of Michel Colombe. The tomb itself, which is in the Italian Renaissance style, has been attributed to the Italian sculptor Girolamo da Fiesole. Scenes showing Samson and Hercules decorate the base.

BEGINNINGS. In the 1st century AD, the former capital of the Turones stretched over a plateau between the Loire and the Cher; its name at that time was Caesarodunum.

TWO TOWNS. At the end of the 3rd century, threatened by invaders, the town retreated behind a rampart protecting its administrative and economic center, which lay to the east; it was here that Saint Lidoire built the first church in Tours, on the site of today's cathedral. To the west, in the 5th century, Saint Perpet built a basilica over the tomb of Saint Martin ▲ *207*. This is how the town arrived at its double structure, which lasted for the next thousand years. After Viking raids, fortifications were built at the end of the 10th century, encompassing the Basilica of St-Martin and creating the new district of Châteauneuf. In 1368 a rampart was built joining the two sectors, with the Abbey of St-Julien between them.

TOWN OF BISHOPS. The town's bishops dominated its history. Saint Martin (371–97) founded a monastery at Marmoutier, and in medieval times his tomb attracted pilgrims from all over Europe. In the 6th century Gregory of Tours confirmed the town's role as a religious center, and Alcuin made it an intellectual and artistic center in the early 9th century.

CAPITAL OF THE KINGDOM. The French court settled here at the end of the 15th century. Louis XI, who lived at Plessis-lès-Tours, introduced the silk industry to the town ▲ *260*. Large private residences were built, especially in Châteauneuf. In later centuries Tours declined: in 1785 the town had only 21,600 inhabitants. However, tourists were attracted by the climate, the valley and the new railway; the town's economy prospered as a result, and the population almost quadrupled between 1789 and 1911. The congress of the Socialist Party (the SFIO) held in Tours from December 25 to 30, 1920 marked the split between the various Socialist factions that led to the formation of the French Communist Party. Tours suffered bomb damage throughout the summer of 1944. Since the 1960's it has become established as the capital of the region.

CATHÉDRALE ST-GATIEN ● *61*

The Cathedral of St-Gatien stands on the site of the first settlement, Caesarodunum. The Romans built their public buildings on this slight hill: the governor's palace, arenas, baths and temples. In the Merovingian and Carolingian eras this remained the focus of the town's administrative and religious life, while the economic center moved toward Châteauneuf. The cathedral was originally named after Saint Maurice, but since the 14th century it has been named after Saint Gatien, who may have been the first Bishop of Tours. The first building, dating from the 4th century,

was altered in the 12th and 13th centuries. The choir was also rebuilt in the 13th century; the transept in the 14th century; the nave in the 14th and 15th centuries; the façade in the 15th century; and the towers in the 16th century.

THE FAÇADE. On the lower section, ornamentation in the Flamboyant style has been applied over the façade of the 12th-century building. The niches of the portal used to hold statues of saints. These were partially restored in the 19th century. The wooden statue in the pier of the central portal may show Saint Gatien; it is a copy of a 15th-century work.

THE TOWERS. They are crowned with cupolas, probably among the earliest examples from the French Renaissance (along with the dome of the tower at St-Antoine de Loches). The north tower, in the Flamboyant style, has a spiral staircase leading to the huge dome. Henri IV admired this masterpiece of the late Middle Ages: "Its towers are twin jewels set in the Garden of France."

THE NAVE. The nave reaches a height of 95 feet under the arches: its narrow width and the unbroken lines of its columns soaring to the tip of the ogival vaulting make it seem much higher than this.

THE TRANSEPT. The master builder Simon du Mans began rebuilding the transept and the first two bays of the nave in the early 14th century. The north transept is built over a crypt (not open to visitors). Soon after it was completed it had to be strengthened with two flying buttresses and a stone reinforcement for the rose window. The stunning rose window presents a circle within a square with four openwork corners (as compared with only two at Notre-Dame in Paris). The south transept houses the organ, which has 16th-century woodcarvings.

THE CHOIR. The superb Gothic chevet (right) can be admired from Place Grégoire-de-Tours. It has five semicircular chapels fanning out from the choir, with 13th-century stained-glass windows.

THE PSALETTE CLOISTERS. The cloisters consist of three galleries. The gallery to the west and the first bay of the north gallery, in the Flamboyant style, date from the 15th century; the other two galleries were built in the early Renaissance. In the northeast corner is a spiral staircase, a miniature replica of the François I staircase at Blois ▲ *148, 150*.

LA PSALETTE
The second story of the eastern gallery of the cloisters used to house the Chapter Library, which had one of the richest collections in France during the Middle Ages.

FROM THE TOP OF THE CATHEDRAL
On the official guided tours, visitors can climb to the top of the south tower (on the right). Arthur Young did so in the late 18th century, as described in his *Travels in France in 1787, 1788 and 1789*: "From the tower of the cathedral there is an extensive view of the adjacent country; but the Loire, for so considerable a river, and for being boasted as the most beautiful in Europe, exhibits such a breadth of shoals and sands as to be almost subversive of beauty."

1,500 etchings and
engravings, many of
them satirical. His
works provide a
detailed record of
17th-century French
society; furniture,
décor and buildings
are depicted with
minute accuracy.

**FROM VERONA
TO TOURS**
*Christ in the Garden
of Olives* (below) and
The Resurrection by
Andrea Mantegna
(1431–1506) were
originally part of the
altarpiece of San
Zeno in Verona.
Napoleon brought
them back from his
Italian campaigns.

MUSÉE DES BEAUX-ARTS

The museum is housed in the former episcopal palace, built
in the 17th and 18th centuries over the foundations of the
Gallo-Roman rampart. One of the towers
of the rampart can still be seen, well
preserved, beyond the portal (built for
Louis XIV in 1668 and placed here in
1775). The curved terraces follow the
outline of the Gallo-Roman arenas, which
are open to the public on certain evenings
during July. Napoleon spent the night of
August 12–13, 1808 here on his journey
back from Spain. In 1870 the museum,
along with the Préfecture, was the
headquarters of the Défense Nationale
(provisional government), which had taken refuge at Tours.

CHÂTEAU DE TOURS

The powerful medieval fortress built by Philip the Bold at the
end of the 13th century consisted of a quadrilateral keep with
four great corner towers, only two of which survive. The
height of the taller of the two, the TOUR DE GUISE, was
increased in the 15th century; it owes its name to the young
Duc de Guise, who was imprisoned here for three years
after the assassination of his father ▲ *146* and escaped on
August 15, 1591. Between the two towers is the LOGIS DE
MARS, rebuilt in the late 18th century, which houses the
Historial de Touraine (a museum of waxwork tableaux of the
region's history) and a tropical aquarium. The 16th-century
LOGIS DU GOUVERNEUR, built on top of the Gallo-Roman
wall, houses an exhibition tracing the development of Tours
through archeological excavations. The marriages of the
future Charles VII with Marie d'Anjou (1413) and of the
future Louis XII with Margaret of Scotland (1436) were both
celebrated at the château.

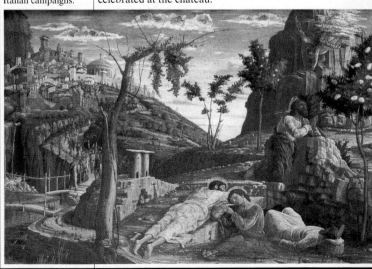

THE FOOTBRIDGE (above). This was built in the 19th century on the site of the first bridge at Tours; locals call it the "Pont de Fil" (string bridge).

CHURCH OF ST-JULIEN

In the 6th century Gregory of Tours founded an abbey to house the relics of Saint Julian of Brioude. This was replaced by a succession of later buildings between the 9th and 11th centuries. In the 13th century a hurricane destroyed part of the church, which was rebuilt in the Gothic style (the belfry porch being all that remains of the Romanesque basilica today). In the 16th century two small chapels were added at the ends of the side aisles of the choir. Behind the organ are fragments of frescos illustrating the story of Moses, taken from an Italian manuscript in the municipal library.
The church is at a lower level than the Rue Nationale, because the quaysides were raised at the end of the 18th century as a protection against flooding.
CLOISTER. The 12th-century chapter house and a monks' dormitory on the second story are the only remnants of the monastery buildings. The cloister was rebuilt in the 16th century and now houses the Musée du Compagnonnage (Guilds Museum). The cellar opposite this, dating from the second half of the 12th century, has been turned into a wine museum. Two wine presses stand in the middle of the cloister: the first dates from the Gallo-Roman era, and the second from the 16th century.
MUSÉE DES VINS DE TOURAINE. The museum, in a large vaulted room, presents items illustrating historical, sociological, oenological and artistic aspects of winegrowing in the Touraine region.
MUSÉE DU COMPAGNONNAGE. This unique museum combines in a single display items relating to the history and work of a variety of craft guilds.

RUE COLBERT

Along with Rue Albert-Thomas, this street formed the original *decumanus* (main east–west axis) of the Roman town. Originally called the Grand-Rue, it still has many half-timbered houses from the 15th and 16th centuries.
MAISON DE LA PUCELLE ARMÉE (no. 39). This 16th-century half-timbered house is said to have been the home of the craftsman Colas de Montbazon, who made Joan of Arc's armor.
PASSAGE DU CŒUR-NAVRÉ (no. 66). Some houses here have collapsed, closing off the top end of this old alleyway opening onto Place Foire-le-Roi. The alley used to have a sign depicting a heart pierced with a sword – *cœur navré* being an old French expression meaning "wounded heart".
PLACE FOIRE-LE-ROI. In 1355 letters of patent from King John the Good established a fair in honor of Saint Christopher on this little square. The taxes levied on the rents and on the goods sold were used in part to provide finance for a new city wall, incorporating Châteauneuf, the old town and the area in between. These letters of patent

CHURCH OF ST-JULIEN
The church was virtually in ruins after being used as a coaching inn during the Revolution. It was saved by Prosper Mérimée (1803–70), author of *Carmen*, who was inspector of historical monuments. Restored by Gustave Guérin, it became a place of worship again in 1859.

MUSÉE DU COMPAGNONNAGE
This presents the history, costumes and skills of the *compagnons* (craft guild members)
▲ *200*, with exhibits including their masterpieces, tools, accessories and other items .

PLACE FOIRE-LE-ROI
Mystery plays, on religious subjects, were performed in the square in the Middle Ages. Legend has it that in the time of François I a pillory stood here and counterfeiters were boiled in a huge pot.

France's craft guilds came into being during the Middle Ages, in the era of the great cathedrals and pilgrimages. The first of these craftsmen's associations, known as *devoirs*, were formed at a time when the traditional corporations had become inflexible and inaccessible. Their journeymen members traveled all over France to perfect their knowledge and skills in their chosen trade; the guilds have survived through the centuries and today continue to train young people by means of the *"tour de France"*.

"CHEF-D'ŒUVRE"
Journeymen made a masterpiece to display the skills they had acquired on the *tour*. Even today a *chef-d'œuvre* must be produced to obtain the title "Compagnon du Tour de France". The finished piece is presented before the *compagnons* and appraised. Right: masterpiece known in Tours as "La Clef des Cœurs" (Key of Hearts), produced by master wheelwright Philippe Leroux in 1887.

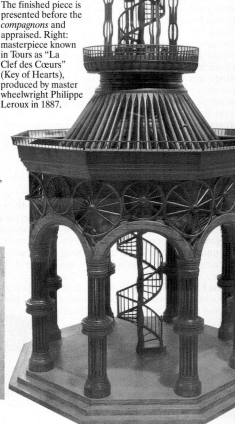

INSIGNIA
At the end of the tour, on the day of their initiation, the *compagnons* received the colors of their corporation and a staff with a metal pommel, decorated with two tassels.

A master blacksmith of the 19th century, dressed in full regalia.

Colors of a *gavot* (highland official), presented in 1859 to Auguste Gouttes, master cabinetmaker of the Devoir de Liberté.

LEGENDS

Legend has it that the origins of the guilds date back to the building of the Temple in Jerusalem (around 965 BC). King Solomon and two of his architects, "Master Jacques" and "Father Soubise", are regarded as the three mythical founders (below) of the "Ordre des Compagnons".

"COMPAGNONNAGE" AT TOURS

In the old days, the *tour de France* was accomplished on foot. When a journeyman left one town to head for the next, his fellow craftsmen organized a special ceremony called the *conduite*: they accompanied the departing apprentice as far as the town gates, where songs, toasts and rituals were performed in his honor.

THE JOURNEYMEN'S "MOTHERS"

The *mères* or "mothers" play a key role in the organization of the guilds. In the past they were innkeepers; nowadays they manage the *cayennes*, or lodges, which house the young apprentices on their *tour de France*. The "mothers" are entitled to wear the colors of the guild. Right: the "mother" of the master cabinetmakers and locksmiths of the Devoir de Liberté.

POMMEL OF THE STAFF
This was as good as a passport, bearing the name of the *compagnon* and his guild, along with the date and place of his admission to membership.

were renewed by Louis XI and then by François I in 1547. This is how the square became known as the "square of the King's fair", although it was used for other markets and fairs, too. The Hôtel Babou de la Bourdaisière (no. 8) was the home of Philibert Babou de la Bourdaisière, a financier who became François I's treasurer in 1520. The entrance portal has magnificent carved doors (left), renovated in the Renaissance style under Louis XIV, and wrought-iron balconies from the 18th century.

Passage des Jacobins. The lovely 16th-century house at no. 12 is known as the Maison de Ronsard because the staircase turret in the courtyard bears a coat of arms similar to that of the poet Pierre de Ronsard (1524–85). The windows are decorated with pilasters.

Rue de la Scellerie

Printers and booksellers set up business here during the Renaissance; today this quarter still has a number of bookstores, along with most of the town's antique stores.

The theater ● 89. The theater (no. 34) was built on the site of the former Cordelier monastery, one of whose doors can still be seen on Rue Voltaire. The monastery was sold as a "national property" under the Revolution, and its chapel was converted into a theater in 1796. The first municipal theater was built here in 1875. All but the façade was destroyed by fire on August 15, 1883; the theater reopened in 1890.

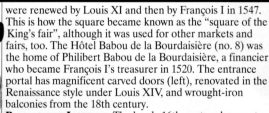

"Le Molière". The café next door to the theater has ceilings decorated with oil paintings by Grandin, dating from 1882. One of the paintings shows Molière crowned with laurels and surrounded by cherubs.

Rue du Cygne. In the Middle Ages the prison stood on this street, which owes its name to a sign showing a white swan surmounted by a cross. This sign exhorted passers-by to make the sign of the cross, to ward off the ill fortune that might one day make them inmates of the prison.

Rue Jules-Favre

Hôtel du Commerce
A paragon of 18th-century architecture (right), it was built for the merchants of Tours. Construction began in 1757. At the far end of the courtyard is a double-flighted staircase with wrought-iron banisters. In the right wing on the ground floor is the old cloth market, with two vaulted halls.

Hôtel de Beaune-Semblançay. Opposite the Hôtel du Commerce is a small garden with the remains of a Renaissance house built by Jacques de Beaune, Baron de Semblançay, finance minister to Louis XII and François I. Most of the house was destroyed in June 1940, but part of the façade survives – with finely carved capitals, and pilasters decorated with diamond motifs and slate (in imitation of marble) – and a gallery with a chapel above.

RUE NATIONALE

This street, which was originally called Rue Royale, is the main north–south axis of the town center; it is nearly half a mile long. It was created in 1765 as part of a project to enlarge the town; Tours, like Orléans and Blois, had grown up along the river and could not expand further in an east–west direction. This change of axis was vital, even though it cut into the fabric of the medieval town.

PLACE ANATOLE-FRANCE

Anatole France lived at St-Cyr-sur-Loire, to the north of Tours. Statues of Rabelais and Descartes (both local figures) stand on the square, on either side of the Rue Nationale.

BIBILIOTHÈQUE MUNICIPALE. The municipal library was built in 1954–7 by Pierre Patout and Jean and Charles Dorian. A matching building was originally planned for the other side of the bridge. The copper-roofed library houses a fine collection of old books.

PONT WILSON

Known locally as the "Pont de Pierre" (stone bridge), the Pont Wilson is 1,400 feet long and 48 feet wide; it is supported by fifteen basket-handle arches, each spanning 82 feet. Its construction was supervised by Mathieu Bayeux (the General Inspector of Bridges and Roads) from 1764 to 1774, then completed by Jean de Voglie, the architect of the bridge at Saumur. Built on piles, because there is no hard rock on the bed of the Loire at this point, it has collapsed several times: in 1789, 1940 and 1978. In 1983 the second arch, which had not been reinforced in the 19th century, was replaced with an identical structure made of concrete faced with stone. While this project was under way, workers discovered an unexploded 1,000-pound bomb from World War Two.

Rue Nationale early this century.

Fountain built by the United States to commemorate the American presence in Tours during World War One.

AN ILL-FATED BRIDGE
The bridge had barely been completed, in 1789, when four of its arches collapsed. On June 18, 1940 engineers from the French army blew up one of the arches as they retreated. The blast sent stones and pieces of cast iron flying into the town, causing damage to roofs and windows (notably those of the Church of St-Julien); one 400-pound block reached as far as Rue Corneille. Finally, the second arch of the bridge collapsed on April 9, 1978, at around 9pm.

THE ORIGINAL BASILICA OF ST-MARTIN

From the 5th century onward pilgrims came from all over Gaul to pray at the tomb of Saint Martin ▲ *207*. The Basilica of St-Martin (above) remained the religious center of France until the end of the Middle Ages. The sanctuary was sacked by the Normans and destroyed several times by fire. Rebuilt in 997, the Romanesque basilica was 360 feet long, with five naves. The vaults were rebuilt in the 12th century, and in the 13th century the choir was rebuilt on the model of Bourges Cathedral. Louis XI had a silver grille built around the shrine of Saint Martin in 1479. During the Revolution the basilica was used as stabling. In 1802, by then in a state of ruin, the basilica was razed to make way for the Rue des Halles. The only sections still standing are the Tour Charlemagne (the tower of the north transept) and the Tour de l'Horloge (the southern tower of the west façade). The best place to stand to imagine the scale of the original building is on Rue des Halles, in front of the Tour Charlemagne.

TOUR CHARLEMAGNE. The tower derives its name from the fact that it was built over the tomb of Luitgarde, the third wife of Charlemagne, who died at Tours in 800. Only the north façade, facing Place de Châteauneuf, remains intact. The south façade was rebuilt after it collapsed in 1928; it was restored in 1963 and now features a bas-relief depicting Saint Martin sharing his cloak. This tower was built over the remains of the 11th-century Romanesque basilica: a capital from this early church, depicting Daniel in the lion's den, can still be seen (from Rue des Halles). In the 19th century a foundry for lead shot was installed here; later the building was converted into a water tower, ruining the first story vaulting.

The Tour Charlemagne, seen from the south side; and the Tour de l'Horloge (clock tower), whose structure and decorations reflect the dominance of Gothic style in the late 12th century.

Nineteenth-century lithograph of the Tour Charlemagne.

The original Basilica of St-Martin (left), just before it was destroyed.

ALCUIN (C.737–804)
The famous English writer and scholar was appointed Abbot of St-Martin by Charlemagne in the 8th century. Alcuin, who had been attached to Charlemagne's court, established a monastic school here, teaching literature, philosophy and

TOUR DE L'HORLOGE. The clock tower dates from the late 12th century. The clock is wound every fortnight: a hazardous undertaking, as the tower has been more or less taken over by pigeons!

THE NEW BASILICA OF ST-MARTIN

Saint Martin's tomb was discovered in 1860, bringing about a revival in the saint's cult and provoking a fierce debate between the Catholic church (which wanted the basilica rebuilt on the original plan) and the civic authorities (who did not want to see this quarter completely disrupted). A compromise solution was found, in the shape of a small basilica, built on a north–south axis, with its sanctuary over the saint's tomb. The Tours architect Victor Laloux ▲ *214* was appointed for the project. The new basilica was built between 1886 and 1902. From the outside the building has a rather inelegant, stacked-up appearance. The interior, by contrast, seems surprisingly spacious, an effect created by the basilical ground plan: three naves separated by monolithic columns of Vosges granite, ending in semicircular apses. The capitals are in the Byzantine style and the naves are roofed with beams. The crypt with the tomb of Saint Martin is beneath the choir, a huge space divided into five bays separated by pink-granite columns. A statue of Cardinal Meignan, sculpted by François Sicard in 1900, stands between two flights of stairs. The walls of the apse are covered with *ex votos*, some brought by famous figures who came here to pray to Saint Martin, among them Maréchal Foch and the future Pope John XXIII. The square in front of the church was designed by Maurice Boille following preliminary plans by Victor Laloux. The calvary depicting Saint Martin, Saint Perpet and Saint Gregory was produced by Henri Varenne.

CLOISTER OF ST-MARTIN. Built by Bastien François in the early 16th century, the cloister now stands in the courtyard of a private building (no. 5, Rue Descartes). It is a fine, though incomplete, example of Tours' early-Renaissance architecture.

MUSÉE ST-MARTIN. This museum is in the Chapel of St-Jean (at no. 3, rue Rapin). Built in the 13th century, the chapel housed the relics of Saint Martin on several occasions, and the canons barricaded themselves here when the basilica was sacked by Protestants in 1552. It has some original stained-glass windows in the chevet, which were altered by Lobin in 1888. The museum displays some remains of the old basilica, as well as a striking model of the building.

theology; the school had a famous *scriptorium*. It is generally regarded as the first school to have been founded in France, and has been described as "the mother of the University of Paris".

CLOISTER OF ST-MARTIN: OUTSTANDING ORNAMENTATION
Its pendentive vaulting is an entirely original creation: the ribs are crossed to form square caissons in an entirely new type of design. The exceptional quality of the carving makes this an architectural masterpiece.

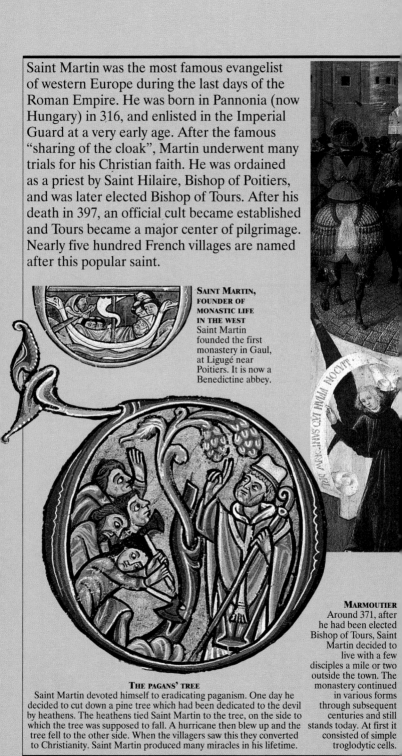

▲ SAINT MARTIN

Saint Martin was the most famous evangelist of western Europe during the last days of the Roman Empire. He was born in Pannonia (now Hungary) in 316, and enlisted in the Imperial Guard at a very early age. After the famous "sharing of the cloak", Martin underwent many trials for his Christian faith. He was ordained as a priest by Saint Hilaire, Bishop of Poitiers, and was later elected Bishop of Tours. After his death in 397, an official cult became established and Tours became a major center of pilgrimage. Nearly five hundred French villages are named after this popular saint.

SAINT MARTIN, FOUNDER OF MONASTIC LIFE IN THE WEST
Saint Martin founded the first monastery in Gaul, at Ligugé near Poitiers. It is now a Benedictine abbey.

MARMOUTIER
Around 371, after he had been elected Bishop of Tours, Saint Martin decided to live with a few disciples a mile or two outside the town. The monastery continued in various forms through subsequent centuries and still stands today. At first it consisted of simple troglodytic cells.

THE PAGANS' TREE
Saint Martin devoted himself to eradicating paganism. One day he decided to cut down a pine tree which had been dedicated to the devil by heathens. The heathens tied Saint Martin to the tree, on the side to which the tree was supposed to fall. A hurricane then blew up and the tree fell to the other side. When the villagers saw this they converted to Christianity. Saint Martin produced many miracles in his lifetime.

"AINT MARTIN'S SUMMER"
en Martin died, in
ember, all the plants
trees on the banks of
Loire burst into flower.
saint's day is celebrated
November 11.

DIVISION OF THE CLOAK

While he was quartered at Amiens with the emperor, Martin tore his cloak in two and gave half to a beggar. The next night Christ appeared to him in a vision, wearing the half he had given away. As a result, Martin was baptized and began his long mission as an evangelist.

The Tours painter André Bauchant depicted Saint Martin preaching in the forests of Touraine (below).

THE LAST BASILICA

Initially a chapel was built over Saint Martin's tomb, in Tours. This was followed by a collegiate church, which was modified repeatedly over the centuries. The present-day basilica ▲ 205 was built at the end of the 19th century by Victor Laloux.

A RENAISSANCE HOUSE
A RENAISSANCE HOUSE
The three forebuildings of the Hôtel Gouin (right, and detail below) were added to a 15th-century façade and richly decorated in Italian Renaissance style, with fluted pilasters, ovum friezes and large foliage scrolls. Most of the house was destroyed by fire in June 1940: only the main façade was saved. The sections that were lost have been rebuilt in their original early-Renaissance style.

PLACE PLUMEREAU

This is the most picturesque and lively part of Tours, the old *carroi aux chapeaux* (hat market). Until the 19th century part of the square was covered over with buildings, including the residence of Charles Plumereau, town councillor of Tours. It is bordered by half-timbered houses from the 15th and 16th centuries ● *73*.

AROUND PLACE PLUMEREAU

HÔTEL GOUIN. This 15th-century house (no. 25, rue du Commerce) was modified in the early 16th century, with additions in early-Renaissance style. It is the oldest Renaissance building in Tours, and the most original. The house's name refers to the Gouin family, a wealthy family of bankers from Brittany who acquired it in the 18th century. It now houses the ARCHEOLOGICAL MUSEUM.

"One might also spend some very pleasant hours with the gabled houses on Place Plumereau; every one of these good old houses has a tale to tell. If you could worm their secrets out of them, you would find out some pretty things about the ladies who lived here at the time of Rabelais.**"**
Maurice Bedel,
La Touraine

RUE CONSTANTINE. This street marks the border of the area destroyed in the war. On one side is the medieval quarter, while the buildings on the other side date from the 1950's. This street was the home of the silk workers ▲ *260* brought to Tours by Louis XI in 1470. The house on the corner of Rue de Maillé is thought to have been Balzac's model for the silk dyer's home in his *Contes drolatiques*.

RUE P. L. COURIER

RUE PAUL-LOUIS-COURIER. At no. 5, in an 18th-century residence, is the CAYENNE DES COMPAGNONS DU DEVOIR (lodge for journeymen ▲ *200*). The wooden dormer window

in the courtyard is a masterpiece produced by a carpenter for admission to the guild. At no. 10 is HÔTEL BINET, which was built in the 15th century; at no. 15 is HÔTEL ROBIN-QUANTIN (private), built for the wealthy silk merchant Charles Robin and his wife Marie Quantin in 1590. The HÔTEL DE JUSTE (no. 17) is said to have belonged to the family of the Italian sculptors Antonio and Giovanni Giusti, who created the famous tomb of Louis XII in the Basilica of St-Denis, on the outskirts of Paris.

RUE LITTRÉ. The Church of St-Saturnin, built in the 15th century, was once the chapel of a Carmelite convent; it was sold off as "national property" under the Revolution. The family who repurchased the church renamed it St-Saturnin – after another church, in Rue du Commerce, which had been destroyed during the Revolution.

PLACE HENRI-DE-SEGOGNE. During restoration work on the old town some of the houses were demolished to bring light and air into the close-knit web of medieval streets. However, a number of chimneys were preserved, so the past would not be forgotten: they can be seen beside the façades of the houses left standing. Small squares have been created on the spaces that were cleared.

RUE DE LA PAIX. This was formerly the Rue de l'Écorcherie, named after the abattoir that stood at the far end. The house at no. 21, with half-timbering at street level, was a canon's house in the 15th century. Near the door is a well: those who used it had to pay a fee to the owner. The door leads to the courtyard called the Jardin des Chanoines (Canons' Garden).

JARDIN DE ST-PIERRE-LE-PUELLIER. This garden is reached through the Jardin des Chanoines (see above) or from no. 17, Place Plumereau. It stands on the site of a convent founded by Saint Clotilda, wife of Clovis, in 512. The Church of St-Pierre-le-Puellier was built in the 12th century, extended in the 15th century, and partially destroyed in the 19th century. Today there is a café in the main section that survived, and the upper story has been turned into a private apartment.

RUE BRIÇONNET. Jean Briçonnet was the first Mayor of Tours, at the end of the 15th century. The MAISON DE TRISTAN (or Hôtel Pierre du Puy ● 74) at no. 16 was built for Tristan l'Hermite, Great Chamberlain of Louis XI, but by 1495 it belonged to Pierre du Puy, a wealthy citizen of Tours. This house and the Château du Plessis-lès-Tours ▲ 259 are the only brick-and-stone buildings in Tours. Opposite (at no. 21) is the HÔTEL CHOISEUL: this building is sometimes attributed to the Duc de Choiseul ▲ 190, who was exiled to the region in the 18th century, but in fact he only rented it. The house at no. 31 is one of the oldest in Tours: its façade dates from the 13th century. The sculpture studio at no. 4 occupies another part of St-Pierre-le-Puellier that escaped destruction: a bay of a side aisle.

STAIRCASE OF THE MAISON DE TRISTAN
Inside the house visitors can admire the magnificent spiral staircase with brickwork vaulting. It is sometimes called the "Escalier à la Rihour", because there is a similar but older staircase in the Palais de Rihour in Lille; it is also known as the "Vis de St-Gilles" (spiral staircase of St-Gilles).

Garden of St-Pierre-le-Puellier; Maison de Tristan (above).

▲ HOUSES ON PLACE PLUMEREAU

Detail of the house at no. 12.

NOS. 11 AND 12. The house at no. 12 is covered with slate. Its woodcarvings convey the vitality of the town in the Middle Ages: they depict pilgrims in their robes, clutching sticks and purses, kings and queens coming to pray at the tomb of Saint Martin ▲ *207*, and royal moneychangers.

HISTORICAL CENTER

This quarter was spared destruction during the bombardments of World War Two. The buildings, which had become very dilapidated, were restored under a program initiated in 1966. To inject new life into the quarter, the university's new Faculty of Literature was built nearby; the streets were made into a pedestrian zone, and the square (once a parking lot) has become a popular meeting place bordered with cafés and restaurants.

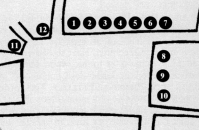

Details of a wrought-iron balcony at no. 10 (right) and of a half-timbered façade (left).

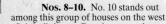

Nos. 8–10. No. 10 stands out among this group of houses on the west side of the square. It is built in neo-Renaissance style and bears the date 1845 on the third story (above the right-hand capital); it also has lovely wrought-iron balconies.

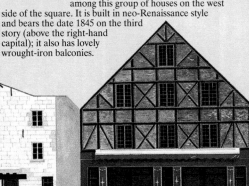

At no. 9 is the Café du Vieux Mûrier, a typically atmospheric café of the old town. Opposite the café stands a mulberry tree: a reminder that for many years Tours derived its prosperity from the silk industry ▲ *260*.

Nos. 1–7. These houses from the 15th and 16th centuries (no. 2 has an 18th-century stone façade) were built on narrow, deep plots of land. The ground floors were built of stone and housed shops; at the rear a spiral staircase in a tower served the upper stories.

Details of the house at no. 11.

Place du Grand-Marché.

"GEMMAIL"
This is a very thick type of stained glass, usually made in a contemporary design. The *gemmiste* arranges thick fragments of colored glass in layers; the completed work is fired in a kiln. The finished *gemmail* is illuminated from behind to display its full range of colors. The first *gemmiste* in Tours was Roger Malherbe-Navarre, who came here in the 1960's.

RUE DU POIRIER.
The house at no. 2, on the corner of Rue Briçonnet, is said to be the oldest building in Tours. The façade, which dates from the 12th century, has been restored with exceptional care.

RUE DU MÛRIER. At no. 7 is the Hôtel Étienne Raimbault, built in 1825 over the remains of houses from the 12th and 15th centuries. In this building is the MUSÉE DU GEMMAIL (see left), a unique museum with a workshop for demonstrations.

RUE DES CERISIERS. The name of this street refers to the Serisiers, a family of silk manufacturers who lived here in the 18th century. At no. 7 is a small 15th-century house: in the 19th century it was a boarding house for young ladies, described by Balzac in the opening pages of *Père Goriot*.

RUE DES ORFÈVRES. At no. 4 is a house built around 1696 by Pierre Taffu, councillor of Louis XIV. On the upper story the windows are decorated with red-colored heads. A little further on is the Rue du Petit-Soleil, named after an inn that once stood here.

RUE DU PRÉSIDENT-MERVILLE. The street marks the western border of the area destroyed during World War Two. The town hall and law courts stood here in the 15th century. No. 3 now houses the Musée d'Histoire Naturelle.

RUE DU CHANGE. The name refers to the fact that in the 6th century Clovis granted the monks of St-Martin the right to mint coins, and this street was the traditional haunt of moneychangers. The façade of the former Church of St-Denis can be seen at the far end of the alley, between nos. 14 and 16. The house with a corbeled turret (at no. 11, on the corner of Rue de Châteauneuf) once belonged to Jean Briçonnet ▲ *209*.

PLACE DE CHÂTEAUNEUF. This was once the vegetable market. At no. 15 stands Hôtel de la Croix Blanche, also

known as Hôtel des Ducs de Touraine, dating from the 15th century. In its courtyard (once the parish cemetery) is the Church of St-Denis, whose main entrance is on Rue du Change (it is not open to visitors).

Rue de Châteauneuf. The former Church of Ste-Croix stands behind no. 17 (near Hôtel Briçonnet, which has a 19th-century neo-Renaissance façade) and no. 19. The remains of the church can be seen from the square on Rue Royer. The nearby Rue du Panier-Fleuri was called Rue de la Pisserie in the Middle Ages, when it was a haunt of prostitutes.

Rue de la Rôtisserie. This street follows the northern outline of the Châteauneuf rampart. The 15th-century Maison de l'Architecte (no. 3) has a mask with a bow tie, symbolizing architecture, added by Albert Archambault in 1972. To the right of no. 3(b) is a magnificent wooden staircase with balustrades dating from the 16th century, which has been moved for restoration work. A vine was planted here some years back; the harvest is celebrated by the "Entonneurs Rabelaisiens" and the grapes are made into jam.

Place du Grand-Marché. This was once the herb market, and also the site of a pillory. Lovely half-timbered houses stand on the west side of the square. On the east side, between nos. 54 and 56, is the Hôtel du Trésor de St-Martin, which has a large 15th-century portal.

Rue Bretonneau. This street was formerly called Rue de la Boule-Peinte: it was once inhabited by craftsmen belonging to the varnishers' and furniture polishers' guilds.

Rue de la Serpe. The house standing at no. 3 is said to have belonged to Jean Bourdichon, a 15th-century painter and illuminator who worked for Louis XI, Charles XII and François I. Between the ground floor and the upper stories are moldings supported by culs-de-lampe and carved figures.

Rue de la Grosse-Tour. A number of masterpieces are on display in the window of the guild of architectural craftsmen, at no. 22.

Rue du Petit-St-Martin. The Chapel of Petit-St-Martin is at no. 22. It was built in the 14th century, supposedly to replace an oratory that marked the place where Saint Martin's body rested after it had been brought by boat from Candes ▲ 270. Today the chapel houses a school for sculpture restoration and is not open to visitors.

The Garlic and Basil Fair
On the feast-day of Saint Anne, when this fair is held, the Place de Châteauneuf is as lively as it ever was; the fair spills over into the surrounding streets.

The "livre tournois"
Coins were minted in Tours from 1493 to 1772. However, the Tours *livre* was not a coin but a counting unit used by traders: it was divided into twelve *sous*, and each sou comprised twelve *deniers*. Due to an edict in 1667, the Tours *livre* was the last unit of currency in France before the present system was introduced.

213

PLACE JEAN-JAURES

In the 18th century this square was known as Place des Portes-de-Fer, because it was enclosed by iron railings with three gates. At that time it was the southernmost entrance into the town.

PALAIS DE JUSTICE. Built in 1840–3, the grand Doric colonnade of the law courts exhibits the classical style in favor at the time.

HÔTEL DE VILLE. The town hall was designed by Victor Laloux (left) and opened in 1904. The balcony is supported by four atlantes created by the sculptor François Sicard (1862–1934). The river gods on either side of the clock are by Antoine Injalbert (1845–1933). The sculptures on the pediments represent Strength and Courage, on the left, matched by Education and Vigilance on the right. The façade, like the staircase inside and the decoration of the building, was designed to glorify the Republic.

BRASSERIE DE L'UNIVERS. This brasserie has a colorful 19th-century glass partition showing festive scenes.

VICTOR LALOUX (1850–1937) Among the many buildings designed by this Tours architect were the town hall, the new Basilica of St-Martin and the railway station in Tours; the Gare d'Orsay in Paris; and the town hall in Lille.

AROUND BOULEVARD HEURTELOUP

The boulevards were created from 1843 onward. Originally lined with elms, today they contain plane trees and maples.

THE RAILWAY STATION. The station was built in 1894–8, following designs by Bonnaudet for the building and Victor Laloux for the façade. The two stone wings support its huge metal framework.

PALAIS DES CONGRÈS LÉONARD-DE-VINCI (above, right). This modern building near the station was created by Jean Nouvel, the architect of the Institut du Monde Arabe and the Fondation Cartier in Paris and the Opéra in Lyon.

HÔTEL MAME. This house (nos. 17–19, rue Émile-Zola) is also known as Hôtel Lefebvre de Montifray ● 75, after the 18th-century Tours merchant who built it. The Mame family ▲ 215 lived here for many years. Its façade and rich 18th-century ornamentation can be seen from the street.

AROUND BOULEVARD BÉRANGER

This boulevard was the favorite place for a stroll in the 19th century.

PRIORY OF ST-ÉLOI. The priory (at the western end of the boulevard) now houses the municipal archives. Founded in

FLOWER MARKET The flower market on Boulevard Béranger, which is held on Wednesdays and Saturdays, presents a magnificent display of colors and heady perfumes. It is the second-largest flower market in France, after the one held in Nice.

the 10th century as the Priory of L'Orme-Robert, it was
rededicated to Saint Éloi (councillor and
treasurer of the Merovingian king Dagobert)
in the 12th century. Legend has it that Éloi
himself made the shrine of Saint Martin here.
CITÉ ALFRED-MAME. This workers' estate was
created by Alfred Mame, in the second half of
the 19th century. It is arranged around a
square. The corners and window frames are
made of brick and stone (right). Each of the
blocks has a central forebuilding.

PARKS AND GARDENS

Two hundred gardeners are employed to maintain the
town's 800 acres of parkland, including the banks of the
Cher. The largest parks are the Jardin Botanique and the
Jardin des Prébendes d'Oé.
JARDIN DES PRÉBENDES D'OÉ. The Prébendes quarter
was originally a marsh. In the Middle Ages this was the
market-gardening district: the gardeners had to pay
their *prébendes* (tithes) to the Provost of Oé, a canon of
St-Martin. This superb landscaped park, covering 10 acres,
was designed by the Buhler brothers in 1872 (they also
designed the Parc du Thabor in Rennes, and the Parc de la
Tête d'Or in Lyon).
JARDIN BOTANIQUE. The botanical gardens opened in
1843. The main entrance is on Boulevard Tonnelé.
Jean-Anthyme Margueron started the gardens in
1838 on a 12-acre site, on what was once the bed of the
Ruau Ste-Anne (a canal created by Louis XI and named
after his daughter Anne de Beaujeu). Part of the park is
reserved for the study of plants by pharmacology
students. An arboretum
contains about two
hundred trees, including
a pyramidal hornbeam
nearly 150 years old. A wide
avenue divides the gardens;
on one side are heathers
and rock plants, on the
other a garden showing the
development of the various
plant families. The avenue
leads to a hothouse and
an orangery.

**ARBORETUM OF
THE JARDIN
BOTANIQUE**
This section
of the park
includes a
miniature zoo
that contains deer,
sheep, pigs, an
aviary, chickens,
turtles, kangaroos,
and even some bears.

▲ TOURS TO VALENÇAY
VIA CHENONCEAU

1. TOURS 2. CORMERY 3. THE LOIRE 4. CHANTELOUP PAGODA 5. AMBOISE 6. CHENONCEAU 7. LOCHES 8. BEAULIEU-LES-LOCHES 9. CHAPEL OF ST-JEAN-DU-LIG...

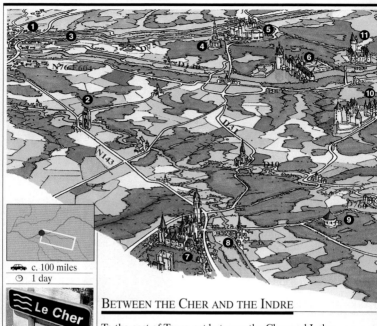

🚗 c. 100 miles
🕐 1 day

Le Cher

"The Cher – indolent, even lazy – ran in a leisurely manner along its spacious river bed, among meadows bordered with acacias, willows and poplars. It passed from the sand of the Sologne to the clay of Valençay, and on to the limestone near Montrichard, getting ready to don its courtly splendor when it reached Chenonceaux."
Robert Sabatier

CHÂTEAU DE MONTPOUPON
A fortress occupied this site from the 13th century onward, guarding the road to Aquitaine. After the Hundred Years' War the quadrangular stronghold was converted into a residential palace in early-Renaissance style ● *68*. Today the château houses a museum of hunting.

BETWEEN THE CHER AND THE INDRE

To the east of Tours, set between the Cher and Indre rivers, is an undulating landscape scattered with woods. In the past this area was split between the provinces of Touraine and Berry; today it is divided between the départements of Indre-et-Loire and Indre. In geological terms it forms a single unit characterized by areas known locally as *gâtines*, which have clay soils that are relatively infertile. In terms of history and architecture the area is an integral part of the Loire valley.

"GÂTINES", WOODS AND FORESTS. Because this is poor farmland, much of it is covered with forest: the tip of the Forest of Amboise at Chenonceaux; the vast Forest of Loches, which begins right outside the walls of the old town; the Brouard Forest overlooking Montrésor ▲ *231*; the Bois du Biard around Montpoupon (below); the Bois de Luçay near Nouans-les-Fontaine ▲ *231*; and finally the *gâtine* forest around Valençay ▲ *232*, which completes the unbroken chain of woodland stretching from the Champeigne of Touraine to the Champeigne of Berry.

DEFENSE. Over the centuries paths and clearings were created in the forests, marshes drained, and towns and fortresses built. The medieval towns of Loches ▲ *224* and Montrésor ▲ *231*, the Château de Montpoupon and the impressive ruins of the impregnable keep at Montrichard bear witness to the days when defense was the priority.

PRAYER. To thank God for his protection man erected buildings to his glory such as the Chartreuse du Liget ▲ *230* and the Collegiate Church of St-Aignan ● *59*: the latter a

Collegiate church and château, St-Aignan.

beautiful Romanesque church with a crypt containing fine mural paintings (detail below) dating from the 12th, 14th and 15th centuries. The town of St-Aignan (above) is best seen from the Chaussée des Ponts: the white silhouette of the collegiate church and the imposing mass of the Renaissance château stand out on the left bank of the Cher; houses huddle around them, covering the slope down to the green river banks.

PLEASURE. In later, more peaceful, times architecture could reflect the pursuit of pleasure and beauty, as exemplified by the châteaux of Valençay and Chenonceaux. The latter inspired Alfred McMahon to write in his *Chronicles of Touraine*: "Like a classical nymph, Chenonceau dips its bare feet into the clear waters of the Cher, turning its dreamy face to the sunset . . ."

PARC DE BEAUVAL (1 mile south of St-Aignan). This ornithological and zoological park was founded at Beauval in 1981. It covers over 20 acres and has some 2,000 birds, as well as monkeys and other species. However, the stars of the zoo are the bears from Jean-Jacques Annaud's movie *The Bear*, and the only pair of white tigers in France.

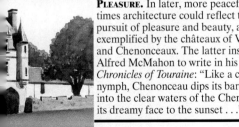

217

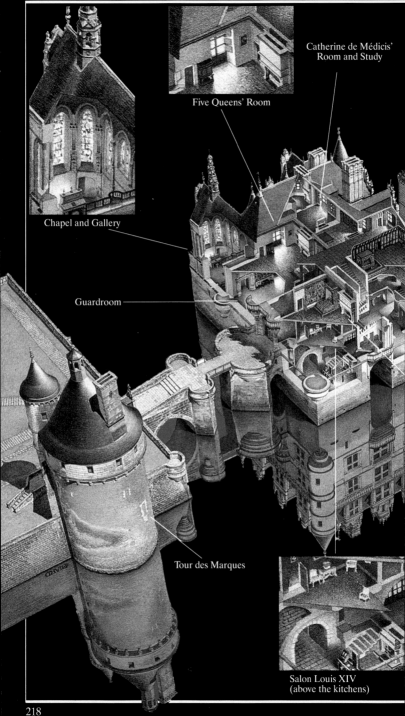

Catherine de Médicis'
Room and Study

Five Queens' Room

Chapel and Gallery

Guardroom

Tour des Marques

Salon Louis XIV
(above the kitchens)

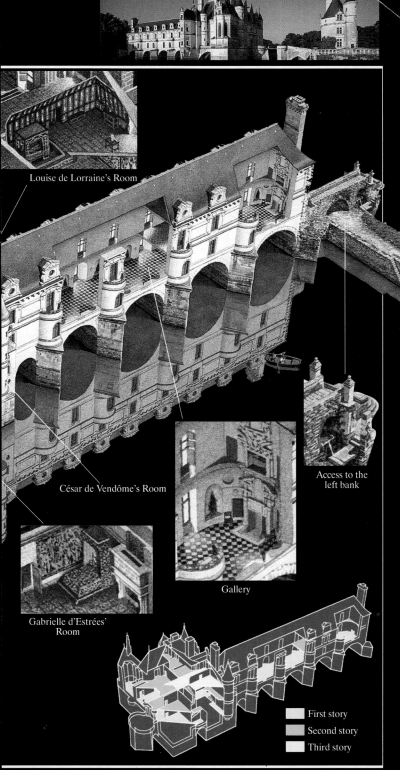

Louise de Lorraine's Room

César de Vendôme's Room

Access to the
left bank

Gabrielle d'Estrées'
Room

Gallery

First story

Second story

Third story

"DIANA'S BATH"
This oil painting on wood (above) by François Clouet (c. 1510–72) celebrates the triumph of the new Diana: Mary Stuart, later Mary Queen of Scots.
Her first husband, François II, is often identified as the horseman in the picture, while the seated woman is said to be Catherine de Médicis.

THE SIX CHATELAINES OF CHENONCEAU
Chenonceau was largely created by women: in this it is unique among the châteaux of France. The six women who supervised the construction, conservation and renovation of this masterpiece of Renaissance architecture were: Katherine Briçonnet from 1513 to 1526, Diane de Poitiers from 1547 to 1559, Catherine de Médicis from 1559 to 1589, Louise de Lorraine from 1589 to 1600, Madame Dupin from 1733 to 1799, and Madame Pelouze from 1863 to 1875. The four shown here are Diane de Poitiers (on the left), Louise de Lorraine (top), Catherine de Médicis (bottom), and Madame Dupin (on the right).

HISTORY OF CHENONCEAU (K7)

This elegant palace bridging the Cher is delightful in every respect. Its exceptionally beautiful setting, its original design and its sumptuous ornamentation make Chenonceau one of the jewels of French Renaissance architecture.

PAYING OFF DEBTS. Around 1230 Chenonceau was just a modest manor house belonging to the Marques family. Subsequently it was demolished (in 1411) and rebuilt by Jean Marques in 1432. A huge burden of debt forced his son Pierre to sell the château to Thomas Bohier, a tax collector who came originally from Tours. Bohier took possession of Chenonceau on February 8, 1513; of the earlier castle he retained only the keep, known as the Tour des Marques, and the foundations of a mill which were used as the basis for his new palace on the Cher. Building work started in 1515. When Bohier departed to fight for François I in Northern Italy, he left his wife Katherine Briçonnet to supervise the work at Chenonceau. Later their son, like Pierre Marques, was forced to give up the château: he handed it over to the crown to pay off debts to the treasury and avoid the fate suffered by Jacques de Beaune-Semblançay ▲ 202.

DIANE'S HOME. The Connétable de Montmorency took possession of the château in the king's name in 1535. By this stage Chenonceau was already sufficiently splendid to be shown to Charles V during his visit to France in 1539 ▲ 162. When Henri II came to the throne in 1547, he gave the château to his mistress Diane de Poitiers. Diane, who was very fond of Chenonceau, decided to build a bridge joining the Bohier castle to the other bank of the Cher. Philibert de l'Orme was entrusted with the commission in 1556 and supervised the work for the next three years.

CATHERINE'S FESTIVITIES. After the death of Henri II in 1559 his mistress fell from favor and Chenonceau passed into the hands of Catherine de Médicis. Catherine's son, the new king François II, was very young; courtly intrigues were rife, and

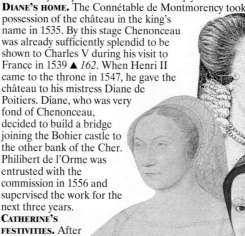

View of the château before the gardens and the terrace of the Tour des Marques were modified.

the first conflicts between Catholics and Protestants had begun. Catherine responded by making Chenonceau a palace of pleasure and intrigue. She held splendid festivities here, known as the "Triomphes de Chenonceau"; and her flying squad of young ladies-in-waiting, drawn from the leading families of the aristocracy, was empowered to seduce and spy on the most powerful lords of the kingdom. Among all these intrigues Catherine did not forget Chenonceau itself. She had a two-story gallery built over Diane's bridge (1570–6); altered the north façade of the main building; and added a small building to the east between the chapel and the library, as well as outbuildings in the courtyard (1580–5). She also planned a new wing at the far end of the gallery, on the right bank of the Cher: however, this was never built.

THE WHITE QUEEN. In 1589, shortly before her death, Catherine de Médicis bequeathed Chenonceau to Louise de Lorraine, the wife of Henri III. A few months after Henri's assassination Louise retired to the château: here she led the life of a recluse, dressed always in white, the royal color of mourning. Chenonceau stood empty for a century after her death.

AGE OF PHILOSOPHERS. In 1730 the tax collector Claude Dupin acquired Chenonceau and restored it to its former splendor. His wife, the natural daughter of Samuel Bernard (a wealthy Protestant financier under Louis XIV), organized grand receptions here, inviting the famous philosophers and intellectuals of the age: Rousseau, Voltaire, Fontenelle, Buffon, Condillac, Montesquieu and Madame du Deffand. The château escaped destruction under the Revolution because it was the only bridge over the Cher between Montrichard ▲ *217* and Bléré.

RENOVATION. Madame Dupin died at Chenonceau in 1799 at the age of 93, and one of her nephews, the Comte de Villeneuve, inherited the château. When he died in 1863, Chenonceau was acquired by Madame Pelouze: she appointed Félix Roguet, architect of the Church of Ste-Clotilde in Paris, to restore the château, following plans by Du Cerceau. Roguet began work in 1865; the project took ten years to complete. Most of his efforts were directed toward the northern façades and the Bohier building. Nearly all the interior decorations were restored at this time. Today the château is owned by the Meniers (the family of chocolate manufacturers), who acquired it in 1913.

DIFFERENT SPELLINGS. Although the Château de Chenonceau can be spelled with or without an "x", the name of the village is usually spelled with one.

ROUSSEAU AT CHENONCEAU
The philosopher Jean-Jacques Rousseau (1712–78) came to the château as the tutor of Madame Dupin's son. It was here that he gave the first performance of his operetta *Le Devin de village*. He later wrote in his *Confessions*: "In 1747 we went to spend the autumn in Touraine, at the Château de Chenonceau . . . We had a very enjoyable time in this beautiful place; we were very well fed and I became as fat as a monk."

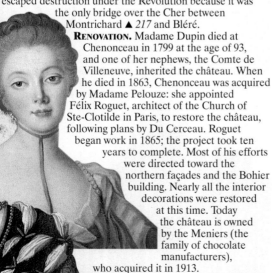

A PROPHETIC MOTTO
The initials TBK (center) are visible on the Tour des Marques: they stand for Thomas Bohier and Katherine. Elsewhere in the château they are accompanied by Thomas Bohier's motto *"S'il vient à point, me souviendra"*, probably meaning "If the château is completed, I shall be remembered."

"The Château de Chenonceau exudes a special sweetness and an aristocratic serenity. It stands at the end of a great avenue of trees, some way from the village which observes a respectful distance; it is built on water, surrounded by woods, and set in a huge park with lovely lawns, with its turrets and square chimneys rising into the air.**"**

Gustave Flaubert,
*Par les champs
et par les grèves*

TOUR OF THE CHÂTEAU

Seen from the banks of the Cher, this castle built out over the water presents a majestic, dreamlike spectacle. Moreover, its scale can be fully appreciated, as can the contrast between its length and the different heights of its three constituent parts: the Tour des Marques, the Bohier castle and the gallery.

TOUR DES MARQUES. The old keep is separated from the rest of the château by a bridge; the Bohiers retained it to give the site a historical flavor. The tower has preserved its medieval appearance, with machicolations and a walkway. However, the east section was embellished in the 16th century, when an elegant turret was added, along with flamboyant carvings in tufa to match the architectural style of the new palace.

THE BOHIER CHÂTEAU. This building looks as if it has simply been placed on top of the arches of the old mill. Its Renaissance architecture is delightful: the building is highly regular in design, with the same measurements, or multiples of them, repeated throughout. Four corner towers emphasize this regularity, which is interrupted only by two annexes built over the piers on the east side: the chapel on the right, and the library on the left.

CHÂTEAU DE CHENONCEAU ▲

Below: the Tour des Marques (left) and chapel (right).

FIRST FLOOR. This story is arranged around a gallery paved with enameled tiles, which opens onto the larger rooms, including the rooms of François I and of Louis XIII, the last king to come to the château. The Salle des Gardes (Guardroom), modified in the 18th century, leads into the small chapel, which has a triangular apse. The two rivals, Diane de Poitiers and Catherine de Médicis, both left their mark on Chenonceau. A room decorated with magnificent 16th-century Flanders tapestries is named after the former; the Cabinet Vert (Green Study) is where the latter worked – its name refers to the fact that she had the walls covered entirely in green velvet. Do not forget to visit the kitchens, which are inside the piers on the river: this arrangement allowed for the direct delivery of goods transported by boat ● *46*.

MIDDLE FLOOR. The second story is reached by a remarkable staircase in the Italian style, with straight banisters and carved keystones: it is one of the château's most striking features. The vestibule, named after Katherine Briçonnet, opens onto four rooms. On the west side are the rooms named after César de Vendôme (the natural son of Henri IV) and his mother, the beautiful Gabrielle d'Estrée. Opposite these is Catherine de Médicis' Room, richly decorated with Italian Renaissance paintings. The final room of this group is the Five Queens' Room, probably named after the two daughters and three daughters-in-law of Catherine de Médicis.

TOP FLOOR. The third story has only one room, presenting a re-creation of Louise de Lorraine's sepulchral surroundings, with funerary motifs and silver tears on a black background.

THE GALLERY ● *69*. The gallery is built in a classical style, set over the five arches of the bridge across the Cher. Originally it was intended as a ballroom: it is nearly 200 feet long, with a fireplace at each end. Visitors can walk through the gallery to reach the left bank of the river, where there is a breathtaking view of the château. Alternatively you can take a boat trip, passing under the arches of the gallery and landing on the island in the middle of the Cher – a magical experience.

THE GARDENS. The château is flanked by two formal gardens. The larger one was created by Diane de Poitiers, and the smaller one designed for Catherine de Médicis. Further to the north is a landscaped garden, the Jardin Vert. In the woods between the gardens and the entrance to the grounds stands a portico decorated with four caryatids, which was added to the Bohier castle by Catherine de Médicis and removed in the 19th century. The outbuildings house a waxwork museum tracing the history of Chenonceau.

THE GALLERY IN WARTIME
A plaque commemorates the fact that Gaston Menier converted the château into a hospital during World War One. Between 1940 and 1942 the gallery (above) spanned an important borderline: the southern door opened onto the Free Territories, while the château itself stood in the occupied zone.

THE VILLAGE
The village's 12th-century church was renovated when the Bohiers built their castle. The house known as the Maison des Pages de François I dates from the same period: it has a polygonal staircase turret and mullioned windows.

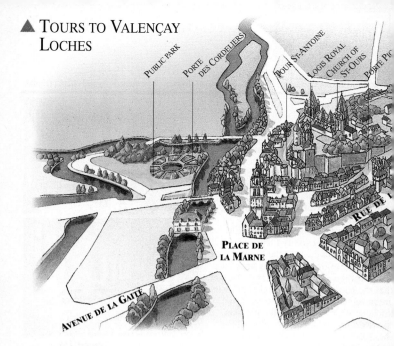

PUBLIC PARK   PORTE DES CORDELIERS   TOUR ST-ANTOINE   LOGIS ROYAL   CHURCH OF ST-OURS   PORTE PIC

RUE DE L

PLACE DE LA MARNE

AVENUE DE LA GAITÉ

History of the Town

● 65 (K8)

The Tour St-Antoine and Porte des Cordeliers, in Loches.

Loches stands at the junction of two Roman roads, overlooking the Indre: this strategic site, with a view over all the surrounding area, enabled the town to oversee movements of troops and merchandise. With its keep, its collegiate church, its royal residence and its old houses, it is one of the most complete medieval towns to have survived to the present day.

A strategic site. Saint Ours, a monk, founded a monastery in the Roman *oppidum* (fortified town) in the 5th century. Charles the Bald (823–77) built a castle which he gave to one of his vassals, whose descendants passed it by marriage to Foulques le Roux, Count of Anjou (the grandfather of Foulques Nerra). This stronghold was a vital asset for the Angevins in their battle against the Counts of Blois. The formidable keep was built at the southern end of the spur in the late

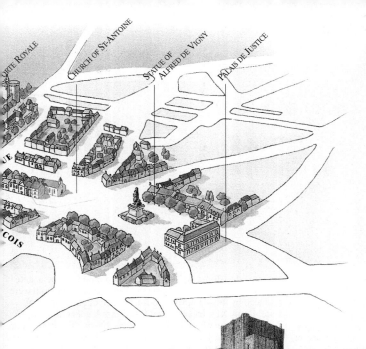

11th century. The Plantaganets kept Loches until 1205, when Philippe Auguste captured it and gave it to one of his officers. **CROWN PROPERTY.** Louis IX was conscious of the town's strategic importance and repurchased it in 1249. The fortress belonged to the kings of France for the next six centuries. Early in this period ramparts and towers were built all around the spur. Later, from the time of Charles VII, the emphasis was on pleasure rather than defense. Nevertheless, Charles took comfort from the town's defensive strength, as his kingdom was under threat from the English.

THE KEEP BECOMES A PRISON. The town was abandoned by Louis XI, who wanted to escape the memories of a childhood spent within its forbidding walls.

PRISON ART
The keep and its annexes housed a wide range of prisoners. Ludovico Sforza, the scheming Duke of Milan (1452–1508) and patron of Leonardo da Vinci, was imprisoned at Loches by Louis XII from 1500 until his death. To pass the time, he decorated his cell with stars, guns and mottos. On the wall of another cell, two ecclesiastical prisoners carved an altar and the fourteen Stations of the Cross.

The town of Loches, 19th-century lithograph.

FANCIFUL RESTORATION
These elevations (above) of the Cité Royale and Logis Royal were created during the course of 19th-century restoration work. The monumental staircase guarded by stone dogs, leading to the interior of the château, was also built at this time. The same is true of the bartizans, the wall walk and other ornamental additions to the turrets and façades of the building. Only the Tour d'Agnès Sorel retains its original simplicity of style.

He moved to Tours ▲ *196*, and the keep then became a state prison: the soldiers and courtiers of the royal stronghold were replaced by those imprisoned for treason or as enemies of state. Louis XIV incarcerated Protestant leaders here after the Revocation of the Edict of Nantes. During the Revolution it was used as a prison for aristocrats and bourgeois from Loches and the surrounding area. The fortress remained a municipal prison until the start of this century, which had the advantage of ensuring that the buildings were maintained.

EVOLUTION OF THE TOWN. The Cité Royale (royal stronghold) was permanently inhabited, which encouraged the development of a small town to the west of the fortress; the other side was flooded by the Indre and its tributaries every winter. Later a second fortified rampart was built, with entrances at either end and in the middle, guarded by huge posterns with portcullises and crenelations . In the 19th century the town outgrew its fortifications and spread over the surrounding fields (where the Palais de Justice was built).

THE CITÉ ROYALE

THE "FILLETTES"
It is said that Louis XI invented the *fillettes* – cruel iron-and-wood cages barely large enough to hold a man – to punish Cardinal Balue (c. 1421–91), a trusted adviser who had betrayed him.

THE PORTE ROYALE. This is now the only way of entering the Cité Royale; in the past there was also a drawbridge to the south, across the old dry moat (now Boulevard Philippe-Auguste). This fortified gateway was rebuilt in the early 15th century and defended by two drawbridges. Visitors can climb up to the top of the gateway (through the museum to enjoy the splendid view.

THE LOGIS ROYAL (royal residence). This little château overlooks the courtyard and a small park to the west; on the eastern side is a terrace above a sheer drop to the banks of the Indre and the houses alongside the river. The southern part of the building dates from the late 14th century; the northern section was completed a century later.

TOUR OF THE ROYAL RESIDENCE. The first room is the RETRAIT DU ROI, the king's bedroom: here visitors can see the remains of a fireplace removed in the 19th century, the walled-up passage to the tower and the remains of a Renaissance tapestry discovered under the paneling of the nearby presbytery. The GRANDE SALLE (Great Hall) was higher in the early 15th century: its beams were visible and

painted in bright colors. This hall is also known as the SALLE
JEANNE D'ARC, because of the meeting here after the victory
at Orléans ▲ *116* when Joan of Arc persuaded the Dauphin
to be crowned, as Charles VII, in Reims Cathedral. The room
contains a group of Audenarde (Flanders) tapestries and the
walls of a staircase first led to the kitchens and servants'
rooms. A richly carved door leads to the later part of the
château, built by Louis XII. In a room with a fireplace
from a nearby farm is a superb triptych by Jean
Bourdichon, a painter and miniaturist from Tours
(c. 1457–1521). This work belonged to the
Chartreuse du Liget ▲ *230*.

**AGNÈS SOREL: THE FIRST OFFICIAL ROYAL
MISTRESS.** One room in the château is dedicated to
Agnès Sorel. Opposite her recumbent statue is one
panel of the diptych by Jean Fouquet ● *88*, ▲ *231, 242*
called the *Virgin of the Milk* (the original is in Antwerp), which
shows the Virgin with the face of Agnès Sorel. This portrait is
significant because Jean Fouquet, Charles VII's official

painter,
definitely knew
Agnès Sorel; all
other portraits
of her are
posthumous,
and based on
this work.
Agnès Sorel
was born in
Picardy; her
date of birth is
not known, so
we cannot be
sure if she was
in her twenties
or thirties when
she died on
February 11,
1450 (she may have been poisoned). A lady-in-waiting to
Isabelle de Lorraine, the wife of René d'Anjou and sister-in-
law of the king, she met Charles VII at Saumur around 1444
and became his mistress. During the course of the five years
she spent with the king she bore him three daughters, who
were legitimated and married according to their royal rank.

COLLEGIATE CHURCH OF ST-OURS ★ ▲ *228*. André
Hallays, a traveler at the start of the 20th century,
enthusiastically exclaimed: "The Collegiate Church of
St-Ours is the wonder of Loches, and one of the
wonders of our religious architecture." The church
(formerly the Collegiate Church of Notre-Dame) has
two bell towers: one from the 11th century, the other a
belfry porch built a century later. In 1165 the roof
joining the two towers collapsed and was replaced by
two *dubes* (hollow pyramids), which may have been
based on the kitchen of Fontevraud Abbey ▲ *272*.
Originally conical, they acquired their present
octagonal form during 19th-century restoration work.
The church is entered through a narthex (added to the
church at the same time as the *dubes*), which has

ALFRED DE VIGNY
(1797–1863)
The statue of
the writer on Place
de Verdun, by
Tours sculptor
François Sicard,
commemorates the
fact that Vigny was
born in Loches on
March 27, 1797.

protected the magnificent early-12th-
century polychrome portal so the colors
retain their original brightness. The
southern side aisle was built in the 12th
century; the northern side aisle, with
ogival vaulting, dates from the 15th
century. An avenue of lime trees, flanked
by old houses, leads from the church to
the keep.

THE KEEP AND ITS FORTIFICATIONS ★
● *65.* The imposing rectangular keep
stands at the far southern tip of the rocky
spur; it is reached by a barbican and a
drawbridge. The keep was built by the
Counts of Anjou around 1070; it
measures approximately 80 by 50 feet and
stands 120 feet high. Further ramparts
were built to reinforce the defenses over
the course of subsequent centuries. In the
13th century three pointed towers were
added to complete the southern defenses of the site. Then
from the mid 15th century onward, as military architecture
evolved, three new buildings were added: the barbican, the
TOUR NEUVE (or TOUR RONDE), at the junction of the town's
ramparts and the keep, and the fearful MARTELET, a hulk of
masonry housing three stories of underground prison cells.

TWO LITTLE-KNOWN MUSEUMS. The MUSÉE DU TERROIR is
housed in the vaulted rooms of the Porte Royale. Founded by
Tours ethnographer Jacques-Marie Rougé (1873–1956), it
contains items relating to the life of the local peasants in
the 19th century. Next door, in a 19th-century bourgeois
residence, is the MUSÉE LANSYER, which displays the work of
Emmanuel Lansyer (1835–93) ▲ *229*, a pupil of Gustave
Courbet. The collection also includes engravings by Piranesi,
Canaletto and Doré, and wash drawings by Victor Hugo.

WALK THROUGH THE TOWN

The Church of
St-Ours (below).
Detail of the portal
(above).

Like the Cité Royale, the old center of the town is surrounded
by ramparts, which are more than half a mile long.
Leaving the fortress by the Porte Royale, at the end
of the Mail de la Poterie you will come to the house
where Louis Delaporte (1842–1925) was born,
which stands in the street named after him. This
explorer revealed the importance and interest of
the ruins at Angkor and assembled a collection
of Indo-Chinese art that formed the basis of the
Musée Guimet in Paris.

RUE DU CHÂTEAU ★. From the Porte Royale, the Rue du Château leads back down toward the town. The house at no. 19 is known as the MAISON D'AGNES SOREL because of the bust over the entrance. The 16th-century house at no. 10, the MAISON DU CENTAURE, owes its name to the bas-relief on the façade (above). The MAISON DE LA CHANCELLERIE (no. 8) is decorated in the Italian style and bears the date 1551 on a cartouche, along with the monogram of Henri II. This house became known as the chancellery from its two inscriptions: *Prudentia nutrisco* ("I am nourished by prudence") and *Justicia regno* ("I govern by justice"). But Loches did not in fact have a chancellery in the 16th century. Finally at no. 1 is a 15th-century house (recently restored) that has a neo-Gothic façade with rather heavy-looking sculptures.

THE TOWN GATES ★. The PORTE PICOIS (left), the northwestern entrance to the town, was built into the rampart, like the Porte des Cordeliers to the northeast and the Porte Poitevine (no longer standing) to the southwest. Porte Picois was built in the 15th century as a fortified gateway, with machicolations and a wall walk: the latter bears the marks of missiles from the Wars of Religion.

BAS-RELIEF ON THE MAISON DU CENTAURE
Originally part of a 17th-century fireplace, this bas-relief was added to the façade during the 19th century. It shows Hercules shooting the centaur Nessus with a poisoned arrow to stop him abducting his wife Deianira.

Bas-relief from the Church of St-Ours.

EMMANUEL LANSYER (1797–1863)
This view of Loches (left) by the painter Emmanuel Lansyer is a perfect illustration of the description by Onésime Reclus, a 19th-century traveler: "Loches is one of the most curious villages of France: it brings one thousand years of history to life in a single day!" The painter bequeathed his house to the town council, along with some of his works and his collection of Japanese prints and armor (below).

HÔTEL DE VILLE ★. The town hall is a perfect example of Renaissance architecture. François I authorized its construction, beside the Porte Picois, in 1519; but the work did not begin until 1535.

AROUND THE TOUR ST-ANTOINE. The TOUR ST-ANTOINE was built between 1529 and 1575 to serve as a bell tower for the adjacent chapel. At no. 3 on PLACE DU MARCHÉ-AUX-LÉGUMES is a late-15th-century turret. At no. 5, rue St-Antoine stands Hôtel Nau, with loggias on three stories, dating from the mid 16th century. On the Grand-Rue is the oldest pharmacy in the town, which has been in business for nearly three hundred years.

ALONG THE RAMPARTS. The steep walls of the collegiate church and the château overhang the picturesque Rue St-Ours. At nos. 13 and 15 are the lovely façades of the MAISON DE L'ÉCUYER DU ROI; then at no. 21 the Renaissance turret of the MAISON DE L'ARGENTIER DU ROI; and at no. 10 the entrance of the former priory. After this continue along Boulevard Philippe-Auguste, which follows the course of the old dry moat.

BEAULIEU-LÈS-LOCHES

To the left of the road leading to Beaulieu-lès-Loches from the Porte des Cordeliers stand the imposing 17th-century hospital and then the Sous-Préfecture, which was once the Hôtel d'Armaillé. On the right-hand side of the road is the manor house of Sansac, built during the reign of François I (a terracotta bust of the king can be seen on the forebuilding). **ABBEY OF STE-TRINITÉ ★.** The old village of Beaulieu, with its 15th- and 16th-century houses, grew up around the famous Abbey of Ste-Trinité, founded by Foulques Nerra ● *37* in 1007. His son Geoffroy Martel extended the church in the mid 11th century and buried his father here. It is one of the largest surviving buildings of this era in France. The abbey's long period of prosperity ended during the Hundred Years' War, when it was ransacked by the English. It never entirely recovered its former glory, and was sold off as national property under the Revolution.

ABBEY OF STE-TRINITÉ
The abbey church and its magnificent bell tower date mainly from the 11th century, with 15th-century additions and embellishments.

A ROUND CHAPEL
The circular design of the Chapelle du Liget is most unusual for a medieval building. Constructed from tufa, it dates from the mid 12th century.

CHARTREUSE DU LIGET ★

The road through the Forest of Loches via the Pyramide des Chartreux leads to the Carthusian monastery at Liget. **THE MONASTERY.** In 1178 Henry Plantaganet ● *38* acquired an area of wood with a spring and gave it to the Carthusians to found a monastery – no doubt hoping to make amends for the assassination of Thomas à Becket, the Archbishop of Canterbury who had refused to submit to his will. Further donations were made by King John of England twenty years later, and a donation by Louis XI in 1234 established a tradition of liberality toward the Carthusians on the part of the French monarchy. A series of portals and gates lead the visitor down toward the monastery buildings. The monumental 18th-century ENTRANCE PORTAL has carved bas-reliefs on the pediment depicting Saint Bruno (who founded the Carthusian order in 1084) and Saint John the Baptist, who was the monastery's patron saint. **CHAPEL OF ST-JEAN-BAPTISTE OF LIGET.** A forest path leads along the side of the monastery to this small Romanesque chapel. It is famous for its late-12th-century mural paintings, which are among the most beautiful of the Middle Ages.

MONTRÉSOR ★

Montrésor was a stronghold under Foulques Nerra, and in the
12th century belonged to Henry II of England until it was
captured by Philippe Auguste in 1188. It was later owned by a
number of famous families, most notably the Bastarnay family
in the 16th century, who founded the collegiate church. In
1849 the château was bought by the Polish Count Branicki,
whose descendants still live here. Branicki, a friend of
Napoleon III, was one of the great financiers of his age.
THE CHÂTEAU. The château is entered through the ruins of a
14th-century building whose arches are protected by splendid
neo-Gothic ironwork. The building was converted into a
comfortable residence in the early 16th century, under Imbert
de Bastarnay (1438–1523); it is surrounded by a double
curtain wall with large round towers from the 12th century.
Inside, little has changed since the 19th century: velvets and
braids provide a setting for Polish objets d'art, Napoleon III
furniture, and paintings by the Italian school, Winterhalter
and Élisabeth Vigée-Lebrun.
COLLEGIATE CHURCH OF ST-JEAN-BAPTISTE. (1520 and 1541)
The chapel is built on a Gothic ground plan, with beautiful
Renaissance decorations. In a side chapel is an *Annunciation*
painted by Philippe de Champaigne (1602-74).

NOUANS-LES-FONTAINES

The village church is dedicated to Saint Martin. The
celebrated Pietà in the choir is attributed to Jean Fouquet.
This artist from Tours, who lived from c. 1420 to c. 1480,
became famous as a portraitist and miniaturist. He is regarded
as one of the most important of the early French painters.

THE CARDERS OF MONTRÉSOR

Until the 19th
century wool from
the local sheep was
carded, spun and
woven in Montrésor.
The 17th-century
wooden market halls
in the town – the
Halle des Cardeux
(carders' market)
and Halle aux Laines
(wool market) – owe
their names to this
traditional craft.

THE "PIETÀ" OF NOUANS

The painter Jean
Fouquet spent a
considerable time in
Italy, after which he
was appointed
official court painter
under Charles VII
and then under
Louis XI. The
somber colors, the
beautifully rendered
drapery, and the
reserved and serious
expressions of the
faces make this panel
painting one of the
masterpieces of
French art.

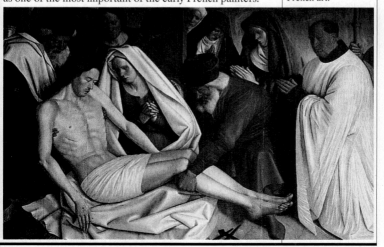

The "pyramide de Valençay",
a famous goat's cheese ● *29*,
and Valençay wine

HISTORY OF THE TOWN

Strictly speaking, Valençay is located in the Berry
region: however, it merits inclusion in the Loire
valley because of its impressive château, similar in
many respects to those on the Loire itself. The
town grew up on a hillside overlooking the Nahon river, as an
important staging post between Touraine and Berry,
consisting of three distinct settlements: the old town, the
Bourg-de-l'Église and the Bas-Bourg. Over the years the
history of the town became intertwined with that of the
château, which underwent many alterations. The Valençay
estate is now one of the largest in France, stretching over
some 50,000 acres. Under the Empire the estate was owned
by Talleyrand, Napoleon's celebrated minister, whose lavish
royal receptions and political intrigues added sparkle and
interest to the life of the town.

HISTORY OF THE CHÂTEAU ★

The oldest part of the château as it stands today dates from
the first half of the 16th century. Later additions were
arranged around the original building in a subtle mix of styles,
creating an elegantly structured architectural group. The
first section of the château was built by Louis d'Estampes,
governor of Blois, and Marie Hurault, daughter of the lord of
Cheverny ▲ *170*, around 1520. Their son, Jacques
d'Estampes, married the daughter of a rich financier in 1540
and extended the château to its full size. Valençay was to
remain under the ownership of financiers for some time,
belonging successively to several "fermiers généraux"
("farmers-general", or tax collectors), including John Law
(1686–1761), the famous speculator who created the first
paper money in France during the regency of the Duke of
Orléans. In 1747 the château was acquired by the farmer-
general Charles Legendre de Villemorien, whose alterations
gave the building its present shape. The splendid palace was
sold to Talleyrand in 1803, with the
encouragement of Napoleon, who saw this
as a way of keeping his
troublesome minister at a
distance, entrusting him with the
reception of high-level guests
and enforced exiles like the
princes of Spain, including the
future King
Ferdinand
VII.

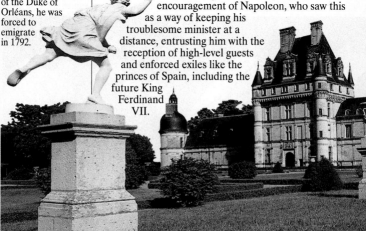

West façade of the main
courtyard of Valençay ● *70.*

When Talleyrand's
nephew died, in
1898, the estate
was split up.

A BLEND OF ARCHITECTURAL STYLES

In the 18th century Legendre de Villemorien demolished the
east wing and the arcaded gallery of the south court, opening
up a beautiful view over the landscape of the valley, as at
Chaumont ▲ *177,* ● *67.*
NORTH WING. This wing dates from the 16th century, with
a round tower (the Vieille Tour) to the west dating from
1520–30. Similar in size to the towers at Chambord ▲ *158,*
it is surmounted by an Imperial-style dome; its machicolations
and wall walk are purely decorative in function ● *68.* The
entrance pavilion at the center, reminiscent of Chenonceau
▲ *218,* was built around fifty years later. It forms a keep
flanked by four turrets and is richly ornamented with dormer
windows, pilasters and chimneys;
its corbeled wall walk and decorative
machicolations match those of the
Vieille Tour. The Renaissance
residential wing facing the courtyard
is more elaborate, with an elegant
gallery of basket-handle arches
(right).
WEST WING. The northern half of
the west wing, on the park side of
the building, was built at the same
time as the Vieille Tour. The southern half was built in the
17th century; its roofs and dormer windows were restored
in the 18th century, following the original design. However,
this uniformity of style was disrupted through the addition
of a new tower, built as a counterpart to the Vieille Tour.
The classical façade on the main
courtyard is a dazzling Ionic
composition reminiscent of some
parts of Versailles (top of page).
INTERIOR. Some of the rooms –
including the Salon Bleu with its
lovely Louis XVI paneling –
display magnificent Regency,
Louis XVI and Empire
furniture along with objets
d'art. On the first story
is a gallery dedicated to
Talleyrand's family. On
the second story, beside
Talleyrand's bedroom,
there are several rooms
where famous visitors
stayed, including the
bedroom reserved for
the King of Spain
(above) and the one
used by the novelist
Germaine de Staël
(1766–1817).

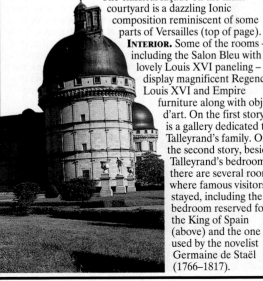

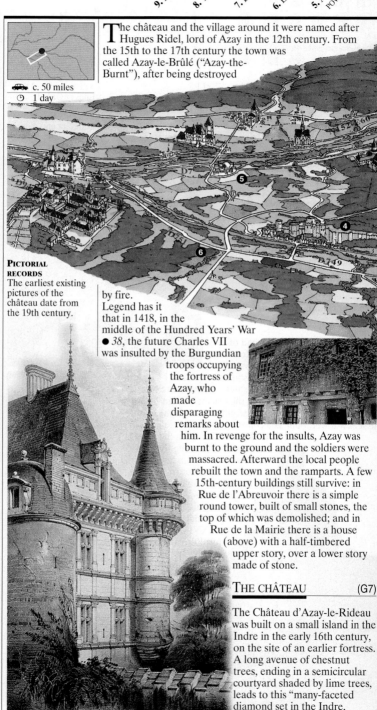

The château and the village around it were named after Hugues Ridel, lord of Azay in the 12th century. From the 15th to the 17th century the town was called Azay-le-Brûlé ("Azay-the-Burnt"), after being destroyed

🚗 c. 50 miles

⏱ 1 day

PICTORIAL RECORDS
The earliest existing pictures of the château date from the 19th century.

by fire. Legend has it that in 1418, in the middle of the Hundred Years' War ● *38*, the future Charles VII was insulted by the Burgundian troops occupying the fortress of Azay, who made disparaging remarks about him. In revenge for the insults, Azay was burnt to the ground and the soldiers were massacred. Afterward the local people rebuilt the town and the ramparts. A few 15th-century buildings still survive: in Rue de l'Abreuvoir there is a simple round tower, built of small stones, the top of which was demolished; and in Rue de la Mairie there is a house (above) with a half-timbered upper story, over a lower story made of stone.

THE CHÂTEAU (G7)

The Château d'Azay-le-Rideau was built on a small island in the Indre in the early 16th century, on the site of an earlier fortress. A long avenue of chestnut trees, ending in a semicircular courtyard shaded by lime trees, leads to this "many-faceted diamond set in the Indre,

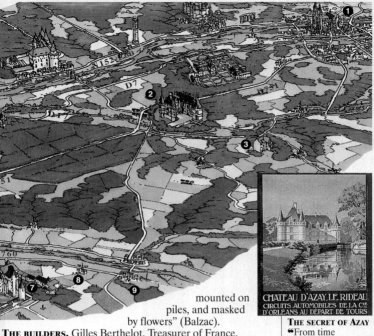

CHATEAU D'AZAY-LE-RIDEAU
CIRCUITS AUTOMOBILES DE LA Cie
D'ORLEANS AU DÉPART DE TOURS

mounted on piles, and masked by flowers" (Balzac).

THE BUILDERS. Gilles Berthelot, Treasurer of France, bought the estate of Azay-le-Rideau and the land around it in the 16th century. He demolished the feudal castle, with the exception of the large tower (which was replaced in the 19th century). Work on his new castle began in 1518, at the same time as Thomas Bohier was completing Chenonceau ▲ *218* and François I was making plans for Chambord. Gilles Berthelot's wife, Philippe Lesbahy, supervised the construction work for long periods while her husband's official duties kept him in Paris.

THE CONSTRUCTION OF THE CHÂTEAU. Some receipts and accounts of expenditure have survived, providing invaluable information about the construction of Gilles Berthelot's château. A large number of laborers, masons and carpenters worked on the building day and night. They used pumps to drain the site and huge iron bars to drive in the piles. They cut and assembled stone from quarries near the château; harder stone had to be brought from quarries further off, in Bourré and St-Aignan, which was transported to the site by river and on carts. The accounts do not provide any clear evidence regarding the name of the architect. It may have been Étienne Rousseau, who seems to have been the only master mason in direct contact with Gilles Berthelot. François I visited the site of the new château on February 2, 1518. After this the work progressed rapidly: the staircase was probably finished by 1524, as it bears two royal emblems: the salamander of François I and the ermine of his wife, Queen Claude, who died in the same year.

THE SECRET OF AZAY
❝From time immemorial this had been the site of a fortress whose function was to defend the crossing of the Indre on the road from Tours to Chinon. The builders who modernized the fortress of Azay in the 16th century did not forget this, as can be seen in the military features they provided, nearly all of which survive today.❞
Jean-Claude Le Guillou

"A SINGLE DESIRE"
This was the motto of Queen Claude, wife of François I and daughter of Louis XII and Anne de Bretagne ● *34*. The ermine is her personal emblem.

235

The Château d'Azay-le-Rideau stands by the riverside, between two branches of the Indre. It was built in a single phase, from 1518 to 1524. Consequently, although never completed, it is the archetypal Loire château, incorporating all the typical features of the genre. Here the feudal elements, such as the turrets, wall walk and moat, are purely symbolic in function, their sole purpose being to demonstrate the high rank of the château's owner. Inside, Azay-le-Rideau was thoroughly modern, with a simple, practical layout in which comfort was the prime consideration.

The château presents a successful blend of medieval traditions and the new classical Italian influences. It was the most perfect château of its era, reflecting the progressive aspects of early-Renaissance architecture.

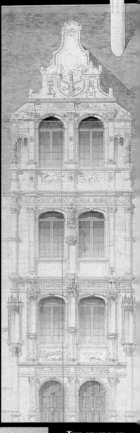

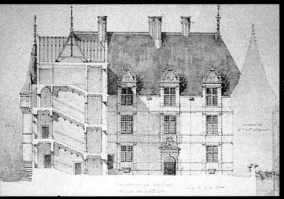

ELEVATION, WITH CROSS-SECTION OF THE STAIRCASE
In contrast to the great spiral staircase of the François I wing at Blois, the staircase at Azay is designed on the Italian model with straight flights of stairs. Its design is innovative, as is its inclusion within the main building of the château: the staircase well opens onto both the exterior and the internal courtyard. The prototype of this staircase design was built at the Château de Bury (now destroyed).

THE STAIRCASE
The staircase occupies a wide central bay, protruding from the north façade. Its structure can be seen on the elevation four stories of vaulted twin bays mark the half-landings. Most of the building's decorative carvings are concentrated here: on the engaged columns, pilasters and entablatures, decorated with foliation, shells and medallions. The staircase breaks up the regularity of the façade, which has vertically aligned windows and horizontal moldings.

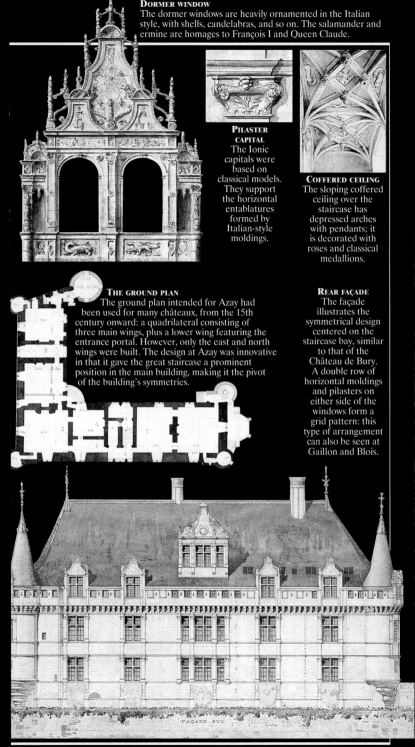

DORMER WINDOW
The dormer windows are heavily ornamented in the Italian style, with shells, candelabras, and so on. The salamander and ermine are homages to François I and Queen Claude.

PILASTER CAPITAL
The Ionic capitals were based on classical models. They support the horizontal entablatures formed by Italian-style moldings.

COFFERED CEILING
The sloping coffered ceiling over the staircase has depressed arches with pendants; it is decorated with roses and classical medallions.

THE GROUND PLAN
The ground plan intended for Azay had been used for many châteaux, from the 15th century onward: a quadrilateral consisting of three main wings, plus a lower wing featuring the entrance portal. However, only the east and north wings were built. The design at Azay was innovative in that it gave the great staircase a prominent position in the main building, making it the pivot of the building's symmetries.

REAR FAÇADE
The façade illustrates the symmetrical design centered on the staircase bay, similar to that of the Château de Bury. A double row of horizontal moldings and pilasters on either side of the windows form a grid pattern: this type of arrangement can also be seen at Gaillon and Blois.

FACADE SVD

PROUD OWNERS . . .
Armand de Biencourt
and his wife Anne de
Montmorency added
their initials to the
doors in the 19th
century (below).

DISGRACE. The ambitious project was interrupted by a
dramatic course of events. A number of families in the
Tours region had grown rich through speculation and lent
money to the crown. After his Italian campaigns the king,
who owed them a great deal of money, accused them of
embezzlement. Jacques de Beaune-Semblançay, his
superintendent of finances, was condemned and hanged in
1527 ▲ 202. Gilles Berthelot did not escape: in 1528 his
possessions were confiscated by François I and given to
Antoine Raffin, one of the king's companion in arms.
Berthelot took refuge at Cambrai, where he died a year
later. For several years Philippe Lesbahy tried to hold onto
Azay; but she finally lost it in 1535, when Raffin took
possession of the estate.

FROM THE 16TH CENTURY TO THE PRESENT DAY. The
château remained in the hands of the same family
until the Revolution. In 1791 it was
acquired by the Marquis de Biencourt,
renowned for his revolutionary ideas.
His descendants kept it until 1899, and
in 1905 it was purchased by the state.

AN EARLY RENAISSANCE MASTERPIECE.
In the mid 19th century the Marquis de
Biencourt took steps to give the château
its present unified appearance: he replaced
the great medieval tower with a tower more suited to the
style of the building, and replaced a small turret in the
troubadour style (dating probably from around 1800) with
a turret matching the others on the main façade. Despite
these later modifications, the château remains an early-
Renaissance building. In its overall appearance it is still
faithful to the medieval tradition – with its high roofs and
chimneys, corner turrets, and wall walk with machicolations.
However, the site was chosen for its pleasant situation
rather than for a defensive purpose. The influence of the
Italian Renaissance is tangible, notably in the structure of
the façades, with windows at regular intervals flanked by
pilasters, horizontal moldings between the stories, and
carved capitals.

THE STAIRCASE. The main entrance of the château is also the
entrance to the staircase. The straight staircase, with one
flight over another, is highlighted by its
central position on the
main façade
and by its

> "YOU WOULD NOT HAVE THOUGHT THAT THIS WAS ONCE A PLACE OF STRATEGIC IMPORTANCE. HOWEVER, IN TIMES GONE BY [AZAY] RESISTED A NUMBER OF SIEGES."
>
> PIGANIOL DE LA FORCE

magnificent decoration of medallions, foliage and shells. The ornamentation features the initial F and the salamander of François I (below), the letter C and the ermine of Queen Claude, and the initials G and P of the builders of the château (Gilles Berthelot and Philippe Lesbahy).

THE INTERIOR OF THE CHÂTEAU. Rich tapestries and furniture from the 16th, 17th and 18th centuries decorate the apartments, which were refurnished by the national commission for historical monuments. The kitchen ceiling has splendid surbased vaulting, decorated with cartouches at the springing points of the arches. The huge fireplace, near the well, bears Berthelot's coat of arms: the escutcheon of Philippe Lesbahy must have been painted over it. The great hall, formerly a reception room, occupies the entire western half of the residential wing. As was customary, its ceiling is higher than that of other rooms in the château; the decoration of the fireplace is especially fine.

THE GROUNDS. To view the other sides of the château and the wall walk, take a stroll in the extensive landscaped grounds which replaced the formal gardens in the 19th century. Also in the 19th century a dam was built across the Indre, in order to transform the moat into a lake. To the west of the château is a small Gothic CHAPEL, restored after sustaining serious damage during World War Two. The view to the south includes the MANOIR DE LA RÉMONNIÈRE (formerly "la Romainière"), from the 16th and 17th centuries. Once a hunting lodge belonging to Azay, it was built over the remains of a Gallo-Roman villa (a number of classical ruins have been found nearby, notably the base of a Roman temple). Today it is a hotel: visitors can stay here or walk in the grounds while viewing the château.

Above: the southeast façade of the Château d'Azay-le-Rideau. Below: aerial view of the west façade and part of the village.

THE INTERIOR OF AZAY IN THE 19TH CENTURY
Armand de Biencourt and his wife Anne de Montmorency were keen to share the artistic treasures that they had inherited, and enjoyed showing the rooms of the château to visitors interested in art and history. Under the Second Empire their home was considered one of the best museums in France.

DECORATION OF THE CHURCH OF ST-SYMPHORIEN
The lower row of statues was partially destroyed to make way for a window installed at a later period (12th or 13th century).

CHÂTEAU DE SACHÉ
This was built in the 16th century, on the site of an earlier fortress.

CHURCH OF ST-SYMPHORIEN

The unusual historiated façade dates from when the church was built (11th century). It is decorated with miter-shaped arches and two rows of statuettes in rounded niches. The vaulted main nave was built between 1025 and 1040, while the left-hand nave dates from the 12th century. The Chapelle Seigneuriale, which doubled as a funerary chapel, was built in the 17th century by Antoinette Raffin, the mistress of Azay at that time. Its façade and the ornamentation of the doorway can be admired from the château grounds. The master glassmaker Max Ingrand (1908–69) ▲ *149* made the four stained-glass windows of the main nave (depicting Saint Martin, Saint Henry, Saint Barbe and Saint Bernadette) and the one depicting the Assumption in the Chapelle Seigneuriale.
BESIDE THE INDRE. The square adjoining the church leads to the banks of the Indre, which separates the town of Azay from the château. From the bridge there is a fine view of the château and an old mill; on the island, which once belonged to the château, visitors can relax, play boules, or doze off to the gentle lapping of the water.

SACHÉ

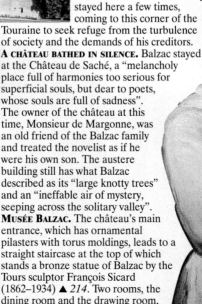

SACHÉ AND BALZAC. Saché is known for its connections with the novelist Honoré de Balzac (1799–1850). He seems to be present everywhere in the valley – which may lead visitors to overlook the fact that he only stayed here a few times, coming to this corner of the Touraine to seek refuge from the turbulence of society and the demands of his creditors.
A CHÂTEAU BATHED IN SILENCE. Balzac stayed at the Château de Saché, a "melancholy place full of harmonies too serious for superficial souls, but dear to poets, whose souls are full of sadness". The owner of the château at this time, Monsieur de Margonne, was an old friend of the Balzac family and treated the novelist as if he were his own son. The austere building still has what Balzac described as its "large knotty trees" and an "ineffable air of mystery, seeping across the solitary valley".
MUSÉE BALZAC. The château's main entrance, which has ornamental pilasters with torus moldings, leads to a straight staircase at the top of which stands a bronze statue of Balzac by the Tours sculptor François Sicard (1862–1934) ▲ *214*. Two rooms, the dining room and the drawing room, have been reconstructed in the

BALZAC'S BEDROOM
This tiny low-ceilinged room under the eaves was furnished sparsely, so that nothing would distract the writer's attention. Balzac worked here, shut away for whole days "like a monk in a monastery", with an oil-lamp for lighting, "asking ideas from the night and words from the silence".

style of the period. A museum on the top floor is dedicated to the writer's life and work. The place where Balzac's presence can be most keenly felt is his bedroom at the top of the house. A single window looks over a "calm, solitary valley, a huge fold of and bordered by two-hundred-year-old oak trees".

CHURCH OF ST-MARTIN-DE-VERTOU. The church (right) is situated at the center of the town. Balzac used to accompany his hosts here from time to time. A wooden porch stands in front of the entrance to the main nave (12th and 13th century). A second nave was added on the north side in the 16th century. To the left of the choir is a plaque inscribed in Latin describing the virtues of the blessed Marguerite de Rouxellé (1608–28), whose tomb became a place of pilgrimage.

ANOTHER FAMOUS RESIDENT OF SACHÉ: CALDER. The American sculptor and painter Alexander Calder (1898–1976), the witty inventor of "mobiles" and "stabiles", moved to Saché in 1955. One of his works – a composite "mobile-stabile" (right) – can be seen in the square in front of the church, in a striking juxtaposition of 20th-century art with a historical setting. Described by his friend Miró as a "solid-looking man with the soul of a nightingale", Calder bought an old house on the hillside on the right bank of the Indre and dubbed it the "Maison de François I", without any historical justification for the name. Later he had a house and huge studio built on a hillside at Le Carroi (north of Saché), with enormous windows that give it the air of a cathedral. Today the building houses the Centre National des Arts Plastiques, which welcomes young artists from France and abroad.

THE VILLAGE OF SACHÉ
The village has a number of old houses; a 12th-century half-timbered inn near to the church (left) is particularly striking.

CALDER'S "STABILES"
This term was invented by the sculptor Jean Arp (1887–1966) to describe Calder's massive sculptures made of sheet metal. Most of them are black in color.

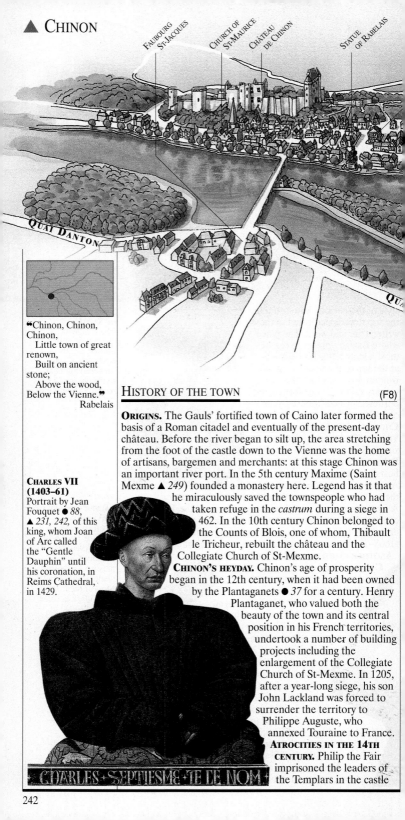

FAUBOURG ST-JACQUES
CHURCH OF ST-MAURICE
CHÂTEAU DE CHINON
STATUE OF RABELAIS

QUAI DANTON

QUA

"Chinon, Chinon,
Chinon,
   Little town of great
renown,
   Built on ancient
stone;
   Above the wood,
Below the Vienne."
               Rabelais

**CHARLES VII
(1403–61)**
Portrait by Jean
Fouquet ● 88,
▲ 231, 242, of this
king, whom Joan
of Arc called
the "Gentle
Dauphin" until
his coronation, in
Reims Cathedral,
in 1429.

HISTORY OF THE TOWN

(F8)

ORIGINS. The Gauls' fortified town of Caino later formed the
basis of a Roman citadel and eventually of the present-day
château. Before the river began to silt up, the area stretching
from the foot of the castle down to the Vienne was the home
of artisans, bargemen and merchants: at this stage Chinon was
an important river port. In the 5th century Maxime (Saint
Mexme ▲ 249) founded a monastery here. Legend has it that
he miraculously saved the townspeople who had
taken refuge in the *castrum* during a siege in
462. In the 10th century Chinon belonged to
the Counts of Blois, one of whom, Thibault
le Tricheur, rebuilt the château and the
Collegiate Church of St-Mexme.

CHINON'S HEYDAY. Chinon's age of prosperity
began in the 12th century, when it had been owned
by the Plantaganets ● 37 for a century. Henry
Plantaganet, who valued both the
beauty of the town and its central
position in his French territories,
undertook a number of building
projects including the
enlargement of the Collegiate
Church of St-Mexme. In 1205,
after a year-long siege, his son
John Lackland was forced to
surrender the territory to
Philippe Auguste, who
annexed Touraine to France.

**ATROCITIES IN THE 14TH
CENTURY.** Philip the Fair
imprisoned the leaders of
the Templars in the castle

COARLES · SEPTIESME · IE DE NOM

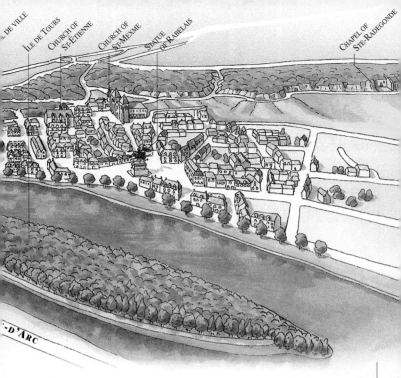

DE VILLE   ÎLE DE TOURS   CHURCH OF ST-ÉTIENNE   CHURCH OF ST-MEXME   STATUE OF RABELAIS   CHAPEL OF STE-RADEGONDE

-D'ARC

JOAN OF ARC ESCORTED TO CHINON
This 13-year-old peasant girl from Lorraine heard voices commanding her to liberate France, which at that time was almost entirely occupied by the English. The young girl asked Robert de Baudricourt, the king's captain at Vaucouleurs, for an escort to accompany her to Touraine to see

at Chinon in 1314, then had them burned alive in Paris. In 1321 his son Philip the Tall exacted the same punishment on 160 Jews of the area, who were charged with poisoning the town's well. The real motive for this massacre, like that of the Templars, was the seizure of their property.

CHINON, CENTER OF THE FRENCH KINGDOM. In the 15th century the Duc de Touraine (the future Charles VII) took refuge behind the town's ramparts. It was here, in 1429, that Joan of Arc convinced him to go to the aid of Orléans ▲ 116. When Louis XI's chamberlain Philippe de Commynes became governor of the town he strengthened the château's defenses and undertook major alterations to the Church of St-Étienne. Cesare Borgia, the son and legate of Pope Alexander VI, met Louis XII at Chinon in the late 15th century: Louis wanted to have his first marriage annulled so he could marry Anne de Bretagne, Charles VIII's widow, and thereby annexe Brittany to France. At the end of the 15th century, François Rabelais ● 97 was born not far from here at La Devinière ▲ 250.

Charles VII. Baudricourt, considering the French cause to be more or less beyond rescue, gave way at their second interview, with the words "Go, go! And happen what may!".

243

Sketch of the south elevation (above) and north elevation (below) of the Château de Chinon by Henri Deverni, 1882.

DEFENSES
A wide and deep dry moat, once spanned by a drawbridge,

separates the Château du Milieu and the Fort du Coudray. Underground passages supplemented the fort's defense system. One of these is said to have led to the manor house of Roberdeau (now destroyed), to the north of the château: this was the residence of Charles VII's mistress, Agnès Sorel ▲ *227*.

North elevation of the Château de Chinon.

CHINON ABANDONED. The kings abandoned the austere château in the 16th century. After this it passed into the hands of Cardinal Richelieu, who obtained permission from Louis XIII to demolish it. This proved to be too costly an undertaking and was not carried out, but time and neglect eventually destroyed a large part of the building. The town's fortified ramparts were demolished in the late 18th century. Shortly before the Revolution a road was built connecting Chinon and Tours via Azay-le-Rideau. Despite the decline of river transport, Chinon was also preserved from isolation by the advent of the railway in the 19th century. A good deal of renovation work was undertaken around this time: the quaysides were built, streets were widened, and the Place Jeanne d'Arc was created.

CHINON TODAY. The Avoine-Chinon nuclear power station was built in 1964, boosting the economy by creating jobs. Chinon's wine ■ *30* has had its own "Appellation d'origine contrôlée" since 1937, and the town still has extensive vineyards, covering an area of 4,200 acres. Local authorities have been developing tourism and the historical heritage; a medieval market is held annually in Chinon, involving two thousand participants in costume and attracting some twenty thousand visitors.

THE CHÂTEAU ● *64*

The Château de Chinon is built on a rocky outcrop overlooking the Vienne: its scale is best appreciated from Faubourg St-Jacques on the other side of the bridge. The château, surrounded by a fortified rampart whose oldest section dates from the 10th century, actually consists of three buildings separated by dry moats: from east to west these are the Fort St-Georges, the Château du Milieu and the Fort du Coudray.

FORT ST-GEORGES (private property). Today little remains of this fortress built by Henry Plantaganet. Its name refers to an adjoining chapel, of which only the crypt survives.

CHÂTEAU DU MILIEU. The drawbridge that defended the entrance to the château was replaced by a fixed bridge in the 18th century. Next to the southern rampart are the GRANDE SALLE DE CHARLES VII, of which only the fireplace survives, and the LOGIS ROYAUX (royal residence) built by Henry Plantaganet. It was here, at the end of February 1429, that the first meeting took place between Joan of Arc (statue, above) and Charles VII ▲ *116*. The Maid of Orleans had been preceded by rumors:

this young girl was claiming that God had commanded her to fight the English and expel them from France. To test her, the king disguised himself as a page and his cousin took his place on the throne. Joan of Arc was not deceived: she went straight up to the "Gentle Dauphin". Contemporaries reported that the king emerged from the ensuing private interview with a radiant expression, convinced of Joan's mission. He supplied her with a small army, and after the victory at Orléans she persuaded him to eradicate all doubts regarding his legitimacy by being crowned, like his ancestors, in Reims (on July 17, 1429). Joan of Arc was sold to the English by the Burgundians; she was declared a heretic after the famous trial and burned alive at Rouen on May 30, 1431. She was rehabilitated in 1450 and canonized in 1920. The displays in the LOGIS ROYAUX include a model of the château in its heyday and tapestries

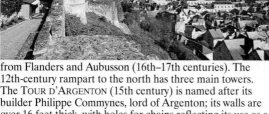

from Flanders and Aubusson (16th–17th centuries). The 12th-century rampart to the north has three main towers. The TOUR D'ARGENTON (15th century) is named after its builder Philippe Commynes, lord of Argenton; its walls are over 16 feet thick, with holes for chains reflecting its use as a prison. The TOUR DES CHIENS, from the 13th century, owes its name to the fact that it housed the royal hounds; it is of great architectural interest, with three stories of rooms with ogival vaulting. THE TOUR DE L'ÉCHAUGUETTE (Bartizan Tower), on the northeast corner, is partly ruined.

FORT DU COUDRAY. The fort is bordered to the west by the oldest curtain wall of the château, which dates from the 10th century. It is separated from the Château du Milieu by a dry ditch, dug out in the early 13th century, which is over 65 feet wide and nearly as deep. The ditch served as a quarry for building work on the TOUR DU COUDRAY (Philippe-Auguste's keep), which overlooks it. To one side was the CHAPEL OF ST-MARTIN (now destroyed) where Joan of Arc came to pray. On the southwest corner stands the magnificent TOUR DE BOISSY built by Philippe Auguste, which offers a panoramic view over Chinon and the

THE ECHO OF CHINON
"There is a remarkable echo from the northern wall of the château, close to the car park. If you ask *'Les femmes de Chinon sont-elles fidèles?'*, the echo queries *'Elles?'*. If you retort *'Oui, les femmes de Chinon'*, the echo replies *'Non'*."
Guide du Val de Loire mystérieux

THE TOUR DE L'HORLOGE
This late-14th-century tower (left) acts as a monumental gateway to the château. It houses a museum which tells the story of Joan of Arc. Its bell, named "Marie Javel", dates from 1399.

CHINON'S WINE
The local wine is known for its slightly earthy, fruity fragrance ■ 30.

▲ Chinon

RVE HAVTE Sᵗ MAVRICE

THE "BONS ENTONNEURS RABELAISIENS"
This winegrowers' brotherhood (below) follows the teachings of François Rabelais ● *97*, ▲ *250*, while celebrating the virtues of Chinon's wine. It meets five times a year in the Cave-Peincte (Painted Cellar).

The cellar's name comes from Rabelais' description of the paintings of dancing satyrs on its walls. Like the Caves Vaslins behind it, this cave was once a stone quarry, used when the château was enlarged in the 14th century. It was used for storing wine from the 15th century onward. In *Pantagruel* Rabelais recalls his visits to the Cave-Peincte where he drank "many glasses of chilled wine" while singing *Bonum vinûm laetificat cor hominum* ("Good wine gladdens the heart"). In the cul-de-sac parallel to this is a wine museum, the Musée du Vin et de la Tonnellerie, which has life-size mechanical figures illustrating work in a vineyard.

river valley. The tower served as a place of worship before the Chapel of St-Martin was built, which explains the presence of an apse. The machicolations around the top were added during the Second Empire. The TOUR DU MOULIN (Mill Tower) stands as a lookout post at the tip of the promontory: its name may be derived from the ovens near the gateway. The Angevin vaulting ● *60* on the first story probably dates from when the tower was built, under the Plantaganets.

BELOW THE CHÂTEAU ★

This quarter (opposite), which was once the center of the fortified town, has retained its medieval street pattern. The main road through the old town is the Rue Voltaire, formerly the Rue Haut-St-Maurice, of which René Boylesve said in his book *La Jeune Fille bien élevée*: "Rue St-Maurice in Chinon is so delightfully pretty! . . . The newest houses date from the 17th century; most are from the 15th and 16th centuries, some half-timbered and decorated with simple carvings, others built in the soft local stone, flanked by corner turrets with conical roofs, and pierced with bright mullioned windows."
THE GRAND-CARROI. The Grand-Carroi ("main crossroads") was the center of the town in the Middle Ages. It was here that the Rue Haut-St-Maurice met the streets rising from the Vienne to the château. One of the most beautiful half-timbered houses in the region can be seen here, on the corner of Rue Voltaire.
RUE JEANNE D'ARC. This street gives pedestrian access to the château. On the corner of Rue Voltaire, standing against a slate-covered house, is the coping of a well. According to legend Joan of Arc stepped on it, to dismount, when she arrived in Chinon; since then the well has never dried up. Not far from here is the Hôtel Torterue de Langardière (c. 1760), which has lovely wrought-iron balconies.
MAISON ROUGE. The Maison Rouge (nos. 38–42, Rue Voltaire) dates from the 14th and 15th centuries. Built of brick and wood, it is a typical example of the town's medieval architecture.
MAISON DES ÉTATS-GÉNÉRAUX. This house built of tufa owes its name to the meeting of the États-Généraux convened by Charles VII in 1428, when the English were laying siege to Orléans; it was held in the hall on the second story. On April 6, 1199 Richard Lionheart is said to have died here, from wounds received at Chalus. The collections of the Amis du

246

"Chinon, like Loches, is a masterpiece of a town. It is crowned with towers, keeps and crenelations, its houses with their pointed roofs are packed in between the rampart and the river, where a line of plane trees affords a perfect riverside promenade: this linear layout has its own special charm. Chinon is a jewel in the crown of Touraine; Chinon, through Joan of Arc, crowned the kingdom of France; Chinon is the glory of our past. How beautiful this town is: so insignificant today and yet in the past so replete with our country's future! Beautiful? Yes, it has the beauty of someone who has accomplished their task and retired from the commotion of the world to live in peaceful retirement. Not that it is overcome with sleepiness, or dozing off gradually at the foot of the hillside; but all that remains of its violent glory are the high ramparts and the empty towers, although something of its past splendors can still be sensed in the Grand-Carroi with its half-timbered houses, in the Carrefour du Puy-des-Bancs, in Rue de la Lamproie and Rue du Grenier-à-Sel, where it is easy to imagine the young Rabelais living a life of reckless pleasure."

Maurice Bedel
La Touraine

Hôtel des Eaux et
Forêts (above); and
Place du Général-
de-Gaulle (below).

Vieux Chinon displayed here feature items relating to river transport and popular traditions. They include a full-length portrait of Rabelais by Delacroix and an 11th-century cope, said to be Saint Mexme's, made of rich oriental fabrics.

PRIVATE HOUSES. Rue Voltaire is lined with private houses from the 15th, 16th and 17th centuries. Don't miss the HÔTEL DU GOUVERNEUR at no. 48. The town's governors lived in this house (built in the 15th and 17th centuries) after the château became inhabitable. The wing at the far end of the courtyard is taken up by a stone staircase with converging flights of stairs. The HÔTEL DU BAILLAGE (no. 71), now the Hostellerie Gargantua, was built in the 15th century: Rabelais' father, a lawyer, used to plead there. At no. 82 on Rue Voltaire, after the Church of St-Maurice, is the 16th-century HÔTEL DES EAUX ET FÔRETS (left), a U-shaped building with a raised courtyard. Opposite this is one of the old gates of the town (17th century), set into the façade of a building dating from the 15th and 16th centuries, which once housed the museum.

CHURCH OF ST-MAURICE. The church was built on the lower side of the street between the 12th and 16th centuries. The main nave has 12th-century Angevin vaulting.

FROM THE HÔTEL DE VILLE TO ST-MEXME

PLACE DU GÉNÉRAL-DE-GAULLE (below). This square used to be called the Place des Halles, because a covered

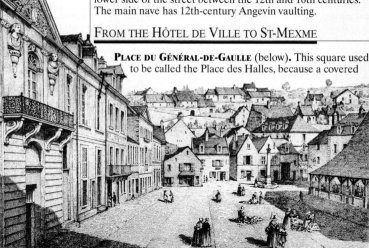

CHAPEL OF STE-RADEGONDE
The chapel is named after the pious Radegund (right), wife of the violent Chlotar I (497–561) who murdered his brother.

market stood on the site of the present-day town hall until the 18th century. From the square you can see a bronze statue of Rabelais by Émile Hébert (1882) and the Rue Rabelais, which is a pedestrian shopping street.

RUE DE LA LAMPROIE. The 18th-century house at no. 15 was built over the house of Rabelais' parents ▲ 250. It is said that Rabelais fished from the house when the water level was high – perhaps catching lampreys?

CHURCH OF ST-ÉTIENNE. Tradition has it that the church was built by a butcher, a draper and a baker; be that as it may, construction work began in the 15th century and the building was completed by Philippe de Commynes, governor of Chinon from 1477 to 1483, whose coat of arms can be seen over the portal. The three stained-glass windows of the choir were made by Léon Lobin in the 19th century, depicting the life of Saint Étienne and two historical events that took place in Chinon: the recognition of Charles VII by Joan of Arc and the meeting of John the Recluse with Saint Radegund.

COLLEGIATE CHURCH OF ST-MEXME. (Left, in 1810, before the bell tower collapsed.) This is one of the loveliest Romanesque buildings ● *58* in Touraine. The monastery was founded by Saint Mexme in the 5th century and elevated to collegiate status around 950; excavations have shown that it was built in seven phases between the 5th and the 15th centuries. It was closed down during the Revolution and then suffered serious damage when the central bell tower collapsed in 1817, destroying the choir and the transept. The forebuilding, from the early 11th century, is magnificently decorated with seventy carved slabs illustrating scenes from the life and passion of Christ. Before entering the nave, note the famous bas-relief of the Crucifixion, now damaged. One of the towers contains a chapel which was painted in the late 15th century: the Last Judgment (on the north wall) and the Fountain of Forgiveness (on the west wall) are still visible.

COTEAU STE-RADEGONDE

The steep path uphill is bordered with caves which were once used as dwellings (one or two are still inhabited). From here there is a view over the newer quarters of Chinon and the Vienne.

CHAPEL OF STE-RADEGONDE ★. (This can be reached by car, via the Route du Tunnel.) It is said that Saint Radegund ▲ *248* (below) came here to ask the English hermit John the Recluse to pray that she would not be forced to return to the court. When her prayer was answered, she decided to take the veil and founded a convent at Poitiers. John the Recluse moved here in the 6th century, after having prayed at the tomb of Saint Mexme. The Chapel of Ste-Radegonde was built in the 11th century on a north–south axis, around the cave where the hermit had lived: his tomb, which was plundered during the Revolution, can still be seen inside. On the vault of the small semicircular apse is the early-13th-century mural known as *La Chasse Royale* (Royal Hunt). Behind the chapel is a small museum of popular arts and traditions.

"LA CHASSE ROYALE"
There are at least three interpretations of this 13th-century mural (detail below). It may depict a subject taken from a chivalric novel, or the legend of Saint Gilles. According to the legend, Charlemagne had committed incest with his half-sister and no one, from his personal confessor to the pope, was willing to absolve him from the sin, until he encountered the hermit Saint Gilles during a hunt. The hermit heaped reproaches on him and commanded him to pray. The emperor and the saint then implored God's pardon together and a hand appeared, which symbolized divine absolution. However, the most generally accepted hypothesis is that the painting depicts the hunt during which John Lackland, accompanied by his mother Eleanor of Aquitaine, met his future wife Isabelle d'Angoulême.

RABELAIS AS SEEN BY PAINTERS
Since all portraits of Rabelais are posthumous, we do not know what he really looked like (above, anonymous 17th-century portrait). In view of this, the very sober-looking image (below) created by Matisse for La Devinière in 1951 is all the more surprising. Matisse opted for the more refined of the two faces of Rabelais described by La Bruyère: "When he is bad, he goes far

beyond the very worst and acquires the charm of the rabble; when he is good, he aspires to the exquisite and the excellent, and can be the most refined of writers."

RABELAIS COUNTRY

François Rabelais (1494–1553) is one of the four famous French writers born in the "Garden of France": the others are Pierre de Ronsard ▲ 258, the philosopher René Descartes (1596–1650) and Honoré de Balzac ● 90, ▲ 240. Between them the works of these four authors illustrate almost every aspect of the French character. Only Descartes – who was born in La Haye, now called Descartes, in southern Touraine – appears not to have been inspired by his native region. Nevertheless, the rigorous style of his philosophical works doubtless had its origin in this area, where the purest French is spoken. The region, especially the area around Chinon, had a strong influence on Rabelais.

LA DEVINIÈRE. This house, Rabelais' birthplace, is located at the heart of Rabelaisia, where the Picrocholine War (an important episode in *Gargantua*) is set. The world view of the Middle Ages had been based on a strict hierarchy ruled over by God; the Renaissance, with its new scientific, technical and intellectual discoveries, overthrew the old order, giving birth to new thoughts and ideals. This new age generated a hunger for knowledge and an unbounded enthusiasm for progress, which were given symbolic expression in the insatiable appetite of Rabelais' giants. La Devinière dates from the 15th century and was probably a winegrower's house.
It contains a collection of documents relating to the life and works of Rabelais, along with local furniture from the 16th and 17th centuries. The troglodyte caves in the basement are open to visitors. In the garden is a map created by the ceramist Jean Luneau in 1989, featuring characters, themes and locations from Rabelais' works.

CHÂTEAU DU RIVAU. Rabelais immortalized the name of Rivau in *Gargantua*, Chapter 49: Grandgousier, Gargantua's father, gives a great feast in honor of the Gargantuist captains who had won the Picrocholine War and showers them with gifts: "And what is

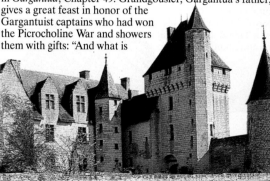

more he gave to each of them on permanent lease (unless they died without heirs) his adjoining castles and estates, to suit each of them: to Ponocrates he gave La Roche-Clermault, . . . Le Rivau to Tolmere." The three cylindrical towers, the moat and the façade behind the main building are remnants of the 13th-century feudal castle. Pierre de Beauvau, the château's owner in the 15th century, obtained permission from Charles VII to fortify it. The outbuildings, now separate from the château itself, date from the early 16th century. The great cylindrical pigeon loft has more than two thousand nesting holes.

ABBEY OF ST-PIERRE-DE-SEUILLY. Rabelais began his education at this 12th-century Benedictine abbey. He later set a scene of the Picrocholine War here (*Gargantua*, Chapter 27: "How a monk of Seuilly saved the abbey precinct from sacking by the enemy"). It was here that Frère Jean of the Entommeures – "who had a great big gob and was well provided in the nose department, who could rush through the hours and rattle through the mass" – attacked the troops of Picrochole, king of Lerné. The abbey now houses a center for environmental education.

CHÂTEAU DE LA ROCHE-CLERMAULT (private property). The château replaced a fortress used by Rabelais as a model in *Gargantua* (Chapter 28: "How Picrochole captured La Roche-Clermault"). Building work came to a sudden halt in 1638, leaving one of the side wings unbuilt. The castle has vast underground passages (said to be the most extensive in the region), with mysterious carvings on the walls. The road to Lerné is lined with troglodyte houses ● *80*.

ON THE BANKS OF THE VIENNE, TAVANT

CHURCH OF ST-NICHOLAS ★. This church, dating from the early 12th century, has a raised choir above a semi-underground crypt. The wall paintings in the crypt have made the church famous ▲ *252, 254*. The carved entrance portal is flanked by two blind arches. The capitals are decorated with motifs, such as sirens and fish, alluding to Tavant's riverside location. In the choir is a painting of Christ in Majesty surrounded by the symbols of the four Evangelists, and a cycle depicting Christ's childhood.

GREAT HUMOR AND SATIRE
Rabelais studied philosophy and Greek before becoming interested in medicine, which he practiced throughout his life. Regarded as the father of French prose, he was a linguistic craftsman and creator of words, expressions and images. His humanist philosophy expresses both the joys of knowledge and the pleasures of the flesh – celebrating food and wine, language, erudition and the spirit of tolerance – all conveyed by satire and parody.

FOUACES ● 97
It was these delicious pancakes (cooked in the oven or under the ashes, then filled with either *rillettes* or cheese) that sparked off the Picrocholine War, the bitter conflict between Grandgousier, Gargantua's father, and the king of the village of Lerné (below).

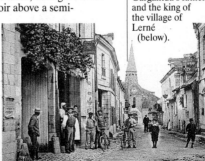

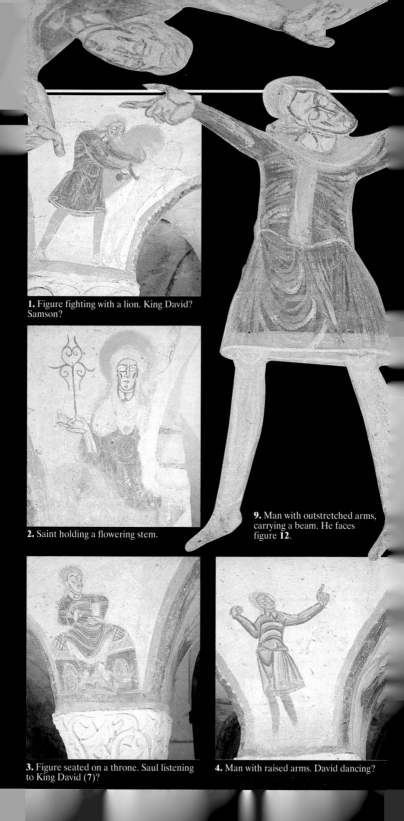

1. Figure fighting with a lion. King David? Samson?

2. Saint holding a flowering stem.

9. Man with outstretched arms, carrying a beam. He faces figure **12**.

3. Figure seated on a throne. Saul listening to King David (**7**)?

4. Man with raised arms. David dancing?

Plan of the crypt ● 58

A UNIQUE CYCLE OF
ROMANESQUE ● 58 PAINTINGS

The Comte de Galembert revealed the paintings' existence at the Archeological Congress of Caen in 1862, in a paper entitled *The Frescos of Touraine*. They were then forgotten again, until a short study by the American Melville Webber appeared in *Art Studies* in 1925. However, it was only through the writings of art historian Henri Focillon (1881–1943) and restoration work undertaken in 1942–5, by a team from the Beaux-Arts directed by Suzanne Flandrin, that this treasure of religious art became widely known. In Focillon's words this is "an art full of poetry and immediacy, life and movement. The figures themselves vibrate with life, their energy intensified by the speed with which they were produced." A reconstruction of the wall paintings can be seen in the Musée des Monuments Français in Paris.

6. Two men walking. Representing months or seasons?

7. King David playing the harp.

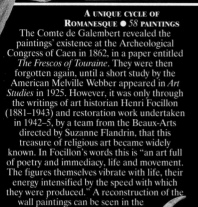

5.

8. Angel carrying a candleholder, as in figure **5** (left).

18. Christ in Majesty, at the far end of the crypt.

10. Figure in armor fighting a monster. The battle between Good and Evil?

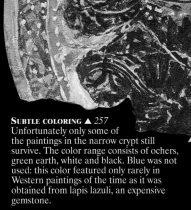

Subtle coloring ▲ 257

Unfortunately only some of the paintings in the narrow crypt still survive. The color range consists of ochers, green earth, white and black. Blue was not used: this color featured only rarely in Western paintings of the time as it was obtained from lapis lazuli, an expensive gemstone.

Symbolism. The significance of some scenes remains obscure. For example, there are two scenes that may depict the allegorical battle between Good and Evil (**10**).

11. Adam delving and Eve spinning.

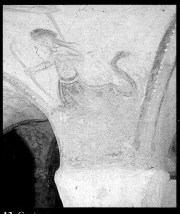

12. Atlas (cf. figure **9**).

13. Centaur.

16. Dishevelled woman. Various interpretations have been proposed. Perhaps she represents Lust, with bare breasts, attacked by serpents? Or Anger, piercing her own breast, as suggested by the Latin inscription *ira* (anger), which is no longer visible? Or even Lust and Anger combined?

17. Descent to Purgatory: Christ seizes Adam and Eve, God's hand holds back the devil.

14. The Virgin of Sorrows, with her arms outstretched.

15. The Deposition.

▲ FRESCO PAINTING

The ancient technique of fresco painting was used in the region from the Middle Ages onward. After 1450, when an increasing number of "gigantic" murals were produced, the painters began to use different grounds, pigments and preparatory methods.

"A FRESCO" PAINTING
In the *a fresco* painting technique the pigments are diluted with water and applied to a ground that is still wet (*fresco* = fresh). This means the artist has to work very quickly: the ground dries in less than a day.

"A SECCO" PAINTING
To overcome this difficulty painters adopted the *fresco secco* technique: the paint was applied to a dry ground of lime and plaster which they saturated with water before painting. This soaking technique, originally used by fresco artists to retouch their works, became the dominant technique in Europe after 1450. It gave the painter greater freedom, though at the expense of durability (fresco paintings are generally better preserved).

RESTORATION
Restorers sometimes retouch frescos discovered beneath whitewash by using watercolors then protecting the paintings with a removable fixative.

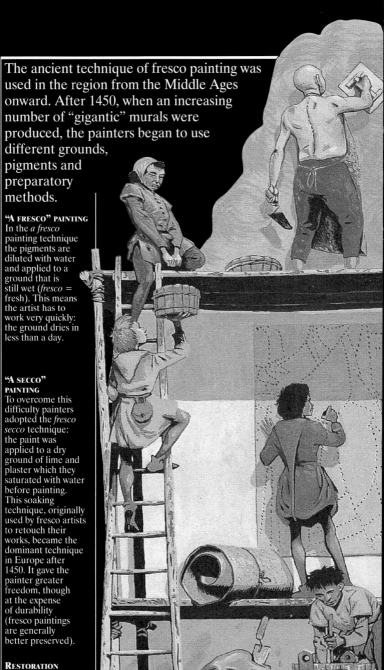

THE WALL. For fresco painting the wall is painted with an undercoat about half an inch thick, made of one part lime mixed with three parts of coarse sand. This coating produces a rough surface which helps bond the second layer (the *arricciato*), a finer mixture about a quarter of an inch thick. The third layer (the *intonaco*) is made of lime-rich plaster; the painting is done while the surface is still wet.

THE PIGMENTS. Frescos are painted on an alkaline surface, which produces variations in the color and luminosity of the paint as it dries. The best pigments are those of mineral or organic origin with a good resistance to lime. For retouching, the pigments were ground in a binding medium such as egg, fig milk or limewater.

THE PIGMENTS
Pigments of mineral origin were ground, then diluted in water. They were applied with thick bristle brushes.

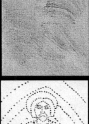

CARTOON TECHNIQUE
The artist marked out the composition by making perforations along the lines of the drawing. The cartoon was applied to the wall and dabbed with charcoal powder to reproduce the image. After 1450 this method gradually replaced the *sinopia* technique (in which a red pigment was used to draw the design on the *arricciato*).

FINISHING
The painted surface was smoothed with a trowel coated with a wax-based solution, and then polished. Sometimes it was varnished with wax.

15. FONTEVRAUD-
L'ABBAYE
14. MONTSOREAU
13. CANDES-
ST-MARTIN
12. AVOINE-CHINON
POWER STATION
11. BOURGUEIL
10. USSÉ

🚗 c. 50 miles
⏱ 2 days

PRIORY OF ST-COSME ★ (H6)

HISTORY OF THE PRIORY. In 1092 the Basilica of St-Martin in Tours founded a priory for five canons on the former island in the Loire

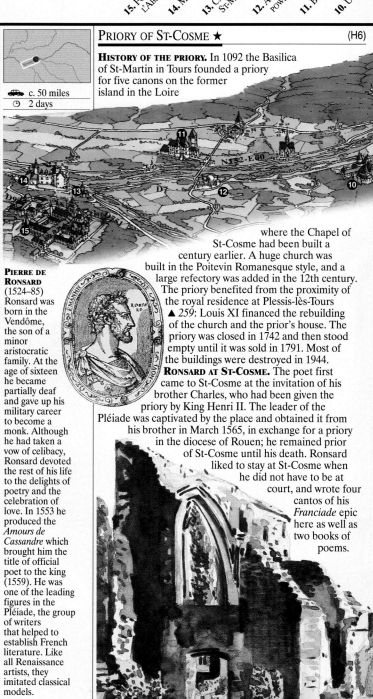

where the Chapel of St-Cosme had been built a century earlier. A huge church was built in the Poitevin Romanesque style, and a large refectory was added in the 12th century. The priory benefited from the proximity of the royal residence at Plessis-lès-Tours ▲ *259*: Louis XI financed the rebuilding of the church and the prior's house. The priory was closed in 1742 and then stood empty until it was sold in 1791. Most of the buildings were destroyed in 1944.

RONSARD AT ST-COSME. The poet first came to St-Cosme at the invitation of his brother Charles, who had been given the priory by King Henri II. The leader of the Pléiade was captivated by the place and obtained it from his brother in March 1565, in exchange for a priory in the diocese of Rouen; he remained prior of St-Cosme until his death. Ronsard liked to stay at St-Cosme when he did not have to be at court, and wrote four cantos of his *Franciade* epic here as well as two books of poems.

PIERRE DE RONSARD (1524–85) Ronsard was born in the Vendôme, the son of a minor aristocratic family. At the age of sixteen he became partially deaf and gave up his military career to become a monk. Although he had taken a vow of celibacy, Ronsard devoted the rest of his life to the delights of poetry and the celebration of love. In 1553 he produced the *Amours de Cassandre* which brought him the title of official poet to the king (1559). He was one of the leading figures in the Pléiade, the group of writers that helped to establish French literature. Like all Renaissance artists, they imitated classical models.

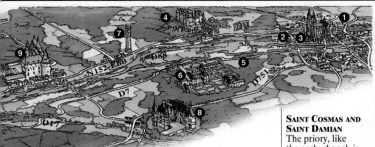

He is buried in the choir of the church (his cenotaph can be seen at the museum in Blois).

TOUR. All that survives of the priory buildings today is the splendid refectory, the *hôtelier* (guest house), the *régulier* (monks' house), the prior's residence (with reconstructions of Ronsard's bedroom and study) and some ruins of the church (the ambulatory and two apsidioles).

CHÂTEAU DU PLESSIS-LES-TOURS   (H6)

BUILT BY LOUIS XI. Plessis-lès-Tours is mentioned in 15th-century documents, under the name of Chastel des Montils or Plessis-du-Parc-lez-Tours. At that time it was owned by the Maillé family. Louis XI bought the estate in 1464 and built a sober château of brick with stone piers. The château gradually became the king's favorite place of residence, and thus the center of the French kingdom.

ROYAL RESIDENCE. Plessis was not deserted by the royal family after Louis XI's death: they stayed here frequently, and work on the château continued for nearly a hundred years. Drawings of the château from the 17th century show that at that time it was considerably larger. It was probably Plessis that made this type of brick building fashionable from the end of the 15th century onward. Near the château was a large park, which served both as a rabbit warren and a menagerie: this was one of the favorite attractions of the king and his guests.

SAINT COSMAS AND SAINT DAMIAN
The priory, like the early chapel, is dedicated to Saint Cosmas; it is probable that the chapel housed the saint's relics. Cosmas and Damian were Syrian doctors who were martyred in the early 4th century. Their cult was very popular in Touraine. The central apsidiole of the Church of St-Cosme has copies of 15th-century statues of the two saints, bearing the tools of their trade; the originals can be seen at the Hôtel Gouin in Tours ▲ 208.

FAMOUS EPITAPH
Ronsard's tomb bears the following inscription: "Pay heed, passer-by! This ground is sacred. Ronsard lies here. The Muses were born with him and died with him, and were buried in the same tomb."

▲ LOUIS XI AND THE SILK INDUSTRY AT TOURS

fondée en 1830

This emblem can still be seen on the pediment over the door of the Le Manach factory.

Today the silk industry of Tours, which was started by Louis XI, employs no more than forty or so people; but in the late 16th century it sustained one third of the town's active population. For many years Tours rivaled Lyon in terms of the volume and quality of silk produced; since then the industry has gradually fallen into oblivion.

THE FIRST FACTORIES

In 1470 Louis XI decided to found a silk factory near to his château at Montils-lès-Tours and brought workers for it from Lyon. The trade gradually became established, and guilds with strict regulations were founded. At this time Tours was the capital of the kingdom: the court, with its taste for luxurious fabrics, contributed to the rise of the new industry.

SERICULTURE

The silkworms were bred in special farms known locally as *verreries* or *verries*. Only the white mulberry (above) provides the right conditions for the larvae of *Bombyx mori*, the white moth that produces silk thread.

SILKWORMS

The worm lives for only six days. It makes its cocoon by spinning a continuous thread of silk that can be up to 1,600 yards long. The cocoons are collected before they can be shed; the chrysalises are destroyed. Only pupae destined for breeding are allowed to become moths.

HEYDAY AND DECLINE

In 1550 the town had 85,000 inhabitants (as many as in 1939) and the silk industry supported nearly 40,000 of them: weavers, dyers, haberdashers, ribbon makers, embroiderers and merchants. The fabrics produced included taffeta, velvet, damask and sumptuous brocades. Later the Tours silk industry was eclipsed by its competitors, mainly Protestant manufacturers who left France after the revocation of the Edict of Nantes and settled in England and Holland. By 1689 only 120 looms were in operation.

> **"THE PANNES [VELVETS] THEY MAKE IN TOURS ARE SO GOOD THAT THEY ARE SENT TO SPAIN, ITALY AND OTHER FOREIGN LANDS."**
>
> CARDINAL DE RICHELIEU

RENAISSANCE

Tours' silk industry revived in the early 18th century, and the local designers were widely reputed. A decree issued by the Conseil d'État in 1787 protected their patterns for fifteen years. Fabrics from Tours won the top prizes at the universal exhibitions of 1867 and 1878. Today only the Roze and

Le Manach factories continue the tradition of making silk in Tours.

Louis XI having mulberry trees planted (A. Bauchant, 1943)

LUYNES
Charles d'Albert, originally from Tuscany, was the head of Louis XIII's government. He left his mark on the Château de Maillé, giving both the castle and the village the new name of Luynes.

PLESSIS AFTER THE ROYAL ERA. In the mid 18th century the château was converted into private houses, and the grounds were used as a nursery for mulberry trees. Later it became a paupers' prison. In the following century the buildings were converted into a factory for lead shot, then into a farm, and even into an immunological institute. The old royal castle was altered beyond recognition. A four-hundred-year-old mulberry can still be seen in the grounds – one of the trees planted by Henri IV, following the tradition established by Louis XI ▲ *260*.

LUYNES

The Château de Luynes belonged to the same Maillé family ▲ *259* that sold Plessis to Louis XI. In 1619 it was acquired by Charles d'Albert (1578–1621), proprietor of an estate at Luynes in Provence.

CHÂTEAU DE LUYNES. This imposing foursquare fortress with circular towers stands on a rocky outcrop overlooking the Loire. Built in the 13th century, it was altered in the 15th and 17th centuries. A dry moat separates it from the hillside to the north and the east. To the west is a brick building with stone piers, reminiscent of Plessis-lès-Tours. The Chapel of the Canonesses, in the Flamboyant style, dates from 1486. The château has come through the centuries intact and has been owned by the same family for three hundred years. Now at last it has opened its doors to visitors, who can admire its gardens and its rich interior decoration. It is an unusually harmonious place, a living illustration of historical continuity. At the foot of the château a number of 15th-century half-timbered houses can be seen around the picturesque marketplace.

SAVONNIÈRES ★

Savonnières (below) is reached by the D88, a small road that runs between the Loire and the Cher, offering a pretty view of one of the most picturesque villages in Touraine.

THE GROTTES PÉTRIFIANTES. These caves were first mentioned by the ceramist Bernard Palissy (c.1510–90) in 1547; they are old quarries which were used in the

"A HOUSE IN THE COUNTRY"
This is what Louis XI wanted his château to be. It was made of brick with stone piers, like the houses that the nobility and wealthy citizens were building by the Loire at this time. Toward the end of his life Louis XI became obsessively fearful of assassins and had the château made impregnable, with iron railings, grilles and spikes. These extreme security measures led Walter Scott (1771–1832) in *Quentin Durward*, and after him the Romantic writers, to depict Plessis as a fortress.

16th century for mining the white chalk, known as *pierre de Bourré*, employed for building the Château de Villandry. Water oozing out of the cave walls leaves a deposit of calcite (as much as half an inch during the course of a year), so objects left there become petrified.

VILLANDRY

THE CHÂTEAU. The Château de Villandry was built by Jean Le Breton, secretary of state under François I, who also created Villesavin ▲ *166*. It was built between 1532 and 1540 on a platform surrounded by a moat, with a design that was typical of the period ● *69*: a main building at the far end of a paved courtyard, with two side wings set at right angles to it. However, at Villandry the wings are not exactly the same length, and they do not form an exact right angle with the main building. These irregularities came about because the château was built over the foundations of an earlier construction, the Château de Colombier. A fourth wing closing off the courtyard was demolished in the 18th century. The façades are surmounted by square mullioned dormer windows, crowned by ornate protruding pediments. There are galleries with porticos, at ground level, around the main courtyard. The elegant façades feature a grid-like arrangement of horizontal and vertical lines. The château was acquired by the Marquis de Castellane in 1754. He made significant alterations to the old Renaissance building, adapting the façades to the classical style. Early this century Dr Joachim Carvallo restored Villandry's 16th-century appearance and re-created the gardens ▲ *264* in Renaissance style. In the east wing of the château is a gallery with a collection of paintings by Spanish masters and sculptures, including a Virgin and Child from the 11th century. From the gardens there is a lovely view over the chevet of the Church of St-Étienne, which dates from the 11th and 12th centuries.

TWO ARCHITECTURAL TRENDS
Villandry stands at the crossroads of two architectural styles. On the one hand, it reflects the style in which the châteaux of the Loire valley had been built for the two previous decades. On the other, it bears the mark of the architectural style fashionable in the Île-de-France region around 1530: this can be seen in the square pavilions that take the place of corner towers.

"SAPONARIA"
The name Savonnières comes from *saponaria*, Latin for soapwort, a plant that was used in fulling cloth.

Early this century Joachim Carvallo undertook to re-create the gardens of Villandry as they would have been during the Renaissance. From the 16th century onward there were two main sources of influence on French garden design: the monasteries with their kitchen garden tradition, and the ornamental gardens of Italy, with their fountains and arbors. One of the first Italian-style gardens was created at Amboise ▲ *188* under Charles VIII, using Italian gardeners.

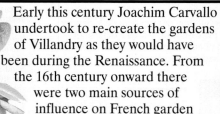

JOACHIM CARVALLO (1869–1936), CREATOR OF THE GARDENS
Carvallo was born in Spain, to a family of modest means. He studied medicine in Madrid then joined the physiology laboratory in Paris of Professor Charles Richet (Nobel Prize, 1913). Here he met Ann Coleman, a wealthy American whom he married in 1899. While looking for a house in the country they came upon Villandry ▲ *263* and fell under its spell. Carvallo gave up his medical work and devoted his life to the château. First he removed architectural features of the 18th and 19th centuries, and then started his restoration project for the gardens, a unique undertaking in France. The gardens he created are maintained by his descendants today.

SOURCES OF INSPIRATION
There were no documents relating to the gardens of Villandry in the 16th century. Joachim Carvallo drew his inspiration from two reference works on Renaissance art: the *Monasticon Gallicanum* produced by the congregation of St-Maur in 1694, and *Les Plus Excellents Bastiments de France* by Jacques Androuet du Cerceau.

MN TO VEGETABLES. Nicolas de Bonnecamp, a 17th-century doctor and ·t, described kitchen gardens in the following words: "The asparagus and artichoke, the piquant celery/ The beetroot, the cauliflower, and spicy sify/ The royal lettuce and the all too tender afange/ With scornful lacity take the place of flowers./ Their size, their tenderness and their e/ Reveal to gourmets the goodness within them./ Thus in these gardens ity and delight/ Join together, to feast the eyes and the dinner table."

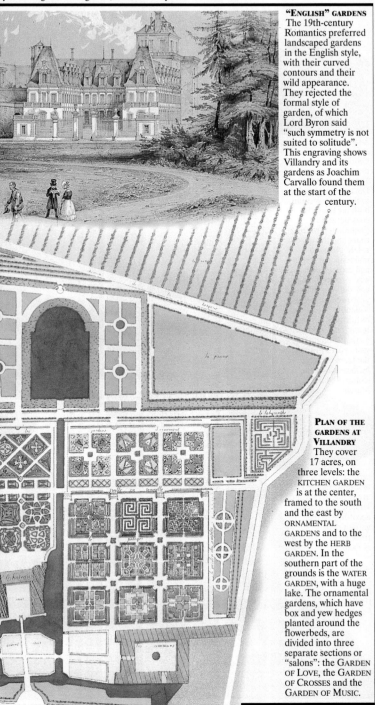

"ENGLISH" GARDENS
The 19th-century Romantics preferred landscaped gardens in the English style, with their curved contours and their wild appearance. They rejected the formal style of garden, of which Lord Byron said "such symmetry is not suited to solitude". This engraving shows Villandry and its gardens as Joachim Carvallo found them at the start of the century.

PLAN OF THE GARDENS AT VILLANDRY
They cover 17 acres, on three levels: the KITCHEN GARDEN is at the center, framed to the south and the east by ORNAMENTAL GARDENS and to the west by the HERB GARDEN. In the southern part of the grounds is the WATER GARDEN, with a huge lake. The ornamental gardens, which have box and yew hedges planted around the flowerbeds, are divided into three separate sections or "salons": the GARDEN OF LOVE, the GARDEN OF CROSSES and the GARDEN OF MUSIC.

Below: view of the kitchen garden.

A GARDEN FOR ALL SEASONS
Gardening plans are drawn up during November and December. They have to take into account both horticultural considerations (including flowering times and the need to rotate plants to maintain soil fertility) and esthetic ones, as well as color schemes and the provision of a year-round display. Villandry has a team of full-time gardeners to take care of this work, including the vast task of pruning the trees and rose bushes during the winter. From March

THE GARDEN OF LOVE. The designs of the four squares of the garden symbolize four aspects of love: hearts (left) and flames for romantic love, swords and daggers for tragic love, horns and fans for adulterous love, and broken hearts for passionate love.

onward vegetables and flowering plants are planted; they are tended and replaced according to the garden plan through to November.

A square of the kitchen garden (right).

THE SYMBOLIC MEANINGS OF CERTAIN VEGETABLES
EGGPLANTS can signify pleasure – but also symbolize poison.
CABBAGES, with their tightly packed leaves, represent happiness and prosperity.
BROAD BEANS are supposed to house the souls of the dead.
PEPPERS symbolize fire, one of the four elements of which the world is made.
PARSLEY is considered to be a magic plant.

THE HERB GARDEN
This garden has around thirty varieties
of aromatic and medicinal plants.

THE GARDEN OF CROSSES
Clipped box hedges make up the
crosses of Languedoc, the Basque country
and Malta (above and below). They are
surrounded by flowers of different colors
according to the season.

**THE KITCHEN
GARDEN IN THE
16TH CENTURY**
In the Renaissance,
new vegetables from
the Americas aroused
a new interest in
kitchen gardens. The
gardens were brought
closer to the main
residence, so that the
owners could
supervise them; they
were decorated
with flowers and
architectural
ornaments
from Italy.

**THE KITCHEN GARDEN
AT VILLANDRY**
It consists of nine
squares that have
identical dimensions,
with varying
geometrical designs
and colors. A total
of around 120,000
vegetable plants
and 15,000 flowering
plants are required
to ensure a year-
round display.

**THE
MUSIC
GARDEN**
Small ponds and
fountains punctuate
the design.

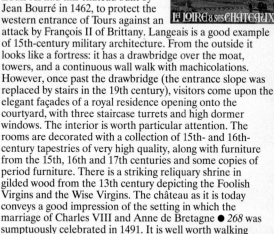

CHEMIN DE FER DE PARIS À ORLEANS

LA LOIRE & SES CHÂTEAUX

LANGEAIS

CHÂTEAU DE LANGEAIS ● 66.
Louis XI had this château built by
Jean Bourré in 1462, to protect the
western entrance of Tours against an
attack by François II of Brittany. Langeais is a good example
of 15th-century military architecture. From the outside it
looks like a fortress: it has a drawbridge over the moat,
towers, and a continuous wall walk with machicolations.
However, once past the drawbridge (the entrance slope was
replaced by stairs in the 19th century), visitors come upon the
elegant façades of a royal residence opening onto the
courtyard, with three staircase turrets and high dormer
windows. The interior is worth particular attention. The
rooms are decorated with a collection of 15th- and 16th-
century tapestries of very high quality, along with furniture
from the 15th, 16th and 17th centuries and some copies of
period furniture. There is a striking reliquary shrine in
gilded wood from the 13th century depicting the Foolish
Virgins and the Wise Virgins. The château as it is today
conveys a good impression of the setting in which the
marriage of Charles VIII and Anne de Bretagne ● 268 was
sumptuously celebrated in 1491. It is well worth walking
round the wall walk, which runs around the entire building.
From here there is a view over the rooftops to the Loire.
Opposite: views of the Loire near Langeais.
THE OLDEST STONE KEEP IN FRANCE. In the château garden
stand the east and south walls of a keep built before the year
1000 by Foulques Nerra, the powerful Count of Anjou
known as the Black Falcon ▲ 278, 297.
THE TOWN. Opposite the drawbridge as you leave the château
is a Renaissance house known as the House of Rabelais,
where the writer is said to have lived. The CHURCH OF ST-
JEAN-BAPTISTE, beyond the small bridge, is striking for its
large transept and its juxtaposition of diverse architectural
styles. The square porch tower with buttresses dates from the
12th century, while the transept was added in 1869; a
photograph of the church before the addition of the transept
can be seen in the 16th-century vaulted porch. In the choir
is a frieze showing two lions facing each other, separated by
a palm leaf, probably from the Carolingian period. On
Rue Foulques-Nerra is the former CHURCH OF ST-LAURENT
from the 12th century: it now houses the MUSÉE DE
L'ARTISANAT, which displays a vast collection of 19th-century
tools and brings to life all sorts of forgotten crafts and trades.

RIGNY-USSÉ

**CHÂTEAU D'USSÉ, FROM THE MIDDLE AGES TO THE
RENAISSANCE.** Gildin de Saumur, the rival of Foulques Nerra,
was the first to settle here: he built a fortress to command the
Loire valley. A passage from inside the castle leads to an
underground refuge – a telling reminder of that turbulent
time. In the mid 15th century Antoine de Bueil, whose wife
Jeanne was the daughter of Agnès Sorel ▲ 227, 244 and
Charles VII, decided to build a château in contemporary
style. A drawbridge gave access to the quadrangular inner
courtyard, which was surrounded by buildings and curtain

**ANNE DE BRETAGNE
AND CHARLES VIII**
The crown of Brittany
was a major stake in
the conflict between
the Capetians and the
Plantaganets. The
marriages of Anne de
Bretagne (1477–1514)
with Charles VIII
(1470–98) and then
with Louis XII
(1462–1515) annexed
the Duchy of Brittany
to the French
kingdom. However,
the two territories
were not officially
united until the États
de Vannes of 1532.

**LANGEAIS
EARTHENWARE**
Charles de
Boissimont
(1817–79) made it
famous throughout
Europe: his factory
produced pieces in
unusual shapes,
decorated with
platinum (which
was cheaper than
gold or silver).

THE BRIDGE AT LANGEAIS (1950)
This bridge has been rebuilt
four times and still plays a vital
role: it is the only bridge across
the Loire between Tours ▲ *193*
and Bourgueil, which are
28 miles apart.

Dormer window
of the Château
d'Ussé.

CHÂTEAU D'USSÉ
With its terraced
gardens, an orangery
(recently restored),
and furniture
collected by the
owners since the
17th century, this
château has a
fairy-tale air about
it. Perrault is said
to have used it as
his model for the
castle in Sleeping
Beauty; Alexis de
Tocqueville called
it "a symbol of the
Old France".

LOCAL DISPUTE
When Saint Martin
died at Candes, his
remains became the
object of a dispute
between the monks
of Poitou and
Touraine. The
Poitevins claimed
the body, but the
Tourangeaux stole
it by night and
brought it back to
Tours by boat.
A solemn procession
was held at Tours,
where the saint
was buried.

walls. The château stands
above a sheer rockface
overlooking the Indre; it is
protected on the forest side
by a deep dry moat and
defended to the west by a
high keep which had a view
over the hill. A century later
the wall facing the valley was
demolished, and the château's doors
and windows were ornamented in the Italian
Renaissance style. A lovely chapel on the hillside
reflects the high status of Ussé's owners, who
founded it as a collegiate church.

FROM THE 17TH CENTURY TO THE PRESENT DAY.
In the 17th century, for the marriage of Maréchal
de Vauban's daughter, the glacis on which the château stands
was transformed into a series of terraces, slopes and steps
decorated with flowers and orange trees. The old keep was
partly hidden by an Italian-style wing with more comfortable
rooms. In the 19th century the Duchesse de Duras bought
the estate and all its furniture; the poet Chateaubriand
visited her and wrote part of his *Mémoires d'outre-tombe*
here. The duchess left the château to her daughter, who
added a façade in the troubadour style and built a gallery
decorated with stained-glass windows on the west façade
(the gallery connected the far end of the château with the
Vauban wing, bypassing the public rooms). After this the
château passed to the Duc de Blacas, a minister of
Louis XVIII; his descendants are the current owners.

CANDES-ST-MARTIN   (E7)

This is one of France's loveliest villages, located halfway
between Chinon and Saumur. Its name derives from the
Gallic word *condate* (confluence): the Vienne river meets
the Loire at this point.
BEFORE CANDES BECAME CANDES-ST-MARTIN. The history
of Candes begins with the Roman occupation, when
fortifications were built around the town. At the end of the
19th century archeologists discovered the remains of a
pagan temple: it had been demolished by Saint Martin, who
came to Candes around 387 to convert the inhabitants and
found the fourth or fifth parish of France. In 397 Martin
returned to Candes to settle differences that
had arisen between the monks, and died here
after completing this task. Candes
immediately became a major
pilgrimage center and a stage
on the pilgrims' route to
Santiago de

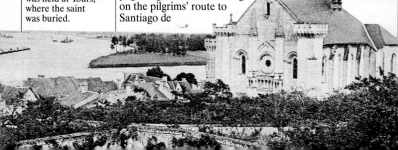

PORTAL OF THE COLLEGIATE CHURCH OF ST-MARTIN
The niches around the doorway contain decapitated statues, carved into the stone of the façade.

At the foot of the statues are crowned heads, as well as interlacing foliage, dragons and sirens.

THE DEATH OF SAINT MARTIN
Detail from a stained-glass window depicting the saint's burial ▲ 270 and the last years of his life ▲ 206. The window, which measures approximately 23 feet by 5 feet, comes from the choir of the Cathedral of St-Gatien at Tours ▲ 196. It was made around 1300.

Compostela. Several kings of France stayed here: Charles the Bald, Philippe Auguste, Charles VII, Louis XI and Charles VIII.

COLLEGIATE CHURCH OF ST-MARTIN. The house where Saint Martin died was beginning to fall into ruin at the start of the 12th century, and the canons built a church in the saint's name around it: this is the present-day CHAPEL OF ST-MARTIN (to the left of the main altar of the collegiate church). The collegiate church itself was built later, from 1175 to 1225: the short time span explains its unity of style. As one war followed another, the church was fortified for self-defense and to shelter the local population from invaders: inside the church is a well, and there are bread ovens in the lofts. The ENTRANCE PORCH to the south is unique and worth a close look. The vaulting, whose ribs resemble the branches of a palm tree, springs from a light monolithic column at the center, which appears to bear the entire weight of the structure. Above the porch, one of the windows of the CHAPEL OF ST-MICHEL looks directly onto the vaults of the collegiate church. The west façade is dominated by a stone cross situated at the junction of two staircases leading to the top of the two square defensive towers. The great portal to the west is surmounted by thirteen empty niches which may have held statues of Christ and the twelve apostles. The church's north façade is remarkable for its synthesis of religious and military architecture, and for its two towers with crenelations and machicolations.

THE INTERIOR OF THE CHURCH. The main nave of the church is very striking, with its pure soaring vaults in the Plantaganet style ● 60. The choir and the apse, with their rounded vaults, date from the late Romanesque era. The vaulting of all three naves, which are of equal height, has intersecting ribs springing from decorative culs-de-lampe. The carvings vary greatly in style, and there are even some rough blocks of unworked stone in the church and on the façades. No doubt a limited budget meant that artists of varying abilities were employed, and that the decorations could not be completed as planned.

THE VILLAGE. In the Middle Ages the town's Roman defenses were reinforced with solid walls surrounded by a dry moat. At

INTERIOR DECORATION OF THE CHURCH
The culs-de-lampe of the nave are carved with plants and figures. Some of the original colored paintwork can still be seen on statues of the apostles, Old Testament prophets and kings, and Saint Martin himself.

The Grand-Moutier Cloisters at Fontevraud (below).

Plan of the abbey (right)

ROBERT D'ARBRISSEL AT FONTEVRAUD
D'Arbrissel (right) founded five priories in 1101, each providing for a different religious community: STE-MARIE or the

GRAND-MOUTIER for nuns; LA MADELEINE for repentant prostitutes; ST-JEAN-DE-L'HABIT for monks; ST-LAZARE for lepers and the nuns who tended them; and ST-BENOÎT (which later became a hospital) for the sick and infirm.

THE KITCHEN
This was restored by Magne in the early 20th century. He reproduced the original appearance of the roofs of the apsidioles, but added lantern chimneytops.

this stage Candes was ruled by the archbishops of Tours, who used the castle as a summer residence. The original CASTLE was ruined during the Hundred Years' War and was rebuilt in 1485. In 1682 the bishop found it uncomfortable and built another RESIDENCE near to the 15th-century Tour de l'Enfant on the ramparts. Opposite the church was a MAISON-DIEU, which took in the sick and also poor pilgrims. Some lovely old houses can be seen in the picturesque little streets of the village.

ROYAL ABBEY OF FONTEVRAUD (E8)

The Abbey of Fontevraud was built in the 12th century on the Benedictine model and covers an area of 35 acres, making it the largest monastic complex in western Christendom. Work on the buildings began in 1101 and continued until 1789: as a result the abbey displays a range of architectural styles. The buildings reflect the taste, techniques and artistic aims of the various periods in which they were built.

BEGINNINGS. The end of the 11th century was an unsettled time, when the Gregorian reforms were slowly beginning to bring order into the life of the clergy, condemning practices such as the sale of ecclesiastical benefits and indulgences. Robert d'Arbrissel (c. 1047–1117) was a priest from Brittany who attempted to implement these reforms, without success. As a consequence he decided to live as a hermit. Soon he was surrounded by disciples and founded his first abbey, situated on the borders of Brittany, Normandy and Anjou. Pope Urban II appointed D'Arbrissel an apostolic preacher and he left his community to take up an itinerant life. Again he gathered a group of men and women from all walks of life and settled on a site in the middle of a forest, near to a spring and the Loire river, on the borders of three bishoprics: Anjou, Touraine and Poitou. This was to become Fontevraud. D'Arbrissel decided that the Order of Fontevraud would include both men and women, and follow the Benedictine rule; he also decreed that it should be directed by a woman. This tradition remained unbroken: Fontevraud had a total of thirty-six abbesses from its foundation until the Revolution (half of them of royal blood).

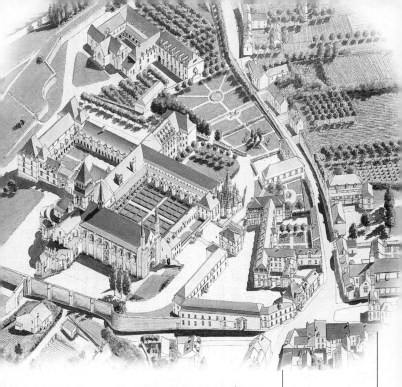

UNTIL THE REVOLUTION. The abbey attracted large donations from the start. More priories were founded, and at its height the Order had priories all over France (123 in all) and also in Spain and England. Fontevraud flourished under the protection of the Plantaganets, who made it their royal mausoleum ▲ *183*. Their decline affected the abbey's prosperity, which only recovered in the 17th century, thanks to the influence of abbesses from the House of Bourbon. Gabrielle de Rochechouart (left), the thirty-second abbess and a very learned woman, was the sister of Madame de Montespan, Louis XIV's mistress: under her rule Fontevraud became a cultural center, where literature and philosophy were discussed. Louis XV entrusted the education of his four youngest daughters to Abbess Louise Françoise de Rochechouart, whom he made a duchess. Under the Revolution all the monks and nuns were expelled, the abbey's furniture was designated national property and sold off, and two of the priories were demolished and used as sources of stone.

THE PRISON ERA. In 1804 Napoleon converted the abbey into a penitentiary for women, men and children. Its intended capacity was seven hundred people, but it actually housed as many as eighteen hundred. Under the Restoration it became a central

ANGUISH
"Of all the central prisons in France, Fontevraud is the most disturbing. This is the one which gave me the strongest impression of anguish and desolation." These words of Jean Genet (1910–86), describe the abbey in his novel *Miracle de la Rose* (1946). He was never imprisoned at Fontevraud himself, but was familiar with prisons from having passed three years in jail as a youth and frequently visited a friend detained at Fontevraud.

The lovely 17th-century spiral staircase at the Priory of St-Lazare.

THE CHAPTER HOUSE
It was here that the chapter of nuns took decisions relating to the life of the abbey. It was built between 1543 and 1562, with a richly worked portal opening onto the main cloister.

prison for nineteen *départements*; the buildings were partitioned, divided or demolished, and the prisoners worked more than twelve hours a day in various workshops and factories. Later it was used as a prison for members of the Resistance during World War Two, then for collaborators in 1945.

ARCHITECTURAL DIVERSITY. The ABBEY CHURCH, the main place of worship, was built in the 12th century. It is impressive for its generous dimensions (300 feet by 50 feet), for the ethereal architecture of the choir, and its Romanesque nave with Byzantine cupolas. In architectural terms the Romanesque KITCHEN is Fontevraud's most famous feature. This round building, 100 feet high with eight apsidal hearths, is built entirely of stone (including the roof, which has a fish-scale pattern). Its unusual appearance has prompted questions regarding its purpose. Was it originally the refuge of the brigand Evraud, who according to legend was converted by Robert d'Arbrissel? Or a funerary chapel? Nevertheless, its seems probable that it was indeed a kitchen, used for curing food and preparing meals for the abbey's three thousand inhabitants. The CHAPEL OF ST-BENOIT has

The walls are covered with scenes from the New Testament (above), painted by the Anjou artist Thomas Pot around 1560. If you look closely at the paintings, you will see that some figures are incomplete. It is a tradition that each Abbess of Fontevraud should be represented in the chapter house, and some of the figures had to be erased to make space for new ones.

Plantaganet-style vaulting, as does the CHAPEL OF THE PRIORY OF ST-LAZARE. Many of the abbey's buildings, including the MAIN CLOISTER and the GRAND-MOUTIER CLOISTERS, were rebuilt or extended in the 16th, 17th and 18th centuries.

TODAY. The abbey was handed over to the Ministry of Culture in 1963. Until 1985 one of the priories continued to house around thirty detainees whose job was to eradicate the most obvious reminders of the prison era. Intensive restoration work has been under way since 1975. Be sure to take a walk in the village. The charming CHURCH OF ST-MICHEL, with its rich interior decoration, stands at one end of a pleasant avenue of lime trees; nearby is the FUNERARY CHAPEL OF STE-CATHERINE.

ROYAL MAUSOLEUM
In the abbey church are the colored recumbent effigies of Henry II (left), the first of the Plantaganet kings of England ● *38*, his wife Eleanor of Aquitaine (bottom), their son Richard the Lionheart (above) and Isabelle d'Angoulême (left), wife of their other son, John Lackland (King John). The history of the House of Anjou is closely interwoven with that of Fontevraud. Henry II's grandfather gave many donations to Robert d'Arbrissel; and his daughter, Mathilde d'Anjou, became the second abbess of Fontevraud. Henry II stayed here with his aunt in 1154 before setting off to pursue his claim to the English crown. Eleanor made substantial donations to Fontevraud after 1170: on her husband's behalf she was seeking to stir up the nobility of western France, and wanted to ensure the support of this powerful abbey. She retired here in 1194, when over seventy years old, while continuing to support her sons in the struggle against Philippe Auguste.

MONTSOREAU (E7)

The Château de Montsoreau stands at the foot of a tufa rockface that stretches along the river. It was the earliest fortress in southern Anjou ▲ *12*, a stronghold built in the Middle Ages to defend the territory against Touraine and Poitou. It overlooks the beautiful, serene landscape around the Loire and Vienne rivers. The old town on the hillside is so close to the village of Candes ▲ *270* that Rabelais' words are still quoted: "Between Candes and Montsoreau grazes neither cow nor calf."

THE CHÂTEAU. From the 11th century onward the castle commanded the river route between Saumur and Chinon, serving as both fortress and tollhouse. At this time the town consisted of the port of Rest-sous-Montsoreau, beside the river, and the town of Montsoreau on the hillside. Today's château was built in three phases between 1445 and the end of the 15th century, by Jean de Cambes, counsellor of King Charles VII. Its contrasting styles of architecture illustrate the transition between feudal fortress and Renaissance palace ● 67.

Two towers of military appearance, with crenelations, loopholes and machicolations, overlook the river. The main building was erected between these two towers from 1510 onward, in a delightful early-Renaissance style with mullioned windows and two small adjoining wings. The right-hand wing contains an impressive staircase, added between 1520 and 1530. The rooms of the second story now house the Museum of Moroccan Goums (the Goums were cavalry units administered by the French army during the colonial period and World War Two). The museum was transferred here from Rabat at the suggestion of the château's owner, the Marquis de Geoffre, in 1956 at the end of the French Protectorate.

THE OLD TOWN. The path up to the old town leads through streets with houses dating from the 15th, 16th and 17th centuries (Ruelle des Trois Pigeons, Place des Diligences, Passage du Marquis de Geoffre, Haute-Rue, Chemin du Coteau). From here there is a lovely view of the château courtyard and the Loire. Take Rue Françoise de Maridor to return downhill.

ALEXANDRE DUMAS AND HISTORY
Charles de Chambes, Count of Montsoreau, married Françoise de Maridor in 1576. She was wooed by Louis de Bussy d'Amboise, who boasted of his success.

The husband was informed of the affair by Henri III, and he had Bussy assassinated at the manor house of Coutancière (on the other side of the Loire) on August 18, 1579. The couple were reconciled: they lived for another forty years and had nine children. Alexandre Dumas (1802–70), author of the *Three Musketeers*, had a passion for reworking historical subjects and gave his own version of these events in his novel *The Lady of Montsoreau*, published in 1845.

SAUMUR

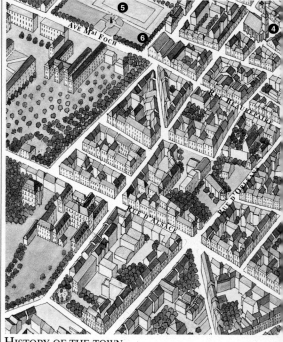

TUFA, HORSES AND WINE
These are the three symbols of Saumur. Tufa ▲ 286, the white local limestone that can be seen on many

of the town's medieval and Renaissance houses, gives the town its bright, distinctive appearance. Saumur is the capital of French equestrianism ▲ 282. Wine ● 30 makes a vital contribution to the region's gastronomic reputation ● 13; it is made from vines grown in terraced rows on the hillsides overlooking the Loire and matured in cellars dug into the tufa.

HISTORY OF THE TOWN

The old province of Anjou ● 12 embraced most of today's département of Maine-et-Loire; the beautiful town of Saumur stands at its far eastern end. Saumur itself, on the south bank of the Loire at its confluence with the Thouet, is the capital of a varied, verdant region known as the Saumurois. The town was once a Carolingian villa. Fortified by Thibault, Count of Blois, in the 10th century, it was conquered by Foulques Nerra ▲ 297, Count of Anjou, in 1026. His successors, the Plantagenets, lost the province in their struggle with Capetian France ● 38, and Philippe-Auguste annexed it to the French kingdom.
ENLIGHTENED PROTESTANTISM. Saumur's enlightened Protestant governor Philippe Duplessis-Mornay (1549–1623) ▲ 281 left his imprint on the town, which had become a

QUAI MAYAUD

PONT CESSART

MONTÉE DU FORT

RUE DU PETIT GENÈVE

refuge for the Huguenots in 1589. Because of the Protestant university he founded, the town became known as the "French Geneva" and for around a century Saumur served as an intellectual and religious center for the whole of Protestant Europe, reaching heights of prosperity that were never equalled after the revocation of the Edict of Nantes and the emigration of the town's Protestant population ● *41*. The Catholic Church responded by organizing major pilgrimages here ▲ *285*, which spawned a flourishing trade in rosaries and religious jewelry.

TOWN OF THE HORSE. In the mid 18th century the town saw a revival, when the École de Cavalerie (Cavalry School) was established here. Saumur became the unchallenged equestrian capital of France, owing its national reputation to the Cadre Noir ▲ *282*, an élite corps of trainers, instructors and riders which upholds the French equestrian tradition.

SAUMUR TODAY. Food (mushrooms, sparkling wine and canned vegetables) makes a major contribution to the town's economy, as does the growing tourist trade.

THE HEROIC SAUMUR "CADETS"
When Germany invaded France in June 1940, the officers and eight hundred pupils of the École de Cavalerie posted themselves along the Loire ● *43* between Gennes and Montsoreau to the enemy from crossing the river. From 19 to 21 June this small, poorly equipped group put up a heroic resistance to the much larger German force, which attacked them from the ground and the air. General Weygand, Commander-in-Chief of the French army, decorated the École de Cavalerie with the Ordre de l'Armée, commenting that it had "written in the annals of equestrianism a page worthy of all its glorious past".

279

"Good King René"
Duke René I of
Anjou (1409–80) was
the son of Yolande
d'Aragon and Louis II
of Anjou; he also held
the titles of
Duc de Bar, Duc de
Lorraine, King of
Sicily and Jerusalem,
and Comte de
Provence. His second
wife was Jeanne de
Laval. Known as
"the Last of the
Troubadours", he was
a disciple of the poet
Charles d'Orléans
▲ 114 and wrote
chivalric romances
which he illuminated
himself, among them
the *Livre du coeur
d'amour épris* (1457).
He was also a
prodigious creator
of buildings in the
Angevin ▲ 298 and
Provençal styles, such
as the châteaux of
Tarascon and Saumur.

History of the Château

No matter how you approach Saumur, it is the château that
you see first, rising above the town on a limestone outcrop.
After the fortress fell under French rule it was rebuilt by Saint
Louis ▲ 296, from 1227 onward. Louis I of Anjou, brother of
King Charles V, carried out major alterations between 1367
and 1376. New polygonal towers were built over the base of
the old round towers, and the keep and a vast residential wing
were added. René I of Anjou (see left) renovated the east
tower (known as the Tour de la Chapelle) and refurbished the
château as a whole. In the 16th century the town's governor
Philippe Duplessis-Mornay ▲ 281 commissioned the Italian
engineer Bartolomeo to fortify the castle. Bartolomeo built a
star-shaped enclosure – anticipating those later designed by
Vauban – with bastions and curtain walls. Between the reigns
of Louis XIV and Napoleon I the château was used as a
prison; subsequently it became a military storehouse. In 1906
the municipal authorities acquired it from the state in grave
disrepair. Restoration work is still in progress.

Tour of the Château ★

Despite its robust fortifications, the Château de Saumur
belongs to the great architectural tradition of Loire châteaux.
The 14th-century keep has two corner bartizans and a
gatehouse; it leads into the Great Court, with a grand
staircase (14th century) decorated in the Flamboyant style.
The belvedere terrace has a magnificent view over the river
and the town.
Musée des Arts décoratifs. This is one of the most
delightful museums in France outside Paris. Located on the
middle floor of the château, it houses the collection of rare
pieces, such as 13th-century Limoges enamels and a large
collection of 16th- and 18th-century French earthenware,
tapestries (left) and woodcarvings (below), left by Count
Charles Lair, a wealthy scholar of Saumur, in 1919.
Musée du Cheval. This museum is housed in the top story of
the château, which has splendid curved beams shaped like
those of a ship's hull. It traces the
history of horses and riding in the
world, from antiquity until today.

Tour of the Town

There are two ways up to the château
from the old town. The Montée du
Petit Genève runs alongside the
former Protestant cemetery and
leads to the panoramic terrace,
while the Montée du Fort, a
steep street with half-timbered
houses ● 72, leads from Place
St-Pierre directly to the
entrance.
Church of St-Pierre. This
church shows a mixture of
architectural styles. The choir
and transept date from the

> **"WE CAUGHT SIGHT OF THE KEEP AND THE WHITE HOUSES OF SAUMUR, A BEAUTIFUL VIEW IN THE DISTANCE . . . THIS TOWN HAS A GRANDIOSE AIR ABOUT IT; IT STANDS AT THE TOP OF A LOVELY HILL."**
>
> STENDHAL

late 12th century, while the nave dates from the 13th century and the façade is built in the Jesuit style. Inside there are beautiful 16th-century tapestries depicting the lives of Saint Peter and Saint Florent, both popular local saints, and remarkable stalls which follow the curving outline of the apse.

QUAI MAYAUD. From the 17th to the 19th century the commercial importance of river traffic led to the construction of mansions and other substantial buildings beside the Loire.

HÔTEL DE VILLE. The town hall, on Place de la République, dates from the 16th and 19th centuries.

THE EQUESTRIAN AND MILITARY QUARTER

Military and equestrian establishments were traditionally located in this part of town. Some of the riding schools and stables are still used by the École Nationale de Cavalerie, others have now been converted for other uses.

MANÈGE DES ÉCUYERS. This riding school was built in 1863 on today's Place Charles-de-Foucault; it was the setting for displays by the Cadre Noir, Saumur's celebrated corps of riding instructors ▲ *282*. On the right-hand side of the square are the old stable buildings, dating from the 19th century.

PLACE DU CHARDONNET. For a long time this was the exercise ground for the equestrian establishments grouped around it. The first carrousel (equestrian display) by the Cadre Noir was held here in 1828, in honor of the Duchesse de Berry. The tradition of the carrousel is still very much alive: it is held on the Place du Chardonnet every year at the end of July, presented by the pupils of the École d'application de l'arme blindée et de la cavalerie and those of the Cadre Noir.

ÉCOLE D'APPLICATION DE L'ARME BLINDÉE ET DE LA CAVALERIE. The academy of the armored corps and cavalry stands near Place du Chardonnet, on Avenue du Maréchal-Foch. The building, in the classical style, was erected between 1767 and 1769. From 1825 to 1969 it was home of the École de Cavalerie, led by the Cadre Noir. It was given its present name in 1945.

RENÉ I'S "CHÂTEAU D'AMOUR"
In the middle ages this Château was so famous that it was depicted in the illuminated manuscript of the *Très Riches Heures du Duc de Berry*, kept at the Château de Chantilly (illustration for September, the month of harvesting, ▲ *277*).

A GREAT PROTESTANT LEADER
Philippe de Mornay (1549–1623), lord of Plessis-Marly, is better known as Philippe Duplessis-Mornay ▲ *278*. Nicknamed "the Pope of the Huguenots", he acted as a lawyer and diplomat in the service of the Huguenot party before becoming chief finance minister to Henri de Navarre (later Henri IV of

France). Duplessis-Mornay took a moderate political line. After he was appointed governor of Saumur, he fortified the castle and the outskirts of the town and created a Protestant university. Together with Hubert Languet he wrote the *Vindiciae contra tyrannos* (1579), one of the most important political treatises of the Wars of Religion, which sought to limit royal power.

Saumur's Cadre Noir is a group of trainers and riders whose aim is to uphold the French equestrian tradition, which dates back to the 16th century, when governor Duplessis-Mornay ▲ *281* founded a riding academy as part of his Protestant university. In 1763 Louis XV entrusted the Duc de Choiseul with the complete reorganization of the French cavalry, and the "best riding school in the world" was built on Place du Chardonnet to house the officers of the cavalry regiments. The cavalry school operated until 1788, and was re-established in 1824. At the first carrousel, held in 1828, the officers presented an impressive display of dressage and jumps which resulted in the foundation of the Cadre Noir, consisting of the school's riding instructors. In 1972 the École Nationale d'Équitation (National Riding School) was founded around the Cadre Noir, whose specialty is the study and teaching of *haute école*, the most elaborate form of dressage. Today the Cadre Noir includes both military and civilian members.

EQUESTRIAN CELEBRITIES
The world of academic equestrianism has its own celebrities. There was Pluvinel (1550–1620), under Louis XIII, and La Guérinière (1688–1751) under Louis XV. After the academic riding school was founded, there was Monsieur Corder, the first *écuyer en chef* (principal rider) of the Cadre Noir; and later Général L'Hotte (left), who gave the French tradition its own distinctive style. A strict hierarchy indicates the level of achievement reached by the riders: *élève-écuyer* (pupil rider), *sous-écuyer* (under-rider), *écuyer* (rider), *écuyer de première classe* (first-class rider) and *écuyer en chef* (principal rider).

THE "REPRISE"
This is a display of the dressage movements performed in high-level competitions. The aim of academic dressage is to restore to the mounted horse all the animal's natural grace of attitude and movement. Right: the passage.

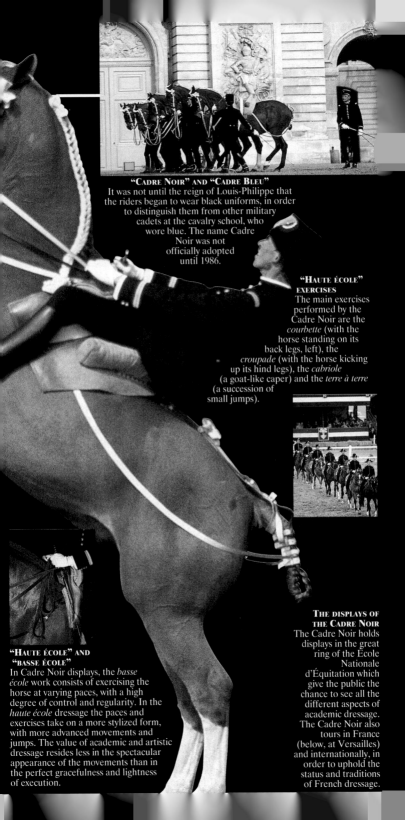

"Cadre Noir" and "Cadre Bleu"
It was not until the reign of Louis-Philippe that the riders began to wear black uniforms, in order to distinguish them from other military cadets at the cavalry school, who wore blue. The name Cadre Noir was not officially adopted until 1986.

"Haute école" exercises
The main exercises performed by the Cadre Noir are the *courbette* (with the horse standing on its back legs, left), the *croupade* (with the horse kicking up its hind legs), the *cabriole* (a goat-like caper) and the *terre à terre* (a succession of small jumps).

"Haute école" and "basse école"
In Cadre Noir displays, the *basse école* work consists of exercising the horse at varying paces, with a high degree of control and regularity. In the *haute école* dressage the paces and exercises take on a more stylized form, with more advanced movements and jumps. The value of academic and artistic dressage resides less in the spectacular appearance of the movements than in the perfect gracefulness and lightness of execution.

The displays of the Cadre Noir
The Cadre Noir holds displays in the great ring of the École Nationale d'Équitation which give the public the chance to see all the different aspects of academic dressage. The Cadre Noir also tours in France (below, at Versailles) and internationally, in order to uphold the status and traditions of French dressage.

MUSÉE DE LA CAVALERIE
The cavalry museum (within the École d'application ▲ *281*) was established in 1936, based on the collection of 19th-century arms and armor assembled by Barbet de Vaux. Its Galerie des Ancêtres traces the development of uniforms, arms and tactics up to 1914; the Salle Bleu Horizon is devoted to World War One.

THE BIRTH OF COCO CHANEL
Gabrielle Bonheur (1883–1971) was born in a train; when the train arrived at Saumur she was taken to no. 27, rue St-Jean, where she grew up. Later she moved to Paris and, under the name of Coco Chanel, founded an haute couture house where she created a new style in women's fashions that made her famous throughout the world.

ÉCOLE NATIONALE D'ÉQUITATION. France's national riding school was founded in 1969 at Saumur-Terrefort (3 miles from Saumur), with an extension at Verrie. The school is dedicated to dressage training, and is also the national training center for French cavalry officers. Training is carried out by the Cadre Noir ▲ *282*, which now includes women in its ranks (left).

L'ÎLE D'OFFARD

From Place de Bilange – where Saumur's market has been held for the last nine centuries – the Pont Cessart (above), completed in 1768, extends across the river to the Île d'Offard.
MAISON DE LA REINE DE SICILE. This is the most striking building on the island: an elegant residence on Rue Montcel, dating from the first half of the 15th century, built of tufa with mullioned windows and two staircase turrets. The house is named after Yolande d'Aragon, Queen of Sicily and mother of René I of Anjou ▲ *280*. She is said to have died here, probably in 1442.

NOTRE-DAME DE NANTILLY ★

This is the oldest of Saumur's four churches. Situated in the southern part of the town, it was built by the monks of St-Florent early in the 12th century in the Romanesque style. The transept was rebuilt in the 14th century, and a century later Louis XI doubled the size of the nave, adding a huge side aisle in the Flamboyant style. The shrine was restored, starting in 1851, by the architect Joly-Leterme, a follower of Viollet-le-Duc. The church has a Romanesque façade influenced by the Aquitaine style, with four high buttresses surmounted by a cornice and a set of blind arcatures.
INTERIOR. The southern apsidiole, which dates from the 12th century, contains a colored sculpture of the Virgin and Child from the same period; known as the Notre-Dame de Nantilly, it is worshiped for its miraculous powers. The spectacular vaulting of the Romanesque nave, 40 feet across, and the highly developed style of the historiated capitals make this a unique example of Angevin Romanesque architecture ● *58*. The church also has a remarkable collection of tapestries from the 16th and 17th centuries.

"THIS IS ONE OF THOSE CORNERS OF FRANCE
WHERE FRANCE IS AT ITS MOST FRENCH."

GEORGE CLEMENCEAU

NOTRE-DAME DES ARDILLIERS ★

This impressive building, in the eastern part of Saumur, can be spotted from a distance by its monumental rotunda crowned by a dome similar to that of Les Invalides in Paris. A first church, in the Flamboyant style, was built on the site between 1534 and 1553, marking the spot where a peasant

had found a statue of the Virgin in 1454. In the 17th century Notre-Dame des Ardilliers became a major center for pilgrimages, and two side chapels were added in the classical style ● *63*. The church was dedicated as a royal chapel in 1614 and given to the Oratorians, making it a visible symbol of Catholicism in a town dedicated to the Protestant cause. The central rotunda, which serves as a vestibule to the shrine, was built between 1655 and 1693 by the architects Biardeau and Gondoin.

CHÂTEAU DE BOUMOIS

This château was built early in the 16th century on the right bank of the Loire, about 4 miles northwest of Saumur. With its tufa stonework and two massive machicolated towers it looks like a plain-fortress, but concealed within its feudal exterior is an elegant residence built in the Gothic style with Renaissance decorations. The door to the staircase leading up to it has a remarkable wrought-iron lock bearing the arms of René de Thory, the first lord of Boumois.

MUSEUM OF ARMORED VEHICLES
The Musée des Blindés and Centre de documentation sur les engins blindés (CDEB) were established in 1982, in a former riding school. The museum's three halls, which are named after three generals (Estienne, Patton and Rommel), display exhibits from the world's largest collection of 20th-century armored vehicles and artillery. The CDEB is at once an information center, a training center, and a technical center for engineers, technicians and specialists (both military and civilian).

CHÂTEAU DE BOUMOIS
Details of the tufa stonework.

▲ SAUMUROIS TROGLODYTIC DWELLINGS

TUFA AND FALUN
Tufa (*tuffeau*) ● 76 is a chalky, white limestone rock from the Turonian level of the lower Cretaceous period (Secondary Era). In the Saumurois region ▲ 278 the rock stratum is sometimes as much as 160 feet deep. Tufa is easy to work, with a tendency to disintegrate under the dissolving action of rainwater. Faluns are conchiferous (shell marl) deposits formed in the Tertiary Era. The thickest stratum, 74 feet deep, is at Doué-la-Fontaine.

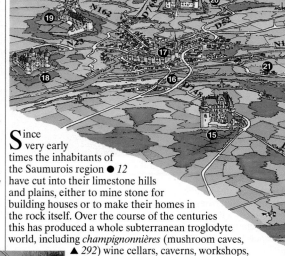

Since very early times the inhabitants of the Saumurois region ● 12 have cut into their limestone hills and plains, either to mine stone for building houses or to make their homes in the rock itself. Over the course of the centuries this has produced a whole subterranean troglodyte world, including *champignonnières* (mushroom caves, ▲ 292) wine cellars, caverns, workshops, hamlets, and even chapels and manor houses. The Saumurois region is unique in possessing two types of troglodyte habitations: both hillside and plain dwellings.

HILLSIDE DWELLINGS (E7)

Troglodyte dwellings are carved into the cliff faces on either side of Saumur (D7), between Montsoreau and Gennes. The tufa rocks provide the white stone that gives the châteaux and houses of the Loire valley their distinctive appearance. Some of the hillside (or "horizontal") troglodytic habitations were formerly quarries. Now rarely occupied as homes, they are mainly used by craftworkers, winegrowers and mushroom farmers.

Falun was extracted vertically, working from ground level – not by tunneling, as for tufa. Houses were built into the walls of the ditches created by quarrying the stone.

VAL-HULIN (E7). Some of the most interesting hillside dwellings are at Val-Hulin (below), near Turquant, between Montsoreau and Saumur. Above this small semi-troglodyte hamlet is a splendid moulin-cavier (cave mill) ● 79, ▲ 294, which has been restored.

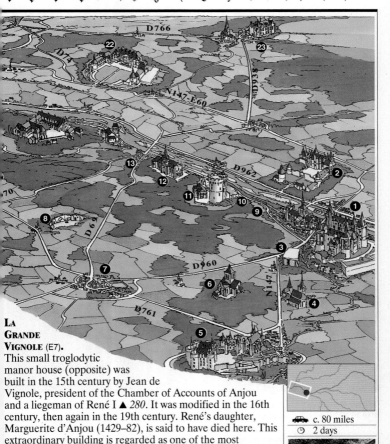

LA GRANDE VIGNOLE (E7).

This small troglodytic manor house (opposite) was built in the 15th century by Jean de Vignole, president of the Chamber of Accounts of Anjou and a liegeman of René I ▲ *280*. It was modified in the 16th century, then again in the 19th century. René's daughter, Marguerite d'Anjou (1429–82), is said to have died here. This extraordinary building is regarded as one of the most remarkable troglodytic dwellings in the whole of Europe.

PLAIN DWELLINGS   (C7, D7)

Troglodytic plain dwellings – made in holes or ditches dug into the falun – can be found within an area of approximately 150 square miles to the south of Saumur, mainly around Doué-la-Fontaine. Falun, a tertiary limestone rock composed of organic debris, contains a great variety of fossils (left, fossilized tooth of a carcarodon, a formidable shark that lived in the ancient Falun Sea). For centuries "vertical" troglodytic dwellings were the main form of habitation for poor farmers in this area (they only had to dig a hole to make their home), and a distinctive lifestyle evolved around them. As recently as a hundred years ago there were still only a few houses above ground level in each village. Today these troglodytic habitations are considered an important part of the region's heritage; there has been a great revival of interest in them, and many unusual sites have been opened to the public.

🚗 c. 80 miles
🕐 2 days

TROGLODYTIC FARM AT MARSON ▲ *288*
The ditch produced by vertical quarrying (see opposite) served as the farmyard. Rooms were carved out from the rock. On the surface the falun was covered with earth, providing a kitchen garden for the underground farm.

287

▲ Saumurois
Troglodytic plain dwellings

INFORMATION CENTER
La Boutinière, a former troglodytic farm to the south of Dénezé, has been turned into an information center on troglodyte dwellings in the region and throughout France. It has a permanent exhibition devoted to the troglodytic world.

ROU MARSON. This romantic, verdant spot is part of a group of three parishes: Rou, Riou and Marson. The Château de Marson – built in Renaissance style, although it dates from 1850 – stands at the foot of troglodytic rocks. Beside the small road leading to the villages of Riou and Les Ulmes there are *caves demeurantes* – troglodyte caves that are still inhabited.

LA FOSSE. This impressive site consists entirely of inhabited caves and their annexes. Dating from the 17th century, it is a typical hamlet of troglodytic plain dwellings. The underground farm is arranged around a courtyard known as the *carré* (square); the slope leading down to the house is called the *courdouère*. The kitchen garden and the orchard were

MUSÉE PAYSAN, ROCHEMENIER
This museum, in two disused underground farms, includes houses, stables, storerooms, ovens and sheds, with original décor and everyday items from the late 19th and early 20th century.

DOUÉ-LA-FONTAINE
The troglodytic Rue des Perrières.

traditionally located over the roof of the farm, the produce being harvested through holes in the roof called *jittes*.

DÉNEZÉ-SOUS-DOUÉ. This carved cavern (16th century) is a strange and fascinating place. Four hundred figures, carved in a simple style, stand out from the wall; hundreds more have been destroyed. The carvings show the initiation rites of stonecutters and record their protests against the royal edict of Villers-Cotterêts (1539), which outlawed certain associations of craftworkers. Near to Dénezé are the troglodyte hamlets of Mousseaux and Saugré.

ROCHEMENIER. This troglodyte village was founded in the 10th century on a falun deposit and consisted of around 250 caves, belonging to forty farms. The village covered an underground area two or three times the size of what could be seen on the surface; today it is completely abandoned.

DOUÉ-LA-FONTAINE (C7, C8)

The town, built entirely on a bank of falun deposits, has been inhabited since prehistoric times. The site was once occupied by a Gallic tribe; in 796 it became one of the four winter residences of Louis the Pious; and at the end of the 10th century Foulques Nerra, the famous Count of Anjou ▲ *297*, built a castle here. The town was modernized from 1765 onward by Joseph-François Foulon (1715–89), later a finance minister. The development of the rose-growing industry

MUSÉE DES ANCIENS COMMERCES AT DOUÉ-LA-FONTAINE
This museum presents a history of retailing (1850 to 1950), from peddling to storekeeping.

boosted its economy. Known as the "City of Roses", it produces more than eight million rose bushes every year.
ROSERAIE DU PARC FOULON. More than five thousand rose bushes grow in this public park, presenting a multicolored, sweet-smelling display of the roses produced locally.
ARÈNES DE DOUCES. This "amphitheater" is in fact an old quarry – tiers were cut into it in the 15th century. Rabelais ▲ *250* may have been thinking of it when, in *Pantagruel*, he talks about the "games of Doué".
RUE DES PERRIÈRES. This street (opposite page, bottom) is lined with troglodyte houses cut into the old falun quarries. The unusual architecture is accentuated by the honey-colored stone and the half-darkness illuminated by shafts of light.
LA SABLIÈRE. This former quarry gallery, embellished with beautiful vaulting, is now a rosewater distillery.
MAISON CAROLINGIENNE. This is part of the oldest rectangular keep in France, dating from the late 10th century and discovered by chance in 1966. It is believed to have formed part of a residence belonging to Robert I, Count of Anjou.
MOULIN DE LA FOURCHETTE. Also known as the Moulin Cartier, this was the last windmill built in Anjou – a rare *moulin-tour* (tower mill) ● *78*, ▲ *294*.

M ontreuil-Bellay, to the southeast of Saumur, is another region of hills, forests and vineyards. Many of the larger towns are perched on hilltops: from the dawn of the Middle Ages onward they acted as defensive outposts, protecting the border of Poitou from Anjou.

BAGNEUX (D7)

This suburb of Saumur has a number of interesting Neolithic remains. The Grand Dolmen de Bagneux is the largest dolmen in France, and one of the largest in Europe. It consists of fifteen sandstone slabs and is a typical Angevin dolmen, similar in form to the one at La Bajoulière (C6). The elongated chamber covers an area of 970 square feet; it is 75 feet long, 25 feet wide, and 11 feet high. A smaller dolmen (23 feet long) can be seen near the cemetery.

LE COUDRAY-MACOUARD (D7)

The charming winding streets of this picturesque village, perched on a hilltop, are lined with houses built between the 15th and 18th centuries.
CHURCH. This was once the chapel of the 12th-century château (now destroyed). It was rebuilt in the 18th century. The retable of the high altar, depicting the Assumption of the Virgin, dates from the same period.
MAGNANERIE. The Impasse Bel-air – a group of troglodyte buildings devoted to silkworm breeding ▲ *260* – includes the *magnanerie*, where the *magnans* (southern French for silkworms) were bred, and an exhibition relating to silk weaving.

PARC ZOOLOGIQUE DES MINIÈRES
This zoo in a former conchiferous-stone quarry has around five hundred animals, kept in an admirably natural environment. The number of animals born here testify to its success. The zoo has some rare species, such as the snow panther, Sumatran tiger and red panda.

DOLMENS ANGEVINS ANGEVIN DOLMENS
The dolmens ● *36* of Anjou were built between 4000 and 2000 BC; most of them are located around Saumur and Baugé, and many are still completely or nearly intact. Most of the dolmens in Anjou have a low, narrow entrance opening onto a large rectangular chamber. Below: the Dolmen de la Madeleine, near Gennes ▲ *293*.

289

A RELIC FROM JERUSALEM IN ANJOU
The Holy Girdle of the Virgin, made of linen and oriental silk, is said to have been brought back from a crusade by Guillaume IX of Aquitaine, as a gift from the

ABBEY OF ASNIÈRES (D8)

Impressive ruins are all that remains of this imposing Benedictine abbey, founded in 1114 by Bernard Thiron, a follower of Robert d'Arbrissel ● 272. The lords of Montreuil made it into a prosperous abbey and their place of burial. The abbey fell into decline after being sacked by the Huguenots in 1500, and was closed in 1746. The square tower of the transept crossing, dating from the 13th century, was restored in the 17th century. The 17th-century dovecote was recently restored: its seven-sided design is unique in Anjou.

LE PUY-NOTRE-DAME (D8)

The town is perched on a vine-covered hill of tufa, 340 feet high, called the Montagne de Marie. In medieval times pilgrims flocked here to worship a relic of the Virgin – a girdle brought from Jerusalem (see left), which was greatly revered by Louis XI.

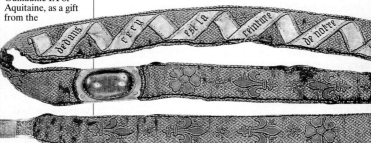

Patriarch of Jerusalem. The two rock crystals were donated by Anne of Austria, who wore the girdle for the birth of Louis XIV. The gold endpieces (above), made by goldsmith Mathieu Dupond, date from 1537.

COLLEGIATE CHURCH OF NOTRE-DAME. The Holy Girdle of the Virgin (above) is displayed in the treasury of the church (12th–13th century). The nave, which has six bays and side aisles, is built in the Poitevin style, while the rounded vaults are in the Angevin Gothic style ● 60. In the choir, the oak stalls carved with human figures date from the 16th century.

MONTREUIL-BELLAY, THE WALLED TOWN ★ (D8)

This magnificent medieval town is perched on a steep rocky spur by the Thouet, a tributary of the Loire. It is the only one of the thirty-two walled towns of Anjou to have preserved its ramparts and its four monumental gates. It is best to enter the town through the Porte du Moulin (16th century), just beyond the bridge over the river. From here you can see the white silhouette of the town through the trees – with a lovely view over the water mill, which was destroyed by fire in 1896 and rebuilt in the Renaissance style.

HISTORY. Montreuil-Bellay was an independent barony for many years. When the Saumur region was annexed to Anjou by Foulques Nerra ▲ 297 in 1026, it became a border town. To the south the 13th-century wall around the Porte St-Jean faces toward Poitou. To the north is the Porte Nouvelle, looking toward Anjou. To the west the Porte du Boëlle, on the Thouet, controlled shipping and tolls.

MONTREUIL-BELLAY
The Tour St-Jean (15th century) is decorated with bosses, a popular form of ornamentation.

THE CHÂTEAU. The present appearance of
the château is the result of alterations
undertaken by the Harcourt family. It has
three sections: the CHÂTEAU-VIEUX
(15th century), with a defensive structure
in front of it with a round barbican from
the 13th century; the LOGIS DES
CHANOINES DE LA COLLÉGIALE (Canons'
Wing) from the late 15th century; and the
CHÂTEAU-NEUF (15th–16th century),

restored in the late 19th century. The Flamboyant oratory is
decorated with magnificent mural paintings. The Collegiate
Church of Notre-Dame (1472 and 1484, restored in 1865) was
originally the castle chapel; it became a parish church in 1810.
THE TOWN. This is a pleasant place for a stroll, with houses
built between the 15th and 18th centuries. From Boulevard de
l'Ardenne there is a spectacular view of the valley.

Heading toward Angers along the Loire, the landscape is
scattered with patches of greenery. This area has a
number of important classical and prehistoric sites, which
provide evidence of early human occupation. Over the
centuries the towns crowning the hilltops to the south of
the Loire have gradually spread downhill toward the
river.

ST-HILAIRE-ST-FLORENT   (D7)

This suburb, west of Saumur, encompasses the
old town of St-Hilaire-les-Grottes and the area
around the Abbey of St-Florent. It stretches along
the left bank of the Thouet, over a hillside dotted
with caves used for maturing wine ■ *30* and growing
mushrooms ■ *26*. The dolmens ▲ *289* of St-Hilaire and Bois-
de-Feu can be seen here.
ABBEY OF ST-FLORENT. This Benedictine abbey was famous
and powerful from the 11th to the 16th centuries; its decline
was hastened by the Revolution, and it fell into ruins after
1805. All that remains today is the base of the choir of the
abbey church, above a remarkable crypt (11th–12th century)
with Romanesque capitals. The narthex (late 12th century) is
a perfect example of the Angevin Gothic style ● *60*.
CHURCH OF ST-BARTHÉLEMY. The church has two naves in the
Angevin Gothic style (late 12th and 14th century). On the
north wall of the church is a plaque commemorating Joan of
Arc's visit to St-Florent in 1429.

**JEANNE D'ARC
IN ST-FLORENT**
Joan of Arc ▲ *116*
came to the Abbey of
St-Florent on March
17, 1429. Marie de
Bretagne, mother of
the Duc d'Alençon,
and Jeanne
d'Orléans, the duke's
wife, were staying
here at the time.
Joan of Arc hoped to
convince the duke,
who was a prisoner
on parole to the
English after three
years of captivity, to
take up arms again
at her side. Her
mission was a
complete success:
the duke sold his
possessions to pay
his ransom and
resumed the fight
against the English.

**THREE HOMES
FOR THE ABBEY**
The monks built their
first abbey to house
the relics of Saint
Florent at
Montglonne, near
St-Florent-le-Vieil,
to the east of
Ancenis. In the 9th
century Norman
invasions forced them
to flee, and they
retreated to Saumur.
When Foulques
Nerra ▲ *297*, Count
of Anjou, captured
the town in 1026, the
monks moved their
monastery again, this
time settling at a
place called St-
Florent-le-Jeune,
near the Thouet,
where the great abbey
prospered in peace.

Château de Pimpéan.

the *pleurote* and the *peuplier*, have been developed in Saumur.

TROGLODYTE CAVES. At the Musée du Champignon, in the caves to the west of St-Hilaire-St-Florent, you can sample different kinds of mushroom and view a collection of fossils and ammonites. Sparkling Saumur wine is also produced in these caves, using the technique introduced in 1811 by Jean Ackerman (1788–1866), son of a banker from Antwerp.

CHÊNEHUTTE-LES-TUFFEAUX (D7)

The small towns of Chênehutte-les-Tuffeaux and Trèves-Cunault, which merged in 1974, present an exceptional group of historical sites and monuments.
THE PLATEAU. This area was inhabited from the bronze and iron ages onward. A Gallic *oppidum* and then a Roman fortification were located here, followed in turn by a Carolingian villa and, finally, by the Abbey of St-Florent. An archeological trail and an exhibition display the wealth of remains that have survived from these times, including sections of wall, tombs, coins and pottery.
THE TOWN. In the town itself, at the foot of the plateau, is the Church of Notre-Dame (12th century), which has a Romanesque ● 58 portal, ornamented with acanthus and foliage motifs, and a bell tower with paired windows.

TRÈVES ● 59 (D7)

The village stands amid green countryside, facing a large island in the Loire. It is dominated by the 15th-century keep, 100 feet high and surrounded by magnificent yew trees. This is all that remains of the fortress, demolished in 1747, built by Robert le Maczon (or le Maçon), Baron de Trèves, chancellor of Charles VII and companion in arms of Joan of Arc.
CHURCH OF ST-AUBIN. This delightful 12th-century building has a 13th-century bell tower and a 15th-century spire. In the nave is a 12th-century baptismal font with four 11th-century masks.
THE VILLAGE. There are a number of 15th- and 16th-century houses. The Logis de la Cour-Condé (early 17th century) has a square corner watchtower.

CUNAULT ★ (D6)

Notre-Dame de Cunault ● 59 was founded by monks from the Île de Noirmoutier who had fled from the Norman invasions of the 9th century. A new collegiate church was built between the 11th and the 13th centuries. One of the loveliest Romanesque buildings in Anjou, it has

Elevation of Notre-Dame de Cunault, a splendid example of Romanesque architecture.

223 capitals and a famous square bell tower (11th century). The entrance on the west façade is built in typical Poitevin style, with a portal (13th century) framed by five archivolts. **Interior.** The church has three naves of equal height. The choir is surrounded by an ambulatory whose chapels contain a colored stone Pietà from the 15th century and the shrine of Saint Maxenceul (13th century) made of painted carved walnut. Opposite the church is the house of a prior, Pierre Cottereau, which dates from the reign of François I.

Gennes-sur-Loire   (D6)

The Angevin-type dolmens of La Madeleine, La Forêt, La Cour d'Avort and La Pagerie show that this site has been inhabited since the Neolithic era. Not far from here stand the menhirs of Bois-Gilbert and Le Bouchet. Roman remains include the site of Gallo-Roman baths, which were supplied by an aqueduct that can still be seen, and the ruins of an amphitheater where excavations have been under way since 1985. The disused Church of St-Eusèbe, perched on the hilltop, still has its square 12th-century bell tower. Next to the ruins of the nave stands a memorial to the cadets of Saumur, commemorating the battles of June 1940 ▲ 279. The Logis de Mardron is a beautiful 15th-century house.
Church of St-Vétérin. The church was built in the 12th and 13th centuries. It has a number of features from the Carolingian period and contains several Merovingian tombs.
Water mill of Sarré. This 16th-century mill is one of the few in the region with its water wheel ● 78 still in use.

The Pays de l'Aubance begins immediately after Gennes. The road follows the winding course of the Aubance river, passing from the bright limestone of the Saumur region to the dark schists of Anjou, through a landscape of vines and copses. Finally, to the south of Angers, the countryside opens onto the famous vineyards of the Coteaux du Layon.

Château de Pimpéan   (C6)

The château with its four square corner towers stands on a hill in an undulating landscape of forests and vines, overlooking the town of Grézillé. It was built in the 15th century by Bernard de Beauvau, seneschal of Anjou and friend of King René I ▲ 280; it was modified in the 17th century. A restoration program undertaken by the current owners is still in progress.

Chapel ★. The chapel stands in the internal courtyard of the château. The building, which dates from the 15th century, is perfectly preserved, with murals that are among the best in Anjou. Particularly striking is the fresco ▲ 256 of angels holding the instruments of the Passion, produced by Coppin Delft of the Flemish school.

"Hélice terrestre de l'Orbière"
Downriver, near St-Georges-des-Sept-Voies (C6), is a monumental sculpture in two parts: one hollowed out of the rock, the other freestanding. This troglodyte group is the studio of sculptor Jacques Warminski, whose drawings can also be seen at the Château de Pimpéan; one room is devoted to troglodyte architecture.

Festival of wine and music
The Pimpéan music festival is held annually in the magical setting of the castle chapel, with recitals held every afternoon from July 31 to August 31. The recitals are followed by tastings of wines produced by the vineyards around the château.

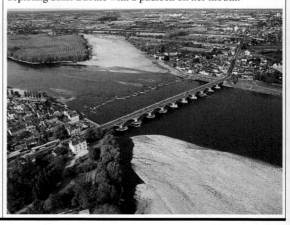

WINDMILLS ● 78
Anjou is said to have had some two thousand mills in the 17th century. Several different types of windmill can still be seen. Tower windmills (*moulins-tours*) with a stone tower have several stories, crowned by a roof that pivots to change the direction of the sails. Cave windmills (*moulins-caviers*), like the Moulin du Pavé (below), have a conical stone tower with a pivoting wooden cabin on top; "Turkish windmills" (*moulins-turquois*) have a cylindrical stone tower.

BRISSAC-QUINCÉ (B6)

This is one of the most extraordinary châteaux in Anjou. Pierre de Brezé, a counselor to Charles VII and Louis XI, built a feudal castle here in the 15th century, on the foundations of an older castle built by Foulques Nerra ▲ 297. It was acquired by René de Cossé, Duc de Brissac, in 1502. His grandson Charles, Maréchal de France and governor of Paris, began building an elegant new residence in 1600, but work came to a halt at his death in 1621. The new building was still incomplete when the feudal castle was partly demolished. This led the present (twelfth) Duc de Brissac to describe it as a "half-finished new château built in a half-ruined old château": the 17th-century residence, for example, is flanked by two medieval towers, dating from the 15th century.

INTERIOR. The 203 rooms, including the huge Salle des Gardes, the portrait gallery, the Salle des Chasses and the bedchamber of Louis XIII, are richly decorated with splendid Flemish tapestries from the 16th century. A beautiful Louis XIII style staircase serves the five upper stories of the pavilion.

CHAPEL. The 15th-century chapel has a funeral stele carved by David d'Angers ▲ 304.

LES PONTS-DE-CÉ (B6)

Providing access to Angers across three branches of the Loire, the Canal d'Authion and the Louet river, this town has been of strategic importance for centuries. It straddles three islands. One of them has a pentagonal keep – all that remains of the château, which was rebuilt in the 13th century.

THE KEEPS. The machicolated keep stands on a curious spur of land, which enhances its impressive appearance. Inside is a museum of Angevin headdresses.

CHURCH OF ST-AUBIN. This church was built in 1003 and extended several times; it has a lovely Romanesque nave.

CHURCH OF ST-MAURILLE. Although built in 1840, this church has lovely carved stalls from the 16th century – including one depicting Saint Babille with a padlock on her mouth.

❝As for the Ponts-de-Cé, this is no longer the old group of bridges it was in the past, which probably went back to Caesar's time, crossing the wide streams of the Loire with 109 arches of all shapes, widths and ages, often knocked down and carried away by the torrents of the river at times of flooding . . . Those old Ponts-de-Cé, which were modified and rebuilt again and again, have now been replaced by a large modern bridge.❞
Albert Robida

IN AND AROUND ANGERS

PRINCELY TITLE
In 1246 Charles, the
younger brother of
King Louis IX
(below), was given

the cadet title of
Count of Anjou. His
descendants reigned
over Naples, Sicily,
Hungary and Poland.

THE ANDECAVI
The Gauls who
inhabited the site of
Angers were called
the Andes by Julius
Caesar and the
Andecavi by Pliny,
Tacitus and Ptolemy;
the name may have
meant "peace-
loving". Domnacus,
chief of the Andecavi,
resisted the Romans
during their conquest
of Gaul, but was
defeated in 51 BC.

HISTORY OF THE TOWN   (B5, B6)

Built on the banks of the Maine, a small tributary of the
Loire, this former stronghold of the Dukes of Anjou, with its
formidable castle, became famous for its tapestries.

INGELGERIANS AND PLANTAGENETS. Angers was once the home
of a Celtic tribe, the Andecavi. At the end of the 9th century it
became the capital of the county of Anjou. After the era of
invasions the town prospered under the Ingelgerian dynasty,
whose most famous representative was the fearsome
conqueror Foulques Nerra (see opposite). His successors, the
Plantaganets, made Angers the keystone of their new Anglo-
Angevin empire (Normandy, Aquitaine, Touraine and
England), built through alliances and conquests ● 37.

CAPETIANS. After fifty years of resistance Angers fell into the
hands of the Capetians, and Louis IX (1214–70) – the future
Saint Louis – fortified the town. In 1360 Anjou was raised
to the status of duchy and annexed to the French kingdom.
Under René I ▲ 280, the last representative of the House
of Anjou, Angers became a flourishing city.

"THE ATHENS OF THE WEST". During the
Renaissance the town saw another golden
age, both culturally and intellectually
(with the development of universities and
colleges) and in terms of architecture
(with the construction of many fine
private residences, ▲ 302–7).
It became known as the
"Athens of the West".

DECLINE AND REVIVAL. Growth
in the 17th and 18th centuries
centered on the manufacture of
sailcloth and rigging. After this
came a long period of decline.

Since the 1960's Angers has compensated by actively encouraging the development of new industries. Today the town has more than 200,000 inhabitants and a very progressive outlook – particularly in the computer sector (represented by Bull, Thomson and Packard-Bell) and with the development of PLANT BIOTECHNOLOGY at the Institut National de Recherches Agronomiques and HORTICULTURE at the Centre National de l'Industrie Horticole.

THE CHÂTEAU

With its tall, somber towers, the fortress has an imposing, powerful presence. Its medieval military architecture ● *64* offers a striking contrast to the delicate patterns of the formal gardens surrounding it.

CENTRE INTERNATIONAL DE LA TAPISSERIE. The museum, established in 1951, displays an unrivaled collection of tapestries dating from the 14th to the 16th centuries. The most famous of them is the Tapestry of the Apocalypse ▲ *300*.

"BLACK FALCON" OF ANJOU (c. 972–1040) In 987 Foulques III, known as Foulques Nerra, inherited the weak county of Anjou.

He was a fierce warrior and rapidly expanded his territory at the expense of his feudal neighbors, including the powerful Count of Blois. He built fortresses (Loches ▲ *224*, Langeais ▲ *268*), fortified Saumur and Angers, built various châteaux (Montreuil-Bellay, Baugé ▲ *312*) and, by way of expiation, founded religious buildings, such as the Abbey of Beaulieu-lès-Loches, which houses his tomb ▲ *230*. His descendants continued his work expanding the lands of "Grand Anjou" ● *37*.

HISTORY OF THE CHÂTEAU

From the 6th to the 9th centuries the residence of the bishops of Angers occupied the site of the present-day château. Foulques Nerra ▲ *297* built a fortress here in the 9th century; only a wall from the great hall survives today.

CAPETIANS. Between 1230 and 1240 King Louis IX erected one of the greatest fortresses of his day on the site of Foulques Nerra's castle. Louis II of Anjou and Yolande d'Aragon added the new chapel and the Logis Royal in the early 15th century. In 1442 their son René I ▲ *280* (below) extended the royal residence and built the Châtelet to close off the main courtyard.

Cul-de-lampe bartizan on one of the two towers forming the Porte de Ville (13th century).

PIERRE DONADIEU DE PUYCHARIC Donadieu was appointed governor of Angers in 1585 and modernized the

château's defense system. When Henri III ordered the destruction of the château, Donadieu bided his time, simply removing the top stories of the towers while waiting for the order to be reversed. The funerary statue (above) is in the Chapel of St-Jean-Baptiste, adjoining the Logis Royal. It was produced by Jacques Sarrazin, one of the greatest French sculptors of the court of Louis XIII, who also created the tomb of Cardinal de Bérulle now in the Louvre.

THE WARS OF RELIGION. Under pressure from the Angevin rebels ● *40*, Henri III authorized the demolition of the château in 1585. However, the governor Donadieu de Puycharic seized the opportunity to improve its defense system by reducing the height of the towers to that of the curtain walls, thus making it possible for artillery to move around the whole circumference of the building.

THE ANCIEN RÉGIME. In the 17th century the château became a state prison. But in 1793, when Angers declared itself a republican town, the château once again played a military role, by halting the advance of the Vendéen army.

MODERN TIMES. In 1951 the national fine-arts commission took over the building, which had been badly damaged during the bombardments of 1944, and began a program of restoration. Transformed into a museum and public park, it remains a place of great historic and artistic interest.

TOUR OF THE CHÂTEAU

The château stands on a sandstone and granite outcrop, above a deep dry moat. It is built in an irregular pentagonal shape, flanked by seventeen cylindrical towers which are nearly 130 feet high and 60 feet in diameter. The towers, built of dark schist with bands of light sandstone, were formerly one or two stories higher and had pepperpot roofs. In the 13th century arrow slits protected the castle; canon holes were added three centuries later. Originally there were two entrances: the Porte de Ville (the present-day entrance) to the north, and the Porte des Champs to the south.

REMAINS OF FOULQUES NERRA'S CASTLE. The wall of the feudal hall dates from the 11th century; the great door with cylindrical and ribbon moldings was added in the 12th century. The high mullioned windows date from the 14th and 15th centuries.

CHAPEL OF STE-GENEVIÈVE-ST-LAUD (12th century). The
northern part of the chapel is set into the Gallo-Roman
ramparts. Only the apse survives today.

THE LOGIS ROYAL AND THE GRANDE CHAPELLE (15th century).
Both were built by Louis II of Anjou. In 1453 René I added
a gallery with windows to the Logis Royal, prefiguring the
galleries of Renaissance châteaux ● 68. The chapel adjoins
the Logis, and has a lovely oratory with a triple arcature
where the lord and lady of the château could pray.

THE CHÂTELET. The gatehouse was built by René I ▲ 280
around 1450 to serve as the château's main portal. Its
pepperpot towers give it an archaic, medieval appearance.

LOGIS DU GOUVERNEUR. This charming 18th-century
residence, built around a 15th-century house, stands
against the eastern wall of the château, hidden away in
the gardens.

THE MOAT. Never filled with water because it was too
far above river level, the moat is now used as a deer park
(right).

GALERIE DE L'APOCALYPSE ★. The gallery runs along the south
wall, close to the remains of the Chapel of St-Laud. It houses
the famous tapestry after which it is named ▲ 300.

"An almost fairy-tale
surprise . . . to see a
herd of dappled deer
grazing"
J. Gracq

**FEUDAL AND ROYAL
ARCHITECTURE**
Left: views of the
Louis IX's fortress,
with its massive
polychrome walls,
including the Grande
Chapelle, the Logis
Royal and the
Châtelet (detail
below right).

**THE GALERIE DE
L'APOCALYPSE**
In 1950 the architect
Bernard Vitry built a
unique gallery
(below) to provide an
appropriate setting
for the Tapestry of
the Apocalypse
▲ 300, allowing
visitors to see it as a
whole and to admire
each of its scenes in
detail.

In 1373 King Charles V sent his brother Louis I, Duke of Anjou, a richly illuminated manuscript of *The Revelation of St John*, also known as *The Apocalypse* (from *apokalupsis*, the Greek for "revelation"). From it Louis commissioned the leading court painter, Jehan de Bondolf (sometimes called Hennequin de Bruges), to design a tapestry with eighty-four scenes – of which seventy-six have miraculously survived. These have been restored and are now displayed in a special gallery at the Château d'Angers.

THE BOOK OF "THE APOCALYPSE"
The mystical last book of the New Testament describes the Last Judgment and the plagues that are to threaten the "inhabiters of the earth". However, it also prophesies the triumph of the "Lamb of God" and the fall of "the great city of Babylon" (above), a symbol of ungodly societies.

"I JOHN SAW THE HOLY CITY, NEW JERUSALEM . . ."
Saint John is depicted as a witness in almost all the scenes of the tapestry. Here he is shown dazzled by the brilliant vision of the new Jerusalem "descending out of heaven from God" – the ultimate symbol of the revelation, a portent of heavenly bliss.

> "AN APOCALYPSE IN FRENCH, ILLUSTRATED WITH FIGURES
> AND SCENES . . . THE KING GAVE IT TO MONSIEUR D'ANJOU
> TO MAKE HIS BEAUTIFUL TAPESTRY."
>
> INVENTORY OF THE ROYAL LIBRARY

RESCUED AND RESTORED

he work was woven in Paris by Nicolas Bataille
and Robert Poisson, using the most advanced
techniques for weaving and fixing pigments.
During the Revolution it was discarded and cut
into pieces. In 1848 Canon Joubert, the keeper
of the treasury of Angers Cathedral, bought back
the pieces for 300 francs and embarked on a
minute restoration, which took fourteen years to
complete. The tapestry has been on display since
1983; it is 350 feet long and 15 feet high.

FABULOUS CREATURES AND ORNAMENTATION

The early scenes have
plain backgrounds
and simple
landscapes. Later
scenes display
luxuriant vegetation
and extraordinary
monsters, with skies
bounded by friezes of
scalloped clouds.

HORSEMEN OF THE APOCALYPSE

The sixth trumpet
of the Apocalypse
summons the
horsemen of hell,
who are to
slaughter one-third
of humanity.
The dark-blue
background
throws into
relief the
movements
and
expressions
of the scene
and highlights
the colors of the
costumes.

BRIGHT COLORS HIDDEN AWAY

In 1981 the lining was
removed for cleaning –
revealing the reverse
of the images, on the
back of the tapestry.
The colors on the
back are dazzlingly
bright, showing how
the tapestry must
have looked
when it was
made (all the
pictures here
are from the
reverse side,
except the
frieze).

Opposite:
Cathedral of St-Maurice.

● 72, 74

THE OLD TOWN

This is the quarter between the cathedral and the château, the area originally covered by the old walled city. Its narrow, winding streets are lined with religious buildings and old houses, many of them half-timbered, including some fine examples of architecture from the late Middle Ages.

PROMENADE DU BOUT-DU-MONDE.
This esplanade created in the 19th century leads from the château toward the old town. It offers views over the Maine to the quarter of La Doutre on the other side of the river.

LOGIS DE L'ESTAIGNIER. In the cobbled Rue St-Aignan, amid the medieval houses (such as nos. 15 and 17) stands a turreted building from 1448 which now houses the Musée de l'Étain (Pewter Museum). The building is also known as the Maison du Croissant, after the order of knights founded by René I ▲ 280.

RUE DONADIEU-DE-PUYCHARIC. This street is typical of the quiet charm of the old town. There are some delightful buildings, such as the Hôtel St-Martial (17th century), which was formerly a canon's residence, and the beautiful Hôtel de Coulanges (16th century), built around a garden that has an old well and a covered walk.

MONTÉE ST-MAURICE. As you climb up this old flight of steps from the bank of the Maine, the cathedral at the top gradually comes into view.

CATHEDRAL OF ST-MAURICE. Construction of the present cathedral was begun on the orders of Bishop Ulger of Douai in the early 12th century, and continued by his successors Normand de Doué and Guillaume de Beaumont.

EXTERIOR. The two 12th-century towers were modified in the 15th century and crowned with stone spires in the 19th century; they stand on either side of the 16th-century clock pavilion. The façade wall, built around 1180, displays a composite style influenced by the Aquitaine tradition. The portal (1170–80), with its four historiated archivolts, is surmounted by a gallery (which replaced an earlier gable in 1537) with eight tall statues of soldiers, including Saint Maurice.

INTERIOR. The oldest part of the cathedral is its single nave, which was built between 1148 and 1153, featuring the earliest Gothic arches in the Angevin style ● 60. As well as the choir, completed in 1274, the church has a large number of magnificent stained-glass windows from the 12th and 13th centuries, which give the building its distinctive luminosity. The large rose windows of the transept (above, the *Last Judgment*) were created by André Robin, master glassmaker of

As well as a remarkable treasury (right, a 15th-century arm reliquary), the cathedral has an organ case in the Rocaille style (above) and mural paintings (14th and 15th century) depicting the life of Saint Maurille (below).

302

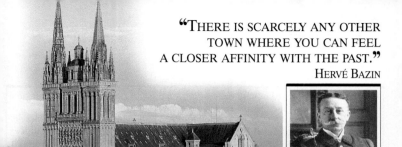

"THERE IS SCARCELY ANY OTHER TOWN WHERE YOU CAN FEEL A CLOSER AFFINITY WITH THE PAST."

HERVÉ BAZIN

the cathedral from 1435 to 1465. The high altar with its canopy in red marble was built in 1757–9 by Antoine-Denis Gervais, the king's architect, imitating Bernini's *baldacchino* at St Peter's in Rome. Of all the churches in Anjou, the cathedral has the richest treasury. Among the most striking pieces are the silver receptacle which contained the heart of Marguerite d'Anjou-Sicile and several reliquaries made of silver, gold and precious stones.

RUE DE L'OISELLERIE. There are three merchants' houses (nos. 5, 7 and 9) with corbeled gables and diamond-pattern timbering. The oldest dates from the 16th century.

ANCIEN ÉVÊCHÉ. The former episcopal palace (no. 2, rue de l'Oisellerie), completed under Bishop Ulger, was restored in the 19th century. It consists of two wings forming a T-shape. The bishop received his vassals in the low hall (12th century).

HÔTEL DE LA GODELINE (no. 73, rue Plantaganêt). This lovely building served as the town hall from 1484 to 1529. It was restored in 1641 and now houses the Maison des Vins and the headquarters of the Wine Council of Anjou and Saumur.

PLACE SAINTE-CROIX. In the Middle Ages this was the commercial center of the town and one of its liveliest districts. The prosperity of the time is reflected by several of the houses, the most spectacular of which is the Maison d'Adam (see below).

HÔTEL DE THÉVALLE. This lovely building from the late 16th century has square pavilions with large dormers and high mullioned windows. It was owned by the powerful Thévalle family, originally from the Maine region.

MAISON D'ADAM ● 73. Built on the corner of two main roads in the early 16th century; this is considered to be the loveliest old house in Angers. Its diamond-timbered façades (right) rise up over five corbeled stories, with a profusion of figures (above) and Flamboyant ornamentation carved in the wood. Up to the 19th century statues of Adam and Eve stood on either side of the Tree of Life, below the remarkable corner bartizan. The house's name derives either

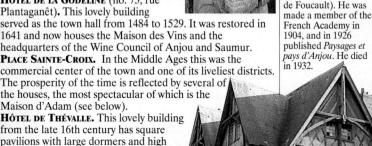

RENÉ BAZIN
Born in Angers in 1853, René Bazin studied at the Catholic University from the time of its foundation and in 1875 became its first Doctor of Law. A Catholic and a nationalist, in 1884 he embarked on his career as a journalist and novelist. He wrote twenty novels inspired by the Angers area and by his Christian faith (including *Stephanette*, *La terre qui meurt* and *Le blé qui lève*), as well as travel books (such as *Les croquis italiens*) and numerous essays (including ones on Pius X and Charles de Foucault). He was made a member of the French Academy in 1904, and in 1926 published *Paysages et pays d'Anjou*. He died in 1932.

DAVID D'ANGERS
Pierre-Jean David
(1788–1856), the son
of an ornamental
sculptor, studied first
at an art school
housed in the Logis
Barrault, and then at
the École des Beaux-
Arts in Paris. He
became known as
David d'Angers and
won the Grand Prix
de Rome in 1811 for
his bas-relief *The
Death of Epaminondas*,
which established his
fame. His close friend
Victor Hugo praised
his "dazzling"
monumental
masterpieces. David
created the pediment
of the Panthéon in
Paris; his most famous
statues are those of
Bonchamps (1824),
Bernardin de St-Pierre
(1851) and Général
Drouot (1853).

This female mask
from the Middle
Ages in gilded copper
(right) is one of the
rare masterpieces
on display in the
museum of the Logis
Barrault (below).

from these statues or from the name of its owner, Michel
Adam, an alderman of Angers, who acquired it in 1714.
RUE SAINT-AUBIN. On this street is the façade of the Hôtel du
Cheval-Blanc (no. 12), a private house from the 18th century
which still has a lovely wooden staircase in the courtyard, with
its original steps and balustrades.

FORMER ABBEY OF ST-AUBIN (Rue des Lices/Rue St-Aubin).
The abbey is said to have been founded around 535 by Saint
Germain, Bishop of Paris. It was extended in the 18th century.
Today the former abbey buildings house the Conseil Général
and Préfecture of Angers. Much of the original abbey was
destroyed when the Rue St-Martin was built; surviving
sections include the cloister (12th century), the Romanesque
arcades (above), the chapter house (12th and 17th century)
and the sacristy (17th century). The 18th-century
monumental railings outside came from the choir
of the abbey church at Fontevraud.
TOUR SAINT-AUBIN (Rue des Lices). This was the
belfry (12th century) of the Abbey of St-Aubin; the
square tower, nearly 180 feet high, terminates in an
octagonal story with four pinnacles.
FORMER COLLEGIATE CHURCH OF ST-MARTIN
(Rue St-Martin). This is the oldest church in Angers.
A Merovingian oratory was founded here by Saint
Loup, Bishop of Angers, in the 7th century. The
building was restored by Foulques Nerra ▲ 297 in
1012. Its transept dates from the
Carolingian era; the columns are from
the 11th century.
médiévale française.
**THE LOGIS BARRAULT (MUSÉE DES
BEAUX-ARTS)** ★. This mansion, in Rue du
Musée, is without doubt the most
impressive in Angers. It has two wings set
at right angles, faced with tufa and
decorated in the Flamboyant style, and a
corbeled staircase tower. The house was
built for Olivier Barrault, treasurer of
Brittany and mayor of Angers, in 1487.
It was altered in the 17th century and
converted into a prison for priests during
the Revolution; it was turned into a
museum in 1801. The displays of the

The Musée des Beaux-Arts has a painting by Ingres (below) depicting the unhappy love of Paolo Malatesta and Francesca da Rimini from Dante's *Inferno*.

Musée des Beaux-Arts consist chiefly of paintings – with some outstanding works by French painters of the 17th century (Philippe de Champaigne, Pierre Mignard) and 18th century (Watteau, Chardin, Fragonard, Boucher, Lancret and Greuze). There is also an impressive collection of sculpture, including works by Houdon, Falconet, Lemoyne and Carpeaux. The second story houses displays of local furniture and sculpture from the Middle Ages and the Renaissance, including a gilded-copper mask (opposite) that is a rare masterpiece of medieval French metalwork.

RUE TOUSSAINT. Substantial remains of the Gallo-Roman ramparts, dating from the 3rd century, can be seen here.

GALERIE DAVID D'ANGERS (no. 33b, rue Toussaint). The gallery is housed in what was once the church of the Abbey of Toussaint (13th century), of which the nave and two side chapels survive. The rectangular choir was added in the early 18th century. The church stood in ruins from 1810 until 1984, when it was restored by Pierre Brunet, chief architect of the national commission for historical monuments, who gave it a splendid glass roof. The municipal authorities decided to use the building to display the works of the famous sculptor David d'Angers (see opposite), giving them the space and prominence they deserved. The gallery was opened by President François Mitterrand (1916–96) in 1984.

HÔTEL DU ROI-DE-POLOGNE. This elegant late-16th-century residence at one end of the Pont de la Basse-Chaîne, close to the château, is one of Angers' most popular buildings. It probably owes its name to the Duke of Anjou who

briefly became King of Poland in 1573, before being crowned King Henri III of France in 1574.

HERVÉ BAZIN
Jean-Pierre-Hervé Bazin, the great-nephew of René Bazin, was born in Angers (in Rue Du-Bellay) in 1911. A novelist and president of the Académie Goncourt, he set some of his stories in Anjou, particularly in the Segréen ▲ *310*. His novels – *Vipère au poing* (1948), *La Mort du petit cheval* (1950), *Qui j'ose aimer* (1956), *Au nom du fils* (1960) and *Madame Ex* (1975) – deal with the theme of oppression within the family and in society.

Natural light from the glass roof highlights the modeling of the splendid sculptures of David d'Angers – such as the plaster casts below.

THE COMMERCIAL QUARTER

This area developed to the east and northeast of the old
city in the 17th and 18th centuries; many buildings were
erected at this time, including a number of ostentatious
private residences. In the 19th century the industrial age
contributed its usual quota of neoclassical houses and
public buildings.

PLACE DU RALLIEMENT. This square, which stands on the site
of a former Christian cemetery (3rd century), has been the
focal point of the town since the Third Republic. Its present
name dates from the Revolution, when volunteers from all
over Anjou gathered here before setting off to join the army.
The auditorium of the municipal theater was rebuilt between
1869 and 1871, after a fire; its ceiling displays a large painting
donated by the Angers artist Jules-Ernest Lenepveu
(1819–98). Lenepveu created the ceiling of the Opéra Garnier
in Paris around the same time.

HÔTEL PINCÉ (MUSEÉ TURPIN-DE-CRISSÉ) ★. This elegant
turreted Renaissance mansion ● 74, at no. 32b, rue Lenepveu,

rivals the attractions of the Logis Barrault
▲ 304. It was built, between 1530 and 1538, for
Jean de Pincé, Lieutenant Criminel (crown
prosecutor) and mayor of Angers. In 1861 the
building was given to the town by the painter
Guillaume Bodinier (1795–1872), who
converted it into a museum. In it Bodinier
displayed the substantial collections of Turpin
de Crissé (1782–1859), a painter and former
chamberlain to the Empress Joséphine. Later
donations brought the museum splendid
collections from the Far East.

RUE SAINT-LAUD ● 73. The street looks just
as it did two centuries ago, with a number
of notable private residences, including
Hôtel Ménage (16th century, altered in the
17th century), Hôtel Bardoul de la Bigottière

(18th century) and Hôtel Chemellier (18th century), where
the sculptor David d'Angers ▲ 304 was born in 1788.

URSULINE CHAPEL (Rue des Ursules). This 17th-century
building houses a remarkable Louis XIII altarpiece,
attributed to Pierre Corbineau. It is one of the most
spectacular examples of Lavallois altarpiece art, which spread
from Brittany to Touraine at this time.

MAISON DE LA "BELLE ANGEVINE" (corner of Place du Pilori
and Rue Lenepveu). This 16th-century half-timbered house is
said to have been that of Renée Corbeau, the beautiful cloth
merchant's daughter who was known as "la Belle Angevine".

RUE DU CORNET. This street below the old market district
has several striking houses, including Hôtel Ayrault-de-
St-Hénis, built for Lieutenant Criminel (crown prosecutor)
Pierre Ayrault, and Hôtel de Maquillé (1789), now the
headquarters of the town's architectural commission.

PLACE LOUIS-IMBACH. In medieval times this was the town's
market square; today it is named after a seed
merchant who fought with the Resistance and died during
deportation to Mauthausen. The building where the city
council was once located was taken over in 1823 by the
Court of Appeal.

> **"THE CUISINE OF ANGERS IS STRAIGHTFORWARD, SENSIBLE AND GOOD-NATURED; IT NEVER STRIVES FOR EFFECT ... ANJOU IS A PARADISE FOR PEACEFUL DIGESTION."**
>
> CURNONSKY, THE "PRINCE DES GASTRONOMES"

MUSEUM OF PALEONTOLOGY. (no. 2, Place Louis-Imbach). This museum, in the former courtroom of the Court of Appeal, was founded in the late 19th century. Its collections are mainly of local origin.

HÔTEL DE LANCREAU-DE-BELLEFONDS (no. 14, rue Pocquet-de-Livonnières). This splendid building, which dates from 1589, consists of three wings set around a main court closed off by an Ionic porchway.

NATURAL HISTORY MUSEUM (no. 43, rue Jules-Guitton).

Since 1958 the town's natural history collections have been housed in the Hôtel Valentin (early 19th century). Left: plates by the botanical painter Pierre-Joseph Redouté (1759–1840).

LYCÉE JOACHIM-DU-BELLAY (Avenue Marie-Talet). The Lycée is housed in the former Abbey of St-Serge, founded in the 7th century. Some of the Benedictine abbey's buildings were restored in the late 17th century and can still be seen today.

CHURCH OF ST-SERGE ★. The former abbey church, flanked by a tower added in 1480, dates from the early 13th century. Its remarkable nave with rounded Angevin vaulting (below) marks the peak of Plantaganet Gothic style.

JARDIN DES PLANTES. The botanical gardens were established in the late 18th century on land belonging to the Church of St-Serge. The former Church of St-Samson is now used for horticultural purposes.

RUE DES ARÈNES. Remains of a 2nd-century amphitheater were unearthed here by local archeologists in 1868, during construction work on the Church of St-Joseph.

JARDIN DU MAIL. These gardens were opened in 1859 alongside an industrial and horticultural exhibition, on the site of a royal-tennis court. The centerpiece is a huge fountain adorned with figures of gods.

HÔTEL DE VILLE. The town hall, opposite the Jardin du Mail, is housed in the classical buildings of the former Collège d'Anjou, built by the Jesuits in 1691. The building was extended in 1823. It was completely renovated in 1981, with the addition of a contemporary extension designed by architect Philippe Morel.

"LA BOULE DE FORT": A LOCAL VARIANT OF BOULES
This is a very popular game in Anjou, especially between Les Ponts-de-Cé and the Bourgueil area. It is a team game, played on a curving wooden or plastic *piste*, using bowls that are weighted on one side. As in ordinary boules, the aim is to get as close as possible to the jack or *maître*. The origins of the game are uncertain, but its popularity revived in the mid 19th century. It is similar to the British game of bowls, the main differences being that it is played indoors and that the bowls are bound with iron hoops.

CURNONSKY
Maurice-Edmond Sailland, born in Angers in 1872, became a journalist specializing in food and restaurants. He signed his first articles with the pseudonym Curnonsky and became the champion of traditional French food, especially the cuisine of Anjou. Founder of the Académie des Gastronomes, he was feared by restaurant owners throughout France and in 1927 was proclaimed the "Prince des Gastronomes". He died in Paris in 1956.

The Pont de Verdun
over the Maine.

QUARTIER DE LA DOUTRE

The La Doutre quarter – from *d'outre Maine* (on the other side of the Maine river) – grew up in the Middle Ages on the right bank of the Maine, around the Abbey of the Ronceray (11th century). It was neglected in the 19th century and has recently undergone a major restoration program.

TOUR DES ANGLAIS. This tower at the end of the Pont de la Haute-Chaîne, which spans the Maine, was once part of the ramparts built by Louis IX in the 13th century.

HÔPITAL SAINT-JEAN ★ (no. 4, boulevard Arago). Built in 1175 by Étienne de Marsay, seneschal to King Henry II of England, this is the oldest hospital in France and a masterpiece of Early Gothic architecture.

MUSÉE JEAN-LURÇAT ★. Since 1967 the museum (below), installed in the former Hôpital St-Jean, has displayed the magnificent tapestry by Jean Lurçat (see opposite) entitled *Le Chant du Monde*, which was to have been some 400 feet long. This work,

created as a tribute to the Tapestry of the Apocalypse ▲ *300*, was woven at Aubusson between 1957 and 1966, when the artist's death brought the project to an end. Ten panels (around 260 feet long) are on display, presenting a pessimistic vision of humanity (*The Great Threat*, *Man of Hiroshima*) and the prospect of renaissance (*Man in Glory and Peace*).

MUSÉE DE LA TAPISSERIE CONTEMPORAINE. This museum was established in a neighboring building in June 1986 and exhibits the donations of Mme Simone Lurçat as well as tapestries by the contemporary weaver Thomas Gleb and other modern artists.

THE HOSPITAL CHAPEL ★. The chapel was built in the 12th and 13th centuries, with magnificent Angevin vaulting. Its

> **"MY WORK WAS STARTED LATE, AND SO HAD OLD AGE CHAFING AT ITS HEELS. IN A WAY YOU COULD SEE IT AS AN INVENTORY OF MY WHOLE LIFE."**
>
> JEAN LURÇAT, ON HIS WORK, IN 1964

stained-glass windows date from the 13th century, the Baroque high altar from the 17th century.

PLACE DE LA PAIX. A paupers' cemetery was located here in the Middle Ages. The square as it is today has a number of imposing buildings, most notably Hôtel de Richeteau (17th century) and Hôtel du Guesclin (1554).

THE RONCERAY. Founded by Foulques Nerra ▲ 297 around 1060, the Abbaye du Ronceray remained the only religious institution for women in Angers. The Romanesque building displays the earliest example in Anjou of a high nave with fully vaulted side aisles. The abbey was rebuilt in the 17th century; since 1815 it has housed the École Nationale des Arts et Métiers.

ÉGLISE DE LA TRINITÉ (second half of the 12th century). This church stands next to the Ronceray. Its single nave has a series of side chapels fanning out in a semicircle. At the entrance to the nave is an unusual carved wooden staircase from the early Renaissance, which was originally part of an organ case.

HÔTEL DES PÉNITENTES. Initially this building (on Boulevard Descazeaux), dating from the 16th century, served as a refuge for monks from the Abbey of St-Nicolas. From 1640 it became a community for prostitutes and other female penitents, founded by Marguerite Deshaies.

FORMER ABBEY OF ST-NICOLAS. The abbey was founded by Foulques Nerra in the 11th century; it was rebuilt in 1725. The grand southern façade, nearly 300 feet long, overlooks the lake and the gardens.

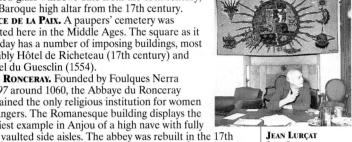

JEAN LURÇAT
Jean Lurçat (1892–1966) was initially a painter and engraver, influenced by Matisse and then by Surrealism; his interest in tapestry began in 1933.
In 1937 he saw the Tapestry of the Apocalypse, an experience which inspired him to create his major work, *Le Chant du Monde* (*Song of the World*). He produced more than 800 tapestries and helped to give weavers their own place in the history of modern art.
Left: *Liberté* (1943), inspired by a very beautiful poem by Paul Éluard.

The exhibitions held at the Musée de la Tapisserie display works by the best artists from France and abroad. Left: *Mai* (1960) by Mario Prassinos (1916–85).

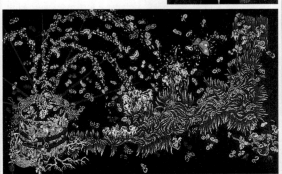

Left: *Champagne* (1959) by Jean Lurçat. Above: a postage stamp issued in his honor.

LE PLESSIS-MACÉ
Right: the fortified keep towering above the
moat. Far right: the tufa balcony of the
château's Renaissance residential wing.

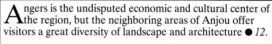

LE PLESSIS-MACÉ
Right: the fortified keep towering above the
moat. Far right: the tufa balcony of the
château's Renaissance residential wing.

"... and should you
decide to linger
afterward ... in the
broad valley through
which the river runs
and the breezes blow,
with so many
sandbanks, poplars
and grapes, you will
have seen the fifth
canton of Anjou and
its greatest beauty"
René Bazin

Serrant, a stylish and
sumptuous château.

A ngers is the undisputed economic and cultural center of
the region, but the neighboring areas of Anjou offer
visitors a great diversity of landscape and architecture ● *12*.

THE VALLEY (A6)

To the southwest of Angers the landscape around the Loire is
composed of hills standing on either side of the alluvial valley.
Here the river has many islands, of which the Île de Chalonnes
is the largest. Beyond the river the landscape is still quite wild,
though criss-crossed by shady lanes and hedgerows, with a few
aristocratic residences dotted here and there.
CORNICHE ANGEVINE ★. The winding road which overhangs
the Louet river between Les Ponts-de-Cé and Chalonnes,
downriver from Angers, is one of the loveliest in Anjou. It has
magnificent views of vineyards, the Loire and the river valley,
and villages with turreted buildings and slate roofs.
CHÂTEAU DE SERRANT ★. The château stands in extensive
grounds, surrounded by a deep moat, on the right bank of the
Loire near St-Georges-sur-Loire. It is built of grey schist and
white limestone, in a satisfyingly harmonious style – even
though it took a century and a half to complete. The first
phase of construction started in 1546, directed by Philibert
Delorme, the architect of Fontainebleau; the chapel was built
later (in 1700–10) by Jules Hardouin-Mansart, architect of the
chapel at Versailles. The residential wing is flanked by two
round towers, each crowned by a pinnacled dome. The main
façade, like the one at Azay-le-Rideau ▲ *234*, features a
staircase surmounted by a pediment. In the chapel the white
marble mausoleum (1705), carved by Antoine Coysevox, is
dedicated to the Marquis de Vaubrun, who was killed in the
Battle of Altenheim in 1675. The château's apartments
display a magnificent collection of furniture and objets d'art,
as well as tapestries from Flanders and Brussels (12th
century), including a series depicting scenes from
Ovid's *Metamorphoses*. The splendid library
contains over 12,000 books.

THE SEGRÉEN (A4, A5)

This region of hills and hedgerows around the
village of Segré, to the northwest of Angers,
stretches as far as the borders of
Brittany, where many
defensive fortresses were built.
CHÂTEAU DU PLESSIS-MACÉ ★.
This château, to the west of
Angers, was originally a
fortress built by the feudal
lord, Macé du Plessis, in the
12th century. Three centuries
later it was modified by Louis
de Beaumont, chamberlain of
Louis XI. It is an imposing
sight, with its 12th-century
ramparts and machicolated
rectangular keep (rebuilt in
1445) surrounded by trees a
hundred years old. This

somber effect is offset by the delightful 15th-century residential wing, with walls of dark schist which contrast with the white tufa of the elegant carved balcony and windows. The chapel, also from the 15th century, is dedicated to Saint Michael; its original altar and a wooden two-story organ loft have survived.

CHÂTEAU DU PLESSIS-BOURRÉ ★. The château is situated to the north of Angers, in the town of Écueillé, between the Sarthe and Mayenne rivers. Jean Bourré, treasurer and confidant of Louis XI, acquired the estate of Plessis-le-Vent in 1462 and in only four years (1468–72) built this dazzling creation of tufa limestone, which appears to be floating on water. It is set in the middle

of a moat so wide that it looks more like a lake. The building's fortresslike appearance is largely due to the fortified entrance, the great towers at the four corners (the southeast tower has a wall walk with machicolations) and the ring of low terraces designed to serve as platforms for artillery. The Renaissance-style residential wing, less austere in appearance, is set in a vast interior courtyard. The guardroom (on the second story) has an astonishing coffered wooden ceiling, decorated with curious allegorical and satirical pictures, such as *Donkey Singing the Mass* (above) and the more obscure *Immodest Venus*, many of them magnificent examples of 15th-century painting.

WINES FAMOUS SINCE THE MIDDLE AGES
■ *30*, ◆ *322*
Although Anjou's most widely known wine is Rosé de Cabernet, the region's reputation is primarily due to the quality of its white wines. To the south of Angers, on both sides of the river, are the Coteaux-de-Loire which produce Savennières, the most celebrated of the dry white wines, as well as the famous wines of La Roche-aux-Moines and La Coulée-de-Serrant (one of the greatest white wines in France). On the left bank, the Chenin Blanc grapes are used to make Coteaux-du-Layon-Village wines, the best of which are Bonnezeaux and Quarts-de-Chaume.

STAUNCH BUILDER OF CHÂTEAUX
Jean Bourré (1424–1506), son of a lawyer from Château-Gontier, entered the service of Louis XI after studying law. He became head of the royal chancellery, governor of Langeais and then treasurer of France. He was made commander of the Château d'Angers under Charles VIII, and built châteaux at Vaux, Jarzé and Plessis-Bourré in the Maine-et-Loire region.

CORKSCREW SPIRES
Towns and villages, such as Graçay, Fougeré, Pontigné, Fontaine-Guérin and Mouliherne, have curious bell towers known as *clochers tors*, which are helicoidal (spiral) and have a twisted appearance. The origin of this type of spire is unknown. The helicoidal spire of the bell tower at Vieil-Baugé was given an extra twist when it was struck by lightning.

THE BAUGEOIS (D5, E5)

The area around Baugé, to the east of Angers, is a sandy plateau covered alternately by deep forest and farmland.
BAUGÉ. The town is situated on the right bank of the Couasnon, at the edge of the Forest of Chandelais, on the border of Touraine.
THE CHÂTEAU ★. The first château was built by Foulques Nerra ▲ *297* around the year 1000. In the 15th century Baugé was a favorite residence of René I ▲ *280*: from 1455 onward he continued the renovation work begun by his mother, Yolande d'Aragon. Above the grand staircase in the north pavilion of the residential wing there is splendid palm-tree vaulting decorated with the arms of Anjou and Sicily. Today the château houses the town hall and a small museum devoted to local history and customs.

HÔPITAL SAINT-JOSEPH ★. The hospital's 17th-century *apothicairerie* (dispensary) displays a rare collection of earthenware pots and jars (left), ranging from the 16th to the 18th century.
CHAPELLE DE LA GIROUARDIÈRE. Since the Revolution the former chapel of the Hospice des Incurables (18th century) has housed the Cross of Anjou ● *37*, said to be made from the True Cross.

The dispensary of the Hôpital St-Joseph at Baugé.

SLATE QUARRYING
According to legend, it was Saint Lézin, Bishop of Angers in the 6th century, who first used slate for roofing. The slate quarries of Trélazé were worked from the 15th century onward and were known as *perrières*. From the 16th century the workers (or *perreyeux*) specialized in particular tasks: those at the lowest level (*fonceurs*) extracted the schist, while those who worked above ground (the *fendeurs*) cut up the thinner blocks to extract the slate. The right to be a *fendeur* passed from father to son. All the workers were accorded the status of miners, as laid down by the Federation of Slate-Quarry Workers, founded in 1904 by a Trélazé quarry worker, Ludovic Ménard (1855–1935).

THE AUTHION VALLEY (D5, D6)

This long valley to the southeast of Angers was once marshland; today the river banks are lined with fields of flowers and corn. A number of aristocratic residences were built here after the area was drained in the 18th century, adding to the charm of the pretty local towns and villages, with their little windmills and tufa houses.
CHÂTEAU DE MONTGEOFFROY. This neoclassical château ● *70* was built by the architect Nicolas Barré for the Maréchal de Contades in 1772. The impressive 18th-century residential wing is flanked by the chapel and two round towers from a 16th-century manor house. The château has an exhibition of documents signed by Louis XV, Napoleon and Louis XVIII. The small temple in the grounds dates from the 19th century.

TRÉLAZÉ (B6)

From the 15th century onward Anjou was famous for its slate, extracted from the schist quarries of Trélazé, for a long time one of the main slate-quarrying towns in the world. However, five of the six mines were forced to close because of the difficult economic climate and competition, notably from Spain. Today Trélazé's slate quarries employ only nine hundred workers, but they still produce 90 percent of the slate used in France.

PRACTICAL INFORMATION

Between Gien and Angers, the Loire flows through four départements: Loiret, Loir-et-Cher, Indre-et-Loire and Maine-et-Loire. This majestic river valley is one of France's best-known regions, famous above all for its many magnificent châteaux. The Loire Valley also offers excellent facilities for tourists, especially those who come to see its cultural attractions. It is close to Paris, and easily accessible by road, by TGV (high-speed) trains and by air. Spring, from May onward, and summer are the ideal seasons to discover the artistic, historical and gastronomic treasures of the valley of the French kings.

TOURIST INFORMATION

For information regarding accommodation and tourist events, contact the regional tourist boards (for the Centre and Pays-de-Loire regions), the departmental tourist boards, and local tourist offices
◆ 320.

REGIONAL TOURIST BOARDS (CRTs: COMITÉS RÉGIONAUX DE TOURISME)
◆ Centre
9, rue St-Pierre-Lentin
45041 Orléans cedex 1
Tel. 02 38 54 95 42
Fax 02 38 54 95 46
◆ Pays-de-Loire
2, rue de la Loire
44200 Nantes
Tel. 02 40 89 89 89
Fax 02 40 08 07 10

DEPARTMENTAL TOURIST BOARDS (CDTs: COMITÉS DÉPARTEMENTAUX DE TOURISME)
◆ Indre-et-Loire
18, pl. de la Préfecture
B.P. 3217
37032 Tours cedex
Tel. 02 47 31 42 60
Fax 02 47 31 42 76
◆ Loiret
8, rue d'Escures
45000 Orléans
Tel. 02 38 62 04 88
Fax 02 38 62 98 37
◆ Loir-et-Cher
5, rue de la Voûte du Château
41000 Blois
Tel. 02 54 78 55 50
Fax 02 54 74 81 79
◆ Maine-et-Loire
Place Kennedy
BP 2147
49021 Angers cedex 02
Tel. 02 41 23 51 51
Fax 02 41 88 36 77

A FEW GOOD REASONS FOR VISITING THE LOIRE VALLEY

◆ The vineyards, the wines, the restaurants . . .
◆ One hundred or more châteaux
◆ The Tapestry of the Apocalypse at Angers
◆ The troglodyte dwellings
◆ The windmills of Anjou
◆ The magnificent château gardens, especially Villandry
◆ The Loire itself, the last untamed river of France

◆ The gentle pace of life
◆ The great writers: from Gregory of Tours, Joachim du Bellay and Rabelais to Balzac, Proust, René and Hervé Bazin . . .
◆ The painters and sculptors: David d'Angers, Leonardo da Vinci, François Clouet, Michel Colombe, Jean Bourdichon, Jean Fouquet, Juste, Corneille . . .

HEALTH

Form E111, available from post offices in the UK, allows EC nationals to receive free emergency health care. Other travelers are advised to take out special

insurance cover before leaving.
◆ For "son et lumière" displays you are advised to equip yourself with mosquito repellent.

TOURIST PROFILE

The Loire Valley is one of the most popular regions of France, attracting nearly ten million visitors each year. It has 730 hotels, with a capacity of 18,000 beds. The majority of these are two-star hotels (accounting for nearly 70 percent of the total). Other types of accommodation are also available, including rural gîtes and guest houses. The most popular historical building in the region is the Château de

Chenonceau, which attracts 900,000 visitors each year, followed by Chambord, with 800,000. The Aquarium de Touraine at Lussault-sur-Loire, which opened in 1994, has already become a major attraction, with nearly 500,000 visitors annually. In recent years the region has successfully developed its varied, delightful countryside as a tourist attraction in its own right.

WHEN TO VISIT

The Loire Valley is known as the "Jardin de la France" ("Garden of France"), a name that takes on its fullest meaning in May and June. Many music and theater festivals are held then, and the monuments and châteaux are not yet overcrowded with

visitors. The weather is generally good: there may be the occasional shower or cold spell but these never last long. The late fall is also a good time to come: during this period the "vendanges" (grape harvesting) are the focal point of local life.

DOCUMENTATION

EC nationals arriving in France need only present an identity card or passport.

Tourists from other countries will need to present a passport, and in some cases a visa.

FESTIVALS

SPRING

February–March	International 20th-century piano competition, Orléans
March–April	St-Cosme spring music festival (Indre-et-Loire)
April	"Fête des plantes et des jardins de Touraine", Montlouis
April–September	Public display by the Cadre Noir at the Grand Manège of the National Equestrian School, Saumur
Late April	"Acteurs-Acteurs": international drama festival, Tours
April 29–May 1	Joan of Arc festival, Orléans
Late May	"Florilège vocal" (choral music festival), Tours
May–June	Festival of classical music, Sully-sur-Loire (Loiret)
Late June	Rock music festival, Tours
	Music festivals in Touraine, Grange de Meslay, Tours
May–September	Summer music and organ festival, Amboise

★ Wine festivals: Vouvray in February, Chinon and Bourgueil in March, Saumur in April, Amboise at Easter . . .

SUMMER

Late June/early July	"Orléans'Jazz", Orléans.
July	Festival d'Anjou: music and arts in the châteaux of Anjou
	National opera festival for children at the Chapelle-St-Mesmin (Loiret)
	"Les Semaines musicales" music festival, Tours
	Festival of musical theater in Touraine, Loches and Chinon
July–September	International festival of parks and gardens, Chaumont-sur-Loire

★ The medieval market of Chinon in August: tumblers, puppets, trades of the past, medieval delicacies . . . experience Chinon as it was in the Middle Ages

FALL

Late September	Jazz in Touraine, Montlouis

★ "Le Mondial du Lion": international equestrian competition at the Lion d'Angers

WINTER

January–February	Regional music festival, Montlouis

SON ET LUMIÈRE

May–September: Château d'Azay-le-Rideau
June–August: Château d'Amboise
June–September: Château de Blois and Château de Chenonceau
July–August: Château de Cheverny, Château de Loches, Château du Lude (Sarthe)

CLIMATE

The Loire Valley is blessed with an especially attractive climate: it is close to the sea, and the maritime influence prevents extremely cold conditions; at the same time the continental influence raises summer temperatures. Anjou and the Touraine are more humid than the areas around Blois and Orléans. The higher humidity levels mean that there are more foggy or misty days. Rainfall is regular, but rarely heavy or long-lasting. Summer storms are more common here than by the sea, ensuring a good level of rainfall during the summer months.

The temperature rarely falls below 5°c during the winter. Spring weather is mild, though cold at night. In summer it can be really hot, reaching 30°c. The fall often brings magnificent Indian summers.

BE PREPARED

Rain can come without warning – sometimes with violent storms, especially in summer. It is a good idea to carry an umbrella and a raincoat with you.

PUBLIC HOLIDAYS IN FRANCE

- ◆ January 1
- ◆ Easter Monday
- ◆ May 1
- ◆ May 8
- ◆ Ascension Day
- ◆ Pentecost Monday
- ◆ July 14
- ◆ August 15
- ◆ November 1
- ◆ November 11
- ◆ December 25

◆ Traveling to the Loire Valley

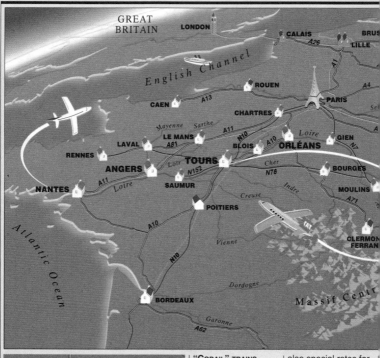

By train

TGV (HIGH-SPEED) TRAIN
These fast, comfortable trains provide a quick, direct service to the Loire Valley.

RAILWAY STATIONS (SNCF)
There is now a single, central telephone number, for all stations, for train times, fares, reservations and sale of tickets.
Tel. 36 35 35 35 or minitel 3615 SNCF

◆ Tours is served by several TGV trains daily, direct from Paris-Montparnasse (1 hr journey time), Lyon-La-Part-Dieu (3½ hrs), Lille (3¼ hrs) and Bordeaux (2½ hrs). The trains stop either at Tours station or at St-Pierre-des-Corps (where there is a regular shuttle service into the town center of Tours).
◆ Several TGV trains run daily from Paris-Montparnasse to Angers (1½ hrs), from Lille to Angers (3¼ hrs) and from Lyon-La-Part-Dieu to Angers (4 hrs).

"CORAIL" TRAINS
These provide a slower but very frequent service. The trains leave Paris nearly every hour for
◆ Orléans (departure from the Gare d'Austerlitz, 1 hr journey time);
◆ Blois (Gare d'Austerlitz, 1½ hrs);
◆ Gien (Gare de Lyon, 1½ hrs).

REDUCTIONS
The SNCF offers a number of reductions: Joker (tickets reserved at least 8 days in advance), Carrissimo (for 12–25 year-olds), Vermeil (for the over-60's), Carte Famille (for families) and Carte Couple (for married or unmarried couples). There are also special rates for different days and journey lengths.

AIR TRAVEL
To NANTES
Nantes International Airport is 55 miles from Angers and 110 miles from Tours. Flights from this airport serve Paris and many other cities in France and internationally. Both French and international airlines fly from Nantes, offering a range of prices and substantial reductions depending on the date of the flight, the length of stay and the age of the passenger.
◆ Information: Aéroport International de Nantes
Tel. 02 40 84 80 00

You can put your bicycle on the train, even on a TGV! It is carried free of charge in the hand-luggage section, or for a charge in the registered luggage section. For information contact railway stations or tour operators.

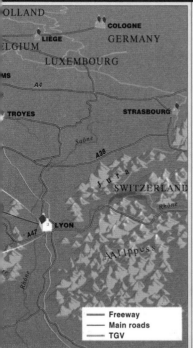

Freeway
Main roads
TGV

To Tours
The airline company TAT offers two flights daily (on Friday and Saturday) between Tours and Lyon, where you can get a connecting flight for other destinations in France or abroad.
◆ TAT (in Tours)
Tel. 02 47 41 23 23
◆ Aéroport Tours-Symphorion (4 miles from the town center)
Tel. 02 47 54 19 46

By car
On the freeway
All the major towns in the Loire Valley can be reached by freeway. The A10 (Paris-Bordeaux) serves Orléans, Blois and Tours. Angers is on the A11 (the "Océane", Paris-Nantes). Traveling from the Lyons region or from the southeast of France, you can reach Orléans on the A72 and the A71, continuing your

journey on the N152 which runs alongside the Loire between Orléans and Saumur.

On the main roads
From the north or the southwest of France, take the N10 (Paris-

HALTE PEAGE

Bordeaux-Hendaye); from the west or the southeast, take the Laval-Bourges-Moulins road.
◆ Road information
Tel. 08 36 68 20 00
or minitel
3615 ROUTES

Allostop
An organization which puts drivers in touch with would-be passengers, who make a financial contribution calculated according to the length of the journey.
◆ Reservations:
Tel. 01 53 20 42 42 (from Paris)
01 53 20 42 43 (from outside Paris)

Regional transport
The region is covered by trains and coaches on the TER network. For information on departure times, connections and journey times, see the "Guide régional des transports" (Regional Transport Guide), available from railway stations and tourist offices
◆ *320*.

SNCF stations
Information on train timetables and ticket prices:
Tel. 36 35 35 35
◆ Orléans
6, rue St-Yves
◆ Blois
Av. Jean-Laigret
◆ Tours
Place du Maréchal-Leclerc
◆ Angers
Place de la Gare

Coach stations
◆ Orléans
Rue Marcel-Proust
Tel. 02 38 53 94 75
◆ Blois
2, Place Victor-Hugo
Tel. 02 54 78 15 66

◆ Tours
Place du Maréchal-Leclerc
Tel. 02 47 05 30 49
◆ Angers
Place de la République
Tel. 02 41 88 59 25

Transport for tourists
The departmental tourist boards organize specialist tours on foot, on horseback, by caravan or barouche, on bicycle or by canoe: these can last one or more days. You can also travel by boat – by renting a barge, for example.

Flying over the Loire
Although expensive, this is a spectacular way of traveling over the region: by hot-air balloon, helicopter or plane. As might be expected, the views are stunning, the river valley offers a mosaic of landscapes dotted with châteaux.
◆ Information at the "Loisirs Accueil" services of the CDTs ◆ *314* or from tourist offices
◆ *320*.

In the Loire Valley, as in many other tourist regions, prices can vary with the seasons. As summer and the holiday period approach they tend to creep upward. . . . The difference is most noticeable in hotels and restaurants, whereas entrance prices for châteaux and other historical monuments stay the same throughout the year.

METHODS OF PAYMENT

CREDIT CARDS

Credit cards are accepted in almost all hotels, restaurants and stores. You can withdraw up to 2,000F weekly using national and international credit cards affiliated to the Visa, Mastercard or Eurocheque networks; up to 4,000F with a Diners card; and up to 6,000F with an American Express card.

◆ All towns of significant size have at least one auto-teller.

TRAVELERS' CHECKS

Hotel chains and a large number of restaurants and stores accept travelers' checks in French francs. Some display signs to this effect in their windows, though it is always wise to ask in advance. Travelers' checks in foreign currencies are not generally accepted: they should be converted in a bank or bureau de change, which will generally charge a commission on the sum of money exchanged.

EUROCHEQUES

Although this is a common form of payment in some other European countries, Eurocheques are not very well received in France: storekeepers are increasingly reluctant to accept them. However, the EC guarantee card which accompanies Eurocheques can also function as a cash withdrawal card, allowing you to withdraw up to 2,000F in currency each week.

LOSS OR THEFT

IDENTITY PAPERS

Contact the nearest police station; also, contact your consulate or embassy in Paris.

EUROCHEQUES AND EC CARDS

Notify the bank that issued the checks as soon as possible.

CREDIT CARDS

Notify the organization that issued the card instructing them to cancel the card, and send a registered letter to your bank. Allow three weeks for a new card to reach you.

◆ Visa
Tel. 01 42 77 11 90
◆ Eurocard and Mastercard
Tel. 01 45 67 84 84
◆ American Express
Tel. 01 47 77 72 00
◆ Diners Club
Tel. 01 47 62 75 75

RESTAURANTS

The Loire Valley offers a wide range of restaurants, allowing visitors to taste local specialties like *matelote d'anguille*, *rillons de Touraine* and the famous *tarte Tatin*. Prices range from 60F for a decent quality menu to 1,000F for a top-class restaurant, with a full range of options between these two extremes. Away from the immediate vicinity of the river there is an excellent choice of menus offering much better value for money. Nearly all restaurants in the Loire Valley area open at noon; in the evening they generally open at 7pm. In the towns, some restaurants serve meals until midnight, while others remain open all night. In more rural areas restaurants will not generally serve meals after 10.30pm.

BANKS

Banks are generally open from 9am to noon and from 2pm to 5pm (some banks in large towns stay open through the lunch hour). Banks are closed on Sundays, public holidays, and Saturdays or Mondays. Independent bureaux de change have longer opening hours and are often open at the weekend.

PRICE GUIDE

1 bottle of Chinon: 40F

1 hot-air balloon flight: 1,000F per person

1 Kilo of "Champignons de Paris": 14F

1 bottle of traditional wine vinegar (75cl): 20F

1 night in a private château: 350–1,200F for two people

1 entrance fee to a château: 10–40F

1 pot of "rillons de Touraine": 68F

1 entrance ticket for the château and Apocalypse tapestry in Angers: 32F

POST OFFICES

Post offices are open from 8am to 7pm Monday to Friday, and from 8am to noon on Saturdays. The normal rate for France and EC countries is 3F for a letter or card weighing up to 20g. Stamps can be purchased from post offices or at a "tabac".

MARKETS

Open-air markets are held in the squares of towns and villages once or twice a week. These are the best places to buy fresh produce: fish, meat, cheese, local vegetables, seasonal fruit and typical local delicacies.

EMERGENCY NUMBERS
Fire: 18
Police: 17
Ambulance: 15

IMPORTANT!
A new code system for telephone and fax numbers in France came into effect in October, 1996. All the information that follows takes this change into account.
CALLING FRANCE FROM ABROAD
Dial the international prefix (00 from the UK and 011 from the US), then 33 for France, followed by a 9-digit number.

TELEPHONE

DIRECTORY INFORMATION
For numbers in France, dial 12. For international information, dial 00 33 12 followed by the prefix for the country concerned.
CALLING ABROAD FROM FRANCE
From France, dial 00, followed by the country prefix (44 for the UK; 1 for the US) and the number you wish to reach.
CALLS WITHIN FRANCE
For all local and inter-regional calls,
dial 0, followed by a 9-figure number.
TELEPHONE BOXES
To use these you will need telephone cards ("télécartes"), which are available in 50 or 120 units (costing 40.60F and 97.50F respectively) from "tabacs", metro stations and post offices.

FOREIGN-LANGUAGE GUIDES

The departmental tourist boards ◆ 314 can provide foreign-language guides for tourists on request.

THE COST OF A TELEPHONE CALL

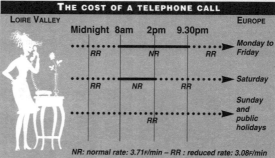

NR: normal rate: 3.71F/min – RR : reduced rate: 3.08F/min

◆ ACCOMMODATION

Pleasant hotel rooms can be found for 250F and above: these are generally in two-star hotels (following the new system of classification). Out of season you can treat yourself to a night in one of the many châteaux and manor houses which have been converted into luxury hotels, for a price in the region of 600F. The Loire Valley also has many guest houses and "gîtes" which offer rooms at a reasonable price, often in opulent settings. Local tourist offices are often the best source of advice for reserving the type of accommodation that best suits your needs.

TOURIST OFFICES

ANGERS
Place Kennedy
Tel. 02 41 23 51 11
Open (summer)
Mon.–Sat. 9am–7pm;
Sun. 10am–1pm and
12–6pm
BLOIS
Pavillon Anne-de-Bretagne
3, av. du Docteur-Jean-Laigret
Tel. 02 54 74 06 49
Open (summer)
Mon.–Sat. 9.am–7pm; Sun. 10am–7pm

ORLÉANS
Place Albert 1er
Tel. 02 38 24 05 05
Open Mon.–Sat.
9.00–19.00; Sun.
10am–noon (and
3–6.30pm during
July–August)
SAUMUR
Place de la Bilange
BP 241
Tel. 02 41 40 20 60
Open (summer)
Mon.–Sat.
9.15am–7pm; Sun.
10.30am–12.30pm
and 3.30–6.30pm)
TOURS
78, rue Bernard-Palissy
Tel. 02 47 70 37 37
Open (summer)
Mon.–Sat.
8.30am–7pm; Sun.
10am–12.30pm and
3–6pm

HOLIDAY VILLAGES

These are village-style groups of holiday homes that offer tourists both relaxation and recreation in a rural setting. They are the ideal place to spend a relaxing holiday at a low price, in both summer and winter. There are around fifty holiday villages in the region as a whole.
◆ Fédération Française des

Stations Vertes de Vacances et des Villages de Neige
BP 598
21016 Dijon Cedex
Tel. 80 43 49 47

HOTELS

Hotels are classified in different categories, according to the new French system: from no stars to the luxury four-star category. Generally the price quoted is for the room and not per

person. It is advisable to make advance reservations at Easter and during July and August. All the major hotel chains are represented in the Loire Valley.

SOME HOTEL ASSOCIATIONS

RELAIS ET CHÂTEAUX AND RELAIS DU SILENCE
Most of the châteaux-hotels in the Loire Valley belong to one of these two associations, whose members are high-quality establishments in exceptional settings.
◆ Relais et Châteaux
15, rue Galvani
75017 Paris
Tel. 01 45 72 90 00

◆ Relais du Silence
2, passage Du Guesclin
75015 Paris
Tel. 01 45 66 77 77
LOGIS DE FRANCE
These hotels, generally in the countryside, are traditional establishments with restaurants.
◆ Logis de France
83, av. d'Italie
75013 Paris
Tel. 01 45 84 70 00

CAMPING AND CARAVANNING

The Loire Valley has some 18,000 camping places in around 260 campsites; as regards classification, 50 percent of the sites have two stars, and 36 percent have three

or four stars. Many have lakes, bathing ponds or swimming pools, tennis courts or playing fields. CRTs publish free brochures listing all the campsites in the region.

Guest houses

Chambres d'hôtes
These private houses in the town or the country offer accommodation to travelers for one or more nights. As well as breakfast, guests are sometimes offered dinner at the "table d'hôte" (residents' table). Prices for a room in this type of establishment vary between 200F and 1,200F (for two persons, including breakfast).
◆ Bienvenu au Château.
This association includes châteaux, manor houses and other exceptional establishments offering accommodation in a spectacular setting.

Gîtes
These are generally traditional houses in the countryside. The prices vary between 700F and 3,000F per week, for 4 to 6 people, depending on classification (from 1 to 4 stars), the locality and the time

of year. "Gîtes" are often very popular and can be reserved from one year to the next: it is advisable to book very early for the summer period.

Gîtes d'étape (hostels)
These gîtes are designed for walkers in particular, although they are also open to other travelers. They cater for groups, offering simple (and increasingly comfortable) accommodation for one or more nights, often including breakfast. Some gîtes d'étape are in troglodytic dwellings. The average price per night is 50F. For information and reservations contact
◆ Relais départementaux des Gîtes de France:
Indre-et-Loire
Tel. 02 47 27 56 10
Loire-et-Cher
Tel. 02 54 78 55 50
Loiret
Tel. 02 38 62 04 88
Maine-et-Loire
Tel. 02 41 23 51 23

Equestrian holidays

The Loire Valley has many equestrian centers, and the region offers magnificent, varied landscapes for horse-lovers to explore. The centers organize courses and treks, with hostel-type accommodation.
◆ Centre de tourisme équestre
49350 Trèves-Cunault
Tel. 02 41 67 92 43
◆ Tourisme équestre Le Sauvageot
49680 Vivy
Tel. 02 41 52 89 52

◆ Association régionale de tourisme équestre Val de Loire-Centre
52, rue Alain-Gerbault
41000 Blois
Tel. 02 54 42 95 60

The École nationale d'équitation de Saumur (National Equestrian School at Saumur) is open to the public from April to September. Visitors can watch demonstrations of jumping, dressage and display riding.
Tel. 02 41 53 50 66

Cycling holidays

The various departmental tourist boards work together with hotels and campsites to organize cycling tours offering accommodation and a range of related services, such as bicycle rental, luggage

transfer, maps and documentation, repair kits and picnics on request.
◆ Information on cycling tours is available from the "Loisirs Accueil" services of the CDTs and from most tourist offices.

Youth hostels

For the addresses of youth hostels (auberges de jeunesse) in the Loire Valley, contact:

◆ Fédération des Auberges de Jeunesse
27, rue Pajol
75018 Paris
Tel. 01 44 89 87 27

Coulée-de-serrant vines.

Troglodytic cellar cut into the rockface.

It is because of the Loire that vineyards have developed in this region: the warm west winds that blow along the river valley create a remarkably warm, sunny microclimate. The vineyards of the Loire Valley were established by the monks of the Cistercian and Benedictine abbeys in the Middle Ages. The Plantagenet and Valois kings enjoyed local wines and encouraged their development, while the proximity of the river furthered the growth of trade from the 12th century onward. For a long time the Loire wines were considered inferior to those of other regions, but over the last thirty years the local producers have achieved high quality standards, creating wines that are both robust and refined.

WINE CLASSIFICATION

The European denomination "Vin de qualité produit dans une région déterminée" (VQPRD) covers the two French categories "Appellation d'origine contrôlée" (AOC) and "Appellation d'origine vin délimité de qualité supérieure" (AOVDQS). The Ministry of Agriculture awards the "Appellation d'origine" classifications according to production standards laid down by the Institut National des Appellations d'Origine (INAO).

APPELLATIONS OF THE LOIRE

These wines can be produced in any of the vineyards of Anjou, Saumurois and Touraine ■ 30.

ROSÉ DE LOIRE
These are dry wines, crisp and fruity, produced from various types of grape (Cabernet-Franc, Cabernet-Sauvignon, Grolleau, Pineau d'Aunis and Gamay Noir).

CRÉMANT-DE-LOIRE
This type of wine is produced from a number of grape varieties grown on widely varying soils (mainly chalky). The fragrance of the wines can be grassy, floral or fruity, depending on where they are made.

ANJOU

Anjou is a traditional winegrowing area, famous for the sweet wines of Coteaux-du-Layon and Coteaux-de-l'Aubance.

A DISTINCTIVE WINE
◆ Le Savennières. This appellation, grown on 185 acres to the west of Angers, has a great tradition of dry Chenin Blanc wine for keeping. The vines flourish on four hillsides facing south–southeast, on soils of volcanic schist and red sandstone. As a young wine Savennières is austere and highly strung, with great vigor and a fragrance of ripe fruits and flowers. It has a distinctive, bitter taste. The wine needs five to ten years to develop from the floral to the mineral and to acquire more body. Two wines are distinguished from the rest of the appellation: Coulée-de-Serrant (17 acres) and Roche-aux-Moines (82 acres).

SWEET WINES
◆ Coteaux-du-Layon, Bonnezeaux and Quarts-de-Chaume. On the hillsides that border the Layon river, the Chenin Blanc vines produce famous sweet dessert wines. The morning mists allow the "noble rot" (Botrytis cinerea) to develop. The best wines are produced from very ripe grapes that have a high concentration of sugar, harvested selectively as the

THE LAND OF CHENIN BLANC

Anjou is the land of the Chenin Blanc grape. A dozen appellations make use of it, for white wines that can be dry or sweet, including smooth dessert wines, and sparkling wines in Saumur. Chenin Blanc wines are generous and full-bodied in warm years; other vintages are drier (even sharp), and long-lived (up to half a century).

"noble rot" appears. These wines have a very dense fragrance of candied fruits; when stored for several decades the flavors become more subtle and complex. The color is golden yellow when the wine is young, acquiring reddish and amber tints over time. The generic appellation is Coteaux-du-Layon (3,700 acres); six parishes and a village (Chaume, which has especially well exposed soils) are allowed to use the appellation. Two wines have their own special appellations: Bonnezeaux (198 acres) and Quarts-de-Chaume (100 acres).

◆ Coteaux-de-l'Aubance.
This appellation (250 acres) produces fruity, soft wines which are less sweet than their Layon counterparts.

EVERYDAY ANJOU WINES
◆ The Anjou AOC covers the entire region, including the Saumurois (200 parishes in all).
◆ The Anjou appellation is traditionally associated with white wines. The wines produced entirely from Chenin Blanc grapes tend to be sweet.

Dry wines are obtained by combining Chenin Blanc with Chardonnay and Sauvignon. All the wines have citrus fragrances with floral notes.
◆ Rosé Anjou wines from Pineau d'Aunis and Grolleau grapes are not sufficiently dry and are falling from favor.
◆ Red Anjou wines, which now account for the majority of production, are made from Cabernet-Franc and Cabernet-Sauvignon grapes. They are fresh, light wines which should be drunk while young.
◆ Anjou-Villages wines are fruity, expansive, strong and fleshy. Their high tannin content allows them to mature.
◆ Anjou-Gamay wines are thirst-quenchers which should be drunk within the year.
◆ Rosé d'Anjou, produced from Grolleau grapes, and Cabernet d'Anjou, made from the two Cabernet grape varieties, are soft, slightly sweet rosé wines.
◆ Anjou-Coteaux-de-la-Loire wines are white wines made from Chenin Blanc grapes, demi-sec or sweet.

SAUMUROIS

The Saumurois region is connected to Anjou by its history and to the Touraine by its soils: here, chalk gives way to schist and sandstone.
◆ Saumur.
The area covered by this appellation encompasses thirty-six parishes.
◆ White Saumur, a lively, floral and mineral wine, is produced from Chenin Blanc grapes, sometimes combined with Sauvignon and Chardonnay.

◆ Red Saumur wine is produced on 1,850 acres of chalky and sandy-clay ground, using the two Cabernet varieties (Franc and Sauvignon). This is a very aromatic wine with elegant tannins, which matures well.
◆ Saumur Brut and Saumur Demi-Sec. The vines cover 3,200 acres on tufa limestone. The whites are made from Chenin Blanc grapes (with an authorized 20 percent addition of

TOURAINE

This vineyard, covering 2,500 acres, goes back to Roman times. It was at its largest in the 19th century, just before the phylloxera crisis. Since the 1950's it has been expanding again, and producing wines of increasing quality.

THE GREAT RED APPELLATIONS
◆ Chinon Vineyards of Cabernet-Franc vines grow on 4,700 acres on the left bank of the Loire, in the triangle formed by the confluence of the Vienne and the Loire. The wines grown on the gravelly areas are high-spirited and easy to drink. On the hillsides and on the plateaus, the clayey, siliceous soils produce finely structured wines. As for the great Chinons for keeping, they grow on the clayey, chalky soils of the Coteaux-de-Cravant and the Coteaux-de-Ligré.

Chardonnay and Sauvignon). They have fine, elegant bubbles and a pale-yellow color.
◆ Saumur-Champigny.
This vineyard of Cabernet-Franc and Cabernet-Sauvignon grows on chalky soils on the banks of the Loire and on more clayey soils on the banks of the Thouet. Only red wines are made, which can be fruity and charming, or robust, spicy and full of character.

◆ Bourgueil.
This appellation is grown on 3,000 acres, on the right bank of the Loire. The area is planted exclusively with Breton vines (Cabernet-Franc). Two-thirds of the vines stretch from the plain toward the terraces of sand and gravel, producing fruity, supple wines which should be drunk young. The remaining third grows on the chalky clay soils of the hillsides. Here, sheltered from the north winds, the vines produce full-bodied, tanninic wines which mature well (known as "vins de tuffeau").
◆ St-Nicolas-de-Bourgueil. The vines of this appellation are grown on terraces and on the clay soils of the hillsides. They are similar in character to Bourgueil wines, though even more supple.

Vintages

	Red wines	White wines	Sweet white wines
1995	7	7	6
1994	6	6	6
1993	5	6	6
1992	6	6	6
1991	3	4	3
1990	9	9	10
1989	10	9	10
1988	7	8	7
1987	4	5	5
1986	6	7	7
1985	8	8	8
1984	5	6	5
1983	6	7	8
1982	7	7	7
1981	7	8	7
1980	6	6	6

Noteworthy older vintages include, for white wines and sweet wines, the excellent 1976, 1971, 1962 and 1959. The sweet wines from the great years of 1989 and 1990 will not achieve their peak until 2020.

Wines and Food Combinations

Hors d'oeuvre, cooked/cured meats: Touraine, Anjou
Foie Gras: Quarts-de-Chaume
Shellfish: Saumur
Oysters: Savennières
Crab, shrimps, etc.: Anjou (white), Touraine (white).
Lobster, crayfish: Vouvray, Savennières.
Freshwater fish: Layon (dry), Touraine (white), Saumur.
Sea fish: Vouvray, Savennières.
Grilled fish: Saumur-Champigny (red).
White meat: Anjou (red), St-Nicolas-de-Bourgueil.
Red meat: Chinon, Bourgueil.
Game, poultry: St-Nicolas-de-Bourgueil, Bourgueil.
Game meats: Chinon, Bourgueil.
Hard cheeses: Touraine, Anjou (red or white).
Soft cheeses: Anjou (red), St-Nicholas-de-Bourgueil.
Goat's cheeses: Anjou (white), Touraine (white).
Desserts: Coteaux-du-Layon, Bonnezeaux.

The Great White Appellations

◆ **Vouvray.** Vouvray wine comes in several different guises: dry, demi-sec or sweet, according to the year. It can be still, "pétillant" or sparkling according to the vinification process.

◆ **Montlouis.** This appellation covers 750 acres, between the Loire and the Cher, on a chalky plateau facing south. It is very similar to Vouvray in character.

Everyday Touraine Wines

◆ **Touraine.** The regional appellation covers the whole of the Touraine region (12,000 acres). The soils are sandy and clay, sometimes with chalk.

◆ **Touraine-Amboise.** This vineyard covers 370 acres on either side of the Loire, producing light red wines made from Gamay grapes; they are more structured and age better when they include Cabernet and Côt grapes as well.

◆ **Touraine-Azay-le-Rideau.** Fine, dry white wines produced on 120 acres by the banks of the Indre; these wines mature well.

◆ **Touraine-Mesland.** These fruity and aromatic wines are produced in the east of Touraine.

◆ **Cheverny.** Fourteen different types of grapes are allowed in this appellation. The fruity red wines are made mainly from Gamay and Pinot Noir.

◆ **Cour-Cheverny.** This appellation is made from a single grape variety, the local Romorantin, which produces very distinctive white wines: delicate and highly strung.

Outlying Vineyards

◆ **Coteaux-du-Loir.** This small appellation produces white wines made from Chenin Blanc grapes and light, fruity red wines made from Pineau d'Aunis, Gamay and Cabernet, as well as some rosé.

◆ **Jasnières.** This white wine made from Chenin Blanc grapes is produced on a single hillside overlooking the Loir, facing due south. According to Curnonsky, "Prince of Gastronomes" ▲ *307*, it is the best wine in the world three times each century. It is an exquisite, dry, mineral wine, which needs ten or so years to attain its full maturity.

◆ **Valençay (VDQS).** Fruity, aromatic wines best drunk young, produced from grapes grown on the chalky, clay soils of the area.

◆ **Orléanais (VDQS).** This vineyard was famous in the Middle Ages. Today, the Gris-Meunier grapes produce deep-rosé wines. The red wines are made from Pinot Noir grapes (known locally as "Auvernat"), while the whites are made from Chardonnay ("Auvernat Blanc").

◆ **Coteaux-du-Giennois (VDQS).** A vineyard of 300 acres growing Sauvignon, Pinot and Gamay vines. The wines are light, crisp and fruity.

Excursion to the Sancerrois

Not far from the Loire Valley are the famous vineyards of Sancerrois (some 5,000 acres in all), overlooking the river from their steep, east–southeast-facing hillsides. To the west, the pale soils produce vigorous, full-bodied wines. To the center the soils are stony and calcareous (called "caillottes"), producing wines that are softer and fruitier. To the east the soils are siliceous ("chailloux"), producing well-structured wines which develop more slowly. It is advisable to leave the red wines to mature for two to three years.

The winegrowers of the Loire may appear rather rough and ready, but this should not mislead you: they value quality more highly than the laws of the market. Some, inspired by their love of wine rather than financial motives, assemble collections of old vintages in their cellars, the like of which wine lovers dream about. Buying directly from producers is of course the best way of getting a bargain – but for real wine lovers it is the direct contact with winegrowers that counts. If you intend to visit a vineyard, it is polite to telephone and let them know beforehand. However, there is no obligation to leave with a case of wine that you do not really want to drink, merely on grounds of politeness.

A cellar in Saumurois.

Troglodytic château in Anjou.

The letter and the figure given after each address refer to the maps of the area inside the covers of this guide.

ANJOU / BONNEZEAUX

DOMAINE DE LA SANSONNIERE
The owner of this estate learned his craft in the Sauternes region. His very low output is an indicator of the quality of the wine. Noteworthy wines include a white Anjou, Christine (55F), a red Anjou (40F) and a Bonnezeaux, Mathilde (160F).
◆ 49380 Thouarcé (B7)
Tel. 02 41 54 08 08
DOMAINE DE HAUTE-PERCHE
This estate to the south of Angers is one of the last producers resisting the urban sprawl. Wines produced on this 75-acre vineyard include an Anjou-Village: the '93

vintage, which is ready to drink, sells for 32F; the '94 vintage sells for 30F.
◆ 9, chemin de la Godelière
49610 St-Melaine-sur-Aubance (B6)
Tel. 02 41 57 75 65
DOMAINE DU FRESCHE
Alain Boré owns the best soils of the hillside and produces a white Anjou wine of exceptional quality, for a very low price. The 1994 and 1995 vintages cost 23F.
◆ 49620
La Pommeraye (A6)
Tel. 02 41 77 74 63
DOMAINE RICHOU
This young winegrower has shown his determination to bring to the Loire winegrowing methods that have succeeded

elsewhere. His success is beyond question; choose from an Anjou-Gamay 94 at 23F and an Aubance from selected

grapes, available from next winter at about 140F.
◆ Chauvigné
49610 Mozé-sur-Louet (B6)
Tel. 02 41 78 72 13

COTEAUX-DU-LAYON

DOMAINE GAUDARD
The white Anjou wines, including Paragères (25F for the '95 vintage), rival the Layons in terms of quality. Fans of sweet white wines will be tempted by the superb Or 1994, at 95F.
◆ Rte de St-Aubin
49290 Chaudefonds-dur-Layon (A6)
Tel. 02 41 78 10 68
DOMAINE MICHEL ROBINEAU
The prices here bear no relation to the quality of the wines

and the effort devoted to producing them. Michel Robineau sorts the grapes again and again to select only the very best; the wines he makes are sold at ridiculously low prices. You will pay 36F to 72F, depending on quality, for wines which would cost twice this amount elsewhere.
◆ 16, rue Rabelais
49750 St-Lambert-du-Lattay (B7)
Tel. 02 41 78 34 67

QUARTS-DE-CHAUME

CHÂTEAU BELLERIVE
The estate may have changed hands, but it has kept its outstanding winemaker, Jacques Lalanne. Lalanne's 1994 Quarts-de-Chaume, Quintessence, is one of the best Loire wines (120F).
◆ 49190 Rochefort-sur-Loire (B6)
Tel. 02 41 78 33 66

DOMAINE DES BAUMARD
Jean Baumard is just as well known for his Quarts-de-Chaume as he is for his Savennières. He has set himself up as a champion of good value for all his wines, and especially for his Quarts-de-Chaume estate acquired in 1954.
◆ 8, rue de l'Abbaye 49190 Rochefort-sur-Loire (B6)
Tel. 02 41 78 70 03

BOURGUEIL AND ST-NICOLAS-DE-BOURGUEIL

DOMAINE DE LA CHEVALERIE
Pierre Caslot has a dozen or more vintages carefully arranged in cellars covering two and a half acres, cut into the tufa limestone. Four wines are represented, from the young vines of Peu-Muleau to the old stock of Les Busardières. The price difference between the different vintages is minimal, allowing visitors to select the best wines from the full range: Les Busardières 1993 and 1995 are recommended, at a price of 42F.
◆ 37140 Restigné (F7)
Tel. 02 47 97 37 18

DOMAINE DE LA LANDE
Marc Delaunay produces a number of wines grown in different types of soil. The Cuvée des Pins comes from vines planted in sandy, stony ground; Cuvée Prestige is grown in siliceous clay ground.

The former will suit those who like a fruity wine; the latter those who prefer a more full-bodied style. Prices range between 35F and 50F.
◆ La Lande 37140 Bourgueil (F7)
Tel. 02 47 97 80 73

DOMAINE DE LA COUDRAYE
How can a wine producer avoid loss of output in years with heavy rainfall? Yannick Amirault's estate has sand and gravel soils which drain the downpours very effectively. The result is wines that are the best of their appellation in wet years. For example, a Cuvée la Source 1993 of the appellation St-Nicolas-de-Bourgueil or the Graviers Vieilles Vignes 1994 at 35F.
◆ 37140 Bourgueil (F7)
Tel. 02 47 97 78 07

SAUMUR / SAUMUR-CHAMPIGNY

LANGLOIS-CHÂTEAU
Bollinger, the champagne producer, owns a controlling interest in this estate, which doubtless explains the meticulous production methods, which are carried out with a Champagne-like precision. The white Saumur from 1994 is well worth mentioning, at 52F. It is matured in casks from the outset.
◆ Rte de Gennes St-Hilaire-St-Florent 49400 Saumur (D7)
Tel. 02 41 40 21 40

LA CAVE DES VIGNERONS DE SAUMUR
This cooperative dispels once and for all the industrial image which is mistakenly associated with these French winemaking institutions. Its production methods are exemplary, and are given perfect expression in a red Saumur from '95 (costing 25F) and a sweet Coteaux-de-Saumur '95 at 80F.
◆ 49260 St-Cyr-en-Bourg (D7)
Tel. 02 41 53 06 08

DOMAINE DE CHAMPS-FLEURIS
In this part of the region, Chenin Blanc vines give way to the Cabernet grapes used to make Saumur-Champigny, which produce a more solid wine. You might prefer Patrice Rétif's two white Saumur wines at 23F and 26.50F: both are admirably balanced, in two tonal ranges.
◆ 49730 Turquant (E7)
Tel. 02 41 38 10 92

DOMAINE DES ROCHES-NEUVES
Thierry Germain came from Bordeaux initially and has emigrated to Saumurois, where he makes wine with the technical precision which established the reputation of his home region. He has made a concession to modern trends with a wine from young vines (made by cold maceration); at the other extreme he produces a stunning wine fermented and matured entirely in the barrel.
◆ 56, bd St-Vincent 49400 Varrains (D7)
Tel. 02 41 52 94 02

CHINON

DOMAINE BAUDRY
Buying wine from Bernard Baudry requires a degree of flexibility. You may still be able to find some of the '94 vintage which was decimated by the frost. Failing this, you may have to fall back on the Cuvée Domaine (at around 37F), on the Grézeaux '95 (announced at 40F) in winter 1997, and on the wine from the old vines after this.

◆ 13, coteau de Sonnay
37500 Cravant (F8)
Tel. 02 47 93 15 79

CHARLES JOGUET
Charles Joguet is synonymous with quality in the region, producing several splendid wines, including the Clos de la Cure '95 at 41.50F and the Varennes du Grand Clos 1992 at 48F. The Clos de la Dioterie, with its seventy-year-old vines, and the Clos du Chêne Vert must be considered among the finest of the region.

◆ 3, rue du Plaisir
37220 Sazilly (F8)
Tel. 02 47 58 55 53

OLGA RAFFAULT
The different branches of the Raffault family are everywhere in the Loire Valley. However, Olga is beginning to steal the limelight from her namesakes. When women make wine they are generally better at it than men: this is true in the Loire as it is elsewhere. Fabulous Chinons: 34F for the '94 vintage, 37.50F for the '93.

◆ 1, rue des Caillis
37420 Savigny-en-Véron (E7)
Tel. 02 47 58 42 16

VOUVRAY

CLOS NAUDIN
Magnificent sweet wines around 90F, depending on vintage, from this wine enthusiast who takes pride in matching his wines with culinary dishes. Also worthy of note is a dry white wine from '95 at 47F, fragrant and full-bodied.

◆ 14, rue de la Croix-Buisée
37210 Vouvray (I6)
Tel. 02 47 52 71 46

DOMAINE HUET
Sweet wines produced by the king of the appellation: only connoisseurs will be able to make out the subtle differences between the Haut-Lieu and the Clos du Bourg. Prices vary according to whether the grapes were from the first selection, from 100F to 170F.
Totally reliable.

◆ 11–13, rue de la Croix-Buisée
37210 Vouvray (I6)
Tel. 02 47 52 78 87

TOURAINE

DOMAINE DE LA CHARMOISE
Henry Marionnet's wines cost less than 30F, but surpass in quality most of the wines of the region. Among the whites, the Sauvignon "M. de Marionnet" is quite sublime and cannot be too highly recommended. As for the reds, the Gamays are made by carbonic maceration, which gives them a unique fruity flavor without chaptalization.

◆ 41230 Soings-en-Sologne (N6)
Tel. 02 54 98 70 73

DOMAINE DES ACACIAS
Charles Guerbois exercises his wit and his knowledge of Latin in the names of his wines: as in the Vinovorax '93, at 35F a bottle, which is unusual for having been harvested in two stages to combine both liveliness and maturity.

◆ Chémery
41700 Contres (M6)
Tel. 02 54 71 81 53

CHÂTEAU-GAILLARD
Vincent Girault has abandoned environmentally unsound practices and mechanical harvesting in favor of organic winemaking. The result is excellent white wines (27F) and above all a Touraine-Mesland (red) from '95 at 28F, a subtle blend of all the best features of the estate.

◆ 41150 Mesland (L5)
Tel. 02 54 70 27 14

This table follows the order of the itineraries as they appear in the guide. All towns and other places of interest are listed in alphabetical order in each itinerary. The letter and figure following the postal code refer to the co-ordinates on the main maps at the beginning and at the end of the guide. The numbers in the right-hand column give pages where you can find further information.

ORLÉANS	45000	O/P2
CATHEDRAL	Open daily June 1–Sep. 15, 3–6.30pm except during services	▲ 114
CENTRE CHARLES-PÉGUY – **HÔTEL EUVERTE-HATTE** Rue du Tabour **Tel. 02 38 53 20 23**	Open Tue.–Fri. 2–6pm. Closed Jan. 1.	▲ 122
CENTRE JEANNE-D'ARC Pl. du Gal-de-Gaulle **Tel. 02 38 52 99 89**	Open daily except Mon., May–Oct., 10–11.30am and 2–5.30pm; Nov–Apr., 2–5.30pm. Guided tour (60 mins). Closed May 1, Dec 31, Jan 1 and Apr. 30.	▲ 118
HÔTEL CABU AND MUSÉE **ARCHÉOLOGIQUE ET HISTORIQUE** Pl. Abbé Desnoyers **Tel. 38 53 39 22**	Open daily except Tue. 10am–noon and 2–5.30pm. Guided tour (60 mins). Closed Jan.1, May 1 and 8, Nov. 1, Dec. 25.	▲ 119
HÔTEL GROSLOT Pl. de l'Étape **Tel. 02 38 79 22 30**	Open daily. June 16–Sep. 25, 9am–7pm; Sep. 26–Dec. 31, 10am–noon and 2–5pm; Jan. 1–June 15, 10am–noon and 2–6pm. Closed May 8 and during special events.	▲ 118
MUSÉE DES BEAUX-ARTS Pl. Ste-Croix **Tel. 02 38 53 39 22**	Open daily except Tue. 10am–noon and 2–5.30pm. Closed Jan. 1, May 1 and 8, Nov. 1, Dec. 25.	▲ 115
ORLÉANS-LA-SOURCE		
PARC FLORAL **Tel. 02 38 49 30 00**	Open daily June 16–Aug. 31, 9am–7pm; Apr. 1.–June 15 and Sep. 1—Nov. 12, 9am–5pm ; Nov. 13—Mar. 31, 2–4pm. Closed Dec. 25.	▲ 124

VAL D'ORLÉANS		
LA FERTÉ-ST-AUBIN	45240	P4
CHÂTEAU **Tel. 02 38 76 52 72**	Open Mar. 17–Nov 11 daily, 10am–7pm; Nov. 12–Dec. 31 Wed., Sat., Sun., (daily during school holidays) 2–6pm; Jan. 1–Mar. 16 Wed., Sat., Sun. 2–6pm.	▲ 125

ORLÉANS TO GIEN		
BRIARE	45250	T4
MUSÉE DE LA MOSAÏQUE **ET DES ÉMAUX** 1, bd Loreau **Tel. 02 38 31 20 51**	Open daily June–Sep., 10am–6.30pm; Oct.–Dec. and Apr.–May, 10am–12.30pm and 2–6pm. Closed Dec. 25,	▲ 137
CHÂTEAUNEUF-SUR-LOIRE	45110	Q2
CHÂTEAU AND PARK **Tel. 02 38 58 41 18**	Visits to the grounds only, all year around.	▲ 127
MUSÉE DE LA MARINE DE LA LOIRE, **DU VIEUX CHÂTEAUNEUF** **ET DE SA RÉGION** 1, pl. Aristide Briand **Tel. 02 38 58 41 18**	Open daily except Tue, Jul.–Aug., 10am–noon and 2–5.30pm; Sep., 2–5.30pm; Oct. Sat.–Sun. 2–5.30pm; Nov.–Dec. and Jan.–Mar., Sun. 2–5.30pm; Apr.–May, Sat.–Sun. 10am–noon and 2–5.30pm; June, Mon., Wed.–Fri. 2–5.30pm, Sat.–Sun. 10am–noon and 2–5.30pm. Guided tour (60 mins). Closed May 1 and Dec. 25.	▲ 127
GERMIGNY-DES-PRÉS	45110	Q3
CAROLINGIAN ORATORY **Tel. 02 38 58 27 03**	Open daily Mar. 16–Sep. 30, 8.30am–7pm; Oct. 1–Mar. 15, 9am–6pm.	▲ 128
GIEN	45500	S4
CHÂTEAU AND MUSÉE **DE LA CHASSE** **Tel. 02 38 67 69 69**	Open daily. Apr. 29–Nov. 3, 9.30am–6.30pm; Nov. 4–Dec. 31 and Feb. 17–Apr. 28, Tue.–Sun. 10am–noon and 2–5pm. Guided tour (90 mins).	▲ 136
MUSÉE DE LA FAÏENCERIE, **MANUFACTURE DE GIEN** 78, pl. de la Victoire **Tel. 02 38 67 00 05**	Open all year around Sun. 10–11.30am and 2–5.30pm; Jun.–Oct., Mon.–Sat. 9–11.30am and 2–6pm; Nov.–Jan., 10–11.30am and 1.45–5.45pm; Feb.–May, 9–11.30am and 1.45–5.45pm. Closed Nov. 1 and 11, Dec. 25 and Jan. 1.	▲ 136
JARGEAU		
COLLEGIATE CHURCH OF ST-VRAIN	Open daily 9am–noon and 2–6pm (when closed, key available from the tourist office).	▲ 126

ST-BENOÎT-SUR-LOIRE	**45730**	**R3**
ABBEY CHURCH Tel. 02 38 35 72 43	*Open daily except first Fri. of the month and during services, 10.30am–3pm. Guided tour (70 mins).*	▲ 130
ST-DENIS-DE-L'HÔTEL	**45550**	**Q2**
MAISON MAURICE-GENEVOIX Pl. du Cloître Tel. 02 38 59 02 24	*Open daily. Sat.–Sun. 10am–noon and 2–6pm.*	▲ 126
ST-JEAN-DE-BRAYE	**45800**	**P2**
MUSÉE CAMPANAIRE FONDERIE BOLLÉE 156, fbg de Bourgogne Tel. 02 38 86 29 47	*Open Apr.–Sep. daily except Tue. 10am–noon and 2–7.30pm; Jan.–Mar., Mon., Wed.–Fri., 2–5.30pm, Sat.–Sun. 10am–noon and 2–5.30pm; Sep.–Dec., 2– 5.30pm. Guided tour (2 hours). Closed Dec. 25 and Jan. 1.*	▲ 126
SULLY-SUR-LOIRE	**45600**	**R3**
CHÂTEAU, RESIDENCE OF THE DUC DE SULLY Tél. 02 38 36 36 86	*Open daily June 1–Sep. 15, 10am–6pm; May 1–June 15 and Sep. 16–Oct. 31, 10am–noon and 2–6pm; Mar.–Apr. and Nov., 10am–noon and 2–5pm. Guided tour (50 min) and visits by candlelight in high season.*	▲ 132
COLLEGIATE CHURCH OF ST-YTHIER	*Open daily 10am–6pm.*	▲ 133
ORLÉANS TO BLOIS		
BEAUGENCY	**45190**	**N3**
CHÂTEAU DUNOIS AND MUSÉE RÉGIONAL DE L'ORLÉANAIS Tel. 02 38 44 55 23	*Open Apr.–Sep. daily except Tue., 10–11am and 2–6pm; Oct.–Mar., 10–11am and 2–6pm. Closed May 1 and Dec. 25. Guided tour (60 mins) in English.*	▲ 139
CHURCH OF NOTRE-DAME	*Open daily. 9.30am–6.30pm (5pm in winter)*	▲ 139
MEUNG-SUR-LOIRE	**45130**	**N3**
CHÂTEAU Tel. 02 38 44 36 47	*Open daily. Jul. 1–Sep. 4, 9am–12.30pm and 1.30–6.30pm; Apr.–June, 10am–noon and 2–5.30pm; Sep. 5–Nov. 6, 10am–noon and 2–5pm; Jan.–Mar. and Nov., 7–Dec. 31. Sat.–Sun. 10am–noon and 2–5pm. Guided tour (60 mins) in English.*	▲ 138
ST-LAURENT-DES-EAUX	**41220**	**N4**
NUCLEAR POWER STATION Tel. 02 54 44 84 09	*Visit by appointment. Two days' notice and proof of identity required. Children under 10 not admitted.*	▲ 139
TALCY	**41170**	**M3**
CHÂTEAU OF THE SALVIATI Tel. 02 54 20 98 03	*Open daily Jul.–Aug., 9am–6pm, Apr.–June and Sep. 9.30am–noon and 2–6pm; Oct.–Mar. daily except Tue. 10am–noon and 2–4.30pm. Guided tour (45 mins). Closed May 1, Nov. 1 and 11, Dec. 25.*	▲ 140
BLOIS	**41000**	**M4/5**
CHÂTEAU AND MUSÉE DES BEAUX-ARTS Tel. 02 54 74 16 06	*Open daily Jan. 2.–Mar. 14 and Oct. 14–Dec. 31, 9–11.45am and 2–4.45pm; Mar. 15–Jun. 14 and Sep. 1–Oct. 13, 9am–5.45pm; June 15–Aug. 31, 9am–7.15pm. Closed Dec. 25 and Jan. 1. Guided tours (60 mins) in English.*	▲ 148
AROUND BLOIS		
CELLETTES	**41120**	**M5**
CHÂTEAU AND PARC DE BEAUREGARD Tel. 02 54 70 40 05	*Open daily Jul.–Aug. 9.30am–6pm; Apr. and Sep., 9.30–11.30am and 2–6pm; Jan. 8–Mar. 31 and Oct.–Dec., 9.30–11.30am and 2–4.30pm. Guided tour (45 mins) in English.*	▲ 167
CHAMBORD	**41250**	**N4**
CHÂTEAU AND NATIONAL PARK Tel. 02 54 50 40 00	*Open daily Jul.–Aug., 9.30am–6.45pm; Apr.–June and Sep., 9.30am–5.45pm; Jan.–Mar. and Oct.–Dec., 9.30–11.45am and 2–4.45pm. Closed Jan. 1, May 1, Nov. 1 and 11, Dec. 25. Guided tour (60 mins) in English.*	▲ 158

CHAUMONT-SUR-LOIRE	**41150**	**L5**
CHÂTEAU, STABLES AND PARK Tel. 02 54 20 98 03	*Open daily Apr.–Sep., 9.30am–6pm; Oct.–Mar.,* *10am–4.30pm. Closed May 1, Nov. 1 and 11, Dec. 25.* *Guided tour (60 mins) in English.*	▲ 177
FESTIVAL INTERNATIONAL DES JARDINS Tel. 02 54 20 99 22	*Open daily. June 15–Oct. 20, 9am–evening.* *Guided tour (50 mins) in English and Dutch.*	
CHEVERNY	**41700**	**M5**
CHÂTEAU, TROPHIES ROOM AND KENNEL Tel. 02 54 79 96 29	*Open daily June 1–Sep. 15, 9.15am–6.45pm; Apr.–May,* *9.15am–noon and 2.15–6.30pm; Sep. 16–Sep. 30,* *9.30am–noon and 2.15–6pm; Oct. and Mar., 9.30am–* *noon and 2.15–5.30pm; Nov.–Feb., 9.30am–noon and* *2.15–5pm. Guided tour in English, Dutch, Polish, Czech* *and Russian.* *Daily visit to the château and the park by hot-air balloon:* *June 1–Sep. 15, 9.15am–6.45pm; Sep.16–Sep. 30,* *9.30am–noon and 2.15–6pm; Oct. 9.30am–noon and* *2.15–5.30pm; Nov. 1–10, 9.30am–noon and 2.15–5pm;* *Apr. 15–May 31 9.15am–noon and 2.15–6.30pm.* *Feeding the dogs Apr. 1–Sep. 15, Mon.–Fri. at 5pm;* *Sep. 16–Dec. 31 and Jan.–Mar., Mon., Wed.–Fri. 3pm.*	▲ 170
FOUGÈRES-SUR-BIÈVRE	**41120**	**L/M6**
CHÂTEAU Tel. 02 54 20 98 03	*Open Apr.–Sep. daily, 9am–noon and 2–6pm; Oct.–Mar.* *daily except Tue., 10am–noon and 2–4.30pm. Closed* *May 1, Nov. 1 and 11, Dec. 25. Guided tour in English* *and Dutch.*	▲ 176
FRESNES	**41700**	**M6**
CHÂTEAU DE ROUJOUX AND MUSÉE HISTORIQUE ANIMÉ Tel. 02 54 79 53 55	*Open daily Mar. 25–Nov. 5, 11am–6pm.*	▲ 173
TOUR-EN-SOLOGNE	**41250**	**N5**
CHÂTEAU DE VILLESAVIN AND COLLECTION OF HORSE-DRAWN CARRIAGES Tel. 02 54 46 42 88	*Open daily May–Sep., 10am–7pm; Mar.–Apr. 10am–noon* *and 2–7pm; Oct. 1–Dec. 20, 2–5pm.* *Guided tour (55 mins) in English and Dutch.*	▲ 166
TROUSSAY		**M5**
CHÂTEAU AND MUSÉE SOLOGNOT (SOLOGNE LIFE) Tel. 02 54 44 29 07	*Open daily Jul. 1–Sep. 2, 10am–7pm; Sep. 3–30, 10am–* *1pm and 2–6pm; Oct. 1–Nov. 1, Sun. 10.30am–12.30pm* *and 2–5.30pm; Apr. 6–May 2, daily, 10.30am–12.30pm* *and 2–6.30pm; May 3–31, Sun. 10.30am–12.30pm and* *2–6.30pm; June daily, 10am–1pm and 2–7pm.*	▲ 172
AMBOISE	**37400**	**J6**
ABBEY CHURCH OF ST-DENIS	*Open daily Jul.–Aug., 10am–noon and 3–7pm;* *Sep.–June, 8am–7pm*	▲ 188
CHANTELOUP PAGODA Tel. 02 47 57 20 97	*Open daily Jul.–Aug., 9.30am–8pm; June–Sep., 10am–* *7pm; May, 10am–6pm; Apr. and Oct., 10am–noon and* *2–5.30pm; Mar. 10am–noon and 2–5pm; Nov. and* *Feb. 15–28, Mon.–Fri. 2–5pm, Sat.–Sun. 10am–noon* *and 2–5pm.*	▲ 191
CHÂTEAU Tel. 02 47 57 00 98	*Open daily Jul.–Aug., 9am–8pm; Apr.–June,* *9am–6.30pm; Sep.–Oct., 9am–6pm; Nov. and Feb.–Mar.,* *9am–noon and 2–5.30pm; Dec.–Jan., 9am–noon and* *2–5pm. Closed Dec. 25.* *Guided tour (45 mins), in English.*	▲ 184
CLOS-LUCÉ MANOR HOUSE AND LEONARDO DA VINCI MUSEUM Tel. 02 47 57 62 88	*Open daily Jul.–Aug., 9am–8pm; Mar. 23–June 30 and* *Sep. 1–Nov. 12, 9am–7pm; Nov. 13–Dec. 31 and* *Feb. 1–Mar. 22, 9am–6pm.*	▲ 185
MUSÉE DE LA POSTE 6, rue Joyeuse Tel. 02 47 57 00 11	*Open Apr.–Sep. daily except Mon. 9.30am–noon and* *2–6.30pm; Oct.–Dec. and Feb.–Mar., 10am–noon and* *2–5.30pm. Closed May 1, Nov. 1, Dec. 25 and at Easter.*	▲ 188

AROUND AMBOISE

CHARGÉ | 37530 | J6

MUSÉE DE LA BATAILLE DE LA LOIRE ET DE LA RÉSISTANCE Tel. 02 47 57 05 24	*Visit by appointment.*	▲ 192

LUSSAULT-SUR-LOIRE | 37400 | I/J6

AQUARIUM DE TOURAINE AND PARC DES MINI-CHÂTEAUX Tel. 02 47 23 44 44	*Open daily Jul.–Aug., 9am–midnight; Apr.–June and Sep., 9am–7pm; Oct.–Nov and Feb. 15–Mar. 31, 10am–6pm. Closed in Jan.*	

TOURS

TOURS | 37000 | H6

ATELIER "HISTOIRE DE TOURS" LOGIS DU GOUVERNEUR 25 quai d'Orléans Tel. 02 47 64 90 52	*Open Mar. 15–Dec. 15, Wed., Sat.–Sun. 3–6.30pm. Closed Easter, Ascension Day, Whit Sunday, Aug. 15, Nov. 1 and 11.*	▲ 198
BASILICA OF ST-MARTIN Rue Descartes	*Open daily Easter–Sep,. 8am–7pm; Oct.–Easter, 8am–noon and 2–6.45pm.*	▲ 204
CHÂTEAU DE TOURS Tropical aquarium Tel. 02 47 64 29 52	*Open daily Jul.–Aug., 9.30am–7pm; Apr.–June and Sep. 1–Nov. 15, 9.30am–noon and 2–6pm, Sun. 2–6pm; Nov. 16–Mar. 31, daily 2–6pm.*	▲ 198
Historial de Touraine (Musée Grévin) Tel. 02 47 61 02 95	*Open daily Jul.–Aug., 9am–6.30pm; Sep.–Oct. and Mar. 16–June 30, 9am–noon and 2–6pm; Nov.1–Mar. 15, 2–5.30pm*	
CLOÎTRE DE LA PSALETTE (PSALETTE CLOISTERS) Tel. 02 47 45 42 04	*Open daily Mar. 28–Sep. 30, 9am–noon and 2–6pm; Oct. 1–Mar. 27, 9am–noon and 2–5pm. Guided tour (45 mins). Closed May 1, Nov. 1 and 11, Dec. 25 and Jan. 1.*	▲ 197
FLOWER MARKET	*Wed. and Sat.*	▲ 214
JARDIN DES PRÉBENDES D'OÉ AND JARDIN BOTANIQUE	*Open daily 8am–evening.*	▲ 215
MUSÉE ARCHÉOLOGIQUE HÔTEL GOUIN 25, rue du Commerce Tel. 02 47 66 22 32	*Open daily May 15–Sep. 30, 10am–7pm ; Mar. 15–May 14, 10am–12.30pm and 2–6.30pm; Oct. and Feb. 1–Mar. 14, 10am–12.30pm and 2–5.30pm. Guided tour (30 mins)*	▲ 208
MUSÉE DES BEAUX-ARTS 18, pl. François Sicard Tel. 02 47 05 68 73	*Open daily except Tue., 9am–12.45pm and 2–6pm. Closed May 1, July 14, Nov. 1 and 11, Dec. 25.*	▲ 198
MUSÉE DU COMPAGNONNAGE ST-JULIEN CLOISTER 8, rue Nationale Tel. 02 47 61 07 93	*Open daily June 16–Sep. 15, 9am–6pm; Apr. 1 –June 15, daily 9–11.30am and 2–5.30pm; Sep. 16–Mar. 31, daily except Tue. 9–11.30am and 2–4.30pm. Closed May 1, Jul. 14, Nov. 1 and 11 , Dec. 25*	▲ 199
MUSÉE DU GEMMAIL AND UNDERGROUND CHAPEL 7 rue du Mûrier Tel. 02 47 61 01 19	*Open Mar. 15–Oct. 15, 10–11.30am and 2–6pm. Guided tour (60 mins). Closed Mon. except public holidays.*	▲ 212
MUSÉE ST-MARTIN CHAPEL OF ST-JEAN 3, rue Rapin Tel. 02 47 64 48 87	*Open Mar. 15–Nov. 15, Wed.–Sun. 9.30am–12.30pm and 2–5.30pm. Closed May 1, Jul. 14.*	▲ 205
MUSÉE DES VINS DE TOURAINE CELLIERS ST-JULIEN (CELLARS) 16, rue Nationale Tel. 02 47 61 07 93	*Open daily except Tue., Apr. 1–Sep. 15, 9.30–11.30am and 2–5.30pm; Sep. 16–Dec. 31 and Mar. 9.30am–12.30pm and 2–4.30pm. Closed May 1, Jul. 14, Nov. 1 and 11, Dec. 25.*	▲ 199
MUSÉUM D'HISTOIRE NATURELLE 3, rue du Président-Merville Tel. 02 47 64 13 31	*Open 10am–noon and 2–6pm. Closed Mon., May 1, Jul. 14 and Dec. 25.*	▲ 212
ST-GATIEN CATHEDRAL	*Open summer 8.30am–noon and 2–8pm; winter 8.30am–noon and 2–7.30pm.*	▲ 196

TOURS TO VALENÇAY

CHENONCEAUX | 37150 | K7

CHÂTEAU, GARDENS AND MUSÉE DE CIRES (WAXWORKS) Tel. 02 47 23 90 07	*Open daily Mar. 16–Sep. 15, 9am–7pm; Sep. 16–30, 9am–6.30pm; Oct. 1–15 and Mar. 1–15, 9am–6pm; Oct. 16–31 and Feb. 16–28, 9am–5.30pm; Nov. 1–15 and Feb. 1–15, 9am–5pm, Nov. 16–Jan. 31. 9am–4.30pm.*	▲ 220

CHEMILLÉ-SUR-INDROIS	37460	L8
CHARTREUSE DU LIGET Tel. 02 47 92 60 02	Open daily 9am–6pm.	▲ 230
LOCHES	37600	K8
COLLEGIATE CHURCH OF ST-OURS	Open daily, except during services: summer 9am–7pm; winter 9am–5pm.	▲ 227
DONJON (KEEP) Tel. 02 47 59 07 86	Open daily Jul. 1–Sep. 15, 9am–7pm ; Sep. 16–30 and Mar. 15–June 30, 9am–12.30pm and 2–6.30pm; Oct. 1–Mar. 14, 9am–12.30pm and 2–5.40pm. Closed Dec. 25 and Jan 1.	▲ 228
LOGIS ROYAL Tel. 02 47 59 01 32	Open daily Jul. 1 –Sep. 15, 9am–7pm; Sep. 16–30 and Mar. 15–June 30, 9am–noon and 2–6.30pm; Oct. 1–Mar. 14, 9am–noon and 2–5pm. Closed Dec. 25 and Jan. 1.	▲ 226
MUSÉE LANSYER AND MUSÉE DU TERROIR PORTE ROYALE 1, rue Lansyer Tel. 02 47 59 05 45	Open Mar. 15–Oct. 15, daily 9am–noon and 2–5.30pm; Oct. 16–Dec.14, daily except Wed. 9–11.30am and 2–3.30pm; Jan. 16–Mar. 14, daily except Wed. 9–11.30am and 2–4.30pm.	▲ 228
MONTRÉSOR	37460	L8
CHÂTEAU Tel. 02 47 92 60 04	Open daily Apr.–Oct., 10am–noon and 2–6pm.	▲ 231
COLLEGIATE CHURCH OF ST-JEAN-BAPTISTE	Open daily 8.30am–7pm, except during services.	▲ 231
NOUANS-LES-FONTAINES	37460	L/M8
CHURCH OF ST-MARTIN	Open daily 8am–7pm, except during services	▲ 231
VALENÇAY	36600	N8
CHÂTEAU AND MUSÉE DE VOITURES ANCIENNES Tel. 02 54 00 10 66	Open daily June 16–Sep. 15, 9am–7pm; Sep. 16–Nov. 15 and Mar. 16–June 15, 9am–noon and 2–7pm. Guided tour (50 mins).	▲ 232
TOURS TO CHINON		
AZAY-LE-RIDEAU	37190	G7
CHÂTEAU Tel. 02 47 45 42 04	Open daily Jul.–Aug., 9am–6.30pm; Sep.–Oct. and Mar. 15–June 30, 9.30am–5.30pm; Nov. 1–Mar. 14, 9.30am–noon and 2–5pm. Closed May 1, Nov. 1 and 11, Dec. 25, Jul-Aug. Guided tour (60 mins) in English.	▲ 234
CHINON	37500	F9
CHÂTEAU Tel. 02 47 93 13 45	Open daily Jul.–Aug., 9am–7pm; Sep.and Mar. 15–June 30, 9am–6pm; Oct. 9am–5pm; Nov. 1–Mar. 14 9am–noon and 2–5pm. Closed Dec. 25. Guided tour (45 mins).	▲ 244
CHAPEL OF STE-RADEGONDE AND MUSÉE DES ARTS ET TRADITIONS POPULAIRES Tel. 02 47 93 17 85 (O.T.)	Visit by appointment with the tourist office.	▲ 249
MAISON DES ÉTATS-GÉNÉRAUX AND MUSÉE DU VIEUX CHINON ET DE LA BATELLERIE 44, rue Haute St-Maurice Tel. 02 47 93 18 12	Open daily Apr. 16–Sep. 30, 10.30am–12.30pm and 3–6pm. Guided tour by apppointment.	▲ 246
SACHÉ	37190	H7
CHÂTEAU AND MUSÉE BALZAC Tel. 02 47 26 86 50	Open daily Jul.–Aug., 9.30am–6.30pm; Mar. 15–Apr. 30 and Sep., 9am–noon and 2–6pm; Oct.–Nov. and Feb. 1–Mar. 14, 9am–noon and 2–5pm. Guided tour (45 mins).	▲ 240
CHURCH OF ST-MARTIN-DE-VERTOU	Open daily 9am–7pm.	▲ 241
SEUILLY	37500	F8
LA DEVINIÈRE Tel. 02 47 95 91 18	Open daily May–Sep. 10am–7pm; Mar. 15–Apr. 30, 9am–noon and 2–6pm; Oct. 1–Mar. 14, 9am–noon and 2–5pm.	▲ 250
TAVANT	37220	G8
CHURCH OF ST-NICOLAS Tel. 02 47 58 58 06	Open Mar.–Nov. daily except Tue.10am–noon and 2.30–6pm	▲ 251

TOURS TO FONTEVRAUD		
AVOINE-CHINON	**37420** F7	
NUCLEAR POWER STATION Museum and installations Tel. 02 47 98 77 77	Visits by appointment. Phone 24 hours before intended visit. Proof of indentity required. Children under 13 are not admitted.	▲ 244
CANDES-ST-MARTIN	**37500** E7	
COLLEGIATE CHURCH OF ST-MARTIN	Open daily except during services.	▲ 271
FONTEVRAUD	**49590** E8	
ROYAL ABBEY Tel. 02 41 51 71 41	Open daily June, 1–3rd Sun. in Sep., 9am–7pm; 3rd Sun. in Sep.–May 31, 9.30am–12.30pm and 2–6pm. Late evening visits by appointment.	▲ 272
LANGEAIS	**37130** G7	
CHÂTEAU Tel. 02 47 96 72 60	Open daily Jul. 15–Aug. 31, 9am–9pm; Sep. and Apr. 1–Jul 14, 9am–6.30pm; Oct. 1–Nov. 2, 9am–12.30pm and 2–6.30pm; Nov. 3–Mar. 31, 9am–noon and 2–5pm. Closed Dec. 25. Guided tours (60 mins) in English.	▲ 268
MUSÉE DE L'ARTISANAT 24, rue de St-Laurent Tel. 02 47 96 72 64	Open daily June 1–Sep. 15, 9am–7pm; Apr.–May and Sep. 16–Oct. 15, 10am–noon and 2–6pm; Oct. 16–Sep. 31 and Feb.–Mar., 2–6pm. Closed Dec. 25.	▲ 268
LUYNES	**37230** H6	
CHÂTEAU Tel. 02 47 95 77 08	Open daily Apr.–Sep., 10am–6pm. Guided tours in English.	▲ 262
MONTSOREAU	**49730** E7	
CHÂTEAU AND MUSÉE DES GOUMS Tel. 02 41 51 70 25	Open daily except Tue., May–Sep., 10am–noon and 2–6.30pm; Mar.–Apr. and Oct., 1.30–5.30pm.	▲ 276
RIGNY-USSÉ	**37420** F7	
CHÂTEAU AND WALL WALK Tel. 02 47 95 54 05	Open daily Jul. 14–Aug. 31, 9am–6.30pm; Apr. 7–Jul. 13 and Sep. 1–25, 9am–noon and 2–6pm ; Sep. 26–Nov. 11, and Feb. 12–Mar. 15, 10am–noon and 2–5.30pm. Guided tour (45 mins).	▲ 268
SAVONNIÈRES	**37510** H6	
GROTTES PÉTRIFIANTES Tel. 02 47 50 00 09	Open daily Apr.–Sep. 9am–7pm; Oct. 1–Nov. 11 9am–noon and 2–6pm; Nov. 12–Dec. 15 and Feb. 5–Mar. 31 daily except Thur. 9am–noon and 2–6pm.	▲ 262
VILLANDRY	**37510** G6	
CHÂTEAU Tel. 02 47 50 02 09	Open Jul.–Aug., 9am–6.30pm; Mar. 31–June 30 and Sep. 1–28, 9am–6pm; Sep. 29–Nov. 11, 9am–5pm; Feb. 17–Mar. 30, 9.30am–5pm.	▲ 263
GARDENS Tel. 02 47 50 02 09	Open daily Jul.–Aug., 8.30am–8pm; May–June and Sep. 1–28, 9am–7.30pm; Mar. 1–30 and Sep. 29–Nov. 11, 9am–6pm; Mar. 31–Apr. 30 9am–7pm; Nov. 12–Feb 28, 9am–5pm.	▲ 264
SAUMUR	**49400** D7	
CHÂTEAU Rue des Remparts Tel. 02 41 51 30 46	Open daily June–Sep., 9am–6pm; Jul–Aug., Wed. and Sat. 8.30pm–10.30pm, late-night visits 10.30pm–midnight; Oct.–May daily except Tue., 9.30am–noon and 2–5.30pm.	▲ 280
CHURCH OF NOTRE-DAME DE NANTILLY Pl. des Récollets	Open daily.	▲ 284
CHURCH OF ST-PIERRE	Open daily 8am–noon and 2–6pm.	▲ 280
MUSÉE DES ARTS DÉCORATIFS ET DU CHEVAL Château Tel. 02 41 51 30 46	Open June–Sep. daily 9am–6pm; Oct.–May daily except Tue., 9.30am–noon and 2–5.30pm.	▲ 280
MUSÉE DES BLINDÉS (CDEB) (ARMORED VEHICLES) 1043, route de Fontevraud Tel. 02 41 53 06 99	Open daily 9am–noon and 2–6pm.	▲ 285

MUSÉE DE LA CAVALERIE Av. Foch **Tel. 02 41 83 93 06 (high season)** **02 41 83 93 17 (low season)**	*Open Tue., Thur. and Sun. 9am–noon and 2–5pm; Sat. before noon and 2–5pm.*	▲ 284
AROUND SAUMUR		**D7**
CHAPEL OF NOTRE-DAME DES ARDILLERS	*Open 9am–noon and 2–7pm.*	▲ 285
CHÂTEAU DE BOUMOIS	*Open Jul.–Aug., daily 9.30am–6.30pm; Palm Sunday and All Saints' Day, daily except Tue., 10am–noon and 2–6pm.*	▲ 285 ▲ 284
ÉCOLE NATIONALE D'ÉQUITATION (TERREFORT) **Tel. 02 41 53 50 66**	*Open June–Aug., daily except Sun and Mon. 9.30am–5pm; Apr.–May and Sep. 9.30am–5pm except Sat. before noon, Sun. and Mon. morning.*	▲ 289
GRAND DOLMEN (BAGNEUX) **Tel. 02 41 50 23 02**	*Open daily Mar. 16–Sep. 30, 9am–7pm; Oct. 1–Dec. 20 and Jan. 20–Mar. 15, 9am–6pm.*	▲ 292
MUSÉE DU CHAMPIGNON (ST-HILAIRE-ST-FLORENT) Rte de Gennes **Tel. 02 41 50 31 55**	*Open daily Feb.–Nov., 10am–7pm.*	

SAUMUR TO MONTREUIL-BELLAY		
DÉNÉZÉ-SOUS-DOUÉ	**49700**	**C7**
CARVED CAVERN **Tel. 02 41 59 15 40**	*Open Jul.–Aug., daily 10am–7pm; Apr.–June and Sep.–Oct., daily 2–7pm; Mar. and Nov., Sat. and Sun. 2.30am–6pm.*	▲ 288
DOUÉ-LA-FONTAINE	**49700**	**C7/8**
ARÈNES DE DOUCES Rue des Arènes **Tel. 02 41 59 22 28**	*Open Apr.–Oct., Tue.–Sun. 10am–noon and 2–6pm*	▲ 289
MOULIN DE LA FOURCHETTE (MOULIN CARTIER) **Tel. 02 41 59 20 49**	*Open Tue.–Sun. 10am–noon and 3–6pm.*	▲ 289
PARC ZOOLOGIQUE DES MINIÈRES Rue de Cholet **Tel. 02 41 59 18 58**	*Open daily Apr.–Sep., 9am–7pm; Oct.–Mar., 10am–noon and 2–6pm.*	▲ 289
LA SABLIÈRE **Tel. 02 41 59 28 23 (high season)** **and 02 41 59 03 59 (low season)**	*Open Jul.–Aug., daily 9.30am–noon and 2–7pm; Mar.–June and Sep.–Dec., Tue.–Sun. 9.30am–noon and 2–7pm*	▲ 289
FORGES	**49700**	**D7**
LA FOSSE (TROGLODYTIC HAMLET) **Tel. 02 41 59 00 32 (high season)** **and 02 41 52 27 60 (low season)**	*Open daily June–Sep., 9.30 am–7pm; Mar.–May and Oct., 9.30am–12.30pm and 2–6.30pm; Feb. 1–28 and Nov., Sat. and Sun. 2–6pm.*	▲ 288
LE COUDRAY-MACOUARD	**49260**	**D7**
MAGNANERIE Impasse Bel-Air **Tel. 02 41 67 91 24**	*Open May 15–Oct. 15, Tue.–Sun. 10am–6pm; Oct. 16–Dec. 24, Sat. and Sun. 2–6pm.*	▲ 289
LOURESSE-ROCHEMENIER	**49700**	**C7**
MUSÉE PAYSAN **Tel. 02 41 59 18 15**	*Open daily Apr. 1–Nov. 1, 9.30am–7pm; Nov. 2–30 and Feb.–Mar., Sat. and Sun. 2–6pm.*	▲ 288
LE PUY-NOTRE-DAME	**49260**	**D8**
COLLEGIATE CHURCH OF NOTRE-DAME	*Open daily June–Sep., 9.30am–7pm; Mar.–May and Oct., 9.30am–12.30pm and 2–6.30pm; Feb. and Nov., Sat. and Sun. 2–6pm.*	▲ 290
MONTREUIL-BELLAY	**49260**	**D8**
CHÂTEAU **Tel. 02 41 52 33 06**	*Open Apr. 1–Nov. 1, daily except Tue. 10am–noon and 2–5.30pm.*	▲ 291
TURQUANT	**49730**	**E7**
LA GRANDE VIGNOLE **Tel. 02 41 38 16 44 (high season)** **and 02 41 52 90 84 (low season)**	*Open daily May–Sep., 10am–7pm; Oct.–Apr. Wed.–Sun. 10am–7pm.*	▲ 287

MOULIN CAVIER (CAVE MILL) **Tel. 02 41 51 75 22**	*Open daily Jul.–Aug., 10am–8pm; May–June and Sep.–Oct., 10am–noon and 2–6pm.*	▲ 286
VAL-HULIN SEMI-TROGLODYTIC HAMLET **Tel. 02 41 51 48 30**	*Open Jul.–Aug., Tue.–Sun. 10am–noon and 2.30–6.30pm; Dec. 15–Feb. 15, Tue.–Sat. 10am–noon and 2.30–6.30pm, Sun. 2.30–6.30pm.*	▲ 286

SAUMUR TO ANGERS

BRISSAC-QUINCÉ	**49320**	**B/C6**
CHÂTEAU **Tel. 02 41 91 22 21**	*Open daily Jul. 1–Sep. 15, 10am–5.45pm; Apr.–June and Sep. 16–Nov. 2, daily except Tue. 10am–noon and 2.15–5.15pm.*	▲ 294

CUNAULT	**49350**	**D6**
CHURCH OF NOTRE-DAME **Tel. 02 41 67 92 44**	*Open daily summer 8am–7.30pm, winter 8am–7pm.*	▲ 292

GENNES-SUR-LOIRE	**49350**	**D6**
CHURCH OF ST-VÉTÉRIN **Tel. 02 41 67 92 44**	*Open daily 9am–7pm.*	▲ 293
GALLO-ROMAN AMPHITHEATER Av. de l'amphithéâtre **Tel. 02 41 59 22 28 (high season)** **02 41 51 83 33 (low season)**	*Open Jul. 1–Aug. 31, daily 10am–noon and 2.30–6.30pm; Apr. 1–June 30 and Sep. 1–30, Sat. 3–5pm and Sun. 3–6pm.*	▲ 293
WATER MILL OF SARRÉ	*Open May–Sep., daily 10am–noon and 2–6pm; Oct.–Apr. by appointment.*	▲ 293

GRÉZILLÉ	**49320**	**C6**
CHÂTEAU DE PIMPÉAN **Tel. 02 41 45 51 40**	*Open May–Oct., 10am–7pm.*	▲ 293

LES PONTS-DE-CÉ	**49130**	**B6**
MUSÉE DES COIFFES D'ANJOU 4, rue Charles-de-Gaulle **Tel. 02 41 44 68 64 (high season** **and 02 41 79 75 75 (low season)**	*Open Jul.–Aug., daily 10am–12.30pm and 1.30–6pm; June and Sep., Sat.–Sun. 2–6pm; Apr.–May and Oct., Sun. 2–6pm.*	▲ 294

ST-GEORGES-DES-SEPT-VOIES	**49350**	**C6**
"HÉLICE TERRESTRE DE L'ORBIÈRE" **Tel. 02 41 57 95 92**	*Open daily May–Sep., 11am–8pm; Oct.–Apr., 2–6pm and by appointment. Evening visits by appointment.*	▲ 293

TRÈVES	**49350**	**D7**
CHURCH OF ST-AUBIN	*Open daily except during services.*	▲ 292

ANGERS	**49000**	**B5/6**
CHÂTEAU AND TAPESTRY OF THE APOCALYPSE **Tel. 02 41 87 43 47**	*Open daily June 1–Sep. 15, 9am–7pm; Sep. 16–Mar. 26, 9.30am–12.30pm and 2–6pm; Mar. 27–May 31, 9am–12.30pm and 2–6.30pm. Guided tour (1½ hours)*	▲ 297
CHURCH OF ST-SERGE	*Open Jul., 1–3rd Sun. in Sep., Mon.–Sat. 9am–7pm, Sun. 2.30–6pm; Oct.–June, daily 9am–7pm except Sun. am.*	▲ 307
GALERIE DAVID-D'ANGERS 33 *bis*, rue Toussaint **Tel. 02 41 87 21 03**	*Open June 12–Sep. 17, daily 9am–6.30pm; Sep. 18–June 11, daily except Mon. 9am–noon and 2–6pm.*	▲ 305
HÔTEL PINCÉ AND MUSÉE TURPIN DE CRISSÉ 32 *bis*, rue Lenepveu **Tel. 02 41 88 94 27**	*Open June 12–Sep. 17, daily 9am–6.30pm; Sep. 18–June 11, daily 10am–noon and 2–6pm.*	▲ 306
BOTANICAL GARDENS Rue Boreau	*Open daily 7am (summer), 8am (winter)–evening.*	▲ 307
LOGIS DE L'ESTAIGNIER AND MUSÉE DE L'ÉTAIN (PEWTER) **Tel. 02 41 88 67 41**	*Open Jul. 16–Aug. 31, daily except Sun.–Mon. 9.30am–noon and 2–7pm; Sep. 1–Jul. 15, daily except Sun. 9.30am–noon and 2–7pm.*	▲ 302
MUSÉE DES BEAUX-ARTS 10, rue du Musée **Tel. 02 41 88 64 65**	*Open June 12–Sep. 17, daily 9am–6.30pm; Sep. 18–June 11, daily except Mon. 10am–noon and 2–6pm.*	▲ 304
NATURAL HISTORY MUSEUM 43, rue Jules-Guitton **Tel. 02 41 86 05 84**	*Open daily except Mon. 2–5pm.*	▲ 307

MUSÉE JEAN-LURÇAT Hôpital St-Jean **Tel. 02 41 24 18 45**	*Open Jul. 1–Sep. 15, daily 9am–6.30pm;* *Sep. 16–June 30, daily except Mon. 10am–noon and* *2–6pm. Closed Jan. 1, Jul. 14, Nov. 1 and 11, Dec. 25.*	▲ 308
ST-MAURICE CATHEDRAL Rue St-Christophe	*Open daily summer 8am–7pm; winter 9am–5pm.*	▲ 297
AROUND ANGERS		
ST-GEORGES-SUR-LOIRE	**49170** **A6**	
CHÂTEAU DE SERRANT **Tel. 02 41 39 13 01**	*Open Jul.–Aug. daily, 10–11.30am and 2–5.30pm;* *Sep.–Oct. and Apr.–June, daily except Tue. 10–11.30am* *and 2–5.30pm.*	▲ 310
ÉCUILLÉ	**49460** **B4**	
CHÂTEAU DU PLESSIS-BOURRÉ **Tel. 02 41 32 06 01**	*Open Jul.–Aug., daily 10am–5.45pm; Sep.–Oct. and* *Mar.–June, daily except Wed. and Thur. 10am–noon and* *2–5.45pm; Nov. and Feb., daily except Wed. 2–5.45pm.*	▲ 311
LE PLESSIS-MACÉ	**49770** **A5**	
CHÂTEAU **Tel. 02 41 32 67 93**	*Open Jul.–Aug., daily 10am–noon and 2–6.30pm;* *June and Sep., daily except Tue. 10am–noon and* *2–6.30pm; Oct–Nov. and Mar.–Apr., daily except Tue.* *1.30–5.30pm; May, daily except Tue. 1.30–6pm.*	▲ 310
BAUGÉ	**49150** **D5**	
CHÂTEAU AND MUSÉE D'ART **POPULAIRE** **Tel. 02 41 89 18'07**	*Open Jul.–Aug., daily except Sun. am 10am–noon and* *2.30–5.30pm; Sep. 1–15, June 15–30, daily except Tue.* *and Sun. am 10am–noon and 2.30–5.30pm.*	▲ 312
MAZÉ	**49630** **C5**	
CHÂTEAU DE MONTGEOFFROY **Tel. 02 41 80 60 02**	*Open June 15–Sep. 15, daily 9.30am–6.30pm;* *Sep. 16–Nov. 1 and Mar. 23–June 14, daily 9.30am–noon* *and 2.30–6.30pm. Guided tour by appointment in English.*	▲ 312

USEFUL ADDRESSES

We have selected the following as good representatives of their various categories. The list covers a range of establishments, including traditional "auberges", gastronomic landmarks that gourmets should not miss, hotels that are friendly and good value. They are all close to the historical sites and châteaux.

ORLÉANS

Postal code 45000
(O/P2)

RESTAURANTS

LA POUTRIÈRE
8, rue de la Brèche
Tel. 02 38 66 02 30
This traditional vine-worker's house has been converted into a luxury "auberge" with a garden and swimming pool. Simon Le Bras is especially fond of shellfish and fish, which he skilfully combines with the vegetables of Orléans and the fruit of the Loire Valley. His cuisine reveals a perfect mastery of the produce, seasonings and garnishes.
Menus 150F (lunch, wine included), 250–350F
À la carte 300–380F

LES ANTIQUAIRES
2–4, rue au Lin
Tel. 02 38 53 52 35
Poultry cooked in the contemporary style, but in Orléans vinegar, which is a condiment dating from the 14th century. Michel Pipet is well-versed in traditional cuisine. The "salade tiède" of calf sweetbreads with foie gras, the sea bass "paupiettes", and the "tarte aux pommes", all demonstrate the same high standards. A highly sophisticated menu, just like the décor.
Menus 155F (midweek), 190–390F
À la carte 280–320F

GIEN

Postal code 45500
(S4)

HOTEL-RESTAURANT

★ **HÔTEL DU RIVAGE**
1, quai de Nice
Tel. 02 38 37 79 00
Fax 02 38 38 10 21
Taste roast pike-perch in a garden by the banks of the Loire. Chef Thierry Renou's cuisine is steeped in the traditional Loire virtues of simplicity and harmony; it would be greatly appreciated if the titles of the dishes were inspired by the same principles. Notable dishes include the stuffed pig's trotters, mushrooms with truffle sauce and "Paris-Gien", a gâteau with raspberries and praline ice-cream. Christian Gaillard, the manager, *is in charge of reception and service.*
Menus 140–380F
À la carte 250–400F
16 rooms, 3 suites
300–520F

ORLÉANS TO GIEN

CHÂTEAUNEUF-SUR-LOIRE

Postal code 45110 (Q2)

HOTEL-RESTAURANT

AUBERGE DU PORT
Tel. 02 38 58 43 07
Closed Wed. and Dec.
A simple "auberge" in the town of Maurice Genevoix, the local writer. The menu includes dishes you will find in Genevoix's novel "Raboliot": fried fish, matelotes, game, and simple veal fricassée with wild mushrooms. The rooms overlook the river and the bridge. Perfect for a walk along the banks of the Loire.
Menus: 75–170F
4 rooms with shower, 165F

CHÉCY

Postal code 45430 (P2)

RESTAURANT

LE WEEK-END
1, pl. du Cloître
Tel. 02 38 86 84 93
Traditional Orléans cuisine presented in a simple rustic setting by a chef with a distinguished background. Fillet of pike-perch and beef "forestière", ragoût of pheasant and jugged hare in the fall. Service and wine list of comparable quality.
Menus: 78 (midweek), 130–200F
À la carte: 180–300F

GERMIGNY-DES-PRÉS

Postal code 45110 (Q3)

HOTEL-RESTAURANT

HÔTEL DE LA PLACE
Tel. 02 38 58 20 14
Fax 02 38 58 21 33
Cordon-bleu cuisine which goes perfectly with the simple Carolingian church and its famous mosaic. *This village hotel is a delightful place to stay or eat. Some of the rooms are very basic, others have a full range of facilities.*
Menus: 59F (midweek), 89–130F
À la carte: 120–220F
11 rooms, 160–220F

JARGEAU

Postal code 45150 (Q2)

RESTAURANT

AUX QUAIS DE LOIRE
23, rue du 71e B.C.P.
Tel. 02 38 59 92 18
Closed Sun. eve and Mon.
Mme Chansard is the manageress of this restaurant, which has a panoramic view over the Loire. Jargeau is the capital of the "andouillette": beyond this, the restaurant also serves "salade solognote", pike-perch and salmon, as well as local poultry. The setting is pleasant and the cuisine is impressive: the chef

HOW TO USE THIS SECTION

The addresses are presented following the order of itineraries in the guide. Within each itinerary, towns and establishments are listed in alphabetical order. The map reference following the postal code refers to the general maps at the front and back of this guide. The telephone and fax numbers incorporate the new system of numbering which came into use in France in October 1996.

was formerly at the Negresco.
Menus: 90–220F
À la carte: 200–300F

ST-BENOÎT-SUR-LOIRE

Postal code 45110 (R3)

HOTEL

HÔTEL DU LABRADOR
7, pl. de l'Abbaye
Tel. 02 38 35 74 38
Fax 02 38 35 72 99
A quiet, partially renovated hotel: some rooms have exposed beams and all conveniences. A lovely setting at the foot of the Abbey of St-Benoît, where you can enjoy the peaceful atmosphere of the river valley with a thought for Max Jacob, who lived here before leaving for Drancy.
45 rooms, 180–360F

ST-JEAN-DE-BRAYE

Postal code 45800 (P2)

RESTAURANT

LA GRANGE
205, fg de Bourgogne
Tel. 02 38 86 43 36
Closed Sun., Mon., and Aug.
There were lots of "mauviettes" (weaklings) about during the reign of Charles IX, when Pithiviers was granted the royal privilege for lark pâté. Here, François Chapot offers classical French cuisine, with plenty of game in season, venison, and wild boar. A good cellar of Orléans wines.
Menus: 100–280F
À la carte: 250–320F

SULLY-SUR-LOIRE

Postal code 45600 (R3)

HOTEL-RESTAURANT

HOSTELLERIE DU GRAND-SULLY
10, bd du Champ-de-Foire
Tel. 02 38 36 27 56
Fax 02 38 36 44 54
Closed Sun. evening.
A summer terrace where you can taste chicken "Bon Roy Henri", pike-perch with baby vegetables cooked in a "papillote", or fillet of perch with beurre blanc and crayfish. The cuisine is steeped in the gentle harmonies of the majestic river valley. Comfortable rooms. Traditional house renovated by Philippe Calciat.
Menus: 150–210F
À la carte: 250–350F
10 rooms, 270F

◆

ORLÉANS TO BLOIS

BEAUGENCY

Postal code 45190 (N3)

HOTEL-RESTAURANT

HOSTELLERIE DE L'ÉCU DE BRETAGNE
Pl. du Martroi
Tel. 02 38 44 67 60
Fax 02 38 44 68 07
The rooms of this old coaching inn (preferable to those in the annex) are completely in character with the town, where you can see fish swimming by from the bridge in summer. A sparkling cuisine, with unusual combinations of flavors: rabbit with gingerbread, pork with honey.
Menus: 90F (lunch), 130–200F
25 rooms, 265–365F

CLÉRY-ST-ANDRÉ

Postal code 45370 (O3)

HOTEL-RESTAURANT

LES BORDES
9, rue des Bordes
Tel. 02 38 45 71 25
Fax 02 38 45 96 95
"Orléans, Beaugency, Notre-Dame de Cléry, Vendôme . . .": these are the words of an old song commemorating the fact that in the days of Villon and Louis XI this was a place of pilgrimage, and a famous stopping point on the road to Compostela. Huge traditional building in its own grounds. A variety of rooms.
Menus: 60–180F
21 rooms, 80–290F
1 apartment, 450F

LA FERTÉ-ST-AUBIN

Postal code 45240 (P4)

RESTAURANT

LA FERME DE LA LANDE
Rte de Macilly
Tel. 02 38 76 64 37
Closed Sun. eve. and Mon.
The restaurant is housed in a former farmhouse of the Château de La Ferté-St-Aubin, which has been carefully restored. The manager is friendly and the chef offers both the pike-perch of the Loire and Gâtinais duckling sweetmeats. In the hunting season you can try Lièvre à la Royale (hare) – a recipe invented by Carême – and tarte Tatin.
8 menus: 138–370F
À la carte: 250–300F

MER

Postal code 41500 (N4)

RESTAURANT

LES CALANQUES
21, rue Saint-Hême
Tel. 02 58 81 00 55
This large 16th-century house, with its

traditional fireplace and exposed beams, has been converted into a fish restaurant. Local fish are served (pike-perch, pike, salmon) alongside Coquilles St-Jacques, sea bass, and shellfish: all prepared with great precision by Philippe Colombet.
Menus: 100–170F
À la carte: 250–300F

MEUNG-SUR-LOIRE

Postal code 45130 (N3)

HOTEL-RESTAURANT

AUBERGE SAINT-JACQUES
80, rue du Général-de-Gaulle
Tel. 02 38 44 30 39
Fax 02 38 45 17 02
You will not find here the fish that Rabelais served his guests at St-Ay, very close by. The parfait of pike and the young rabbit with onions created by chef Le Gall (winner of the Trophée de la cuisine et de la pâtisserie) exemplify his excellent, simple cuisine.
Menus: 90F (midweek)–220F
À la carte: 250F
12 rooms, 190–260F

OLIVET

Postal code 45160 (O2)

HOTEL-RESTAURANT

LE RIVAGE
635, rue de la Reine-Blanche
Tel. 02 38 66 02 93
The fish of the great river itself, and of the Loiret and the nearby lakes of the Sologne, make a major contribution to the elegant cuisine of François Tassain. This idyllic refuge, situated on an island, also serves Sologne pigeon, calf sweetbreads with crayfish and morel, and the "cendré d'Olivet" praised by Balzac.
Menus: 155–300F
À la carte: 250–350F
18 rooms 370–590F

SAINT DYÉ-SUR-LOIRE

Postal code 41500 (M/N4)

HOTEL-RESTAURANT

MANOIR DE BEL-AIR
(3 miles north of Chambord)
Tel. 02 54 81 60 10
Fax 02 54 81 65 34
Closed Jan. 20–Feb. 20
An old ivy-covered building where you will find both traditional Loiret-et-Cher cuisine and dishes from Beauce: the Loire connects these distinct gastronomic regions, which overlap only at harvest time (Sologne quail) and grape-picking (game). By the riverside.
Menus: 118–218F
40 rooms, 240–400F

TAVERS

Postal code 45190 (N3)

HOTEL-RESTAURANT

LA TONNELLERIE
12, rue des Eaux-Bleues
(near the church, approach from Beaugency on the N152)
Tel. 02 38 44 68 15
Fax 02 38 44 10 01
"My hoops on my back, my tools in my hand, I preserve for the people's pleasure". This is the motto of the "tonnelier" (cooper) – and also of Alain Pouey, who serves part-smoked pike-perch and "rillons" of Touraine flavored with herbs, in an elegant, tastefully decorated setting.
Menus: 125–230F
À la carte: 280–450F
12 rooms, 700–880F
8 suites, 800–1,235F

VILLENY

Postal code 41220 (O4)

HOTEL-RESTAURANT

LES CHÊNES-ROUGES
Tel. 02 54 98 23 94
Fax 02 54 98 23 99
Closed Sun. eve. and Mon. (exc. June–Aug.) and Feb.
A hunting lodge by the side of a lake in the forest. The rooms look out over the reeds, which hide the cross-shaped sluice gate. A landscape of birch trees. Serves seasonal cuisine: game in winter, fish from the lakes in summer (bleak, dace, tench and sometimes rainbow perch).
Menus: 170–185F
9 rooms, 600–800F

BLOIS

Postal code 41000 (M4/5)

RESTAURANTS

L'ORANGERIE DU CHÂTEAU
1, av. du Docteur-Jean-Laigret
Tel. 02 54 78 05 36
Facing the royal

BRACIEUX

Postal code 41250 (N5)

RESTAURANT

★ LE RELAIS DE BRACIEUX
1, av. de Chambord
Tel. 02 54 46 41 22
Closed Tue. eve. and Wed.
This former coaching inn first became the Café de la Gare, and then was converted into a substantial restaurant sixty years ago. Today the restaurant is decorated in a tasteful contemporary style. Bernard Robin

château. Jean-Marc Molveaux presents the full range of Loir-et-Cher cuisine, combining dishes from Vendômois, Touraine, Beauce and Sologne. Molveaux comes from Savoie himself, which makes his achievement all the more notable. He uses top-quality local produce (game, fish, fresh vegetables).
Menus: 125–320F
À la carte: 270–360F

AU RENDEZ-VOUS DES PÊCHEURS
27, rue du Foix
Tel. 02 54 74 67 48
Closed Sun. and Mon. lunchtime.
Fresh and salt-water fish are a specialty in this restaurant which was once a grocery store in the old town, a favorite haunt of locals. Éric Reithler creates his dishes opportunistically, making use of what is freshly available: cold lobster soup, oysters, Dublin Bay prawns. The desserts must also be mentioned: Blois "pistoles", Vendôme pralines.
Menu: 145F
À la carte: 250–310F

has served his own version of classical cuisine here since 1975, without forgetting local specialties: carp "à la Chambord", pike mousseline, and the delicious Sologne-

AROUND BLOIS

CANDÉ-SUR-BEUVRON

Postal code 41120 (L5)

HOTEL-RESTAURANT

HOSTELLERIE DE LA CAILLÈRE
36, rte des Montils
Tel. 02 54 44 03 08
Fax 02 54 44 00 95
Closed Jan. 2–Feb. 28
Jacky Guidon creates a high-quality cuisine in his peaceful, pleasant establishment, set amidst trees and fields. Classical cuisine with a new twist: pike-perch with citrus fruits and ginger, duck breast in honey, cinnamon and almonds. A wide selection of Loire wines. Tasteful rooms.
Menus: 88F (midweek)–278F
À la carte: 220–280F
14 rooms, 330–360F

CHAMBORD

Postal code 41250 (N4)

HOTEL-RESTAURANT

HÔTEL DU GRAND-SAINT-MICHEL
Tel. 02 54 20 31 31
Fax 02 54 20 36 40
Closed Nov. 12–Dec. 20

style "pâté de pommes de terre". An unforgettable experience, with exceptional wines; the game is unrivalled.
Menus: 200–550F
À la carte: 330–640F

Opposite the château, a fairytale spectacle straight out of "Cinderella" or "Beauty and the Beast". Once the tourists have left, take a stroll in the grounds in the evening, while the chefs prepare the grilled salmon with beurre blanc, or the wild boar stew. Touraine wines a specialty.
Menus: 130F
À la carte: 200F
40 rooms, 260–420F

CHAUMONT-SUR-LOIRE

Postal code 41150 (L5)

RESTAURANT

LA CHANCELIÈRE
1, rue de Bellevue
Tel. 02 54 20 96 95
A small, rustic establishment which has already gained a reputation, in the grounds of the famous château. Poultry from local smallholdings with morel, "poulet au sang" following the recipe from Berry, the famous Sologne duck (stuffed the day before and cooked slowly). Quality, good prices and courteous service.
Menus: 79–205F

CONTRES

Postal code 41700 (M6)

RESTAURANT

LE SAINT-VINCENT
Oisly (4 miles away, on the D675 and D21)
Tel. 02 54 79 50 04
Closed Sun. eve. and Mon.
An unpretentious façade at the heart of the village, but an excellent menu and an elegant rustic setting. The friendly chef presents an original, varied cuisine, with unexpected combinations: pork confit with rhubarb sauce, guinea-fowl with spiced wine, etc. A good selection of local wines.
Menus: 90–220F

ONZAIN-EN-TOURAINE

Postal code 41150 (L5)

HOTEL-RESTAURANT

★ DOMAINE DES HAUTS-DE-LOIRE
Route d'Herbault (take the D1)
Tel. 02 54 20 72 57
Fax 02 54 20 77 32
The Bonnigal family has turned this old hunting lodge into a delightful hotel. The cuisine of chef Rémy Giraud, a native of Vendôme, is both expert and approachable, drawing on local traditions. The entrées are light and delicious: caramelized foie gras of duck with rhubarb, shellfish ravioli with broad beans. The Vendôme pigeon cooked with mushrooms is full of flavor. The Vouvray wines go perfectly with the "crème chocolatée", flavored with tea and blackberry. High-quality setting and service.
Menus: 290–475F
À la carte: 380–500F
10 suites, 1,600–1,800F

COUR-CHEVERNY

Postal code 41700 (M5)

HOTEL-RESTAURANT

CHÂTEAU DU BREUIL
(2 miles away, on the D52)
Tel. 02 54 44 20 20
Fax 02 54 44 30 40
Closed Jan. 2–Feb. 20, Sun. eve. (out of season) and Mon. lunchtime.
All the splendor of an 18th-century residence in its own grounds, and serving top-quality food. Patrick Léonce creates exquisite combinations: artichoke and lobster medallions in "barigoule" sauce, bass in a pastry crust with cèpes. Delightful setting and good service.
Menus: 195–375F
À la carte: 400–450F
16 rooms, 530–890F

MONT-PRÈS-CHAMBORD

Postal code 41250 (M5)

HOTEL-RESTAURANT

LE SAINT-FLORENT
(6 miles south of Chambord, on the D923)
Tel. 02 54 70 81 00
Fax 02 54 70 78 53
A pretty, simple hotel in the heart of château country. The menu features traditional Sologne dishes such as pig's trotters, carp with Chinon. The game terrine is delicious.
Menus: 81–210F
18 rooms, 200–265F

AMBOISE

Postal code 37400 (J6)

HOTEL-RESTAURANT

★ LE CHOISEUL
36, quai Charles-Guinot
Tel. 02 47 30 45 45
Fax 02 47 30 46 10
Closed Nov. 26–Jan. 20
The elegant, austere building of the Choiseul stands at the foot of the château, on the quayside – by the side of the "moving road", as the Loire used to be called when it was used for shipping. The chef Pascal Bouvier deftly combines a modern repertoire of flavors and tastes, as in his "nonette de foie gras de canard", celery and balsamic caramel with wild herbs, or the fondant of oysters with green lentils from Berry. The roast loin of lamb with bacon sauce and

AROUND AMBOISE

NOIZAY

Postal code 37210 (I6)

HOTEL-RESTAURANT

CHÂTEAU DE NOIZAY
Rte de Chançay
(5 miles to the east on the D46)
Tel. 02 47 52 11 01
Fax 02 47 52 04 64
Closed Nov. 12–Mar. 15
A château dating from the 16th century, set amid ancient trees, with young peas goes perfectly with a Touraine-Amboise wine. Lovely rooms and very attentive service.
Menus: 200–400F
À la carte: 300–420F
28 rooms, 540–990F
4 suites, 1,200–1,600F

extremely elegant rooms. The chef, Didier Frebout, uses local produce and adapts his cuisine to the changing seasons, displaying a mastery of flavors: "petits-gris" (snails) and "rillons de Touraine", foie gras in Vouvray wine, pike-perch in Chinon.
Menus: 145–340F
À la carte: 240–360F
14 rooms, 950–1,300F

ST-OUEN-LES-VIGNES

Postal code 37530   (J5)

RESTAURANT

L'AUBINIÈRE
Rue J.-Gauthier
Tel. 02 47 30 15 29
Closed Mon. eve. and Wed. (except July and Aug.)
The cuisine of Jacques Arrayet is seasonal, with exquisite, intense flavors: tomatoes in warm oxtail vinegar, red mullet steak with red peppers, lobster with coriander. In summer

★ **JEAN BARDET**
57, rue Groison
Tours
Tel. 02 47 41 41 11
Fax 02 47 51 68 72
Closed Mon. lunchtime Apr.–Oct., Sun. eve. and Mon. Nov.–Mar..
Jean Bardet is a cook, a gardener and a poet, who is able to share his passions with others. "Pike with beurre blanc tastes best in rainy weather," he declares, while uncorking a bottle of chilled wine. A Montlouis 1989 (Domaine Delétang), for example, to match the flavors of turbot

---

you can eat on the terrace, at the heart of this village near Amboise.
Menu: 110F (midweek), 190–340F
À la carte: 300–400F

TOURS

Postal code 37000   (H6)

RESTAURANTS

CHARLES BARRIER
101, av. Tranchée
Tel. 02 47 54 20 39
Closed Sun. eve
Charles Barrier is a long-established chef in the classical tradition: he is one of the great French chefs of the last thirty years. The elegant setting matches the culinary pleasures: lobster terrine with tomato in the Breton style, and young-guinea fowl with foie gras and fondant potatoes. Often imitated, rarely equalled.
Menus: 230–470F
À la carte: 370–500F

LA ROCHE LE ROY
57, rte Saint-Avertin
Tel. 02 47 27 22 00
Closed Sat. lunchtime, Sun. eve. and Mon.

poached with asparagus. The hazel grouse of the Racan area, a rare bird with dense, tasty flesh, goes best with a Bourgueil (Domaine de la Chevalerie) by Pierre Caslot (1986). The best

---

In an old manor house in Tours, Alain Couturier excels in the preparation of local, seasonal dishes: pike-perch with beurre blanc, matelote of eels with Chinon wine, fricassée of hazel grouse with morel mushrooms. The wine is kept in a cellar hollowed out of the rock.
Menus: 160F (lunch), 200–350F
À la carte: 240–400F

AROUND TOURS

ROCHECORBON

Postal code 37210   (H6)

HOTEL-RESTAURANT

LES HAUTES-ROCHES
86, quai de Loire
Tel. 02 47 52 88 88
Fax 02 47 52 81 30
Hotel closed mid-Jan.–mid-Mar.. Panoramic view over the Loire and troglodytic caves, in an extraordinary location. Chef Didier Edon has a predilection for seafood dishes (burbot, smoked duck, turbot supreme, "persillade" of squid with pickled tomato), but he also cooks pigeon with exceptional skill.
Menus: 150F (lunch), 270–355F
8 rooms, 3 suites, 995–1,200F

restaurant in the area. Very comfortable rooms, lovely gardens. Warm welcome and service.
Menus 270–720F
À la carte 500–700F
16 rooms, 650–1 200F
5 suites, 1,400–1 800F

RESTAURANT

L'OUBLIETTE
34, rue des Clouets
Tel. 02 47 52 50 49
Closed Sun. eve and Mon.
This restaurant has a troglodytic dining room hollowed out of the tufa rockface: a natural setting for the creations of Thierry Duhamel, which vary according to the season and availability of local produce. Lobster with Vouvray and baby vegetables, pan-fried Dublin Bay prawn with asparagus. Good Vouvray wines at very reasonable prices.
Menus: 948–290F
À la carte: 280–320F

SEMBLANÇAY

Postal code 37360   (H5)

HOTEL-RESTAURANT

HOSTELLERIE DE LA MÈRE-HAMARD
Pl. de l'Église
Tel. 02 47 56 62 04
Fax 02 47 56 53 61
Closed Sun. eve. and Mon. (except Apr. 15–Oct. 15).
An old house set in a garden, with simple, comfortable rooms. The dining room is just as traditional as the cuisine, which uses exclusively fresh produce (pike-perch, salmon, game in season). Friendly welcome and service.
Menus: 99–250F
9 rooms, 200–255F

VALLIÈRES (PAR FONDETTES)

Postal code 37230   (H6)

RESTAURANT

AUBERGE DE PORT-VALLIÈRES
Tel. 02 47 42 24 04
Closed Sun. eve. and Mon.
Jean-Jacques Thomas considers that "terrine

de couenne" (pork terrine) brings out the flavor of the local wines. Food is served from nine in the morning: asparagus, pig's trotters, roast venison and fried fish. Small selection of excellent wines.
Menu: 85F

◆

TOURS TO VALENÇAY

CHENONCEAUX

Postal code 37150 (J6/7)

HOTEL-RESTAURANT

HÔTEL DU BON-LABOUREUR ET CHÂTEAU
6, rue du Docteur-Bretonneau
Tel. 02 47 23 90 02
Fax 02 47 23 82 01
Closed Nov. 13–Dec. 16 and Jan. 3–Feb. 15
This "auberge" in the village, close to the château, serves traditional local food. The rooms are extremely comfortable, and the dining room opens onto a lovely patio. Antoine Jeudi likes to use local produce: eels marinière "en matelote", "magret de canard" with Chinon.
Menus: 150–300F
À la carte: 280–320F
28 rooms, 320–700F
4 suites, 800–1,000F

LE GRAND-PRESSIGNY

Postal code 37350 (I9)

HOTEL-RESTAURANT

L'ESPÉRANCE
Tel. 02 47 94 90 12
Closed Mon. and Jan.6–Feb.3.
Paulette and Bernard Torset run this establishment in a traditional, opulent-looking house. Traditional dishes made

ROMORANTIN

Postal code 41200 (O6)

HOTEL-RESTAURANT

★ GRAND HÔTEL DU LION-D'OR
69, rue Georges-Clemenceau
Closed Fe. 19–Mar. 21
One of France's great restaurants. This house near Valençay once belonged to a friend of François I; today it is an elegant hotel with a patio at the heart of the small town, run by two generations of the Clément family. Didier Clément, the chef, uses from locally grown produce: pan-fried foie gras with apples, turbot with vermouth-flavored "mousse de St-Pierre", Touraine pigeon cooked with spices. Pleasant rooms at the heart of the village.
Menus: 100–195F
À la carte: 280–320F
10 rooms, 150–200F

LE PETIT-PRESSIGNY

Postal code 37350 (I9)

RESTAURANT

LA PROMENADE
Tel. 02 47 94 93 52
Closed Sun. eve and Mon.
Jacky Dallais learned the art of creating unusual dishes from Jacques Manière. He demonstrates his skill with "pain brûlé" accompanying "parmentier de foie gras et artichaut", white asparagus and veal with "gribiche" sauce. The comfortable setting and attractive décor of this village restaurant and the friendly service make this a must for all gourmets.
Menus: 120–350F
À la carte: 350–400F

the best produce (Dublin Bay prawns, lobsters, eels), with a mastery of cooking methods and spices (stuffed pigeon, calf sweetbreads), and close attention to the

MONTRICHARD

Postal code 41400 (L6)

RESTAURANT

GRILL DU PASSEUR "CHEZ SUZANNE"
Pont de Montrichard (at Faverolles-sur-Cher)
Tel. 02 54 32 06 80
A pleasant restaurant on the Cher, with superb red meats roasted on a spit in the fireplace, and good local wines. By night the view over the old town is stunning: the waters of the Cher flow under the bridge at the foot of the 12th-century keep, which once protected the town from invaders.
À la carte: around 150F

◆

TOURS TO CHINON

BEAUMONT-EN-VERON

Postal code 37420 (F8)

HOTEL-RESTAURANTS

CHÂTEAU DE DANZAY
Tel. 02 47 58 46 86
Fax 02 47 58 84 35
An elegant 15th-century château set in the heart

fine details. Impeccable service, and the best wines of the Loire.
Menus: 420F (lunch)-600F
À la carte: 520F
6 suites, 1,500–2,100

of the famous vineyard of Véron. Excellent rooms with four-poster beds and medieval-style wooden furniture, in keeping with the château's historical past. The restaurant, open only in the evening, offers a range of regional dishes, which are skilfully prepared.
Menus: 290–350F
10 rooms, 650–1,500F

LA GIRAUDIÈRE
Tel. 02 47 58 40 36
Fax 02 47 58 46 06
Restaurant closed Tue., Wed. lunchtime and Nov. 15–Mar. 15; hotel open all year
17th-century manor house with dovecote, set in its own grounds. A peaceful, delightful setting, with tasteful, opulent rooms. The restaurant is open daily, with a modest range of dishes: braised ox-tongue with truffle sauce, "civet de canard" (duck stew). Some very good local wines.
Menus: 110–300F
20 rooms, 200–395F
5 suites, 320–480F

L'ÎLE-BOUCHARD

Postal code 37220 (G8)

RESTAURANT

★ AUBERGE DE L'ÎLE
3, pl. Bouchard
Tel. 02 47 58 51 07
Closed Sun. eve, Mon. and Jan. 2–Feb. 20
The terrace of this modest auberge overlooks the bridge on the Vienne; the setting has a timeless quality. The menu offers a range of typical Loire dishes, including: asparagus in puff pastry with lamb sweetbreads, and roast pike-perch with a "ragoût de grenouilles et de morilles" (ragoût of frog and morel). Chinon wine goes splendidly with the pig's trotters with potatoes and mushrooms, in a "sauce diable". The local goat's cheese, Sainte-Maure, goes with the white wines of the region: Cheverny, Amboise, Azay-le-Rideau . . . names shared by famous châteaux and excellent wines.
Menus: 95–260F
À la carte: 260–300F

★ AU PLAISIR GOURMAND
2, rue Parmentier
Chinon
Tel. 02 47 93 20 48
The cuisine of chef Jean-Claude Rigollet is inspired by regional traditions, with his "fouée à l'ancienne", "mousseline de brochet" (pike mousse), leek terrine with rillons, and tart of calf sweetbreads. The pike-perch in Chinon wine is equally traditional. By contrast, Rigollet shows his inventiveness with the Dublin Bay prawns with courgettes and vanilla, best accompanied by a Coteaux-du-Layon wine. This lovely Renaissance building in the heart of old Chinon is beautifully decorated: it is a must for visitors to the land of Rabelais. Extensive list of local wines. The restaurant is managed by Danielle Rigollet.
Menus: 175–340F
À la carte: 280–320F

CHINON

Postal code 37600 (F8)

RESTAURANT

L'OCÉANIC
13, rue Rabelais
Tel. 02 47 93 44 55
Closed June 8–16
Chinon stretches alongside the waters of the Vienne, where fishers catch the pike-perch which feature prominently in the region's cuisine. This restaurant in the old town has achieved a well-deserved reputation. It serves excellent seawater and freshwater fish, presented very simply and accompanied by local wines, at reasonable prices.
Menus: 98–155F

HOTEL

LE DIDEROT
4, rue Bufon
Tel. 02 47 93 18 87
Fax 02 47 93 37 10

MARÇAY

Postal code 37500 (F8)

HOTEL-RESTAURANT

★ CHÂTEAU DE MARÇAY
Tel. 02 47 93 03 47
Fax 02 47 93 45 33
Closed Sun. eve and Mon. out of season and Jan. 28–Mar. 16
This magnificent château built of tufa limestone and slate, dating from the late Middle Ages, stands in landscaped gardens which symbolize the "Garden of France", with vineyards all around. The rooms

This peaceful hotel near to the Place Jeanne-d'Arc occupies an 18th-century building of tufa limestone with a lovely half-timbered staircase. The service is excellent and the prices are reasonable. All the rooms are different. Homemade jellies are served at breakfast, beside an old fireplace.
28 rooms, 250–400F

MONTBAZON

Postal code 37250 (H7)

HOTEL-RESTAURANT

CHÂTEAU D'ARTIGNY
Rte d'Azay-le-Rideau
Tel. 02 47 26 24 24
Fax 02 47 65 92 79
Closed Jan. 1–13.
When François Coty, the perfumer, was unable to buy Chambord, he resigned himself to reproducing an in the château and its outbuildings are furnished very tastefully, with top-level facilities. The chef, Pascal Boudin, presents a range of classical dishes which draw inspiration from local produce and traditions: poached eggs with cream of wild mushrooms, sole soufflé with herbs from the garden, and exquisite desserts. Guests can eat on the terrace in summer. Extensive wine list, very attentive service.
Menus: 145–385F
À la carte: 340–420F
34 rooms, 495–1,350F
6 suites, 1,420–1,680F

18th-century château. Now this building has been converted into a luxury hotel, offering the best in service and facilities. An extensive menu is served in the round dining room: fish dishes, asparagus, hazel grouse with truffles. Magnificent wine list.
Menus: 250–440F
À la carte: 380–450F
51 rooms, 520–1,640F
4 suites, 2,300–2,680F

◆

TOURS TO FONTEVRAUD

BOURGUEIL

Postal code 37140
(F7)

RESTAURANTS

AUBERGE DE TOUVOIS
Rte de Gizeux
(3 miles to the north, on the D 749)
Tel. 02 47 97 88 81
Touraine is the "green heart" of the

Loire Valley, the land of "primeurs" (early wines), good cheeses, and an abundance of fruit. This auberge by the forest is run by Pascal Calmettes: it is an idyllic place, serving traditional cuisine (millefeuille d'escargots, kidneys with three types of mustard) and Bourgueil wines.
Menus: 85–125F
À la carte: 240–280F

GERMAIN
Rue A.-Charier
Tel. 02 47 97 72 22
A reliable restaurant. Charcuterie (cooked/ cured meats) plays a vital role in the gastronomy of this region: the pâtés, sausages, rillettes and rillons are best accompanied by a straightforward Sauvignon or a delicate Vouvray.
Menus: 90–180F

FONTEVRAUD-L'ABBAYE

Postal code 49590
(E8)

RESTAURANT

LA LICORNE
Allée Ste-Catherine
Tel. 02 41 51 72 49
This restaurant, set in the gardens of an 18th-century residence, offers a classical style of cuisine, which changes throughout the year depending what is in season and the local produce that is available.

Salmon with anchovy sauce, aubergines gratin, roasted calf sweetbreads with Layon wine: any of these provides a perfect accompaniment to the local wines.
Menus: 110–280F
À la carte: 300–380F

LUYNES

Postal code 37230
(H6)

HOTEL-RESTAURANT

DOMAINE DE BEAUVOIS
Rte de Cléré
(2½ miles to the northwest, on the D49)
Closed Jan. 11–Mar. 9
A magnificent house in a verdant setting, with its own swimming pool at the end of the lawn. Stéphane Pineau offers "classic wines of the estate, with traditional dishes", including the sole roulade with Vouvray and the pigeon in a salted pastry crust.
Menus: 200–360F
À la carte: 340–380F
36 rooms, 920–1,400F

MONTSOREAU

Postal code 49730
(E7)

HOTEL-RESTAURANT

HÔTEL DE LA LOIRE
Tel. 02 41 51 70 06
Fax 02 41 38 15 08
A unique setting at the confluence of the Loire and the Vienne, which

meet amid valleys and forests. A reliable, family-run establishment, and a good base for exploring Candes and the Basilica of St-Martin. Simple rooms and good-quality local cuisine.
Menus: 79–160F
14 rooms, 160–265F

◆

SAUMUR

Postal code 49400
(D7)

RESTAURANTS

L'ESCARGOT
30, rue du Maréchal-Leclerc
Tel. 02 41 51 20 88
Closed Wed. out of season
The restaurant serves snails, of course, but also the "rillons" described by Balzac as a "piece of pork fried in its own fat, which looks like a cooked truffle". Saumur wines a specialty. The menu includes traditional dishes, like a tasty "boudin de brochet" (pike sausage) with Dublin Bay prawns.
Menus: 73–165F
À la carte: 200–150F

LES DÉLICES DU CHÂTEAU
Courtyard of the château
Tel. 02 41 67 65 60
Pierre Millon runs this restaurant in the former chapel of the Château de Saumur, dating from the 14th century, looking down over the town and the river. It is a unique place, especially in summer when guests can eat on the shady terrace. An imaginative menu, featuring fish, local vegetables and fruits, and game in season.
Menus: 175–285F
À la carte: 290–390F

GUEST HOUSE

★ DOMAINE DE MESTRÉ
Fontevraud-l'Abbaye
Tel. 02 41 51 75 87
Fax 02 41 51 71 90

A delightful farm, which has been run by the same family since the 18th century, set in a landscape of hills and trees near to the

confluence of the Loire and the Vienne. Rooms and dinner are offered at an attractive price. Guests can taste produce from the farm itself, including chicken, veal, and cheese from the dairy. An old-fashioned farm with a warm, traditional atmosphere; it welcomes many visitors from outside France.
Dinner: 135F
12 rooms, 230–380F

SAUMUR TO MONTREUIL-BELLAY

OIRON

Postal code 79100 (E9)

HOTEL-RESTAURANT

RELAIS DU CHÂTEAU
Tel. 02 49 96 54 96
Fax 02 49 96 54 45
The young chef Éric Bernier is highly skilled at combining different flavors and textures in a very original way. His dishes bear the hallmark of culinary genius: the "verdurette de gésiers confits" (gizzard), the pike-perch with oyster sauce, and the noisettes of lamb with port and cinnamon.
Menus: 75–158F
À la carte: 240 280F
15 rooms, 130–230F

THOUARS

Postal code 79100 (D9)

HOTEL-RESTAURANT

LE CLOS SAINT-MÉDARD
Tel. 02 49 66 66 00
Fax 02 49 96 15 01
Pierre Aracil's restaurant, with its austere style of décor, is set in a robust medieval building. The cuisine is full of flavor and rustic in style: eels in flaky pastry with horseradish, "pot au feu de St-Jacques" with Maissais butter, and beef and ragoût of pig's trotters.
Menus: 98–320F
4 rooms, 230–280

SAUMUR TO ANGERS

CHÊNEHUTTE-LES-TUFEAUX

Postal code 49350 (D7)

HOTEL-RESTAURANT

LE PRIEURÉ
(4½ northwest of Saumur, on the D751)
Tel. 02 41 67 90 14
Fax 02 41 67 92 24
Taste the atmosphere of Anjou in this delightful Renaissance manor house set in extensive grounds, overlooking the Loire. The luxury rooms and the dining hall have views over the river. Jean-Noël Lumineau highlights local products in a typically Angevin menu. A good selection of Loire wines.
Menus: 230–400F
À la carte: 350–400F
20 rooms, 2 suites, 500–1,350F

LES ROSIERS-SUR-LOIRE

Postal code 49350 (D6)

RESTAURANT

JEANNE-DE-LAVAL
54, rue Nationale
Tel. 02 41 51 80 17
A large auberge by the river. Michel Augereau, employed by his father Albert, is establishing himself as a chef of considerable skill, after training with Joël Robuchon. His typically Angevin cuisine features variations on local themes: crayfish, Loire fish with beurre blanc, ballottine of pigeon with truffles. A good list of Loire wines.

Menus: 180–420F
À la carte: 380–470F
8 rooms, 300–550F
(at the Hôtel des Ducs d'Anjou)

ANGERS

Postal code 49000 (B5/6)

HOTEL-RESTAURANTS

PAVILLON PAUL-LE-QUÉRÉ
3, bd Foch
Tel. 02 41 20 00 20
Fax 02 41 20 06 20
Closed Sun. eve.
Paul Le Quéré makes skilful use of local produce, as it becomes available on the market: artichoke and asparagus combined with Dublin Bay prawns (cooked with pepper) and burbot cooked with herbs in a rustic sauce. A lovely classical building.
Menus: 150–470F
6 rooms, 500–800F

HÔTEL D'ANJOU RESTAURANT "LA SALAMANDRE"
1, bd Foch
Tel. 02 41 88 99 55
Fax 02 41 87 22 21
Closed Sun.
This is the main hotel in the town for receptions and celebrations. The restaurant features the classical cuisine of Daniel Louboutin: grilled bass with basil cream sauce, pigeon rissole with truffle sauce. A perfect prelude to visiting the Tapestry of the Apocalypse.
Menus: 120–195F
À la carte: around 300F
53 rooms, 355–580F

AROUND ANGERS

BÉHUARD

Postal code 49170 (B6)

RESTAURANT

NOTRE-DAME
12, pl. de l'Église
Tel. 02 41 72 20 17
Upriver from the remarkable confluence of the Maine and the Loire is a church (which has survived repeated flooding) and this magnificent village restaurant, which serves specialties of Anjou: mussels, fried Loire fish, smoked goose, eels, duck. Accompanied by a crisp Anjou wine.
Menus: 85–185F

ST-GEORGES-SUR-LOIRE

Postal code 49170 (A6)

RESTAURANT

RELAIS D'ANJOU
Tel. 02 41 39 13 18
The old press-house, opposite the abbey, has a barrel standing on the terrace. The cuisine is classical and local at once: terrine of pike with crayfish, boudin of lobster with cabbage, Anjou pigeon with garlic cloves.
Menus: 105–280F

ST-SYLVAIN-D'ANJOU

Postal code 49480 (B5)

RESTAURANT

AUBERGE D'ÉVENTARD
(Rte de Paris N 23)
Tel. 02 41 43 74 25
Good, classical cuisine from Jean-Pierre Maussion, a native of the Loire. All the local specialties are here: andouillette with shallots, farm-raised chicken, Anjou pigeon with Savennières. One of the best places to sample traditional Angevin cuisine.
Menus: 135–365F

APPENDICES

ESSENTIAL
◆ READING ◆

◆ BENTLEY (J.):
The Loire, Philip,
London, 1986
◆ GOUVION (C.):
Châteaux de la Loire,
Thames & Hudson,
London, 1986
◆ LONGNON (J.) and
GAZELLES (R.)
(introduction): *Les
Très Riches Heures
du Duc de Berri*,
Thames & Hudson,
London, 1969/
Abrams, US, 1984
◆ MYHILL (H.):
*The Loire Valley –
Plantagenet and
Valois*, Faber and
Faber, London, 1978
◆ SEYDOUX (P.):
Châteaux of the Loire,
Thames & Hudson,
London, 1992
◆ WALDEN (H.): *Loire
Gastronomique*,
Conran Octopus,
London, 1992

GENERAL
◆ READING ◆

◆ ARDAGH (J.) and
JONES (C.): *Cultural
Atlas of France*, Facts
on File, New
York/Oxford, 1991
◆ AUDEBERT (B.) and
TOURNAIR (J.): *La
Châtre et la Vallée
Noire*, Editions Souny,
Limoges, 1985
◆ BAILEY (A.) et al:
The Taste of France,
Webb and Bower
(Publishers) Ltd.,
Exeter, 1983
◆ BAROLI (M.): *La Vie
Quotidienne en Berry
au temps de George
Sand*, Hachette, Paris,
1982
◆ BAZIN (R.):
*Paysages et Pays
d'Anjou*, Calmann-
Lévy, Paris, 1926
◆ BEDEL (M.): *La
Touraine, gens et
pays de chez nous*,
De Gigord, Paris,
1935
◆ BOYLESVE (R.):
Portrait de la France,
Vol. IV, Émile-Paul
Frères, Paris, 1926
◆ BURY (J.P.T.):
France 1814–1900,
Methuen, London,
1949
◆ BURNAND (R.): *La
Vie Quotidienne en
France 1870–1900*,
Hachette, Paris, 1943
◆ CHAMBERLAIN (S.):
*Bouquet de France
– an epicurean tour of
the French provinces*,

Hamish Hamilton,
London
◆ CHIROL (S.) et
SEYDOUX (P.): *Le Val
de Loire. Des
châteaux et des
manoirs*, Paris,
Le Chêne, 1991
◆ CLÉMENT (M-Ch. &
D.): *La Sologne
gourmande*, Albin
Michel, Paris, 1993
◆ COLLAS (R.): *Heurs
et malheurs des
soieries tourangelles*,
Le Clairmirouère,
Blois, 1987
◆ COURTE (L.),
GATEUAD (P) and
STEPHAN (B.): *La Loire
en sursis. Croisade
pour le dernier fleuve
sauvage d'Europe*,
Sang de la Terre,
Paris, 1990
◆ DYER (C.):
*Population and
Society in Twentieth-
Century France*,
Hodder & Stoughton,
London, 1978
◆ GENEVOIX (M.):
*Images du val de
Loire*, Imprimerie
Nationale, Paris, 1900
◆ GUERLIN (H.): *La
Touraine, Le Blésois,
Le Vendômois: Choix
de Textes prédédes
d'une étude*,
H. Laurens, Paris, 1911
◆ HALÉVY (D.): *Visites
aux Paysans du
Centre (1907–1934)*,
Grasset, Paris, 1935
◆ MASTROJANNI (E.):
*Le Grand Livre des
vins de Loire*, Solar,
Paris, 1991
◆ MENDRAS (H.) AND
COLE (A.): *Social
Change in Modern
France: Towards
a Cultural
Anthropology of the
Fifth Republic*,
Cambridge University
Press, Cambridge,
1991
◆ ROUGÉ (J.M.):
*Le Folklore de la
Touraine*, C.L.D.,
Chambray-lès Tours,
1975
◆ ROWE (V.): *Châteaux
of the Loire*, Putnam,
London, 1958
◆ ROWE (V.): *The
Loire*, Eyre Methuen,
London, 1974
◆ PARIS (T.): *The River
Yonne and the Canal
du Nivernais from the
Seine to the Loire*,
Enterpris, Bideford,
c. 1992
◆ WALDEN (H.):
*Régions gourmandes.
Le Pays de Loire*,
Hatier, Paris, 1993

◆ *Walking in the Loire
Valley*, trans WILSON
(A.): Robertson
McCarta, London
1990
◆ WEBER (E.):
*Peasants into
Frenchmen: the
Modernization of Rural
France, 1870–1914*,
Chatto & Windus;
London, 1977
◆ ZELDIN (T.): *Histoire
des Passions
Françaises* (5 vols.),
Éditions du Seuil,
Paris, 1980–1

◆ HISTORY ◆

◆ BOUSSARD (J.): *Le
Comté d'Anjou sous
Henri II Plantagenêt et
ses fils (1151–1204)*,
Slatkine, Paris, 1977
◆ DALLAS (E.), *The
Imperfect Peasant
Economy, the Loire
Country, 1800–1914*,
Cambridge University
Press, Cambridge,
1990
◆ DAVID-DARNAC (M.):
*The True Story of the
Maid of Orleans*,
trans. De Polnay (P.),
W.H. Allen, London,
1969
◆ DUBY (G.) and
MANDROU (R.):
*A History of French
Civilisation*,
Weidenfeld &
Nicolson, London,
1964/Random House,
New York, 1975
◆ FARMER (S.):
*Communities of
St Martin – Legend
and Ritual in Medieval
Tours*, Cornell
University Press,
Ithaca and London,
1991
◆ FRANCE (A.): *The Life
of Joan of Arc*, trans.
Stephens (W.), John
Lane, The Bodley
Head, London, 1909
◆ GAULTIER (J.):
*Histoire de la Châtre
et Berry*, Éditions de
vagabond, Paris, 1982
◆ GOUBERT (P.): *The
Ancien Régime*,
Weidenfeld and
Nicolson, London,
1973/ Harper and
Row, US, 1970
◆ GOUBERT (P.):
*French Peasantry in
the Seventeenth
Century*, Cambridge
University Press,
Cambridge, 1982, US,
1986
◆ KEEN (M.): *The
Pelican History of
Medieval Europe*,

Penguin,
Harmondsworth,
1968
◆ McLEOD (E.):
*Charles of Orleans,
Prince and Poet*,
Chatto & Windus,
London, 1969
◆ MAUROIS (H.):
A history of France,
Jonathan Cape,
London, 1949

◆ ARCHITECTURE ◆

◆ BABELON (J. -P.):
*Les Châteaux de
France au siècle de la
Renaissance*, Picard,
Paris, 1990
◆ BILLY-CHRISTIAN (F.),
RAULIN (H.):
*L'Architecture rurale
française*, Paris,
Berger-Levrault, 1986
◆ BINNY (M.):
Châteaux of the Loire,
Penguin Books,
London, 1993
◆ DEFARGES (B.) and
BERLAND (J.-M.):
Val de Loire roman,
Zodiaque, La Pierre-
qui-Vire, 1965
◆ DUTTON (R.): *The
Châteaux of France*,
B.T. Batsford, London,
1969
◆ GASCAR (P.):
Chambord, Delpire
Éditeur, Switzerland,
1962
◆ GUILLAUME (J.):
*Léonard de Vinci et
l'architecture
française: la villa de
Charles d'Amboise et
le château de
Romorantin*, Revue de
l'Art, no. 25, 1974
◆ HALL (M.): *Château
de Blois, Loire*,
Country Life, April 11,
1996
◆ JEANSON (D.):
*La Basilique Saint-
Martin de Tours*,
C.L.D., Chambray-lès-
Tours, 1988
◆ LELONG (C.):
La Touraine romane,
Zodiaque, La Pierre-
qui-Vire, 1977
◆ LEVRON (J.):
Châteaux of the Loire,
trans. Coburn (O.),
Nicolson Eyre,
London, 1963
◆ LESUEUR (F. and P.):
Le Château de Blois,
Picard, Paris, 1970
◆ LESUEUR (F. and P.):
*Léonard da Vinci et
Chambord*, Études
d'art nos. 8, 9 and 10,
Paris-Alger, 1953–4
◆ MARTIN-DEMÉZIL (J.):
Chambord, Société
Française

d'archéologue, Paris, 1986
◆ NICOLAY-MAZERY and NAUDIN (J.-B): *The French Château: Life, Style, Tradition*, Thames & Hudson, London, 1991
◆ PORCHER (J.): *Anjou roman*, Zodiaque, La Pierre-qui-Vire, 1987
◆ SARRAZIN (A.): *Maisons rurales du Val de Loire: Touraine, Blésois, Orléanais, Sologne*, Vincent Freal, 1976
◆ SEYDOUX (P.): *Châteaux et manoirs du Blésois*, Paris, La Morande, 1990
◆ SULLAM (J.) and WAITE (C.): *Villages of France*, Weidenfeld & Nicolson, London, 1988

◆ **FINE ARTS** ◆

◆ BLUNT (SIR A.): *Art and Architecture in France 1500–1700*, Pelican History of Art, Penguin Books, Harmondsworth, 1970
◆ DEMANGE (F.): *Images de la Révolution. L'imagerie populaire orléanaise à l'époque révolutionnaire*, Musée des Beaux-Arts d'Orléans, 1989

◆ **LITERATURE** ◆

◆ ALAIN-FOURNIER: *Le Grand Meaulnes (The Lost Domain)*, trans. Davison (F.) Oxford University Press, Oxford/New York, 1986
◆ BALZAC (H. DE): *Droll Stories*, Garden City Publishing Company Inc., Garden City, New York, 1928
◆ BALZAC (H. DE): *Le Curé de Tours*, Pléiade/Gallimard, Paris, 1971
◆ BALZAC (H. DE): *Eugénie Grandet*, trans. Ellen Marriage, Everyman's Library, London, Alfred Knopf, New York, 1992
◆ BALZAC (H. DE): *La Grenadière*, Pléiade/Gallimard, Paris, 1971
◆ BALZAC (H. DE): *Le Lys dans la Vallée (The Lily of the Valley)*, trans Waring, (J.),

J.M. Dent & Co., London/New York, 1987
◆ BALZAC (H. DE): *La Rabouilleuse*, Pléiade/Gallimard, Paris, 1971
◆ BAZIN (R.): *La Terre qui meurt*, Calman-Lévy, Paris, 1978
◆ BETHAM-EDWARDS: *East of Paris*, Hurst and Blackett, London, 1902
◆ DU BELLAY (J.): *Poète du XVIe Siècle*, Pléiade, Gallimard, Paris, 1953
◆ BENJAMIN (R.): *L'Homme à la recherche de son âme*, La Palatine, Geneva, 1943
◆ COLETTE: *Claudine à l'École*, Livre de Poche, Paris 1973
◆ COLETTE: *Looking Backwards*, trans. David Levay, Peter Owen, London, 1975
◆ DUMAS (A.): *La Reine Margot*, Dutton, New York/Dent, London, 1968
◆ FLAUBERT (G.): *Par les champs et les grèves*, Encre, Castillon-en-Couserans, 1984
◆ DE LA FONTAINE (J.): *Relation d'un Voyage de Paris en Limousin*, 1663
◆ GENEVOIX (M.): *Raboliot*, Éditions du Seuil, Paris, 1980
◆ GENEVOIX (M.): *Solognots de Sologne*, Chêne, Paris, 1977
◆ HUXLEY (A.): *The Devils of Loudun*, Penguin, Harmondsworth, 1971
◆ HUGO (V.): *Œuvres Complètes: Voyages*, Robert Laffont/Bouquins, Paris, 1987
◆ JAMES (H.): *A Little Tour in France*, from *Collected Travel Writings: the Continent*, The Libraries of America, New York, 1993
◆ PÉGUY (C.): *Œuvres Poétiques Complètes*, La Pléiade, Gallimard, Paris, 1957
◆ PROUST (M.): *À la recherche du temps perdu*, La Pléiade, Gallimard, Paris, 1954
◆ QUIGNARD (P.): *Les Escaliers de Chambord*, Gallimard, Paris, 1989
◆ RABELAIS (F.): *Gargantua and Pantagruel*, trans. Sir Thomas Urquhart

and Pierre le Motteux, Everyman's Library, London, Alfred A. Knopf, New York 1994
◆ RABELAIS (F.): *The Complete Works of François Rabelais*, trans. Frame (D.M.), University of California Press, Berkeley 1991
◆ RONSARD (P.): *Œuvres complètes*, Pléiade, Gallimard, Paris, 1950
◆ SAND (G.): *François le champi*, Michel Lévy Frères, Paris, 1858
◆ SAND (G.): *Les Maîtres sonneurs*, Calmann-Lévy, Paris
◆ SAND (G.): *La Mare au Diable*, Calmann-Lévy, Paris
◆ SAND (G.): *The Miller of Angibault*, Weldon & Co., London, 1848
◆ SAND (G.): *Mémoires d'un touriste*, Albatros, Paris
◆ STENDHAL: *Mémoires d'un touriste*, Paris, Albatros, 1986
◆ TINDALL (G.): *Célestine, Voices from a French Village*, Sinclair-Stevenson, London, 1995
◆ DE VIGNY (A.): *Cina-Mars, ou une Conjuration sous Louis XIII*, Folio/Gallimard, Paris, 1980
◆ VIVIER (R.), ROUGÉ (J.-M.) and MILLET (E.): *Contes et Légendes de Touraine*, Arrault, Tours, 1945
◆ WAUGH (E.): *The Diaries of Evelyn Waugh*, Michael Davie, Book Club Associates, London, 1976
◆ WORDSWORTH (W.): *The Prelude – or growth of a poet's mind*, ed. de Selincourt, OUP, London/New York 1970
◆ WORDSWORTH (W.): *Residence in France*, Oxford University Press, Oxford/New York, 1970
◆ ZOLA (E.): *La Terre*, G. Charpentier et Cie, Paris, 1887

TRAVELERS'
◆ **TALES** ◆

◆ EVELYN (J.): *The Diary of John Evelyn*, ed. de Beer (E.S.), 1955

and Pierre le Motteux,

◆ GERNHARD (C.G.): *Through France with Berzelius: Live Scholars and Dead Volcanoes*, Pergamon Press, Oxford, 1989
◆ LEE (V.): *Genius Loci – notes on places*, John Lane, The Bodley Head/John Lane Company, New York, 1908
◆ LOCKE (J.): *Locke's Travels in France, 1675–1679*, ed. Lough (J.), Cambridge University Press, Cambridge, 1953
◆ MORRIS (J.) ed: *Travels with Virginia Woolf*, The Hogarth Press, London, 1993
◆ TAINE (H.): *Journeys through France - being impressions of the provinces*, T. Fisher, Unwin, London, 1897
◆ WHARTON (E.): *Abroad – Selected Travel Writings 1888–1920*, Robert Hale, London, 1995
◆ WRAXALL (N.): *A Tour through the Western, Southern and Interior Provinces of France*, 1784
◆ YOUNG (A.): *Travels in France during the years 1787, 1788 and 1789*, Cambridge University Press, Cambridge, 1950

◆ **GUIDES** ◆

◆ DUIJKER (H.): *Loire, a wine-lover's touring guide*, Het Spectrum, Utrecht, 1994
◆ EPERON (A.): *The Loire*, Pan, London, 1992
◆ SEELY (J.): *The Loire Valley and its wines*, Lennard, London, 1989
◆ WADE (R.): *The companion guide to the Loire*, Collins, London, 1979

LIST OF ILLUSTRATIONS ◆

We would like to thank the following people and institutions for their help:

M. Patrick Boyer
M. Carvallo
Mme Florence Dauge
M. Dontenwille
M. Dupavillon
Mme Favard
M. Giquel
Mme Godefroy Durand-Ruel
M. Pierre Huteau
Mme Le Platre
M. Yves Maufra
M. Perraguin
M. Jean Poulain
Mme Muguette Rigaud
M. Steinberg
Mlle Claudine Varin
Mme Barbara Wright
Les Archives Départementales du Loir-et-Cher
La Bibl. du Patrimoine, Paris,
La Bibl. Dép. d'Indre-et-Loire à Tours
La Bibl. Mun., Tours
La Bibl. Mun., Vendôme
La Documentation de l'Inventaire, Orléans
La Photothèque de la Ville-de-Tours
Le Musée de l'Hôtel de Ville à Amboise
Le musée régional de l'Orléanais à Beaugency
Le Musée archéologique de Blois
Le Musée des Beaux-Arts de Blois
Le Musée des Amis du Vieux Chinon
Le Musée de Sologne, Romorantin-Lanthenay
Le Musée de Sologne, Romorantin-Lanthenay
Le Musée Lansyer, Loches
Le Musée des Beaux-Arts, Tours
Le Musée du Compagnonnage, Tours
Le musée municipal, Vendôme
Les Amis de Rabelais et de La Devinière
La Galerie La Cymaise, Paris
Pierre Aucante
Anne and Alain Beignet
Anne and Serge Chirol
Martine and Alain Doron
Jean-Paul Grossin
François Joly
Patrick Lavaud
Jean-Pierre Moreau
Jean-Luc Péchinot
Pierre Pitrou
Jean-Noël Thibault
Les Éditions CLD, Tours
Les Éditions du Zodiaque